hypermedia & the Web

WORLDWIDE
SERIES IN
COMPUTER
SCIENCE

Series Editors   **Professor David Barron, Southampton University, UK**
Professor Peter Wegner, Brown University, USA

The Worldwide Series in Computer Science has been created to publish textbooks which both address and anticipate the needs of an ever evolving curriculum thereby shaping its future. It is designed for undergraduates majoring in Computer Science and practitioners who need to reskill. Its philosophy derives from the conviction that the discipline of computing needs to produce technically skilled engineers who will inevitably face, and possibly invent, radically new technologies throughout their future careers. New media will be used innovatively to support high quality texts written by leaders in the field.

Published titles   Ammeraal, *Computer Graphics for Java Programmers*
Ben-Ari, *Ada for Software Engineers*
Ercegovac, *Introduction to Digital Systems*
Gollmann, *Computer Security*
Goodrich & Tamassia, *Data Structures and Algorithms in Java*
Kotonya & Somerville, *Requirements Engineering:*
Processes and Techniques
Preiss, *Data Structures and Algorithms with Object-Oriented*
Design Patterns in C++
Reiss, *A Practical Introduction to Software Design with C++*
Winder & Roberts, *Developing Java Software*

Hypermedia & the Web

An Engineering Approach

David Lowe

University of Technology, Sydney, Australia

and

Wendy Hall

University of Southampton, UK

JOHN WILEY & SONS

Chichester • New York • Weinheim • Brisbane • Singapore • Toronto

Copyright © 1999 by John Wiley & Sons Ltd,
Baffins Lane, Chichester,
West Sussex PO19 1UD, England

National 01243 779777
International (+44) 1243 779777

e-mail (for orders and customer service enquiries): cs-books@wiley.co.uk
Visit our Home Page on http://www.wiley.co.uk
or http://www.wiley.com

Other Wiley Editorial Offices

John Wiley & Sons, Inc., 605 Third Avenue,
New York, NY 10158–0012, USA

Weinheim • Brisbane • Singapore • Toronto

Library of Congress Cataloguing in Publication Data
Lowe, David.
    Hypermedia & the Web : an engineering approach / David Lowe and Wendy Hall.
        p. cm. – (Worldwide series in computer science)
    Includes bibliographical references and index.
    ISBN 0 471 98312 8 (pbk. : alk. paper)
    1. Interactive multimedia. 2. World Wide Web (Information retrieval system) I. Hall, Wendy, 1952–   . II. Title.
III. Series.
QA76.76.I59L69 1999
006.7–dc21
                                                                                            98–28199
                                                                                            CIP

British Library Cataloguing in Publication Data
A catalogue record for this book is available from the British Library.

ISBN 0 471 98312 8

Typeset from the authors' disks by The Florence Group, Stoodleigh, Devon.
This book is printed on acid-free paper responsibly manufactured from sustainable forestry, in which at least two trees are planted for each one used for paper production.
Printed and bound by Antony Rowe Ltd, Eastbourne

*For my wife Cathy and my parents John and Joan, you have
my love always – your encouragement and support are unceasing.
David*

*To Pete – who makes everything possible.
Wendy*

Contents

Foreword

This rich, multi-faceted book is particularly appropriate at this time. Hypermedia is changing from a cottage industry of hand-crafted pages to a spectrum of applications that culminates in enterprise-wide systems. The intuitive, trial-and-error methods that have worked in the past do not meet today's needs, much less those of tomorrow. As the authors state, what is needed is an engineering approach – 'a systematic, disciplined, and quantifiable approach to the development, operation, and maintenance of hypermedia applications'. In this book, they explore what such an approach would look like, and they show how it could be applied to a hypothetical hypermedia design problem. They also discuss several systems that are alternatives to the Web and exhibit capabilities not found in it.

The book is really three books in one, each interesting and worthwhile in its own right. Yet, true to the concept of hypermedia, the authors weave the parts into a coherent whole by returning throughout to a few basic themes – product, process and cognitive load. Each time, the theme is viewed from a different perspective, expanding the reader's understanding of the depth and diversity of the issue.

Product is concerned with the tangible nature of a hypermedia application. It includes the various forms of information, such as text, graphics and sound, their basic organisation, the associations that link the various parts, and different modes of access, such as searching versus browsing. A key issue for hypermedia engineering is to develop an abstract representation of the application that can be scrutinized, tested and ultimately implemented. As a starting point, they draw on software engineering models, but they show that a richer, more complex set of techniques will be needed for hypermedia products than those currently available.

Process is concerned with methods and techniques for building the hypermedia application, described in the product model, in a systematic and predictable way. Again, their starting point is software engineering. They explore characteristics of both the waterfall and the spiral, iterative models. Yet, again, they argue that there is currently no process model which is adequate for hypermedia engineering. For example, there is no good approach for the long-term maintenance of a hypermedia database. By recognising the limitations of available approaches and by developing new techniques to achieve specific hypermedia objectives, a viable process model will gradually emerge, but it will not happen overnight.

Whereas Part One examines issues from a conceptual point of view, Part Two applies those insights in a sustained way to a hypothetical problem – the HyperBank is updating its operations from conventional to hypermedia technology. The discussion of product considers how to choose a particular model in which to develop this application, and lists the many different kinds of documents needed to specify aspects of it. The discussion of process considers both the waterfall and spiral models, how they could be applied, and differences in the design process that would result from using one in preference to the other. The authors also consider the overall organisation of information, the link structure that binds the parts of the site together, and the look and feel of the user interface.

In much of the research coming from the non-Web hypermedia community, the WWW is treated in a begrudging fashion. The authors of *Hypermedia and the Web: the Engineering Approach* do not fall into this trap. They take pains throughout Parts One and Two to show how the principles and practices they are considering can be applied to large, complex Websites, as well as to hypermedia applications implemented on other platforms. Developers of Websites will find a wealth of useful information and reflection. However, lest they leave with impression that the Web is the only technology in which a site can be built, the authors include discussions of several other hypermedia systems.

Part Three provides an in-depth look at five research projects – Microcosm, Matilda, Hyperwave (formerly Hyper-G), RMM and AHM. The first two of these were developed by the authors. They also consider a number of other systems and architectures in less detail. These chapters will be particularly informative for readers whose only exposure to hypermedia has been through the Web. They also note several of the more important limitations of WWW, such as its lack of support for authorship and links that break, and point out that these limitations have been overcome in other hypermedia systems. Since several of these alternatives have Web interfaces, designers have the option to build their sites within them, taking advantage of their additional features, while providing access through a conventional Web browser.

Whereas Part Three could have been written as a separate exhibition of non-Web hypermedia systems, the discussions are continuously tied into the larger fabric of the book. For example, the authors point out specific ways in which these systems lend themselves to product and process models. They note features in an application design that are supported by some systems but not others. And they discuss how several of these systems address cognitive load for factors such as navigation.

Thus, the book is a richly diverse tapestry of design and development considerations. Issues are examined in the abstract, with respect to a sustained hypothetical example, and finally, in relation to several systems that complement the World Wide Web. Readers will not find a 'cookbook' set of procedures that can be applied mechanically, but if they invest the time and effort to ponder these issues along with the authors, they will emerge with a much deeper, more nuanced understanding of them. Should they be confronted with designing a hypermedia application at some future time, they will do so with a great deal more confidence and understanding than they would otherwise.

We may eventually achieve an engineering discipline that will allow us to build, operate and maintain large hypermedia sites in a systematic, disciplined and quantifiable way. We don't have that discipline today, but the authors have sketched a vision of it, and they have shown us a path we can follow to start building it. Let us hope that others will join their effort and help them achieve that goal.

John B. Smith,
Chapel Hill, NC
1998

Preface

'In fact, every time one combines and records facts in accordance with established logical processes, the creative aspect of thinking is concerned only with the selection of the data and the process to be employed, and the manipulation thereafter is repetitive in nature and hence a fit matter to be relegated to the machines.'

(As we may think, Vannevar Bush)

There has recently been a strong focus on the burgeoning information revolution. As a number of enabling technologies (such as communications networks, databases and computing hardware) continue to evolve and mature, the ability to quickly and easily access information improves. Hypermedia and Interactive Media systems, such as CD-ROMs and the World Wide Web, have provided a platform for allowing these technologies to be widely used, and have experienced phenomenally rapid growth in both usage and potential[1].

The result is that we have an unprecedented ability to rapidly obtain and use information from a growing range of sources. This glut of information is reaching the stage where the time required to absorb and analyse it is becoming prohibitive. Many people are finding it increasingly difficult to maintain relevancy. A typical problem is that we have access to so much information that we are finding it difficult, if not impossible, to sift through it and identify those areas which are relevant to us.

This problem is particularly visible with the World Wide Web, where we have vast quantities of information interlinked. The information scope which is immediately accessible is no longer bounded by a single

---

[1]As an example of the rapid growth of the Web, a survey carried out by SIMBA Information Inc., a leading market research and media company, suggests that the Web-only revenue from advertising is estimated at US$110 million in 1996 and is expected to rise to US$1.86 billion by 2000.

document site or personal Web page, but covers the entire Web – often in a transparent fashion.

This problem is not likely to be easily resolved. If we are to avoid being 'drowned' in this sea of information, then we need to improve our techniques for using these information sources. Hypermedia is a tool which allows us to organise information in a way which is more in accordance with how we naturally access and manipulate information.

For hypermedia to be effective we must develop techniques for effectively creating quality hypermedia applications. This book is based upon the belief that a systematic, disciplined, quantifiable approach – in short, an engineering approach – to the development, operation and maintenance of many hypermedia applications is essential. We hope to provide the foundations upon which necessary skills, knowledge and understanding of hypermedia systems engineering can be developed.

The focus in this book can best be described by using an analogy (one which we will develop in more detail in Chapter 1). Much of hypermedia and Web development is very analogous to software development thirty years ago. Traditionally, software applications were largely hand-crafted, tools were focused around implementation and performance issues, almost no process modelling or management existed and metrics were primitive or non-existent. As software applications grew in scope and complexity, this *ad hoc* approach broke down, leading to a phenomenon known as the 'software crisis'. Many applications failed to meet their specifications or were completely unmaintainable. Over the next 20–30 years, this was (and still is being) addressed through the development of software engineering development paradigms, process modelling and management, metrics, development methodologies and techniques, quality assurance, and a range of other activities which support the development process. Demonstrated gains include improved software quality and reliability, improved development visibility for both management and users, increased user confidence and satisfaction, reduced software development and maintenance costs and better management control.

Unfortunately, hypermedia and Web development is currently at the stage that software development was thirty years ago. Most applications are developed using an *ad hoc* approach. There is little understanding of development methodologies, measurement and evaluation techniques, development processes, application quality and project management. The focus in much of the development is usually squarely on technical issues such as interface implementation. Rarely is the development process adequately considered or understood. It is these problems which this book aims to address. Like software engineering texts, this book will not provide an explicit approach; indeed, such an approach does not yet exist, and it may not even be appropriate to provide a general approach for all types of hypermedia development. Rather, this book focuses on the issues we need to understand in order to undertake effective development, and provides pointers as to the directions in which we should be heading if we are to effectively manage the development of hypermedia and Web applications.

Underlying the ideas in this book are two primary emphases. First, that hypermedia development is a process. This process includes more than just media manipulation and presentation creation – it includes analysis of needs, design, management, metrics, maintenance, etc. The second emphasis is the handling and management of information in order to achieve some desired goal. The context of this book is the combination of these two emphases – the use of a suitable process in creating hypermedia applications which are effective in managing and utilising information.

Before we look at the aims of this book in more detail, it is worth making it explicit that here we have something of a love–hate relationship with the World Wide Web. The Web is by far the most significant existing platform for supporting delivery of hypermedia and interactive multimedia. Over the last few years it has become ubiquitous, and is now both widely used and abused. We would be remiss if we did not provide a degree of focus on the Web and it's technologies. At the same time, however, we recognise that the Web has some quite fundamental flaws with respect to supporting flexible open hypermedia systems. Because of this, we often criticise the Web (rather mercilessly in places) and applications or Websites which use Web technologies. It should nevertheless be borne in mind that even where we criticise the technologies which underlie the Web or the way in which these technologies are used, we still recognise the pre-eminence of the Web as a vehicle for supporting hypermedia. Indeed, much of Part Two is about how we can develop applications which overcome the Web's flaws. This is, in essence, the origin of the title of the book – we focus on both hypermedia and the Web, and how an effective engineering approach to development can result in quality applications, irrespective of possible flaws in the underlying technologies.

Goals of the Book

Hypermedia and the Web has essentially three primary goals:

1. **To provide a resource which can lead to significantly improved development.**
   In this book we aim to provide an understanding of hypermedia development which will lead to improving current practice. Whilst definitely not a 'how-to' guide for any particular tool, package, authoring environment or platform, this book can be viewed as a general 'what-to' guide for hypermedia development. In other words, this book looks at *what* aspects need to considered during the development process; it looks at *what* the issues are that affect decisions made; and it looks at *what* we can do to substantially improve our current practice.

2. **To engender an awareness of the need for a more disciplined approach to the development of hypermedia.**
   We strongly believe that hypermedia development needs to move from the current, largely *ad hoc*, approach to development to a more disciplined approach. If this is not achieved, then we shall increasingly find that large complex applications are not delivering the expected performance or quality, and that the development process becomes increasingly complex, difficult to manage and expensive. In this book, we wish to develop an awareness of these problems and an understanding of the implications if they are not effectively addressed.

3. **To demonstrate how the field is likely to evolve over the next five years.**
   Finally, we recognise that the hypermedia field is evolving *very* rapidly. What is best practice now is likely to be outdated and uncompetitive within a very short span of time (certainly less than a few years, and probably measured in months). As a result, any book such as this would be quite remiss if it did not develop (in parallel with developing an understanding of current best practice) an understanding of how hypermedia development and development best practice is likely to evolve within the foreseeable future. An important goal of this book is to show how those development issues which are still problematic are likely to be addressed, and the implications for how development will be carried out in the future.

Who Should Read the Book?

This book considers the hypermedia development process and how to perform hypermedia development in a way which is consistent with sound engineering principles. It considers current practice and trends, issues affecting the development and use of hypermedia applications, and discusses and demonstrates best practice. The book should thus be of interest to anyone involved in any of the broad range of development activities within hypermedia, including anyone involved in application development, media capture or creation, user interface development, application analysts and designers, information experts, Web developers and managers, content experts and project managers. In all of these cases, an appreciation of the role of specific activities within the overall development process would be of great benefit.

The book provides significant interest for designers of hypermedia applications and those managing such projects. Examples include the development of CD-ROMs and Websites on company intranets. The book looks at how concepts of handling information are likely to affect the development process, and how the information can be effectively structured and accessed. In particular, aspects related to how information can be reused and how applications can be maintained are likely to affect how hypermedia applications are designed.

Content and interface experts need to be aware of the way in which text, graphics, sound, video, images, etc. are used within hypermedia applications in order to understand what content is most appropriate in a particular context, and how best to structure and present this information. This book will help develop an understanding of how structuring and presentation can be most effectively achieved now, and how the field is likely to change over the next five years. Authoring architectures, techniques for managing large complex information spaces and information modelling are some of the key concepts covered here.

This book should be of interest to both researchers and practitioners. For researchers it shows current trends and provides an overview of areas which are still open research questions. For practitioners, it demonstrates current approaches to development, and shows how they can be most profitably improved and applied. It also considers directions in which the field is heading, gives insights into aspects which need to be considered, and provides a strong understanding of the types of systems which are likely to be used in the future.

Finally, it is assumed that the reader has some familiarity with at least the fundamentals of hypermedia and multimedia (such as experience with the World Wide Web). Beyond this basic assumption, little or no technical knowledge is assumed.

Acknowledgements

Special acknowledgement is due to Professor Athula Ginige. Athula has co-authored Part Two of the book, as well as contributing numerous ideas to other areas of the book.

A large number of other people have helped us bring this book into existence; contributing comments and advice, reviewing drafts, providing information, and a plethora of other contributions.

We would like to thank Gaynor Redvers-Mutton from Wiley for her support for this project from the start (and before), her insightful comments and guidance in the preparation of the manuscript.

Our appreciation also goes to Lynda Hardman (at CWI – Centrum voor Wiskunde en Informatica – in The Netherlands), Tomas Isakowitz (at the The Wharton School, University of Pennsylvania) and Keith Andrews (at the Institute for Information Processing and Computer Supported New Media at Graz University of Technology, in Austria) for their invaluable assistance in developing the research chapters on AHM, CMM and Hyper-G, respectively.

We are also grateful to numerous other people who have contributed ideas on their research, commented on the text, and been tolerant of our interpretations of their work. These include Komei Harada, Jocelyn and Marc Nanard, Norbert Streitz, and many others. Numerous other people have read and provided invaluable advice and comments. We are especially indebted to Ron Meegoda, Andrew Bucknell, Nectar Costadopolous, Hugh Davis, Dave DeRoure and Les Carr.

Introduction

Outline of the Book

We began by claiming that we need to develop a discipline of what we have referred to as 'hypermedia engineering'. The goal of this book is to begin this process by outlining practical steps which can be taken in setting up a development process that adheres to current best practice, and has the greatest achievable probability of resulting in high quality hypermedia applications.

This book is broken into three parts. Part One (Chapters 1–6) covers the fundamentals of hypermedia engineering and development. If we are to develop hypermedia applications effectively, then we need to have a strong understanding of the structure and goals of hypermedia applications.

We begin in Chapter 1 by explaining the need for a discipline of hypermedia engineering, and in Chapter 2 consider what exactly we mean by the term 'hypermedia'. We provide both a historical context and a goal-based perspective, and end with a working definition of hypermedia which can be used to guide our approach to the development of hypermedia applications. In Chapter 3 we look at how we represent both hypermedia information and the structure of hypermedia applications themselves. From here we consider what characteristics are typically built into hypermedia applications.

In Chapter 4 we describe the development process and the concept of hypermedia *engineering*. We show that the goal of the development process is twofold: to develop hypermedia applications which have desired characteristics; and to undertake this development as effectively and efficiently as possible. Hypermedia engineering provides us with a mechanism for achieving this goal.

Chapters 5 and 6 look at issues which must be addressed during the development process. These are separated into product (Chapter 5) and process issues (Chapter 6). Product issues are those which must be considered during the development, and which have a direct or indirect impact on the quality of the product (as perceived by a user and relative, of course, to the requirements of the applications being developed). Process issues are concerned with the effectiveness of the development process itself. Examples include factors which affect development productivity and repeatability.

Part Two of the book (Chapters 7–9) applies the fundamentals developed in the first part of the book to showing how hypermedia applications can be most effectively developed.

We look at the errors, pitfalls and failings which are common when creating hypermedia applications, and show how they can lead to difficulties either in the development process itself (such as runaway budgets, blown out timeframes, or loss of development focus) or with the resulting product (such as unusable or inadequate interfaces, poor performance, and incorrect, incomplete or badly structured information). In addition, we demonstrate how these problems can be circumvented. We look at best practice within the constraints of current understanding and technology, and provide practical tips, hints and recommendations which have the potential to significantly improve the effectiveness of current development practice and the quality of applications developed. We also identify the (many) problems and issues which even best practice has yet to adequately address. The final chapter of Part Two considers future directions in hypermedia engineering and development, and how we may be able to overcome those difficulties which still remain.

Part Three looks at a number of existing research and development projects. This is intended as a vehicle for demonstrating how the field of hypermedia may evolve, and how many of the existing problems with hypermedia development can be overcome. Each of the projects considered demonstrates how specific issues in the development process can be addressed.

In the final chapter, we revisit many of the concepts covered, and finish with some 'crystal ball gazing'.

Part One

Hypermedia Development Fundamentals

Hypermedia cannot truly develop as an effective communications medium until we are able to develop applications which not only assist in information procurement, but also facilitate effective information utilisation. This requires an understanding, on the part of developers, of the issues which need to be addressed during the hypermedia development process, and appropriate approaches for addressing these issues. The underlying focus of this book is on the need for a development process which has been devised with a consideration of managing information and its uses in communication. We call this 'hypermedia engineering'. This is distinct from a current strong focus on managing media rather than information. Although information management has been the focus of much work on hypermedia applications, usage, interaction, etc., it has only recently been actively considered during the full lifecycle development process. The book illustrates why this trend is critical to the continuing evolution of hypermedia applications and our ability to effectively develop these applications.

This first part introduces hypermedia applications and hypermedia development (including hypermedia authoring), and focuses on issues which need to be addressed during the development process and current theory as to how this might be achieved. In particular, the information management and communication aspects which are addressed during the development process are considered. For hypermedia development to evolve and improve (both in terms of application quality and process success), we need to improve the way in which we currently approach managing, storing, manipulating, accessing and representing information and its structure.

1

Introduction

*The essence of knowledge is, having it, to apply it;
not having it, to confess your ignorance.*

(Confucius)

Chapter Goals

This chapter aims to introduce and provide an overall context for the book. In particular, we wish to develop an understanding of hypermedia and the Web, the current crisis which exists with respect to their development, and the critical need for a more disciplined approach to development of these applications – an approach which we refer to as *hypermedia engineering*. The objectives of this chapter are to:

- Develop a common understanding of hypermedia to establish a consistent framework for later discussions.

- Consider a rudimentary taxonomy of hypermedia applications in order to define the domain of interest of this book.

- Describe characteristics of large scale hypermedia applications and show how these relate to the development process.

- Compare the development process of hypermedia to software development from 30 years ago – and the conclusion is drawn that we are in the midst of a crisis!

- Introduce the concept of *hypermedia engineering* and how it can help us develop an effective approach to development, thereby improving the crisis.

The above quote was chosen to begin this book, since it so neatly encapsulates what hypermedia has, to date, failed to achieve. Hypermedia, the conjunction of hypertext and multimedia, undoubtedly has incredible potential as a vehicle for improving our ability to effectively use information. Unfortunately, hypermedia, and especially its ubiquitous incarnation as the Web, has only just begun to fulfil this potential.

Current hypermedia applications are beginning to mature in their ability to support the first aspect of the above quote – 'The essence of knowledge is, having it'. The more advanced current applications do provide reasonable access and retrieval of information, albeit often within a constrained domain. They do not yet, however, help us achieve the second half of the problem – appropriate application of the knowledge or information.

A further, and potentially much more significant, problem is the way in which hypermedia applications are currently developed. The dominant approach of *ad hoc* development can, given a combination of expertise and sufficient luck, give acceptable results when the applications being developed are sufficiently small and/or highly structured. Similarly, artistic and literary works, such as hypertext fiction, are such that a 'scientific' approach is not particularly appropriate. However, with larger or less structured applications we are likely to run into development problems which include runaway budgets, blown out timeframes, loss of development focus, unusable or inadequate interfaces, poor performance, and incorrect, incomplete or badly structured information. Current approaches to development are lacking in a broad range of areas: effective processes, process models, project management, metrics and documentation guidelines, to name a few. Until these areas are addressed, we will be unable to consistently develop high quality large-scale hypermedia applications.

In this book we investigate the above issues, and propose guidelines to assist in the adoption of current best-practice in the development of hypermedia applications. We look at the goals of hypermedia applications, and the characteristics which need to be embedded to achieve these goals. The issues that need to be addressed during the development process in order to achieve applications with the desired characteristics are considered, and we look at current practice, then investigate how it can be improved to achieve best-practice for hypermedia development – what we have chosen to refer to as 'hypermedia engineering'. Finally, directions in which hypermedia development is likely to progress over the next five years are examined.

The ultimate goal is to provide a deeper understanding of the purpose of hypermedia and hypermedia development, and the skills necessary to radically improve current practice of hypermedia development, whether in the development of interactive CD-ROMs or setting up and maintaining a large WWW site.

1.1 Hypermedia

What is hypermedia? For many people the most common experience of hypermedia is the World Wide Web. Although Websites are only a single type of hypermedia application (and an often criticised one at that), they do demonstrate many of the fundamental characteristics of a hypermedia application. A simple interpretation of hypermedia is that it is an application which allows us to navigate through an information space using associative linking. This leads to ideas such as non-linearity and interactivity, as demonstrated in Figure 1-1. Here we can see that traditional media, such as a book or film, is linear – there is a single path through the material. With hypermedia we (i.e. the developer of the hypermedia applications) provide multiple possible paths through the information;

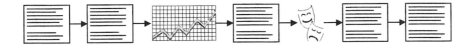

Linear 'linking' of traditional media

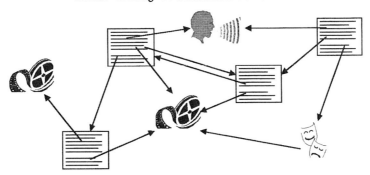

Nonlinear 'linking' of hypermedia

Figure 1-1

Demonstrates associative linking. In most applications this 'structure' would not be visible to the user

we do not constrain the reader to a predetermined path. Instead, the user can interactively browse through the information following any of the possibly very large number of paths.

Different applications will implement this basic concept in different ways. The basic 'nodes' of information may be separate windows or overlayed screens. The links may be unidirectional or bidirectional, embedded into the information or dynamically generated. The overall effect is still an application which uses a network of associatively related information.

Although this definition of hypermedia provides a starting point for understanding what makes hypermedia different from traditional media, it is unfortunately rather simplistic. In particular, it encourages us to focus on the technical structure of hypermedia rather than the ultimate purpose of a hypermedia application. This will, in turn, skew our approach to developing hypermedia applications. In the following chapter we look at a more goal-oriented understanding of hypermedia, and begin to consider the implications of this. For the time being, however, we can view a hypermedia application as being an information management system which is based around associative linking of the information.

Hypermedia applications typically have various primary characteristics. As pointed out above, the most significant of these is non-linearity (hence *hyper*media). Other characteristics include the use of multiple forms of media (hence hyper*media*) and multiple types of access mechanisms. We convey information by using media types which are best suited to the particular information. For example, consider how you might convey the colour 'blue' or Beethoven's 9th Symphony using just text. The use of different access mechanisms provides the user with different ways of locating and assimilating the information. The simplest examples include browsing and searching.

A number of secondary characteristics can also be identified which elucidate the above points. Integration of media into a cohesive whole is obviously important. A major flaw in many existing hypermedia applications is that much of the information, especially non-textual media, has been patchworked together. It is not sufficient to simply create non-linear structures – they need to be created in a way which is meaningful to the user. Developers also need to consider the mechanisms which will be used in developing and maintaining non-linear structures. Aspects such as information cost-management, copyright considerations, access control and security are also important.

The specific relevance of each characteristic will be highly dependant upon the application domain, the user profiles, the application size, the approach to the design which was adopted, and a host of other factors. Nevertheless, it is important to remember that the primary goal of hypermedia remains enabling access to, and utilisation of, information.

A Note on Terminology

Before we progress any further, it is worth clarifying our use of certain terms. The hypermedia field is still evolving, and in a number of cases the terms have yet to acquire well accepted precise meanings.

The terms *hypertext* and *hypermedia* are often used interchangeably. In this book, we treat hypermedia as an extension of hypertext which makes use of multiple forms of media (such as text, audio, video, animation, graphics, etc.). Nevertheless, the literature, and common use in many cases, uses hypertext as a general term covering both applications which use only text and applications involving multiple forms of media. In this book we will use hypermedia as a general term covering both forms.

The terms *application* and *system* are also used in varying ways. In this book when we refer to *application* (or hypermedia application) we are referring to the end result of the hypermedia development process, the product which has been developed for end-users. When we refer to *system*, unless explained otherwise, we are referring to the tools and infrastructure used by developers in creating or supporting applications. It is worth pointing out that in some cases these systems are also used as a delivery and presentation system for the application. In these cases we will refer to a *presentation system* in which case the presentation system plays an integral part in supporting the application.

As an example, when we create Websites (*applications*) these sites will be developed using a variety of tools (*development systems* – such as authoring tools, media editing packages, database systems, etc.) and then supported by the infrastructure of the World Wide Web (*delivery and support systems* – such as Web servers, CGI scripts, database engines, etc.) and accessed using Web browsers (*presentation systems*).

1.2   Hypermedia Applications

Before we look at hypermedia in more detail, it is worth diverting our attention to consider the possible application domains and types which are the focus of this book. We can categorise hypermedia applications in many different ways: categorisation by application domain, by presentation technology, or by the degree of openness, for example.

A more useful categorisation to us at the moment is shown in Figure 1-2. In this categorisation we have separated applications along two axes: application size and application development focus. Those applications in the first category are characterised by small size, a low-level of structure, a short lifespan, and virtually no need for ongoing development or revision, but a strong focus on quality presentation. Examples of this type of application include marketing and promotional material, advertisements, public relations announcements, etc.

The applications in the second category are again characterised by small size, though they may have a longer lifespan and the focus is more on the structure and content of the information rather than on its specific presentation. Examples of this type of application include hypertext

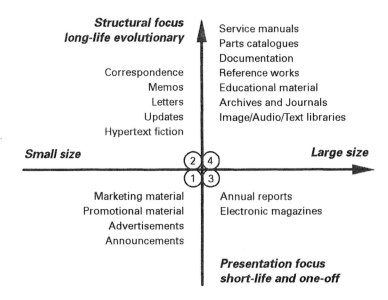

Figure 1-2

Hypermedia applications can be categorised on the basis of size and development focus

fiction, correspondence, memos, letters, etc. For the first two categories, the scale of the applications is relatively small, and as a result, *ad hoc* development approaches can often be adequate, though an awareness of cognitive aspects such as interface design and information structuring is still important.

Applications in the third category are larger sized applications, but as with applications in the first category, they are characterised by a short lifespan, virtually no need for ongoing development or revision, and a strong focus on presentation. Examples include material such as annual reports and electronic magazines. This type of application, though large and therefore complex to create is usually unlikely to require ongoing development and change over an extended time period. As a result, issues such as reuse of the information and maintenance of the application is unlikely to be a significant concern.

The final category of application (category four) is characterised by a large scale, a focus on content and how it is effectively conveyed and managed, and a long lifespan during which ongoing change to content and technology is likely to occur. There are numerous examples of this type of application, including sets of procedures, manuals, documentation of assorted types, reference works, educational material, archives, journals and catalogues. These applications are often referred to as *mission critical*, because they can provide information which is critical to the day-to-day operation of many organisations. With this type of application, several new issues become important, including the fact that the application size means that issues such as navigability become important, and the long lifespan means that maintainability and reuse are relevant.

In this book it is category four applications, and to a lesser extent category one applications, which are the prime focus. Although an awareness of many design issues can be important for small scale applications, it is really only when we deal with large scale applications that a truly disciplined approach to the development becomes critical. Let us now consider what characteristics of these large scale applications are important in determining the approaches we might adopt to their development.

1.3   Large Scale Hypermedia Applications

The defining characteristic of large-scale hypermedia applications is, obviously, size. The size of an application has significant implications for how we develop and use the application. Small-scale applications can often be satisfactorily developed using an *ad hoc* approach. After all, a small size implies that most issues can be easily perceived and handled by one or two developers. Any problems encountered during the development can usually be easily rectified with minimal effort.

This is not true of large-scale applications. To understand why this is so, we should consider some of the characteristics of large-scale applications, but first let us define what we mean by 'large-scale' applications. This is not easy since the scale, and the difficulties associated with a large scale, are heavily dependant upon the type of application being developed. For example, an application which contains a large amount of very highly structured data (such as 1000 sets of pages of company employee records) may be much easier to develop than a smaller application containing only 50 'pages' of very eclectic information such as educational course notes. As a specific example, consider the problem of structuring the content of this book in a hypermedia form, as compared to structuring the information in a large telephone book (which is likely to have a much greater amount of data). The variation in content structure is much less in the latter case.

Nevertheless, as a typical guideline and subject to the above caveats, applications above about 100 nodes tend to become difficult to develop effectively without a consistent rigorous approach. As an example, a typical and well known large scale CD-ROM application, Microsoft Encarta'95, has over 26,000 articles and 300,000 links. Even Encarta may be small compared to applications such as News servers.

As applications grow in size the effort required to develop the applications also obviously grows. The relationship is, however, not necessarily linear. As an example, ignoring factors of application domain, an application with 1000 nodes will have 10 times as much content as an application with 100 nodes. We may be able to achieve economies of scale in generating or capturing the content. For example, the design of filters to convert legacy data will only need to occur once. The capture of the content for a 1000 node application may therefore not be significantly larger than for a 100 node application.

In other cases, the relationship is exponential rather then decaying, for example, the structuring of the captured information. Consider the situation where each node has links to 10% of the other nodes in the application. A 10 node system will have 10 links. A 100 node system will have 1000 links. A 10 000 node system will have 10 000 000 links! This is, of course, oversimplistic, but it does illustrate a typical trend. As the application size grows, not only does the number of links grow, but the overall structure becomes more complex, making it more difficult to create each link.

The growth in development effort which accompanies a growth in application size is therefore not just a reflection of the growing amount of material and structuring which must be dealt with, but also the growing complexity of the application.

Other factors also come into play when developing large-scale applications which are not significant for small-scale applications. As the size grows, the range of media being used and how these media are combined grows, both of which create difficulties which must be addressed during development. Another factor is the increasing complexity of information access mechanisms; as the application grows it becomes more important to provide sophisticated mechanisms to assist users in managing the complexity. This can take the form of assisting users in understanding the structure of the information, navigating around the information, and providing mechanisms for identifying specific information within the application. As an example, whereas search engines are not typically required for simple applications, they are almost mandatory for most classes of large-scale applications. But even search engines are often insufficient. For example, given a simple search criteria, most commonly used Web search engines return hundreds or possibly thousands of 'hits'. A failure to address these types of issues is often manifested as the classic 'lost in hyperspace' problem, where a user becomes disoriented or lost within the application.

Another important aspect of large-scale applications which must be considered is that they will usually have long lifetimes and involve progressive or iterative development and refinement. Whereas small-scale applications can be easily created, used for a short period and then discarded, the investment in a large-scale application is much greater. The result is that, with large-scale applications, ongoing maintenance, updates and refinement becomes important. Consequently, the applications should be developed with this in mind. The application framework or structure must be extensible, and mechanisms for carrying out the maintenance understood.

Given all of the above, it becomes possible to define a set of typical characteristics of large-scale applications, including both functional characteristics (those associated with the function or behaviour of the application) and non-functional characteristics (those associated with the form of the application). Typical functional characteristics include support for:

- effective navigation
- searching and indexing
- information contextualisation
- handling of information security and cost
- appropriate presentation mechanisms
- support for customisation
- effective use of resources
- handling of temporal media.

Typical non-functional characteristics include:

- link and content validity (covering aspects such as correctness, relevance, completeness and integrity)
- suitable organisation of concepts
- consistency and seamlessness of the structure
- efficiency
- maintainability and evolvability
- reusability of information
- reliability and robustness
- testability, ability to be validated and verified
- interoperability, flexibility, portability, genericity
- appropriate handling of political and social aspects
- cost-effectiveness.

In developing applications, most of these characteristics become progressively more difficult to manage as the application size and scope grows. Any approach to development should ensure that applications contain the appropriate balance of these characteristics.

1.4   The Development Crisis

The Software Crisis

It is worth briefly considering a field which has evolved in an analogous fashion to hypermedia – that of software development.

Like software, the complexity of hypermedia can be deceptive. The basic concepts in software programs – basic programming statements and syntax – and hypermedia applications – nodes and links – are both, at least on the surface, quite simple. The difficulty arises in managing the incredibly complex interactions which can occur when many of these simple elements are combined into large-scale, complex applications.

Like hypermedia development, software development involves the creation and maintenance of large, complex, interlinked and inter-dependant applications. Traditionally, software applications were largely hand-crafted, tools were focused around implementation and perfor-mance issues, almost no process modelling or management existed, and metrics were primitive or non-existent. As software applications grew in scope and complexity, this early approach broke down. This led to a phenomenon known as the 'software crisis' (Gibbs, 1994) (the term was coined in 1965), with many applications failing to meet their specifica-tions or being completely unmaintainable. Example problems included:

- Unclear or ambiguous specifications.
- Poor project management due to a poor understanding of needs.
- Inadequate tools for development and management.
- Lack of user involvement in the development process.

Even the discussion of problems facing software developers at that stage was similar to those being discussed in hypermedia today. A prime example is the discussion of 'spaghetti code' in software and 'spaghetti linking' in hypermedia. This was (and is still being) addressed through the development of software engineering development paradigms, process modelling and management, metrics, development methodolo-gies and techniques, quality assurance, and a range of other activities which support the development process (Gibbs, 1994). The focus has shifted from raw code being produced, to the process being used to ensure that the application is of a high quality. Potential gains include (Howell, 1992):

- improved software quality and reliability,
- improved development visibility for both management and users,
- increased user confidence and satisfaction,
- reduced software development and maintenance costs,
- better management control,
- a more comprehensible and easier to maintain system.

The Hypermedia Crisis

Unfortunately, hypermedia development is currently at the stage software development was at thirty years ago. Most hypermedia applications are developed using an *ad hoc* approach. There is little understanding of development methodologies, measurement and evaluation techniques, development processes, application quality and project management. The focus in much of the development is on technical issues such as interface implementation – rarely is the quality of end applications adequately considered or understood.

Many of these problems are best illustrated by current practice in Web development. Much of the development is carried out without a true understanding of the skills required, the issues which need to be addressed, or the effectiveness of the results.

We are potentially about to suffer a hypermedia crisis!

Current approaches to developing hypermedia are, in many cases, failing to deliver applications which have acceptable quality, especially in terms of information access and usability. Those applications which are considered good examples are often more the result of the high level of expertise of a few individuals, along with considerable luck. As hypermedia applications grow in scope and complexity, current practice will need to develop too, or risk failing to deliver. This is particularly true for applications on the Web where separate interlinked sites can result in very complex structures.

The problems developers are liable to suffer if this crisis is not addressed include applications which do not satisfy their goals, do not provide access to the desired information, do not assist in the use of this information, are not maintainable, and are cost-ineffective. Indeed, the problems parallel those with software.

Very large amounts of money are being committed to developing hypermedia products. Large scale CD-ROMs are becoming more common. Many companies are spending in the millions of dollars developing and maintaining Websites. The development of these applications is very likely to be over-budget, over-cost and over-time.

This failure is largely due to a lack of process. As hypermedia applications grow in scope and complexity, an evolution (or possibly revolution) similar to that which occurred in software development needs to occur. Just as the focus in software development shifted from programming to process, the focus with hypermedia must shift from the use of specific authoring tools in handcrafting applications to broader process issues which support the development of high quality, large-scale applications. This includes aspects such as specifying hypermedia applications, the development of appropriate frameworks, tools and techniques, validation methods, metrics, etc. As with software tools, hypermedia development tools are important, but they must be used appropriately within an overall development process which gives them a suitable context.

Factors which affect the development process and its components, such as our choice of paradigm, process model and methodology, include application scale and size, approach, intended audience, etc. For example, small applications can still be readily handcrafted, but for large applications, and especially those which will evolve over time, we need to adopt a more formal and thorough approach if we are to avoid a 'hypermedia crisis'. We need to adopt a 'hypermedia engineering' approach.

1.5 Hypermedia Engineering

What, then, is hypermedia engineering? Later we will develop a formal definition, and explain the justification of this. For the time being, we just give the definition (based on a similar definition for software engineering from the IEEE (1991)) and explain briefly what we mean.

Definition

Hypermedia engineering The employment of a systematic, disciplined, quantifiable approach to the development, operation and maintenance of hypermedia applications.

In other words, hypermedia engineering is about the employment of an engineering approach – an approach which is managed, scientifically based, and yet practical and pragmatic. We use the term 'engineering' because we believe that the employment of an appropriate process is critical to the effective development of large scale hypermedia applications. At present, current hypermedia development practice is to a large extent focused around the use of specific tools (such as HyperCard – as shown in Figure 1-3 – or an assortment of Web authoring tools such as HotDog, FrontPage and Net Fusion) in creating and linking the pages of information which make up a hypermedia application. However, this is only a small part of the whole development process. Many, if not most, of the aspects given above are either overlooked entirely (such as the use of metrics) or performed in a very *ad hoc* manner (such as managing the whole development).

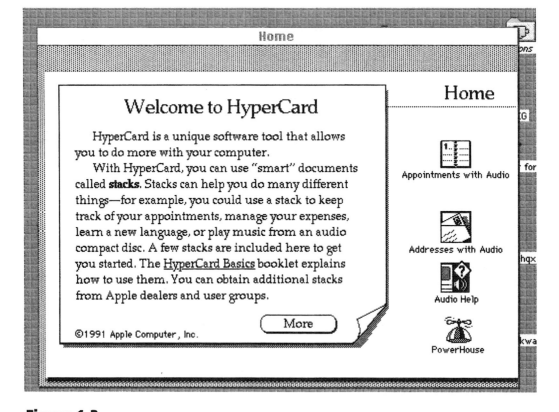

Figure 1-3

HyperCard is an example of a typical hypermedia authoring and presentation tool

Products and Product Models

Before considering the specifics of what an engineering approach to hypermedia development covers, we shall look at two fundamental concepts which run throughout the book: product and process. Let us begin by considering *product*.

We can view hypermedia applications as *products* that we wish to develop. As discussed previously, these products will have certain desired characteristics. For example, consider a World Wide Web application which supports accessing product catalogues for a furniture store. This application might have desired characteristics such as wide accessibility (since we wish the catalogue to be available to as large a potential market as possible), maintainability (since the information on the furniture products changes regularly), sophisticated query mechanisms (since customers of the furniture store will often be looking for specific items), and high quality presentations (since the catalogue items need to be presented in a way which encourages sales).

To achieve the optimal blend of desired characteristics, we create applications that have a given structure or form. This product structure will include aspects such as how we store and represent the information and the mechanisms used to access the information. The given structure of an application will be largely dictated by the characteristics we desire that application to have. With the furniture catalogue example, the application will be based on the World Wide Web, since this improves accessibility. Underlying the application we could have the information on the furniture products (text and audio descriptions, pictures, etc. of the furniture) stored in a database. When the Web server receives a request for information from a client, the application generates the page dynamically from the stored data. This would allow flexible maintenance of information on the furniture. Separation of the presentation (in the Web client – such as Netscape Navigator) from the information (stored in the underlying database and combined into Web pages by the Web server) would allow flexible and sophisticated presentations.

Every application will have a specific structure best suited to its desired characteristics. It is, however, possible to identify certain patterns in the structure or forms of applications. For example, some applications will tend to be built around a pattern of the content and presentation being combined together into linked components. Other applications will be built around a pattern which separates content and presentation (such as in the furniture store catalogue example). We can create *product models* which capture the essential elements of these patterns. Each type of product model will be suited to supporting particular hypermedia characteristics. For example, we can define an 'information-centred' model that separates content from presentation (as with the furniture store example). This type of model would be appropriate for systems requiring constant maintenance of the underlying application content.

Processes and Process Models

Obviously, the act of creating hypermedia applications requires some form of development *process* – a set of activities which are carried out and which result in a hypermedia application. At some point, we will have the genesis of the idea for a hypermedia application. We then undertake various development activities which if adequate enable the application itself to come into existence. Over time it is likely that the application will evolve, improve and be adapted. Finally, it may be 'decommissioned'. In other words, we have a hypermedia development lifecycle.

Hypermedia engineering is about managing all aspects of this lifecycle in the most effective manner. This involves using a *process* which is best suited to creating the desired application, but also doing so in a way which is cost-effective, repeatable and manageable. The process essentially covers the development phases we carry out (such as identifying the specific requirements of an application) and the way in which these phases combine into a cohesive whole.

As with the discussion above on how the structure of a hypermedia *product* depends upon the desired characteristics, the process we use will also depend upon the characteristics we wish to build into the application. The structure of the *process* will also depend upon the structure of the *product*. For example, consider the situation where we wish to convert an existing encyclopaedia into a Web-based hypermedia application. Since the project is relatively large, our process may start by undertaking an analysis of the functionality desired by potential users of the system.

Again, as with models of hypermedia product structure, we can generate *process models* – or models which provide an abstract representation of the structure of the process we are adopting. Figure 1-4 illustrates a typical model of one possible approach to the development lifecycle of software applications. This lifecycle model describes the various phases a software developer must go through in the process of creating a software application. Equivalent models for the entire development lifecycle of hypermedia applications are only now beginning to be developed. In many cases (such as the models implicit in RMM, discussed later in this book), they are based on traditional engineering process models, such as that in Figure 1-4, though in many cases the appropriateness of these models is doubtful. In most cases, it will still be a while before these embryonic models have evolved to the point where they are suitably adapted explicitly for the particular needs of hypermedia applications.

We can still consider the types of activities we might wish to include in a process model. Possibilities, which will be discussed in detail in Chapter 5, include:

- project planning
- functional analysis
- information analysis
- feasibility analysis
- nonfunctional analysis
- navigation analysis

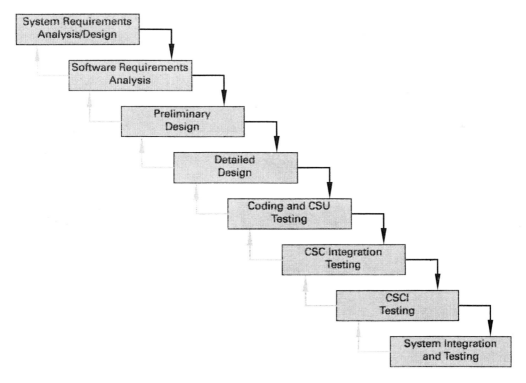

Figure 1-4

DOD-STD-2167A software development process model

- architectural design
- navigation design
- behaviour design
- application implement
- evaluation
- maintenance
- creative authoring
- ...

- user-interface design
- information capture
- content design
- testing
- navigation verification
- process measurement
- project management

If we are to consistently develop high-quality hypermedia applications in a timely and cost-effective manner, then we need to begin to develop and adopt both appropriate product and process models.

In essence, hypermedia engineering is about being able to identify a suitable product model for our application, identify a process model which supports the development, implement this process model as an actual development process, and result in the desired product. We still have a considerable amount to learn about how this can be achieved. Nevertheless, there is much that we can currently do which will provide substantial benefits.

Hypermedia Engineering as a Distinct Discipline?

An obvious question at this point is whether hypermedia engineering is likely to be any different from engineering in other domains, such as software engineering? Although the specific development approaches, methodologies and tools used in developing hypermedia are substantially different from those used in other domains, the processes within which these methodologies fit generally seem to have similarities. Nevertheless, the differences are significant enough that we need to be very careful about applying conventional 'engineering' approaches.

> 'Fundamental differences [between hypermedia and other disciplines] however, make a pure transposition of techniques both difficult and inadequate. An important part of hypertext design concerns aesthetic and cognitive aspects that software engineering environments do not support'

> (Nanard and Nanard, 1995)

As an example, hypermedia projects typically involve significantly finer grained maintenance than development in other domains, which affects how the maintenance should be managed within the development process. Despite these differences, and the subsequent need to explicitly consider hypermedia engineering as distinct from the engineering of other systems and applications, we can learn much from other disciplines. This shall be illustrated throughout this text.

This is, of course, not to imply that hypermedia engineering will be the solution to all problems, or will be appropriate in all cases. For example, hypertext fiction and other literary hypertexts require creativity rather than engineering. As discussed in Section 1.2, large scale, long-lived applications are the core focus of this book, and the most appropriate target for an engineering approach.

1.6   Developing an Effective Approach

The way in which we approach development will vary from application to application, and from platform to platform. To develop an effective approach we need to understand the range of applications and platforms which can be developed and used, and the issues that affect how we approach the development. In the remainder of this chapter, we will look briefly at applications and environments. The rest of Part One focuses on issues which must be addressed to develop an effective development process.

A number of good overviews of hypermedia applications exist (for example, see Nielsen (1995)). The range of applications covers online documentation, user assistance, software engineering, manuals, reference works, catalogues, advertising, idea organisation, education and edutainment, museums and libraries, interactive fiction and news. In each case the approach adopted for development will typically be adapted to the specific requirements of the application, much as the software engineering approach for banking applications is likely to quite different to the approach adopted for real-time embedded applications.

For example, with advertising applications the process will need to closely consider how to most effectively present the information in a way which supports typical marketing considerations, such as product name recognition and product appeal. With news applications this is unlikely to be a significant consideration. The focus is more likely to be on cross-linking news, analysis and archival information.

The environment used to support the application will also have a significant impact. Considerations include local applications versus distributed applications, local data versus networked data, single platform versus multi-platform, single-user versus multi-user, level of hardware support, and level of computing resources available. Any approach to development will need to take into account the constraints and benefits of the various possible environments.

Local applications are those which typically run on a single machine without requiring any network or multiprocessor support. Distributed applications are those which distribute some or all aspects of the application across multiple machines or processors. This type of environment allows a hypermedia application to take advantage of scarce resources, such as using a CD player located on one machine, a video card on another, and a high performance processor on a third. Such an environment will require that the development of applications take into account aspects such as resource management and coordination of communication among the various application components.

The information base being used for the application can be localised (such as with a CD-ROM) or distributed (as with the Web). In the case of a local information base, significant consideration needs to be given to the bounds placed on the information which is to be incorporated. Conversely, it means that the developer has a much tighter control over the entire structure, and hence consistency, in terms of both information and interfaces. With a networked information source it is significantly easier to evolve and extend the information base. Look at how readily additional information is added to the Web – whereas with local information bases this would typically require the expensive production and distribution of 'update' material. An unfortunate corollary of this is that, with increasing levels of information networking, it becomes progressively more difficult to ensure consistency and correctness of the information.

A major consideration in development is the specific platform(s) to be supported. If the application is a custom, in-house, localised application then it may be reasonable to expect it to be developed on a single platform, thus minimising development effort. Alternatively, if the application is to be widely distributed then it is likely that multiple platforms should be supported. Although many authoring tools support cross-platform development, the implications extend beyond this to other stages of the development, e.g. management of the cross-platform development, designing generic interfaces, and maintaining multiple versions of an application.

The development process will also be affected by whether the application is intended to be single-user or multi-user. A multi-user application will need to take into account aspects such as multiple access and consistency maintenance (where multiple users are editing the information space simultaneously), and possibly the ability to personalise the information and interfaces.

The hardware and software support which is available in different environments will also have a major impact on the development process. The types of interfaces and performance which can be supported will be affected, which will in turn affect what types of requirements can be met and how the application is designed to support these requirements.

As an example of the above concepts, let us consider the Web. The Web is typically an anarchic, very large, highly distributed, multi-platform, multi-user conglomeration of intertwined hypermedia applications. If we are to develop applications for the Web, then our development process should incorporate, for example, the following provisions:

- *Analysis of interconnectivity*: much of the strength of applications on the Web comes from their ability to interconnect with the vast amount of material elsewhere on the Web. In developing an application we need to be able to analyse the Web and identify existing material which we can use (by linking to this material).

- *Distributed nature of the Web*: material accessed across the Internet is typically constrained by available bandwidth. The design of a Web-based application must take into consideration both the material being made available, as well as the mechanisms which are used to access that information. A simple example is the use of thumbnail images to provide an indication of the content of full-size and large data-content images. A more complex example, is the design of the whole application structure in order to minimise navigation requirements.

- *Maintenance*: the maintenance of Websites is complicated by the fact that they usually incorporate links to sites which are outside the developers control. This has maintenance implications in that at any time links can become stale or incorrect. The lifecycle process needs to consider the mechanisms and costs associated with regular maintenance and validation of the interface between the local site and the remainder of the Web.

- *Multi-platform, multi-browser support*: the information underlying the application will be viewed on varying platforms and using a variety of browsers. The developer has the option of either explicitly constraining this set (for example, requiring the use of, say, Netscape Navigator rather than Microsoft Internet Explorer), or developing the application in a generic a fashion as possible. This will have implications for aspects such as planning, design, evaluation and navigation (some browsers support navigation facilities not available in others – such as Netscape 'cookies').

- *Multi-user support*: the users of most Websites may have significantly different backgrounds, requirements and contexts. In the development of a Web based application, consideration needs to be given to how to support these varying requirements and contexts, usually in as transparent a fashion as possible.

2

Hypermedia

'We live on an island surrounded by a sea of ignorance.
As our island of knowledge grows, so does the shore of our ignorance.'

(John A. Wheeler)

Chapter Goals

In this chapter we take a much more detailed look at what exactly we mean by the term 'hypermedia'. We provide both an historical context, and a goal-based perspective, and end with a working definition of hypermedia that can be used to guide our approach to the development of hypermedia applications. The objectives of this chapter are to:

- Look at cognitive aspects of hypermedia to begin to develop an understanding of the underpinning philosophy.

- Analyse numerous existing definitions. We see that these tend to have a technology focus, and do not help us understand the implications for development.

- Derive a definition for hypermedia which helps us understand how to effectively develop hypermedia applications.

- Establish the concept of hypermedia as a vehicle for information utilisation.

- Develop a solid understanding of information concepts and how they relate to hypermedia.

What is hypermedia development? This entire book is about hypermedia development, and yet the term is not yet well understood or defined, even within the research and academic literature. Individual books, papers, documents, manuals and presentations use the term to cover a surprisingly diverse mix of activities. These include, though are not limited to, media management (such as data capture, storage and manipulation), creative and artistic processes (such as content design and interface creation), implementation activities (such as the use of both 'authoring' and presentation tools and development languages) and application development (such as hypermedia application design, process planning and development process management).

Before we can begin to consider this broad array of activities and the roles they play within the development of hypermedia applications, we need to understand exactly what we mean by the term *hypermedia development*. The logical place to begin is to consider hypermedia and then development, and only then to investigate an understanding of hypermedia development. We do not aim to provide a definitive introduction to hypermedia; this is provided in numerous articles and books elsewhere (for example, Berk (1991), Nielsen (1995) and Woodhead (1991)). Rather, its purpose is to set the context for the rest of this book – providing a specific definition of hypermedia which will enlighten the discussion for the remainder of the book. We begin by considering current interpretations of the term 'hypermedia'. We look at how hypermedia has evolved, providing an historical perspective which helps us understand not only the current state of hypermedia applications, but also the current state of approaches to developing hypermedia applications.

From here we derive our own interpretation of what hypermedia should be, and hence what the development of hypermedia applications is likely to involve. This definition is strongly influenced by what we wish a hypermedia application to achieve, and as such, we consider the goals of hypermedia applications in terms of information transferral, and the characteristics of applications that are likely to help us achieve these goals. Finally, we look at several examples which illustrate many of the aspects discussed, and briefly consider both the good and bad characteristics of these applications.

2.1   What is Hypermedia?

We begin this chapter by considering the question 'What is hypermedia?' To understand how to approach hypermedia development, we need to understand what we mean by the term hypermedia development. To understand hypermedia development, we need to understand what we mean by the hypermedia application we are developing. In other words, by developing an understanding of hypermedia which extends beyond a mere collection of technical wizardry and flashy displays, we provide a context in terms of our interpretation of the purpose/goals of hypermedia which allows us to develop an understanding of how to most effectively approach the development of the next generation of truly effective hypermedia applications.

The term 'hypermedia' is becoming more and more widespread. But what exactly is hypermedia? This sounds like a relatively simple question. It is not! Along with terms such as hypertext and multimedia, it is bandied about the press as though it were a cure-all for all information management woes. Despite this, or possibly partly because of it, the term is still rather ill-defined. Before trying to identify or develop a useful definition, let us divert for a moment and consider the way that human memory works.

Hypermedia and Human Memory

Human memory is associative: we associate pieces of information with other information and create complex knowledge structures. We often remember information via association, i.e. a person starts with an idea which reminds them of a related idea or a concept, which triggers another idea. The order in which a human associates an idea with another idea depends upon the context under which the person wants information i.e. a person can start with a common idea and can end up associating it to completely different sequences of ideas on different occasions.

When writing, an author converts his knowledge which exists as a complex knowledge structure into an external representation. Physical media such as printed material and video tapes only allow us to represent information in an essentially linear manner. Thus, the author has to go through a linearisation process to convert his knowledge to a linear representation. This is not natural. So the author will provide additional information, such as a table of contents and an index, to help the reader understand the overall information organisation.

The reading process can be seen as a transformation of external information into an internal knowledge representation combined with integration into existing knowledge structures. These processes are shown in Figure 2-1a. For this, the reader breaks the information into smaller chunks and rearranges these based on the reader's information requirement. We rarely read a textbook or a scientific paper from start to end – we tend to browse through the information and then follow the information trails that are interesting to us (Ginige and Fuller (1994)).

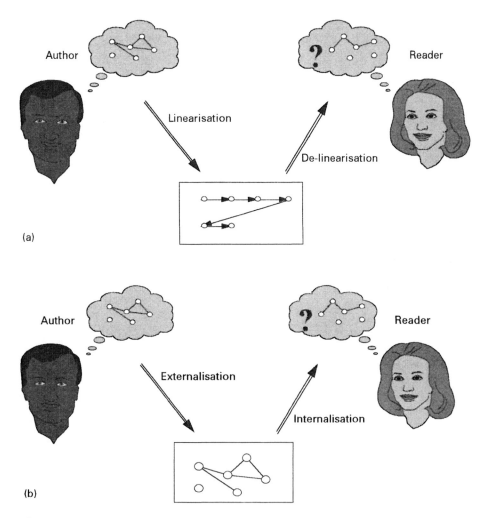

Figure 2-1

(a) Process of writing and reading using traditional linear media. (b) Process of writing and reading using non-linear hypermedia

Hypermedia, using computer supported links, allows us to partially mimic writing and reading processes as they take place inside our brain. We can create non-linear information structures by associating chunks of information in different ways using links. Further, we can use a combination of media consisting of text, images, video, sound and animation to enrich the representation of information. It is not necessary for an author to go through a linearisation process of the author's knowledge when writing. Also, the reader can have access to some of the information structures the author had when writing the information, which helps readers to create their own representation of knowledge and to integrate it into existing knowledge structures. This process is shown in Figure 2-1b.

In addition to being able to access information through association, hypermedia applications are strengthened by a number of additional aspects, including an ability to incorporate various media, interactivity, vast data sources, distributed data sources and powerful search engines. These make hypermedia a very powerful tool to create, store, access and manipulate information.

Definition of Hypermedia

Let us now refine our concept of hypermedia by considering more formal definitions. Table 2–1 provides a number of definitions of both hypertext and hypermedia which provide varying perspectives on hypermedia.

If we look at these definitions we can find specific points which we might argue with, or can result in confusion. For example, the term 'non-linear' is often used when defining hypertext and hypermedia, but can be quite misleading. Any given navigation path through a hypermedia application will be linear – a hard constraint set by the unalterable single dimensional nature of time. It is the explicit support for a network of potential or possible paths through the information which gives us non-linearity, even though a specific actual path will still be linear.

Similarly, many hypertext and hypermedia definitions include references to databases (such as the Shneiderman and Kearsley definition). Again, if taken out of context, this can be misleading. The term 'database' often carries connotations of a high degree of structure, and while this is typical of some hypermedia applications, it is not a defining characteristic (consider, for example, the WWW). A database can be considered to be a repository from which data can be accessed.

Table 2–1

Hypertext/Hypermedia definitions

'A memex is a device in which an individual stores all his books, records and communications and which is mechanized so that it may be consulted with exceeding speed and flexibility. It is an enlarged intimate supplement to his memory.'
  Vannevar Bush, 'As we may think', *Atlantic Monthly*, July 1945.

Hypertext: 'a combination of natural languages text with the computer's capacity for branching, or dynamic display'
  Ted Nelson, 'Getting it out of our system': *Information Retrieval: A Critical Review*, G. Schechter (ed.), Thomson Books, Washington, DC, 1967.

Hypertext: 'a database that has active cross-references and allows the reader to 'jump' to other parts of the database as desired'
  Shneiderman B, Kearsley G. *Hypertext Hands-On!: An Introduction to a New Way of Organizing and Accessing Information*, Addison-Wesley, 1989.
  (see also http://www.win.tue.nl/win/cs/is/debra/cursus/definition.html or search the Web for 'Hypertext Shneiderman Kearsley' for a discussion of this definition)

Hypermedia: 'Multimedia Hypertext. Hypermedia and Hypertext tend to be used loosely in place of each other. Media other than text typically include graphics, sound, and video.'
Hypertext: 'Text which is not constrained to be linear.'
  World Wide Web Consortium 'Hypertext Terms'
  http://www.w3.org/pub/WWW/Terms.html April 1995

'It is tempting to describe the essence of hypertext as its ability to perform high-speed, branching transactions on textual chunks. But this is a little like describing the essence of a great meal by listing its ingredients. Perhaps a better description would focus on hypertext as a computer-based medium for thinking and communication'
  Conklin J. 'Hypertext: An Introduction and Survey', *IEEE Computer*, September 1987, 17–41.

'Hypertext denotes an information medium that links verbal and nonverbal information. . . . Electronic links connect lexias 'external' to a work – say, commentary on it by another author or parallel or contrasting texts – as well as within it and thereby create text that is experienced as nonlinear, or, more properly, as multilinear or multisequential. Although conventional reading habits apply within each lexia, once one leaves the shadowy bounds of any text unit, new rules and new experience apply.'
  Landow G. *Hypertext: The Convergence of Contemporary Critical Theory and Technology*, The Johns Hopkins University Press, 1996.
  (see also http://www.stg.brown.edu/projects/hypertext/landow/ht/contents.html or search the Web for 'Landow Hypertext')

Hypermedia is different from 'traditional' databases, especially from the perspective of the user interaction. Indeed, it may be more accurate to refer to hypermedia applications as 'infobases', rather than databases. This does not, of course, preclude the use of databases as an enabling technology within hypermedia applications. Indeed, the structured information organisation and document management functionality of databases can be effectively used in conjunction with hypermedia style information organisation (i.e. associative linking) to provide a degree of synergy between the two. Database structures can provide a structuring of information spaces which is often overlooked in the traditional hypermedia structures, such as those in HyperCard and the Web.

Indeed, examples of applications, albeit rather contrived, could be found which satisfied most of the given definitions in turn, yet which would not be regarded as hypermedia applications. What then holds up as a definition of hypermedia? The breadth of the ways in which hypermedia is interpreted or defined can be seen in the following two less well recognised quotes:

> 'Hypertext: "is basically the same as regular text – it can be stored, read, searched, or edited – with an important exception: hypertext contains connections within the text to other documents."'
>
> Kevin Hughes, 'What is hypertext and hypermedia?', May 1994 (see http://www.eit.com/goodies/www.guide/guide.02.html or search the Web for 'Web Hypertext Hughes').

> 'Hypertext: "is a web of possibilities, a web of reading experiences. . . . Hypertext is the language of exploration and discovery"'
>
> Charles Deemer, 'What is hypertext?', 1994. (see http://www.teleport.com/~cdeemer/essay.html or search the Web for 'Hypertext Deemer').

To provide a basis for the remainder of this book we will answer the question 'What is hypermedia?' in an unusual fashion. We will not provide the more usual product-based definition, such as most of those in Table 2–1. Rather, we shall provide a goal-based definition (which we will refine later in this book) which allows us to focus on the purpose of hypermedia (and hence the characteristics which we wish to build into applications) rather then the technologies of hypermedia.

To start let us consider the definitions in Table 2–1 anew, not individually but as a whole. The underlying theme (especially when we consider the *int*ent of the definitions, rather than the *cont*ent of the definitions) is one of using information inter-relationships to provide support for flexible access and management of information. For example, why should hypermedia provide support for information interlinking in complex non-linear networks? Surely it is in order to allow us to navigate this information in complex but flexible patterns to identify specific items of information or information patterns – the associative linking of information parallels the mechanisms by which our mind retrieves information. Another example: why do we use databases? Surely it is in order to manage the data in a way which facilitates information access and manipulation. Why use multiple forms of media? Surely it is because of the information carrying capacity of the various forms of media.

This leads us to an initial tentative definition of hypermedia as:

Definition

Hypermedia An application which uses associative relationships among information contained within multiple media data for the purpose of facilitating access to, and manipulation of, the information encapsulated by the data.

This definition does not contradict those given in Table 2–1, rather it complements them. This definition is intended to make explicit certain factors relating to hypermedia and its purpose. We will return to this definition throughout this book, refining and using it constantly.

Let us consider this definition. It contains two key elements: access to and manipulation of information; and associative relationships amongst the information. The first of these provides the core tenet which underlies this entire book – *the purpose of hypermedia is to provide access to and manipulation of information*. This should be foremost in our consideration when we are looking at how to develop hypermedia applications. For the time being, we will ignore what exactly we mean by 'information' – but we return to this later, as it is critically important that we understand the idea of information if we are to develop applications which allow us to handle information.

The second aspect of the definition relates to the associative relationships among the information. What makes hypermedia different from other information management systems is that it uses the complex associative inter-relationships among the information which underlies hypermedia applications – hence the common focus on non-linearity and networks. We shall divert for a moment, and consider just what these relationships mean in terms of hypermedia.

Hypermedia Linking

Hypermedia systems, indeed information in general, contains various types of relationships between elements of information. Examples of typical relationships include similarity in meaning or context (*Vannevar Bush* relates to *Hypermedia*), similarity in logical sequence (*Chapter 3* follows *Chapter 2*) or temporal sequence (*Video 4* starts five seconds after *Video 3*), and containment (*Chapter 4* contains *Section 4.2*).

Hypermedia allows these relationships to be instantiated as links which connect the various information elements, so that these links can be used to navigate within the information space. We can develop different taxonomies of links, in order to discuss and analyse how they are best used.

One possible taxonomy is based on the mechanics of the links. We can look at the number of sources and destinations for links (single-source single-destination, multiple-source single-destination, etc.), the directionality of links (unidirectional, bidirectional) and the anchoring mechanism (generic links, dynamic links, etc.).

A more useful link taxonomy is based on the type of information relationships being represented. In particular, we can divide relationships (and hence links) into those based on the organisation of the information space (structural links) and those related to the content of the information space (associative and referential links). Let us take a brief look at these links in more detail.

Structural links

The information contained within the hypermedia application is typically organised in some suitable fashion represented using structural links. We can group structural links together to create different types of application structures. If we look, for example, at a typical book, then this has both a linear structure (from the beginning of the book linearly to the end of the book) and usually a hierarchical structure (the book contains chapters, the chapters contain sections, the sections contain . . .). Typically, in a hypermedia application we try to create and use appropriate structures. Example structures are discussed in more detail in Section 3.2. These structures are important in that they provide a form for the information space, and hence allow the user to develop an understanding of the scale of the information space, and their location within this space. This is very important in helping the user navigate within the information space. Structural relationships do not, however, imply any semantic relationship between linked information. For example, a chapter in a book which follows another is structurally related, but may not contain any directly related information. This is the role of associative links.

Associative links

An associative link is an instantiation of a semantic relationship between information elements. In other words, completely independantly of the specific structure of the information, we have links based on the meaning of different information components. The most common example which most people would be familiar with is cross-referencing within books ('for more information on X refer to Y'). It is these relationships – or rather the links which are a representation of the relationships – which provide the essence of hypermedia, and in many respects can be considered to be the defining characteristic.

Referential links

A third type of link which is often defined (and is related to associative links) is a referential link. Rather than representing an association between two related concepts, a referential link provides a link between an item of information and an elaboration or explanation of that information. A simple example would be a link from a word to a definition of that word. One simple way of conceptualising the difference between associative and referential links is that the items linked by an associative link can exist independantly, but are conceptually related. However, the item at one end of a referential link exists *because* of the existence of the other item.

It is important to note that many hypermedia systems (most noticeably the WWW) do not provide a mechanism for differentiating between the different link types. As a result, the same mechanism is used to represent these different types of links. A common result is that users are not readily able to differentiate between the structure of the information space and the content of the information space – resulting in difficulty in navigation.

As a final point on linking, it is useful to note that we could take a holistic perspective and recognise that every item of information is related to every other item of information within some context. Hypermedia, however, is about sifting through this almost-infinite web of interconnections, to identify and use those that help with the goal of information access and manipulation within some context. As was originally recognised by Vannevar Bush (1945) over 50 years ago, these associative relationships are analogous to the way in which our mind appears to achieve such a high level of efficacy in information retrieval.

Current State of Hypermedia

Although the underlying ideas of hypermedia are still being actively refined, debated and improved, we are now at a point where many of the technical limitations associated with handling various forms of media, such as image, video, animation and audio, have been removed – at least to a limited extent. Similarly, we have begun to develop an understanding of how to manage the various technologies in a reasonably cohesive fashion (much of this has been a result of the development of the WWW over the last few years). However, we have not yet reached an effective understanding of the *processes required* to develop applications which help us to *effectively utilise* information. We need to reconsider what hypermedia should be helping us to achieve.

If we look at the current state of hypermedia applications, we can identify at least two major limitations. First, we have yet to satisfactorily address problems of effective location of information. To be able to use information we must be able to identify or locate the information we need. Our current applications typically rely on primitive manual authoring of static links, with little subsequent assistance to a user. Similarly, current applications rarely attempt to develop an understanding of the users context and how to respond to this.

In some respects, this is a core element of the reason for using a hypermedia structure – we identify information based on association. This will, however, only be effective if the associations are appropriate, comprehensive and contextual. Although the WWW and most other hypermedia applications support some forms of associative linking, this is limited (it is often neither typed nor structured), incomplete (typically being manually generated, or based on poor automatic indexing) and often lacks mechanisms for providing contexts to aid in comprehension. Additionally, and this is where much recent attention has been focused, the application should be designed in such a way that assists us in identifying appropriate relationships (i.e. links). This covers factors such as screen and interface design, use of indexes and tables of contents, node or page size, and a host of other design characteristics.

Potentially, a much more significant problem relates back to the purpose of hypermedia. Most current applications, including the WWW, are to a large extent predicated on Bush's more restrictive idea of associative information retrieval, rather then Nelson's broader concept of 'hypermedia' being about supporting information usage. This is evidenced by the lack of consideration given to dealing with issues such as information contextualisation, support for intelligent browsing and navigation (beyond mere associative linking in flat networks), information structuring, mechanisms for active annotation and restructuring of networks based on feedback.

The field has evolved in such a way that it has gradually led us towards the current situation of an overly narrow perception of hypermedia as a vehicle for *information provision* or *procurement*, rather than the broader concept of a vehicle for *information utilisation*. The 'non-linearity' and 'interactivity' which current hypermedia applications incorporate are only implemented to help us find an item of information, not to help us use that information. This has been reflected in the development of hypermedia applications, authoring tools and the entire approach to hypermedia development. This is partially a result of the dominance of the WWW and its basic paradigm of flat arbitrary linking and information downloading. There are, however, positive signs that this is gradually changing, such as discussions on typed links, the use of URN's (Universal Resource Name) rather than URL's (Universal Resource Location) and enhanced levels of interactivity and mechanisms for supporting these, such as VRML and Java applets.

In this book, we will be considering hypermedia development as the field of developing hypermedia applications which fulfil this wider definition of information utilisation rather than simply information procurement.

2.2 Goals of Hypermedia

We believe that hypermedia has evolved into essentially a paradigm of information *procurement*, whereas we believe that a paradigm of information *utilisation* is more appropriate. To demonstrate this, we shall briefly consider an historical perspective on hypermedia.

An Historical Perspective

Having developed a working definition of hypermedia in the previous section, it is worth looking at how hypermedia applications have developed within the context of this definition. Large numbers of hypermedia histories and timelines exist elsewhere (Hughes, 1994; Nielsen, 1995). Rather than reiterate this material, let us look at a few of the pivotal events within this history which impact on our interpretation of the goals of hypermedia applications.

Vannevar Bush and memex

Vannevar Bush is generally recognised as the first person to begin speculating about hypermedia. It is worth repeating parts of a critical section of the article from 1945 where this began (Bush, 1945) (we have italicised parts of the text for emphasis):

> 'The real heart of the matter of selection, however, goes deeper than a lag in the adoption of mechanisms by libraries, or a lack of development of devices for their use. Our ineptitude in getting at the record is largely caused by the artificiality of systems of indexing. ... The human mind does not work that way. *It operates by association.* With one item in its grasp, it snaps instantly to the next that is suggested by the association of thoughts, in accordance with some intricate web of trails carried by the cells of the brain.
>
> Man cannot hope fully to duplicate this mental process artificially, but he certainly ought to be able to learn from it. In minor ways he may even improve, for his records have relative permanency. The first idea, however, to be drawn from the analogy concerns selection. *Selection by association, rather than by indexing, may yet be mechanized.*
>
> Consider a future device for individual use, which is a sort of mechanized private file and library. It needs a name, and to coin one at random, "memex" will do. A memex is a device in which an

individual stores all his books, records, and communications, and which is mechanized so that it may be consulted with exceeding speed and flexibility. *It is an enlarged intimate supplement to his memory.'*

What troubled Bush, and led to the ideas in his article, was the gap between our growing knowledge and our inability to manage and access this knowledge effectively. Bush's vision was of an 'enlarged intimate supplement to his memory' – something which provided such a straight-forward and natural method of accessing information that it could almost be viewed as part of our memory. Despite Bush's technical descriptions of how such an approach may work (naturally constrained by the technology of the time), the real underlying message, and the reason why the article has been so enduring, is that we need a method of managing our expanding stores of information and knowledge *in a way which facilitates rapid and natural access.* Bush was not concerned with specific technological implementations, rather with how best to provide support for accessing information.

Bush also introduced a number of related concepts which are still being investigated and developed today. For example, he discussed the use of 'trails'. His concept was that experts or 'trail-blazers' would identify useful or appropriate paths through the tangle of information. These trails could be recorded and used as a guide for others. Although reflected in current implementations such as guided tours, Bush's ideas went beyond this to consider contextualised tours and aids in navigating through complex sets of information.

Ted Nelson and hypermedia

During the first half of the 1960s, Ted Nelson revived Bush's original ideas, and developed his ideas of hypermedia, though he didn't coin the term hypertext until 1965. Again, the focus was very strongly on access to and manipulation of information. Where Nelson differed from Bush is that where Bush saw 'hypermedia' as a mechanism for managing and retrieving our stores of information, Nelson saw it as a way of extending the ways in which we use and manipulate information (Nelson, 1993b)

'We would not be reading from paper any more. The computer screen, with its instant access, would make paper distribution of text absurd. Best of all, no longer would we be stuck with linear text, but we could create whole new gardens of interconnected text and graphics for the user to explore! (It would be several years before I would choose the word "hypertext" for this vision.) Users would sit holding a light-pen to the screen, making choices, browsing, exploring, making decisions. This would free education from the tyranny of teachers! It would free authors and artists from the tyranny of publishers! A new world of art! knowledge! populism! freedom! The very opposite of what everyone thought computers were about!'

Nelson's writings constantly used, and still use, a starting point of *what can be or should be achievable* with hypermedia – the technology is an implementation side-issue which is used because it is necessary to support the ideas. As with Bush, Nelson's ideas started with concepts of information utilisation, but where he differed was that he viewed information as active, rather than Bush's passive information which exists only to be retrieved.

Nelson named his system Xanadu after the 'magic place of literary memory' in the poem *Kubla Khan* by Samuel Taylor Coleridge. Xanadu was intended to record not just documents and links between them, but all versions of all material. Documents were stored as the original and a collection of progressive changes. Documents could also have 'windows' to other documents – an idea which evolved into Transclusion, a concept aimed at managing not just information reuse but copyrighting and information charging. Xanadu also strongly emphasised the separation of the user interface and the database server. Unfortunately Nelson's vision for Xanadu has yet to be fully achieved in an implemented system (Nelson, 1993a).

Doug Engelbart and NLS

NLS, developed by Doug Engelbart in the 1960s (Englebart, 1988), evolved from Engelbart's work on H-LAM/T (Human using Language, Artifacts, and Methodology, in which he is Trained). Engelbart envisioned the user and the computer in a dynamic symbiosis which amplified the native intellect of the user, augmenting human capabilities. NLS, the oN Line System, was an experimental system which could store and access a broad range of documentation. As with Nelson, Engelbart was beginning with a focus on managing abilities to use information, and then progressing to tools which could support this.

The development of hypertext systems

During the 1970s and 1980s, the concepts begun by Bush, Nelson and Engelbart began to appear in an assortment of hypertext systems and hypertext authoring environment. Early examples included ZOG (Robertson, McCrackon and Newell, 1981) (which evolved into KMS in the early 1980s), Hyperties (Schneiderman, 1987), NoteCards (Halase, Moran and Trigg, 1987) and Intermedia (Yankelovich, Meyrowitz and van Dam, 1985) in the mid-1980s, and HyperCard (Apple Computers, 1989) in 1987. If we look at the development of these systems, as well as those that followed them, we see a shift in focus away from information use as embodied by Nelson's ideas of 'making choices, browsing, exploring, making decisions' towards a significantly more highly constrained perception of hypermedia as being almost a data structuring tool. This is exemplified by systems like HyperCard, which narrow down hypermedia almost solely to a collection of nodes and links. The result is a system which barely supports information retrieval, and is used more as a presentation mechanism.

Indeed, this trend went even further, resulting in a growing focus on specific information representations and tools which manage these representations. This was partly a result of the efforts to overcome technical limitations of handling digital media, and partly a result of a failure to understand *how* to tackle the more difficult issues of supporting effective use of information. This unfortunate trend was continued with the development of the World Wide Web.

Tim Berners-Lee and the World Wide Web

The WWW (Berners-Lee, 1991) (or just 'Web') was originally proposed by Tim Berners-Lee in 1989, and has since received both high praise and scathing criticism from a variety of sources. The high praise is a result of the incredible success it has achieved as a mechanism for providing rapid access to an incredibly diverse range of information. The criticism is typically a result of the things which the Web has failed to support. Examples include active support for flexible indexing and searching, consistency maintenance, and a host of specific technical constraints such as generic links (Lewis *et al.*, 1996), and universal resource names and identifiers (Berners-Lee, 1994). Much of the research and development effort over the last five years has been focusing on overcoming many of these problems. From the perspective of how the implementation of the Web has influenced our understanding of hypermedia, we find that the Web has tended to focus on *information provision*, rather than the broader concept of *information utilisation*. This will be discussed further in the next section. It is worth pointing out that we are not criticising the Web *per se*: the Web has achieved admirable progress in supporting access to information. Rather, our criticism is for an acceptance of the Web as being a *sufficient* solution to many information access and management problems. We need to consider how to learn from the Web, but move beyond it to more usable, reliable and robust applications.

Why Hypermedia?

In the context of the above observations, let us look at why we use hypermedia – in other words, the goals of hypermedia. These goals will not only be a result of what we wish to achieve, but also the technological constraints under which we are working.

Why do we use hypermedia? Obviously, hypermedia is not an end in itself. We must have a reason for using hypermedia. It provides a vehicle for achieving some end. If we consider this end – the goals of hypermedia – then we can gain an insight into what hypermedia is really trying to achieve, and hence the direction in which our development efforts should be moving. As discussed above, the historical context of hypermedia is demonstrated as either information procurement, or information utilisation. This is reflected in the quote at the beginning of the first chapter:

> The essence of knowledge is, having it, to apply it; not having it, to confess your ignorance.
>
> (Confucius)

If we treat knowledge as being based on information (this relationship will be discussed in considerably more detail in Section 2.3), then we can extract three essential components:

- information: The *essence of knowledge* is, having it, to apply it.
- having information   The essence of knowledge is, *having it*, to apply it.
- applying information   The essence of knowledge is, having it, *to apply it*.

Let us consider the first part of this. If we ignore (for the time being only) the relationship between information and knowledge and focus just on information, then the obvious question is 'What is information, within the context of hypermedia?' Hypermedia is not an end, but rather has been developed to support some action, activity or goal. If we are to provide this support, then we need to understand what information is relevant and appropriate.

Appropriateness may be a function of completeness, timeliness, correctness or a range of other criteria, defined by user, context and environment. For example, if we are using a hypermedia application to try to locate a single contact for a given person (email, postal, telephone, etc.), then completeness (of all possible 'solutions') is not necessarily a requirement, whereas correctness would be paramount. This leads us to the first goal of hypermedia:

Hypermedia Goal 1

To support (using the associative relationships between information sources) the carrying out of actions which result in the identification of appropriate information (with appropriateness being based on a given set of contextually defined criteria).

What does this statement really mean? The most obvious implication is that we must be able to find information which is relevant and appropriate, and then once found, recognise it as such. This is partly the basis of the associative relationships used in hypermedia. Associative relationships provide a mechanism for moving about within a given information map – they can be viewed as the roads connecting various information sites. These roads, relationships or links will only be useful though if we know where they lead. The relationship is not sufficient in itself; for it to be useful, we need to be able to find relationships which are relevant within the context that we are considering. This raises a broad range of issues such as:

- How do we 'label' relationships in order to support understanding of their destinations? Is labelling and subsequent linking even appropriate (see the 'tyranny of the link debate' (Hall, 1994))?
- Relationship relevance is heavily dependant upon context. How do we incorporate context into relationship or link provision?

- Should relationships move beyond being essentially static entities to incorporating mechanisms for supporting intelligent contextual sources and destinations (this is reflected in work on typed links, generic links, multi-destination linking, etc.).

As well as linking, another avenue for identifying relevant information is the more traditional field of information indexing. We can supply searchable indexes of information spaces, the effectiveness of which is a function of their coverage, the intelligence of the indexing mechanisms and the types of searches which are supported. The better search engines which currently exist on the Web typically provide comprehensive coverage of the material available on the Web, but severely restricted searching mechanisms, especially with respect to supporting contextual searching. For example, they typically cannot adapt their searching mechanisms based on an understanding of personal taste or background. The main exceptions to this which are beginning to appear are the use of active agents, which can build up user profiles. A good example are the systems developed by *Firefly* – look at:

```
http://www.firefly.com/
```

Alternatively, look at the July/August 1997 issue of *IEEE Internet Computing*.

The essence of knowledge is, having it, TO APPLY IT

How do we apply information? What does 'applying' information mean? This is often the most difficult aspect of any hypermedia application, and hence it often gets overlooked. A dictionary definition (*Oxford English Dictionary*, *2nd Ed.*, Clarendon Press, 1989) of *apply* is: "apply: *v*. 5. to put to a special use or purpose; 6. to put to use; to employ". This may mean any number of things. We need to be able to modify information, annotate information, restructure the information, add, combine and compare information, analyse the information and interpret the information. Note that many if not all of these activities require a context within which the activity can be carried out. We can summarise this as:

Hypermedia Goal 2

To support the carrying out of actions which facilitate the effective use of information.

This goal essentially tells us that hypermedia is about (or at least should be about) more than information retrieval. It should be capable of supporting users in effective utilisation of the information which is retrieved. This is only achieved effectively in rare cases at present, such as where applications have incorporated modelling mechanisms that allow users to manipulate the information being presented (consider, for example, an application which allows a user to manipulate a three-dimensional model of a piece of furniture they are considering purchasing in order to develop an understanding of how it might look in certain positions or with certain fabrics). What functionality might satisfy this goal? The most critical aspect is that hypermedia applications should be able to provide a context to support interpretation of the information which is provided. Other possibilities include support for annotation, analysis and reconstitution of the information.

The essence of knowledge is, HAVING IT, to apply it

This aspect is probably the most subtle. What exactly does 'having' information mean? Within the WWW paradigm, it is often interpreted simply as 'information downloading' or the procurement of information (and possibly presentation of the information, though this is not necessarily required). This however, is too simplistic an interpretation.

Another dictionary definition (*OED*): 'procure: *v* 5. To obtain by care or effort; to gain, win, get possession of, acquire', and a definition of possession is 'control or occupancy of property'. This leads us to a definition of information procurement as *to carry out some action which results in control of the information*. Note that there is no indication of the more traditional idea of 'possession' of the information, nor any technological connotation (such as 'download'). Rather, we wish to have control of the information, to be able to use it in any way which is appropriate. A final goal of hypermedia can then be given as:

Hypermedia Goal 3

To support the carrying out of actions which result in control of appropriate information.

This definition does not, at first glance, tell us anything more about 'having information' than the idea of simply procuring information.

However, it does tell us that the physical or logical location of the information (even when we are making use of the information) is not relevant. What matters is that we have obtained control of the information. This means that we are in a position to analyse or manipulate the information – we can make use of it in any fashion which is appropriate (within the constraints set by ownership, copyright, etc.). The implications of a sense of 'control of information' rather than 'possession of information' might be well demonstrated by a simple example.

Consider a WWW server which maintains information on published books. We wish to know how many books have been published on hypermedia authoring, so we follow a link to a page of information which lists all the published books in this area. But we do not need this information directly – we simply want to count the books. This list of books could remain on the server, *under our control*, but never in *our possession*. We could then manipulate this information (in this case, perform a count) with only the result being given into our possession and subsequently presented.

The most obvious implication of the idea of control rather than possession is that we do not need to possess information (and hence possibly pay for the information – see the work on transclusion (Nelson, 1995) for an introduction to how this might occur), which is only of interest as an avenue to locating some ultimate item.

In summary, this gives us the following goals for a hypermedia application:

Goals of Hypermedia Applications

To support (using the associative relationships between information sources) the carrying out of actions which:

- ... result in the identification of ...

- ... facilitate the effective utilisation of ...

- ... result in control of ...

appropriate information (with appropriateness being based on a given set of contextually defined criteria).

2.3   Data, Information and Knowledge

In the previous sections we have referred to 'information' on a large number of occasions. This is not surprising given that hypermedia is ostensibly about handling information in one way or another. Despite this, the concept of information is often quite poorly understood and used in a wide variety of ways (and with a wide variety of interpretations) within the multimedia and hypermedia community. This results in a very unstable foundation when considering hypermedia.

If we are to effectively develop hypermedia applications (or even discuss them in an unambiguous fashion), then we need to have suitable working definitions of information and related concepts. In this section we will provide definitions of the concepts of data, information and knowledge. These definitions will be used as the basis for many of the discussions throughout this book. We do not claim that these definitions are definitive, nor necessarily even consistent with the more fundamental ideas on information theory (indeed, in many cases even these contradict each other). What we do have, however, is a set of practical definitions which can be used in discussing and developing hypermedia applications. For more information on information (no pun intended) and its interpretation, you could look at any of the following: Barlow (1994), Belkin (1978), Buckland (1991) and Niteki (1984).

The definition of information we will use is based around the hierarchy shown in Figure 2-2. In this we consider three layers of concepts or entities with which we are dealing: data, information and knowledge.

Data?

Definition

Data   Artifacts which exist as a vehicle for conveying information.

What exactly is data? Data includes the artifacts which we are able to use as the basis of information – such as writing, images and sounds. These artifacts can be physical (such as marks on a sheet of paper), electronic (bit patterns in a computers memory) or some other form (such as electro-chemical potentials in the brain).

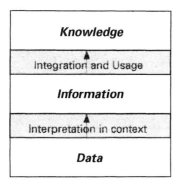

Figure 2-2

The basic Data-Information-Knowledge hierarchy. In simple terms data is the collected symbols and artifacts, information is the interpretation of these artifacts within some context, and knowledge is the integration of the information into a knowledge base such that it can be effectively utilised

This can be clarified with a simple example. Consider a sheet of paper with writing on it (such as this page). To someone able to read (at least in the language in which this book is written), this page will convey significant information. To someone unable to read (indeed, someone entirely unfamiliar with the concept of written communication), this page would appear to be a meaningless jumble of scrawls with no information content. Similar arguments apply to audio (consider speech in an unknown language) and images (how would a blind person who had just gained their sight for the first time perceive the images they saw?) In other words, the symbols themselves are not information – they merely carry information which must be extracted. This idea of data is quite similar to the concept of signifier within semiotics (Chandler, 1994).

This leads us to the role of media formats and data representations. The data must adhere to some structure which allows the required information to be extracted. The ease with which this extraction can occur will depend upon the nature and complexity of the representation. We will consider this in more detail later.

Information?

Information   The interpretation of data within a context set by *a priori* knowledge and the current environment.

When we read a page of text we are interpreting the textual symbols (i.e. the data) in the context of *a priori* knowledge (what we know about the language in which the text is written) and our current environment and context (why we are reading the page, where and how we are reading the page, etc.). For example, the words 'hypermedia applications use associations between concepts' involve many levels of interpretation (and levels of information). These could include:

- If we were illiterate and had no knowledge of written languages (and hence no relevant *a priori* knowledge) then these symbols would be meaningless – we would extract no meaning.

- If we were literate, understood a language which used the Latin alphabet, but did not know any English, then our *a priori* knowledge (of the shapes of Latin letters and the concept of groupings of letters forming words) would allow us to extract the information that this message contained six words, the first with 10 letters, the second with seven letters, and so on.

- If we understand the basics of hypermedia then we would be able to understand the meaning implied in the given message.

What we are essentially doing is identifying mappings from concepts (the concept of a letter and its shape, the concept of letters grouping together to form words, the concept of hypermedia, etc.) which already exist in our knowledge base to the information that is captured by the data. Again, this is similar to the semiotics notion of the relationship between signifier and signified concept.

The implications of this for us, in terms of developing hypermedia, are that to facilitate the extraction of information we need to consider the *a priori* knowledge which we are assuming of the users of the application and how to support the creation of the data-information mappings at the full range of levels. It also means we need to consider the context within which the application is being used. This is much more difficult for hypermedia than for traditional media since with hypermedia we can typically arrive at a point within the information space in many different ways. We typically cannot assume that a reader has followed a specific path in arriving at that point.

Knowledge?

Definition

Knowledge   The base of personal information which is integrated in a fashion which allows it to be used in further interpretation and analysis of data.

As described above, the extraction of information from data can be viewed as the identification of appropriate mappings from the data symbols to concepts in our knowledge base. These mappings will only be useful if we are able to use them in some way. This use can either be the direct usage as support for making a decision or carrying out some action, or in the augmentation of our knowledge base.

We view knowledge as being the personal base of information that we have accumulated and integrated in a fashion which allows it to be used further. As a trivial example, we could tell you that the word 'utility-media' (a rather cumbersome, non-existent, made-up word) is a new word which means media (images, text, etc.) that have been augmented with functionality to support active use of the media (such as media with built-in indexing mechanisms). If this word has gone beyond just infor-mation, to be incorporated into your knowledge base, then we could use this word, and your knowledge would provide an appropriate interpre-tation each time, i.e. you would be able to identify the mapping from the symbol 'utilitymedia' to the concept described above (which is in turn a set of mappings between other concepts, *ad nauseam*).

Implications

Although the definitions of data, information and knowledge we have provided are in some respects overly simplistic (from both an informa-tion studies perspective, and from a signal processing perspective), they are intended to provide working definitions that can be used to guide us in understanding the requirements of hypermedia development. Based on our definitions, we can make the following observations.

Within the hypermedia context, data has no direct purpose of its own; it exists solely as a vehicle for conveying information. So factors which lead to an inability to handle the data effectively (for example, if an application fails to maintain video and audio synchronisation), or which modify the way in which we present the data (such as progressive presentation of images on Web pages), will have a direct impact on the user's ability to interpret the data, and hence extract and use information. This should be taken into account in developing the data handling mechanisms to be used with in hypermedia applications.

The underlying data in hypermedia is not meaningful to a user until it has been interpreted within the context of both the *a priori* knowledge of the user and the environment within which the user is using the application. This tells us that any hypermedia application must have been developed with an understanding of both the *users* and the *conditions* under which they will be using the application. Factors such as the expected level of knowledge of the users and the objectives and expectations of users when they are using the application need to be taken into consideration. A useful exercise to determine meaningfulness during the development of a hypermedia application would be to profile the users. This will be considered later in the book.

A corollary to the above point is that in developing hypermedia applications, we need to be particularly aware of the environment in which data is being presented, as this will have a major impact on the users ability to identify and use information. The user's environment will be a function of factors such as the way the data is presented and the 'recent history' of the user. Consider, for example, a neutral article on alcohol use (hypothetically titled 'Alcohol – social lubricant or dangerous drug'). The potential interpretation of such an article will be very different if linked from an article on wine tasting versus an article on alcohol-related road fatalities.

In developing hypermedia applications, we need to be aware of the extent to which we are aiming to facilitate changes in the user's knowledge base. Where this is the case (especially, for example, with applications such as educational or instructional titles) we need to consider how the information presented will be integrated into the user's knowledge structures, and what mechanisms we may provide to evaluate and support this process.

One final important point is worth making before moving on. As discussed in the previous section, in most (if not all) cases we will be aiming to develop applications which allow users to use the information (rather than just retrieve information). For this to occur effectively, users must understand the information they are retrieving, i.e. users must be able to see the linkages between the information being made available and their own knowledge. Effectively, this implies that the information will almost always become part of the user's knowledge base (even if only very temporarily).

3

Hypermedia Modelling

If you don't know how to do something,
you don't know how to do it with a computer.
(Anonymous)

Chapter Goals

Having developed an understanding of hypermedia in the previous chapter, we now focus on the modelling of hypermedia information. We aim to show how we represent both hypermedia information and the structure of hypermedia applications themselves. From this point, later chapters will be able to consider what characteristics are typically built into hypermedia applications – and therefore how we approach their development. The objectives of this chapter are to:

● Consider the functionality of the digital domain, especially with respect to how we can represent and manipulate data. This leads on to a consideration of support for hypermedia interactivity.

● Develop an understanding of the types of information structures which can be constructed, and how these structures help us manage information.

● Look at current hypermedia models, and how these models help us understand how to represent information, and how to create applications which work within the constraints of these representations.

● Develop a detailed understanding of the characteristics of hypermedia applications, and in particular, to look at how different characteristics help achieve the goals of hypermedia applications.

Hypermedia *applications* are about helping users manage data, information and knowledge in a cohesive manner. Hypermedia *development systems* help developers create applications which achieve this. We have shown that an understanding of information is important to our understanding of hypermedia. From a pragmatic perspective, hypermedia is about managing knowledge, but knowledge management will be controlled by our ability to manage and represent information. In the development process we use to create applications, we need to consider how this might be achieved. Managing information will, in turn, be controlled by our ability to manage and represent data. Again, we need to consider how to achieve this.

Management and representation of data is becoming increasingly well understood. Mechanisms for representing audio, image and video data are being progressively refined (taking into account such diverse requirements such as data compression, accessibility, synchronisation, retrieval, etc.). Applications to manage data (such as multimedia databases and high-speed networks adapted for media delivery) are also evolving rapidly.

Unfortunately, a similar level of understanding does not exist regarding information representation and management. Although there is a significant body of work on modelling information, this has yet to be effectively mapped into the hypermedia domain, and the implications for hypermedia application development are, at best, poorly understood.

3.1   Data Representation

We need to consider how we represent data, and how this influences what we can achieve with hypermedia. In the previous chapter, we developed a goal-based definition of hypermedia, and looked at the role of data, information and knowledge within hypermedia. In particular, we emphasised the need to have a strong understanding of information and how it is used, in order to be able to appreciate how to effectively manage information in the hypermedia development process.

Up to this point, we have to a large extent avoided considering the fact that how we manage information will be constrained (or at least strongly influenced) by what is possible given the current technical limitations imposed by data formats. Indeed, we have largely ignored even the fact that hypermedia is implemented on computer hardware. We shall begin by considering just what functionality is provided within the digital domain.

Functionality of the Digital Domain

Information in hypermedia applications consists of different media such as text, images, video, audio and animation. Text and images are known as *static media*. Video, sound and animation are known as *dynamic* or *temporal media*, as these types are time dependant. When building hypermedia applications on computers, these media are obviously represented digitally. This digital representation, and the ways in which they can be manipulated on a computer, provided a significantly enhanced level of functionality over traditional media representations (for example, the ability to simply change the colour map for an image to manipulate its contrast).

From a technical point of view, if we are to make the most effective use of the functionality which is provided, then we should have an understanding of the following issues:

- Digital representation of media.
- Storage requirements.
- Structuring and retrieval methods.
- Compression.
- Capture, creation and editing.
- Display or playback methods.
- Media synchronisation.

Many of these issues are beyond the scope of this book, and are covered in great detail elsewhere. Gibbs and Tsichritzis (1995) provide a good overview of the representation and functionality supported by different media types.

From the perspective of developing hypermedia applications two of the most important considerations (which we shall look at in more detail) are supported operations and resource considerations.

Supported Operations

What types of operations are supported by different media? Different types of media will provide varying levels of support for operations on the media. Table 3–1 lists some of the more common (and important)

Table 3-1

Typical range of operations supported by different media types in the digital domain. The items in italics are still very poorly understood (Partially collated from (Gibbs and Tsichritzis (1995))

Text	Audio	Graphic	Image	Animation	Video
character manipulation	sample manipulation	primitive editing	pixel operations	primitive editing	pixel operations
string manipulation	waveform manipulation	structural editing	geometric manipulation	structural editing	frame manipulation
editing	audio editing	shading	filtering	rendering	editing
formatting	synchronisation	mapping	compositing	synchronisation	synchronisation
sorting	conversion	lighting	conversion	searching	conversion
indexing	searching	viewing	indexing	indexing	mixing
compression	indexing	rendering	compression		indexing
searching		searching	searching		searching
encrypting		indexing			video effects

types of operations which can be applied to different media. It is worth noting that the extent and ease of support for these operations will be dependant upon the particular representation (i.e. data format) used in each case. For example, pixel manipulation of a JPEG image will be significantly more complex than pixel manipulation of a BMP (bitmap) image.

We can break the operations which we perform on media into three categories: presentation, manipulation and analysis. By presentation, we mean the ability to present the media. Obviously, every type of media will support various forms of presentation. With static media this is relatively straightforward. One example of the extent of presentation support provided by different media is the idea of scalability. Examples of this include whether an image representation includes the ability to easily extract a thumbnail image for indexing presentation, and whether it allows progressive transmission and display of images. With temporal media it becomes slightly more complex, as the media format can actively support (or fail to support) characteristics such as media synchronisation and time manipulation. For example, is it possible to easily play a video clip at double speed? Backwards?

Manipulation operations are those that relate to the ability to edit and modify the media. With text we can easily perform a very large and complex set of operations. We can reformat text, restructure it, change styles, etc. With other media the range of operations is both theoretically much wider, and pragmatically more constrained. For example, the range of possible manipulations which can be performed to video data is very broad – editing, restructuring, enhancement, moving or replacing objects in scenes, changing characteristics of objects (such as changing a car from blue to red). However, many of these manipulations are either very computationally intensive or very time consuming (needing to be performed by hand).

The most significant class of operations (in terms of supporting hypermedia functionality) are those that analyse media in some way. This includes operations such as indexing and searching. A simple example serves to illustrate the effect on hypermedia of varying operations quite well. During the authoring process, we may wish to create a link from all occurrences of the words 'hypermedia engineering' to an article discussing this concept. We can readily use a text search engine (based on simple textual pattern matching) to locate possible candidate anchors for the links. To perform a similar operation on image data would be much more difficult. The fields of object recognition and computer vision do not yet provide reliable general purpose schemes for identifying arbitrary objects in images. Automatically searching for all Elm trees in a large image database is impractical, if not impossible, at present. The functionality of automatic indexing is possible for text, but not for images. (The QBIC application is a good example of how these inadequacies are being overcome for image data. See http://wwwqbic.almaden.ibm.com/ or search the Web for 'QBIC').

Media Analysis Supporting Interactivity

Hypermedia purports to *integrate* a number of different *media* into an *interactive* whole. Note the key words in this description: integrates, media and interactive. To-date, most hypermedia applications have not successively reached this goal. Although they tend to be interactive and integrated, and include multiple forms of media, these media are not combined into a cohesive whole, i.e. all forms of media are not used to provide the interactivity. In fact, most existing hypermedia applications would be more appropriately called multiple media hypertext applications. They tend to be hypertext applications (i.e. the textual information provides the interactivity), with the additional media acting as annotations, but not truly integrated into the application.

The few minor exceptions to the lack of visual information interactivity predominantly revolve around hand-crafted, small scale applications. However, these applications are sufficient to illustrate the significantly enhanced functionality which can be achieved with active visual information. For a good example of this, look at the map images in the *Virtual Tourist* on the WWW – http://www.vtourist.com/. These small scale applications have tended to be hand-crafted using low-level tools (such as MapEdit – a shareware Unix tool), and contain hard-coded static syntactic descriptions of the image data.

We can better understand the poor use that is made of media other than text by considering the use of textual data within hypermedia, an area that has received considerable research attention. Textual data can be readily stored, analysed, manipulated and generated synthetically by combining other sources of text. Essentially, text can be treated as consisting of lexical components or discrete entities – hypercomponents – (words, sentences, paragraphs, etc.) which obey a series of syntactic and semantic rules describing the inter-relationships. Within hypermedia applications these hypercomponents can be used to create nodes, anchors, links, etc. These elements provide the navigation functionality, which allows us to use the associative linking at the core of any hypermedia application.

The evolution of media other than text is still at a much lower level, and they are predominantly treated as passive media. For example, visual information in its raw form is highly unstructured and yet very common-place (documentary video tapes, image and photographic collections and databases, etc.). Many visual information applications (such as medical imaging, robotics and interactive multimedia) make use of the visual information in a highly structured format. Conceptually, visual informa-tion can be treated in the same way as text; consisting of discrete entities which obey certain syntactic rules. The primary difficulty, however, lies in analysing these entities and the associated rules, and then interpreting these. When this is achieved, visual and audio can become an active media as powerful (and in many cases, more so) than textual information.

Examples of some systems which have started to address these problems include HyperImages (Lowe and Ginige, 1995), which has used computer vision techniques to automatically generate hypermedia links (albeit within a very constrained domain), the Miyabi system (Hirata *et al.*, 1993), which provides a framework for generic media-based navigation, and MAVIS (Lewis *et al.*, 1996), which uses image feature matching to support generic links.

3.2   Information Structures

Having discussed data representations, the next step is to consider infor-mation models. However, we shall first consider why we need to model information, and the types of information structures which are tradi-tionally modelled.

Why Model Information?

Information models allow us to clarify the role of information and to be clear about the structure of the information we are using. Consider a simple example: hypermedia utilises the associations between concepts to support location of information. How do we model these relation-ships? Is the relationship between one document and another? Between one point in a document and an entire other document (such as is typical in the Web)? Are the relationships bidirectional (such as those which were supported in Intermedia), or unidirectional (such as those supported in the Web)? The specific answers to these questions, although important, don't affect the underlying point that, unless we have a model of the information and the way we intend to structure it, we won't be able to manage the information effectively.

One additional point which is worth making with respect to both data and information models is that different representations can capture the same content, but provide support for significantly different functionality. The best way to illustrate this is through a simple example. Consider Figure 3-1, where we have a simple graphical image that we can represent as either a collection of pixel coordinates or as set of drawing vectors (this is an oversimplification, but will suffice for our demonstration). Both of these representations capture the same image, and we can easily map from one representation to the other. The difference between the representations is the characteristics which are made explicit. From the underlying image (i.e. the data), we can extract information such as which points lie on the boundary, the number of lines and vertices in the object boundary, the boundary length, etc. It will be simpler to extract the number of boundary lines from the vector representation, but it will be simpler to identify whether a particular point lies on the boundary from the bitmap representation, i.e. the different representations provide more direct support for the extraction or identification of different forms of information.

A similar situation applies to hypermedia information structures. An application's ability to provide active direct support for different types of navigation and information management will depend heavily upon the types of links, nodes and data structures which are supported.

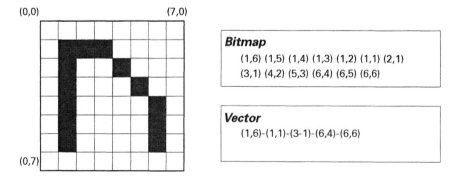

Figure 3-1

Two alternative representations of the same graphic image

Information Structures

What types of hypermedia information structures can exist? How do these structures affect the forms of navigation which are possible? A number of factors can be identified which affect the design of information structures. Examples of some of these factors include:

- Information retrieval and accessibility.

- Information security.

- Information reuse and maintainability.

- Inter-relationships between information sources.

- Provision of differing viewpoints on the information.

All of these factors (and many others) will impact strongly on the way in which we represent and structure the hypermedia information being used. We need to identify and use appropriate information structures which maximise the support for the underlying concepts of accessibility and manipulation of information. These structures will impact heavily on the development process.

When we structure information during the development process, we are trying to make explicit the knowledge representations which are inherent within the information. Since we are using the information to convey certain ideas, we will typically only make explicit certain subsets of the knowledge representations. For example, information related to a given concept will relate to other information differently depending upon the overall context. For example, George Bush and Bill Clinton are obviously related in the context of American politics (there may be a link labelled 'was succeeded by'), but are totally unrelated in the context of famous people named Bill. We therefore need to develop methods of structuring the information in such a way that they support the desired knowledge representations.

The basic structuring techniques that have been almost universally adopted are to break the information into atomic blocks, commonly called nodes, and typically containing an item of information which loses all usefulness if broken down any further. Typically, nodes may be images, audio tracks, blocks of text, video shots, etc. The next stage is to structure these nodes, which can involve one or both of two activities. The first is to group these atomic information building blocks into progressively more complex patterns. For example, a simple document may contain a block of text, an image and a short video sequence. The size of the presentation pages or nodes is still an issue open to debate: some developers recommend that pages should be kept small (nothing beyond a single screenful of information) to emphasise each individual concept and to improve the structuring of the information; other developers recommend much longer pages which preserve the natural linear structure of the plot or argument (with appropriate interlinking within the page). In our opinion, the size of the presentation nodes will be a function of the application and the way in which the information is being structured, and it is inappropriate to set specific constraints or recommendations.

The final activity is to then interlink the documents or nodes to create the often complex structures which support navigation and browsing within the information space.

Types of Information Structures

The information structures we create during the development process can be classified in various ways. Four common structures are linear, hierarchical, network or graph and matrix (see Figure 3-2). Applications can use more than one information structure. For example, training material, at the highest level may have a linear structure. The user first has to complete topic one before progressing onto topic two, but within a topic information can be organised into a hierarchical structure where the user can go through different sub-topics in any order. Alternatively, we can overlay different structures onto the same underlying information, so that it can be accessed and used differently, depending upon the context. Often the structure used will reflect the types of links we are trying to represent. For example, a hierarchical structure most often reflects *structural* links, whereas a network structure is most often based around *semantic* links.

Linear structures

Linear structures can be used in a number of ways within a hypermedia application. They can be used to retain the sequential structure of an original paper document. Typically, it makes good sense to retain the linear structure of the originating document, although printed material is linear because of the constraint of the media. The original author has ordered the information in a way which should contain value. The reader of this document within an electronic application should have access to

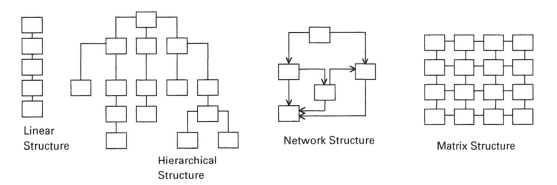

Linear Structure

Hierarchical Structure

Network Structure

Matrix Structure

Figure 3-2

Different information structures which can be used within hypermedia applications

this order in the same way as the reader of the paper version will have access to this structure.

Hypermedia application developers sometimes implement link applications that bind a series of nodes together in a sequential manner. These are sometimes referred to as guided tours, or hypertrails, and are commonly used as instructional aids. Guided tours can replicate the way teachers organise the presentation of information (nodes) in a logical progression and are useful when a hypermedia application is being used to provide procedural instructions. Procedures are comprised of a number of discrete actions which must take place in a particular order. Each action can be described in a node, and these nodes can be linked into a guided tour in the order these actions should take place.

Hierarchical

Hierarchical structure can be used to retain the original structure of the information contained in a hypermedia application. Books are often organised into chapters which have sections and subsections. This hierarchical structure can be replicated within a hypermedia database through the use of hierarchical links. A reader can go to a hypermedia application's table of contents or index and select a point within the information space to read in the same way as is done in the paper domain. Once again, it makes good sense to retain the structure that the author of the paper version of the document has constructed.

There are a number of hypermedia applications and systems that use hierarchical links extensively. Applications constructed using hypermedia systems such as KMS, Guide and AUGMENT/NLS use hierarchical structure as the base structure. Every node in these applications is part of a single hierarchy: the root node is usually the starting point for readers using these applications, and from this entry point all nodes within the application are reachable. This type of system is very similar in many respects to folding editors.

Network or graph

The third type of structure available in hypermedia applications is the graph or network. This structure is composed of associative links, which are of a semantic or pragmatic nature and are truly non-sequential. They bind common or related concepts together within the information space. The ability to use these associative links and the resulting network in effective browsing of the information space is one of the main advantages of hypermedia applications.

To a large extent, hierarchical links are used to represent information structure, while network links are used to represent semantics. In practice, a combination of these is often used to form a hybrid structure.

Matrix

In many cases we will have categorisations of information, but the categorisation is not single dimensional. Matrix structures allow us to capture the multidimensionality of various sources of information. For example, consider the case where we have a hypermedia application which provides details on procedures for car repair. We can have a matrix structure where the horizontal axis of the matrix is divided into information on different mechanical problems (wheel suspension faults, ignition problems, etc.), and the vertical axis of the matrix is divided into information describing symptoms, causes, solutions, tools and procedures. This would result in a single cell of the matrix describing, for example, the symptoms of problems with the suspension.

A matrix structure will often be appropriate to be used as a top level of a hypermedia structure, providing an indexing mechanism to lower levels of detailed information.

Examples of Information Structures

What link structures to include in a hypermedia application and how they are to be designed is dependant upon a number of factors. Both content and context need to be taken into consideration. The *content* of the application consists of the information to be included and how it is to be accessed. The important issues to resolve are:

- What material is to be included?
- What is the underlying structure of the information, and what subsets of this structure do we wish to support?
- How should this information be accessed (i.e. table of contents, index, full text and key word search)?

The *context* of the application is how it is to be used. Is the end application to be used as an information retrieval application? Is it to be used for education or training purposes, or is it primarily an entertainment product? Who is going to use it? Are they children or adults? How familiar are they with computers? These are just a few of the criteria that must be examined to decide how to structure the information and how to present the information.

Some illustrative examples:

- *Training material.* A linear structure is more suitable to present this type of material as the reader should learn the modules in a sequential manner. Developers can include questions at various points and provide additional information if the user provide wrong answers.
- *Educational material.* A hierarchical structure is suitable for computer-based training material. This base structure can be enhanced by providing links to a glossary and references.
- *Encyclopedia.* A network structure is more suitable to organise information in encyclopedia. This will enable access to the same information from different contexts.

As has been mentioned, the case is not usually as black and white as pictured in these examples. Most commonly a hybrid structure which has aspects of all of the above examples will be developed and used.

3.3   Hypermedia Information Models

Sitting above the layer of information structures we have models of the hypermedia information, which serve a variety of purposes. First, they allow us to provide a consistent framework within which we can build hypermedia applications. Beyond this, they can also be used for such purposes as ensuring interoperability of hypermedia applications and/or commonality of data formats.

Specific models are useful in the development of architectures for hypermedia applications and development systems. By architecture we mean the overall form or structure of an application or system. For example, the Web imposes a specific client-server architecture. When we are undertaking a particular development project, we will be highly constrained by the architecture of both the development system and the application, which are usually related. For example, when undertaking Web development we have no option but to adhere to the hypermedia model envisioned by the original developers of the Web and those who have subsequently modified or extended it through development of enhancements.[2]

It is, nevertheless, highly useful to have an understanding of the model upon which the particular development environment is predicated. It will mean that we will have a stronger understanding of what is possible and what is not directly supported – such as bidirectional linking in the Web.

Requirements of a Hypermedia Information Model

Before looking at several example hypermedia information models, we consider the requirements of any model. Looking at the requirements of a hypermedia model is doubly useful, apart from providing details of what must be considered when constructing the framework for any hypermedia application, it also gives a strong insight into many of the issues which need to be considered in general application development.

Hardman, Bulterman and van Rossum (1993) give a good list of the types of requirements for a hypermedia information model. They list:

- *Composition with multiple, dynamic data*: the model must support the ability to group different media items into a presentation and the expression of timing constraints among these items.

---

[2] Such as HTML extensions, Java applets and browser plug-ins.

- *Higher level presentation specification*: it is inadequate to be able to just express presentation specifications for individual media elements. The media elements will be used together with scarce presentation resources (such as screen real estate). We need to be able to develop higher level presentation specifications for groups of media in order to facilitate application maintenance. Hardman *et al.* use style sheets in word processors as an analogy.

- *Combining composite components*: a mechanism needs to be supplied which allows the expression of information required for combining presentations into composite presentations in a way which takes into account the scarce presentation resources.

- *Temporal relations*: a hypermedia model needs to express time-based relationships. Hardman *et al.* claim that these temporal relationships should be part of the presentation specification. There is disagreement as to whether this is most appropriate, given that the temporal relationships can be viewed as simply another form of structural information. We agree with Hardman *et al.*, however, that it is ill-advised to use the conceptual linking mechanism to support the temporal relationships.

- *Context for links*: a major constraint in most existing hypermedia applications is that they do not support any notion of link attributes, link contexts or control of context based on linking. A useful functionality for hypermedia is to be able to control the application context depending upon which links are followed (e.g. 'If I follow link *A* change just this part of the application. If I follow link *B* change the whole application').

In addition to the above requirements, we would add a few additional requirements:

- *Separation of data and information*: we believe that hypermedia models need to explicitly separate the data (i.e. the artifacts being used to encode the information) and the identification of the information. The classic example of this not being done is the Web, where the identification of information (such as information components to be used as anchors) is embedded into the same documents containing the raw data (i.e. the HTML files). This tends to lead to difficulty in reuse and maintainability. Most other hypermedia models explicitly separate (at least logically, if not physically) the data and the information. A good example of this approach is the use of linkbases in Microcosm (Hall, Davis and Hutchings, 1996).

- *Separation of information and application*: a hypermedia model which separates the information underlying applications from the applications themselves will facilitate much greater reuse of information. We can view such an approach as having a set of information upon which we layer different applications.

- *Separation of application and presentation*: if we separate the presentation mechanisms from the application, then the portability and genericity of applications will be substantially enhanced. As an example, the Web achieves this to a certain extent by specifying structural elements (such as 'heading level 1') rather than presentation style (such as 'bold, 14 point, times-roman font).

One final requirement is a little more controversial, though again we believe that it is important:

- *Openness*: open hypermedia allows the importing of new objects into the application (Davis *et al*. 1992). This enables the integration of hypermedia applications with the broad range of other applications likely to be used by any given user. This will substantially enhance the usability of all applications involved, with user applications benefiting from the interlinking provided by the hypermedia, and hypermedia benefitting from the broadened functionality provided by the various applications.

Let us now look at several typical hypermedia information models.

The Dexter Model

The Dexter Hypertext Reference Model evolved out of two small workshops, the first of which was held in the Dexter Inn in New Hampshire in 1988. This model was an attempt to capture the main abstractions that exist in a range of hypermedia applications. Its stated goal is to provide a basis for both comparing hypermedia applications and improving interoperability (Halasz and Schwartz, 1994).

The Dexter model represents a hypermedia application as three layers (see Figure 3-3). The bottom layer – the *within-component layer* – represents the contents and structure *within* the components of the application.

The Dexter model does not attempt to model this layer, but rather leaves the representation at this level up to other reference models designed specifically for modelling the structure and content of particular forms of information.

The middle layer – the *storage layer* – is the core of the Dexter model. This layer models the basic structure of a hypermedia application composed of nodes (or component, in Dexter terminology) and links between the nodes. A 'database' is composed of a hierarchy of components (which are either *atoms*, i.e. primitive components, or *composites*, i.e. composed of other components) which are interconnected by links. This linking can be used to support any of the types of structures discussed earlier – such as linear, hierarchical or network. The interface between the storage layer and the within-component layer is based around the concept of *anchors*. The within-component and storage layers describe a passive data structure for the hypermedia application.

The top layer – *run-time layer* – captures the functionality to access and manipulate the data structures. This layer revolves around the instantiation of components (i.e. presentation to the user) which can then be manipulated. A *session* entity is responsible for keeping track of the mappings between components and their instantiations.

The Dexter model actively supports the concepts of information nodes and interlinking between the nodes. However, the model does not handle the issue of granularity particularly elegantly. When an information component is stored as a single document, it can be mapped to a single

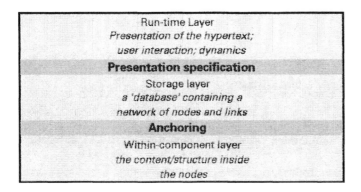

Figure 3-3

Layers of the Dexter Hypertext Reference Model (adapted from Halasz and Schwartz (1994))

component in the storage layer. If we wish to identify components at a finer level of granularity, then the model requires the use of anchors to mark a subset of the component. This implies that the same mechanism is being used for both interlinking and hypermedia document structuring.

The implicit structure of the document (i.e. sentence 1 *follows* sentence 2) is represented in the same way as the relationships between concepts (i.e. the hypermedia links) – thereby blurring the distinction between the information imposed structure and the application imposed structure – though for many current applications this may not be relevant. This is discussed in more detail in the section on the Matilda framework. A number of papers giving a more detailed discussion of the Dexter model and its relevance to the development of specific hypermedia applications are given in the February 1994 edition of *Communications of the ACM*.

Amsterdam Hypermedia Model

This model was developed partially to address perceived shortcomings of the Dexter model, especially with respect to the handing of temporal media and link contexts. The Dexter model has no inherent concept of time (unless it is included in the within-component layer, but this does not allow the expression of timing constraints between components). Nor does the Dexter model include any concept of context for an anchor or presentation information beyond individual components. The Amsterdam Hypermedia Model (AHM) attempts to address these shortcomings by merging ideas from Dexter and the CMIF multimedia model (described in Chapter 14). We discuss AHM in much more detail in the third part of the book.

The Hypertext Abstract Machine

Campbell and Goodman (1988) distinguished three levels of a hypermedia application: presentation level; Hypertext Abstract Machine (HAM) level; and database level. The database level manages issues such as data storage, multi-user access, networking issues, security considerations, concurrency, etc., and roughly equates to the within component layer in the Dexter model. The presentation level handles the user interface, and is responsible for presenting the information from the HAM in a consistent and effective way. It will need to consider factors such as the use of available resources, provision of suitable contexts and personalising the interface. This level roughly equates to the run-time layer in the Dexter model. The HAM is where the fundamental structure of the hypermedia is modelled (such as nodes, links and the relationship between them). The specific mechanisms which are built into this layer will determine what forms of hypermedia functionality are supported. For example, if bidirectional linking is supported, then we can implement simpler cross-referencing.

It is also to be expected that the HAM level will be the prime candidate for standardisation, as both the presentation and database levels are to a large extent dependant upon particular platforms and environments. HyTime (the standard ISO/IEC 10744:1992 for Hypermedia/Time-based Structuring Language (Newcomb, Kipp and Newcomb, 1991)) is a good example of a standard which fits within the HAM level.

Client-Server Models

A number of models based around the client-server paradigm have been proposed. These models typically have a server where the information is stored and a client which is the user interface, the client makes requests of the server, to which the server attempts to respond in an appropriate fashion. This model is not a hypermedia model, but rather a computational model which can be used to support hypermedia functionality.

Two examples of hypermedia environments which make use of a client-server model are the Web and Hyperwave (previously called Hyper-G) (Maurer, 1996). We shall consider Hyper-G in considerable detail in the third part of this book.

Let us examine the Web in a little more detail. One of the difficulties with the Web is that it originally began life not so much as a hypermedia application, but as a set of protocols which provide a common interface to different applications. As such it was not originally developed, and has not subsequently evolved, in the context of a formal model of hypermedia. As mentioned above, the client-server model which forms the basis of the Web is not a hypermedia model, and does not attempt to address hypermedia issues. It is certainly possible to map many Web concepts and the architecture of the Web to various models, and this often provide valuable insights. Nevertheless, the hypermedia aspects of the Web (such as the interlinking mechanisms and node size and structure) lack many of the requirements (described in the previous section) of an effective model. There have been a number of attempts to rectify some of these problems, such as the DLS (Carr *et al.*, 1995), but these are yet to have any substantial impact on the Web community.

The Web uses a very simple node-link model of hypermedia which is not based on any specific model. Information is presented in nodes, and the nodes are interconnected with simple links. The Web concept of links is very simple: links are simple, point-to-point, uni-directional, non-contextual, and do not have any form of typing. The Web has developed (and continues to develop) a complex array of modifications and add-ons to circumvent the constraints which result from such a simple model of hypermedia.

With nodes, the mechanisms used to present information have evolved substantially from the original very simple text only nodes, to the current situation of very complex media compositions supported by various browsers. Examples include the use of browser frames to improve contextualisation of information, Java applets to improve the integration of media, three-dimensional VRML models and other integrated media displayers (such as QuickTime) to broaden the range of accessible media, and plug-ins to improve browser functionality.

The nodes are still, however, the basic information units. It is really the links which give the hypermedia functionality (as opposed to the multimedia functionality embedded in the nodes). Again, there are a variety of modifications which have been made to the basic Web to facilitate various improvements to the very constrained hypermedia functionality supported by the Web. Examples include the use of plug-ins to provide multiple destination links, and applications which provide a map of the inter-relationships between information on a Website. Most of the modifications have, however, focused on non-hypermedia aspects such as interface improvement and better media handling.

3.4   Hypermedia Application Characteristics

We have now developed a reasonable understanding of hypermedia, its goals and its constraints. The last main aspect we wish to consider prior to looking at the development of hypermedia applications are the characteristics of these applications. If we are to have a hypermedia application which achieves the goals we have delineated, then that application is likely to have certain characteristics. If we can identify what these characteristics are, we should be able to determine how to ensure (or at least maximise the likelihood) that they exist in any application we develop.

One factor which is important to remember is that the hypermedia systems used to develop applications and the presentation systems used to present applications (which may often be the same system) will typically place strong constraints on our ability to achieve certain characteristics. For example, the Web restricts our ability to use concepts such as generic links, multiple destination links and overlapping link anchors. During the design of an application, we need to be aware of the constraints of the alternative development and presentation systems which may be used, select an appropriate system, and derive ways of working within the constraints imposed.

Before considering the characteristics of hypermedia applications, let us revisit the goals of a hypermedia application:

Goals of Hypermedia Applications

To support (using the associative relationships between information sources) the carrying out of actions which:

- ... result in the identification of ...

- ... facilitate the effective utilisation of ...

- ... result in control of ...

appropriate information (with appropriateness being based on a given set of contextually defined criteria).

We can identify two different categories of hypermedia characteristics: functional and non-functional. Functional characteristics are those which affect the functionality provided by a hypermedia application, and will be the characteristics which are most directly visible to any user of an application (especially in terms of the above goals). Non-functional characteristics are those characteristics of a hypermedia application which do not affect the functionality, but are nevertheless important within the context of achieving the goals (especially on an ongoing basis).

A simple example will help to illustrate the difference between functional and non-functional characteristics. A typical operation in the Web is to follow a link from one page of information to another page of information. However, we have certain expectations of the way in which this operation will be supported, and what occurs when we carry out this operation. Given a page of information on Beethoven with an anchor from the text 'the choral symphony', we would expect that some suitable mechanism would be provided to allow this link to be followed (such as the usual Web browser mechanism of clicking on the highlighted text). This navigation ability can be considered a functional characteristic. Following the link would produce information related in some way to Beethoven's 9th Symphony. In other words, we have an expectation of relevance and correctness when considering links and link navigation. These are non-functional characteristics – they are not part of the *behaviour* of the application, but they influence our ability to achieve the desired goals of the hypermedia applications.

It is also worth pointing out that the characteristics of an application can be used as the basis for the evaluation of an application. This is discussed in Section 6.6 alongside the issue of metrics and quality assurance.

Functional Characteristics

Navigability: the most obvious (and most widely discussed and dissected) of all hypermedia characteristics is the support for navigation which it provides. Irrespective of the underlying hypermedia model, a mechanism needs to be supplied which allows association-based navigation around the information space. In the Web this is implemented simply, using a single linking mechanism. In contrast, a system such as Microcosm allows arbitrary media elements to be selected and possible multiple relevant links (which may be generic or local) to be presented. If we are dealing with hypermedia rather than just hypertext, then the navigation mechanisms must be able to be applied to media other than text – we need to be able to navigate based on graphics, images, animations, video and audio. This particular aspect of the characteristics is one of the least well supported in most existing hypermedia systems.

Information maps and overviews: many hypermedia applications provide mechanisms to assist users in understanding the overall structure of the information space and the users location within this space. The most common mechanism is some form of information map showing the link structure (both structural and semantic links).

Information trails: related to the user's ability to navigate around the information space is the ability to remember where the user has been, and allow the user to return to these places. This is typically implemented using mechanisms such as bookmarking, history lists, navigation request lists, etc.

Searching and Indexing: although association-based browsing is the necessary core of hypermedia, it is not (in all but the simplest cases) sufficient. The support of searching and indexing functionality must be a characteristic of hypermedia applications in order to effectively achieve the goal of identifying information. Additionally, the searching and indexing mechanisms should be sophisticated enough to handle contextual searches and non-textual media (i.e. *appropriate* information).

Document management: many hypermedia applications provide some form of functionality to support the management of the underlying documents. Indeed, some applications (such as those built using Hyperwave) use the document management tools as the underlying core interface. Document management is often carried out using conventional database technologies.

Information contextualisation: a major factor affecting the user's ability to understand what is appropriate and what is not appropriate is the context in which the information is presented. This is partly facilitated by the way in which the information is presented. Additional functionality can also assist in the process, however, such as the above-mentioned idea of information maps and document management tools.

Information security and cost: if we are to control information, then we need to include functionality for supporting aspects such as information security and the cost of information. A simple example of this is the inclusion into Websites of password-protected pages. This characteristic extends to our ability to address issues of transmitting or accessing sensitive information (such as credit card details) charging for access to information (at levels of granularity from access to entire Websites to access to, and control of, single words).

Presentation: a suitable presentation metaphor is critical to our ability to identify appropriate information and to control and use it in an effective fashion. We cannot use information if we are unable to sense it (note that presentation does not necessarily imply a screen, for example consider how audio is 'presented'). This sensing must be supported in a way which facilitates interpretation.

Customisability: different users will operate in differing ways. If we are to maximise the users ability to utilise information effectively then a hypermedia application should be able to be customised to the particular needs of individuals. Note that this is not just customisation of the presentation but all aspects of the application. Open hypermedia applications embody this characteristic particularly well.

Effective use of resources: the speed of an application, the way it uses memory and CPU, and its bandwidth requirements are all factors which will have a major effect on our ability to *effectively* use information. A characteristic of any hypermedia application should be that it takes into account the environment within which it is working, and provides functionality to manage these resources. A common example is the use of progressive downloading and presentation of images in the Web as a mechanism for coping with the bandwidth constraints of the network resources.

Handling of temporal media: temporal media present a series of unique problems. These include synchronisation, interaction, use of resources, etc. They are, however, an important part of hypermedia, and a hypermedia application which cannot handle temporal media is effectively crippled with respect to providing the ability to use *all* forms of information.

Nonfunctional Characteristics

Information characteristics

Link validity (correctness, relevance, completeness, and integrity): a major consideration which affects our ability to gain access to, and effectively use information is the validity of the relationships between information components. Issues such as correctness and completeness of linking are not yet well understood (and are the focus of considerable research attention) (Robertson, 1997). What may be a perfectly valid link in one context may be highly inappropriate in another context. Experiments have shown that, given a set of concepts, a set of experts will be likely to identify (often vastly) different link sets. Similarly, link completeness is not a simple issue. Information spaces can easily be underlinked (many links between related concepts are missing) or so heavily linked that links become meaningless or context and navigation becomes totally unmanageable. Another traditional link validity problem is dangling links where the link destination is invalid. Some development systems (such as Hyperwave) address this by controlling the documents and links in such a way that it is possible to ensure that dangling links do not occur.

Content validity (correctness, relevance, completeness and integrity): in a similar way to link validity, we have node or content validity. This will include aspects such as the completeness of the local information space, the relevance and global cohesiveness of the information space and the correctness of the material being presented. (In fact, correctness may not be a requirement – consider for example information which is intended to be opinion. What is important is that such information can be recognised as what it is, i.e. what we might call context-correctness.) Other facets of content validity will include aspects such as uniqueness and authoritiveness (where appropriate). Content and link validity are both especially difficult issues to handle in distributed hypermedia systems such as the Web.

Concept organisation: apart from the network structure imposed by the linking mechanisms, the other major characteristic which determines the structure of the information is the way in which the concepts are partitioned into nodes and how these nodes are organised (such as into a document hierarchy). This includes things like node size, cohesion of the information within nodes, and the ways in which different media are combined within nodes. There is still significant debate about many of the factors, and mechanisms for handling them are still poorly understood.

Consistency and seamlessness: the content structure, the presentation of this structure and the functionality of the interface are all major factors affecting our ability to locate and use information. Consistency of these elements will have a major impact on our perception of the information space, our ability to navigate within it, and our ability to use the tools provided as part of the application. Where the application is inconsistent, the user will have an additional cognitive burden interpreting the inconsistency. Similarly, seamlessness between the application and other applications or systems will be important. If the interface between the application and other systems is too disjoint, then the user will have difficulty crossing this boundary. Similarly, if the boundary is completely seamless the user may not be aware of having crossed the boundary. This may be desirable in some cases, but in others it can lead to confusion if the user believes they are still within the information space of the original application.

Other characteristics

Efficiency: the efficiency of an application will cover usage of resources such as memory, CPU, bandwidth, etc. In many cases, the efficiency (or lack of efficiency) may not directly impact on the supported functionality, but may have a significant effect in related applications, or impact on other applications (such as the case where a networked hypermedia application swamps a network and limits the bandwidth available to other users or applications).

Maintainability and evolvability: we shall focus to a large extent on maintainability later in this book. We look at software applications as a useful analogy. For commercial software applications, on average over 80% of the lifecycle costs for software are maintenance costs – i.e. costs incurred after initial delivery of an application. There is no reason to expect that the situation will be any different for hypermedia applications. Anything which can be done to improve the maintainability of hypermedia applications has the potential to result in both significant cost savings as well as higher quality applications (since they will be more readily corrected and updated).

Reusability: a major characteristic of hypermedia applications is the extent to which they support the reuse of both data and information. Current usage on the Web, for example, does very little to promote the reuse of information, apart from the obvious ability to cross-link information sources. Indeed, the embedding of both data and information into the single HTML format often inhibits reuse.

Reliability and robustness: a non-functional characteristic which is important in almost any application is the reliability of the application. This covers aspects such as the reliability of the application ('Will this information always be valid?') reliability of the application engine ('How often does my Web browser crash – and und᷃ ᷃ what circumstances?') and reliability of the operating environment ('What does my Web browser do when the network becomes congested').

Testability, validation, verification: as with reliability, these are relatively well established concepts within the field of applications development. If we are to develop a hypermedia application then it is likely to be important that we are able to test (i.e. make measurements on) the application, verify that the application has achieved what we wanted, and validate that what we wanted was appropriate. Although these sound trivial, similar problems to those that exist in software are likely to make this quite difficult. For example, in hypermedia, the number of possible navigation paths is likely to be very large. In all but the most simple cases, it is unlikely that the developers of the application will be able to foresee and test all possible navigation paths. How, then, can we be sure that all paths provide consistent and reasonable information streams and appropriate contexts, especially if the links are dynamically generated?

Interoperability, flexibility, portability, genericity: again, these are relatively well understood concepts. To what extent will our hypermedia applications work under varying conditions (on different platforms, under different environments, using different devices)? How simple is it to port an application to these different conditions? How readily will the application integrate into a broader framework to work with other applications?

Political and social aspects: how does our application deal with issues such as legal constraints, policy issues and social conventions? Are mechanisms in place, or can they be added, to deal with illicit or unethical material? Has the application given any consideration to copyright and trademark issues? (A trivial example – all copyright material can be tagged to automatically provide notification of the copyright status before it is viewed). Can the application handle the adoption of information management policies? (Again, a trivial example – a company using an application wants all employees to get used to dealing with metric rather than imperial measurements – can the application be configured to enforce this?) As an example of failing to consider these issues, at the time of writing the Curtis Management Group Worldwide (the official licensing agent for the James Dean Foundation) had a lawsuit pending against American Legends, which has a James Dean Website, based on claimed illegal use of several photographs and a signature. This case is likely to set a key legal precedent for copyright on the Internet.

Cost-Effectiveness: finally, how cost-effective is the application. A hypermedia application will really only be appropriate if the cost of developing and using the application results in the achievement of goals more effectively than could have been achieved using some other mechanism.

Relationship between Characteristics and Goals

If we look at a summarised version of the goals given previously: *To support, using associative **relationships**, the carrying out of **actions** which result in the **identification**, effective **utilisation** and **control** of **appropriate** information*; we can identify the contribution of each of the characteristics given above to these goals. In particular, the characteristics will contribute to one or more of:

- Using associative relationships,
- Carrying out of actions,

Table 3-2

Relationship between hypermedia applications characteristics and goals of the applications

	Goals					
	Relat.	Actions	Identify	Utilise	Control	Appro.
Navagability	✓	✓	✓	✓	✓	✓
Information trails	✓	✓	✓	✓	✓	✓
Searching and indexing		✓		✓		✓
Information contextualisation	✓	✓		✓		✓
Information security and cost		✓		✓	✓	✓
Presentation	✓	✓	✓	✓	✓	✓
Customisation		✓	✓	✓	✓	✓
Effective use of resources		✓		✓	✓	✓
Handling of temporal media	✓	✓	✓	✓	✓	✓
Link validity	✓	✓	✓	✓	✓	✓
Content validity		✓	✓	✓	✓	✓
Concept organisation	✓	✓	✓	✓	✓	✓
Consistency and seamlessness	✓	✓		✓	✓	✓
Efficiency	✓				✓	
Maitainability and evolvability	✓	✓	✓	✓		✓
Reusability	✓		✓	✓		✓
Reliability and robustness			✓			✓
Testability, validation and verification	✓		✓	✓	✓	✓
Interoperability, flexibility, portability			✓	✓	✓	✓
Political and social aspects					✓	✓
Cost effectiveness						✓

- Identification of information,
- Utilisation of information,
- Control of information,
- Appropriateness of information.

Table 3–2 shows which characteristics contribute considerably to each aspect of achieving the goals of a hypermedia application.

4

What is Hypermedia Engineering?

'The most original authors are not so because they advance what is new,
but because they put what they have to say as if it had never been said before.'

(Johann Wolfgang von Goethe)

Chapter Goals

From previous chapters we have developed a solid understanding
of hypermedia applications and their characteristics. This chapter
aims to develop an understanding of the development process and
the concept of *hypermedia engineering*. We show that the goal of
the development process is twofold: to develop hypermedia
applications which have desired characteristics; and to undertake
this development as effectively and efficiently as possible.
Hypermedia engineering provides us with a mechanism for
achieving this goal. This chapter aims to:

- Develop a definition of the goals of hypermedia development,
  and consider the implications of this definition in detail. In
  particular, we differentiate between product issues – related
  to the application being developed – and process issues – how
  we go about creating that application.

- Develop a definition of *hypermedia engineering* which focuses on
  a systematic, disciplined, quantifiable approach to development.

- Consider those activities, technologies or approaches which
  contribute to hypermedia engineering. In particular, we
  consider process, paradigms, methods, activities, etc.

- Look at activities which will typically be carried out in a hypermedia development project, and how these are integrated into
  an overall process.

- To delineate approaches to managing the overall process, and
  the issues which impact on this process.

We began Chapter 2 by asking the question 'What is hypermedia development?', and both Chapters 2 and 3 were spent developing an understanding of the general concept of hypermedia. Having developed an understanding of hypermedia and hypermedia applications, we can now return to that original question of hypermedia development. We can be pedantic and say that hypermedia development is simply the development of hypermedia applications, but this then begs the question of what do we mean by 'development'?

A simple explanation would be that development is the carrying out of activities which result in the creation of a desired application. Towards the end of the previous chapter, we considered the characteristics which are desirable in a hypermedia application – such things as navigability, provision of search mechanisms, maintainability and appropriate concept organisation. What we haven't considered are the mechanisms by which we might ensure that an application we develop has these characteristics. It is this which is really at the core of hypermedia development.

We can view hypermedia development as the process of developing hypermedia applications, which have a desired balance of characteristics, in the most effective manner possible. For the development to be effective (in terms of application quality – development cost trade-off) these activities need to managed in an appropriate fashion. This is why we have referred to hypermedia engineering rather than hypermedia development in the title of this chapter. The development of hypermedia applications should not be an *ad hoc* affair. Rather, it should be performed in a consistent scientific fashion.

This really then gives us two components to hypermedia development – developing quality applications (based on desired characteristics), and adopting a process which does this efficiently and effectively. In this chapter we will consider these two aspects briefly, expanding on them over subsequent chapters. We look at why the development is carried out and what guidelines give focus to the activities which make up the development process. We shall consider the development process itself and what it encompasses, and the relationship between the (often misused) terms hypermedia engineering, hypermedia development, hypermedia design and hypermedia authoring.

4.1   The Goal of Hypermedia Development

We have described hypermedia as a means and not an end (i.e. hypermedia has no inherent value in itself – it's value derives from its ability to assist in information access and use). In much the same way, hypermedia development is only a means and not an end. We do not carry out the development of hypermedia for its own sake; the only reason for the existence of any form of development is the application which is produced as a result of the development.

Based on this observation, let us then begin this section by providing a definition of the goal of hypermedia development:

> **Definition**
>
> **Goal of Hypermedia Development**   The goals of hypermedia development are:
>
> **product**:   to develop high quality hypermedia applications which have the optimal balance of desired characteristics;
>
> **process**:   to carry out the development in the most effective and efficient manner possible consistent with achieving the desired application.

Process and Product

If we consider this goal, there are two major components – product and process (or alternatively, outcome and action). The first part of the goal deals with the result of the development – creation of a hypermedia application, or the product we develop. The second part of the goal deals with the act of development itself, or the process we carry out. Let us consider these two components in more detail.

The point of any development process is to develop some product (whether this 'product' is tangible is not relevant at the moment). Therefore, to understand the development process we need to understand the product being developed (hence the lengthy discussions of the previous chapter). The form and function of the product will determine the form and function of the process. In developing a suitable process, we must consider the product and the relationship between process activities and product outcomes.

Apart from the product itself, we also need to consider purely process issues. For example, we may have a process which results in the ideal product, but may still be impractical for reasons of cost, repeatability, timing, management or other similar factors. The implications here are that we want to have a process which ensures that the most cost-effective solution is obtained.

Typically, product and process issues will affect the development process in different ways. For example, employing world experts on hypermedia design may result in a very high quality application, but would result in a prohibitively expensive process. As with any development process, there will need to be a managed trade-off between the various constraints and costs.

It is important to bear in mind that what is important is not the action, but the outcome. So the action should be defined by the outcome, and not *vice versa*. We can therefore gain insights into the actions (what actions are appropriate, how these should be coordinated, etc.) by considering the outcomes. Let us consider the outcomes in a little more detail.

A Quality Product

In the definition given previously about the goals of hypermedia development, we referred to 'a quality hypermedia application'. In the previous chapter we considered the idea of a 'hypermedia application', but did not refer to the idea of quality. What then is a 'quality' hypermedia application?

Towards the end of the previous chapter we considered a large number of hypermedia application attributes, each of which may be important in any given application. What we did not consider was that often they may be in conflict, or they may be of varying importance. Let us consider an example: We may have a dedicated educational package which uses a case study to demonstrate some educational principle. In this type of application, content and linking validity and concept organisation is likely to be of utmost importance, whereas management of information security and cost effectiveness may be only secondary.

Since any development has an associated cost, we can consider a 'quality' application to be an application which has the optimal combination of desired attributes balanced against the cost of achieving these attributes. In other words, quality is not an absolute measure, rather it is relative to the application context. In some cases, quality may mean good value for money; in other cases, it may mean absolute correctness. In the previous chapter, we gave a list of possible attributes which contribute to quality. In each case the process will have an effect on this attribute. The goal of the process is to find the best balance of these attributes. For various applications, these attributes will take on varying importance, and often increasing quality in one area can only be obtained at the expense of quality in another area.

Quality cannot be added to the hypermedia application at the end of the process, it needs to be taken into account during the entire development process. Quality (good, bad or otherwise) is embedded in the application as a result of the development. In fact, it should be the driving factor during the development.

Process Affecting Product: An Example

One of the attributes we considered in the previous chapter was information relevance. The contents of an application must be relevant to the objectives of the application. This implies not just including information because it is semantically related to the 'topic' of the application, but including it because it enhances the ability of the application to achieve its stated objectives. Let us consider an example.

We are developing an educational hypermedia application which has the objective of improving users' understanding of the use of language in Shakespeare's plays. In developing such an application we may access a large repository of text, images and video clips of various productions of these plays, but we will typically only include those that illuminate aspects of the discussion being presented. Inclusion of unnecessary material will simply overload the hypermedia application and make the information space which the user is browsing more complex than necessary – and hence inhibiting the actual goal.

What this implies for the development process is that at some stage we need to consider what material is relevant and what is not. To do this we must understand the goals of the application being developed and the role that content will play in achieving this goal. For example, we would define the goal of the above application as being the improvement of users understanding of the use of language in Shakespeare's plays. From here we would need to consider how a hypermedia application could facilitate this – maybe through the provision of a series of discussions of language, linked to examples which illuminated each discussion.

We would also need to consider the prospective audience and how this affects the content. Providing the original manuscript of Shakespeare's plays may be useful if the intended audience were university-level English scholars, but not if they were young primary school children.

This then illustrates that a number of activities must be included in the development process to manage the desired characteristic of information relevance. We need to take the next step and consider what the cost (time, resources or financial) will be of these activities. As with any characteristic, there will be a law of diminishing returns (in terms of improving the specific characteristic) as we spend more resources on the activities designed to handle that characteristic.

Figure 4-1 illustrates (in a hypothetical fashion) that the relationships between the amount of effort we apply to specific activities and the resultant change in quality with respect to a particular characteristic will not be the same in all cases. If we are to plan or manage the process, then we need to have an understanding of these relationships.

Finally, it is worth pointing out that in many cases there is not yet sufficient experience or understanding to obtain explicitly the type of relationships shown in Figure 4-1. We can apply effort to certain activities in order to improve the quality of a hypermedia application with

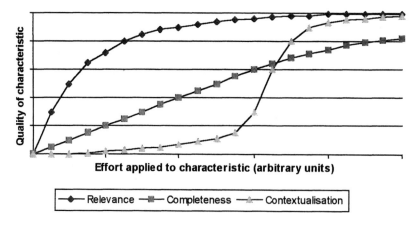

Figure 4-1

Relationship between development effort and application quality varies from application characteristic to application characteristic

respect to a particular characteristic. As shown in this hypothetical graph, the relationship between effort and quality varies from characteristic to characteristic. Unfortunately, enough experience does not yet exist to accurately define specific relationships, though we can identify trends. Often the closest we can come is a series of heuristics or 'rules-of-thumb' which guide us. For example, we may know that using certain approaches or tools, the relationship between effort and quality of linking, for a fixed application size, is roughly linear, but the relationship between application size and effort, for a fixed quality, is exponential. This will be particularly useful in the case where there is some threshold below which effort does not significantly result in any reasonable quality, or above which additional effort has no significant effect (as with 'contextualisation' in Figure 4-1).

We can therefore view hypermedia development as the process by which we create a hypermedia application in such a way that we balance individual desired attributes whilst minimising the net cost of the development.

4.2   Hypermedia Engineering

Definition

What then is hypermedia engineering? Before we answer this, let us consider software engineering. Thirty years ago, software development barely existed as a discipline (either practical or theoretical). It was at much the same stage that hypermedia development is now. Since then, software engineering has evolved into a significant sub-discipline of computing science and applications engineering. Many of the problems which triggered this evolution are similar to those now becoming increasingly significant in hypermedia development. Consider the following definitions:

> 'Engineering is about the systematic application of scientific knowledge in creating and building cost-effective solutions to practical problems'
>
> (D. Berry, *Academic Legitimacy of the Software Engineering Discipline*, S.E.I. Technical Report CMU/SEI-92-TR-34, Carnegie Mellon University)

'software engineering: (1) The application of a systematic, disciplined, quantifiable approach to the development, operation, and maintenance of software; that is, the application of engineering to software. (2) The study of approaches as in (1).'

(IEEE Standard Glossary of Software Engineering Terminology, Spring 1991 Edition) (IEEE, 1991)

Using these as a starting point, we can begin to consider what might be a reasonable definition of hypermedia engineering.

Definition

Hypermedia engineering The employment of a systematic, disciplined, quantifiable approach to the development, operation and maintenance of hypermedia applications.

In other words, hypermedia engineering is about the employment of an engineering approach – an approach which is managed, scientifically based, and yet practical and pragmatic. Obviously, the process of creating hypermedia applications requires some form of development – a set of activities that is carried out and which result in a hypermedia application. These activities should be carried out in a way which is consistent with both an approach designed to most effectively yield results (an engineering approach) and the goals of hypermedia (managing information using associative linking). For example, we need to be able to:

- Understand the goals and requirements of the application being developed.
- Design suitable interfaces and information structures.
- Provide mechanisms for helping users to use the application effectively (and we need to understand what 'effective utilisation' actually means).
- Manage the process of development in an effective manner
- Use metrics to measure aspects of the development in order to control development progress.
- Document appropriate aspects of the development.

- Carry out the development in a way which ensures that the application can be maintained.

- etc.

Many of these activities or requirements are either virtually non-existent or extremely primitive in most current hypermedia development practice. For example, we still do not have effective or accurate metrics for measuring most of the characteristics detailed at the end of the previous chapter (which of course means that, since we cannot measure these characteristics, it is very difficult to know whether what we are doing is improving them).

Concepts

Up to this point, we have been using a large number of terms (such as process, methodology, product, design, etc.) fairly loosely. To improve our ability to discuss hypermedia and hypermedia development unambiguously, it is now worth to refining our understanding of various concepts (see Figure 4-2).

A hypermedia application will have a *lifecycle* – the entire period of existence of the application from conception, through development, delivery and maintenance to final application cessation or retirement. Within this application lifecycle we will carry out some form of development. This development can be modelled in various ways – resulting in assorted *process models*. A process model essentially describes the phases or stages of development, and how these are integrated into a overall development process. It does not describe the specific development activities.

As an example of a process model consider the model shown in Figure 1-4. This shows the DOD-STD-2167A process model for software development. In 1988, the U.S. Department of Defense established a government standard software development process, defining an eight step process. Unlike most software process models, the first and last steps of the process focus on an overall system (both hardware and software) recognising the context within which the software will exist. The middle six steps are focused on the development of the software components of a system. At each stage of the development, specific deliverables are defined. DOD-STD-2167A generates an extremely large amount of documentation, which can be useful in large projects involving numerous development teams, but which can become burdensome for small projects. As a result, tailoring of the process model is actively encouraged to suit the specifics of any given development project. DOD-STD-2167A also places a large emphasis on management involvement in the development process, especially with respect to evaluation. For example, the criteria which are used to evaluate documents or other deliverables include:

- Internal consistency (including lack of contradiction and consistency of usage of terms).
- Understandability (including appropriate style).
- Traceability.
- Consistency between documents and/or other products.
- Appropriate use of analysis, design and implementation techniques.
- Appropriate allocation of resources.
- Adequate test coverage, cases and procedures and testability of requirements.
- Adequacy of quality factors.

We can design different process models to suit different types of development, which will in turn be suited to different types of applications. A model incorporating iterative refinement of an initial prototype may be best suited to small scale trial applications. Educational applications probably require a model which incorporates consideration of learning objectives. No model will be completely adequate for all applications – each model has its advantages and disadvantages. A competent hypermedia engineer would be aware of the available models, and would use the most appropriate model for each problem, taking into account the limitations and strengths of the model chosen.

To demonstrate a typical process model, we should look at the waterfall model – a traditional applications process model. This model views the development process as including a series of discrete phases organised in a linear sequence. In its simplest form, each phase is completed and 'signed-off' before beginning the next stage. The stages typically used are to analyse and specify the requirements of the application, then to design the application, to implement the hypermedia application, test the final application, and finally, to use and maintain the application. Although this form of model is useful from the viewpoint of project management,

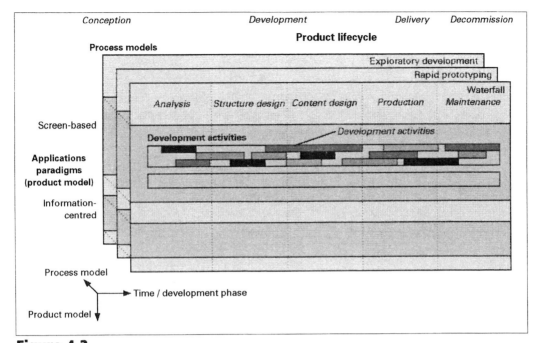

Figure 4-2

Development is carried out within the context of both a process model and a product model

in practice the various stages typically overlap, and feedback is usually provided from each stage to the previous. This results in an iterative approach. The problem with an iterative approach is that it then becomes difficult to assess the progress of the development, and so usually only a small number of iterations are used. There are a number of criticisms of the waterfall model, including that it freezes the specification at too early a stage of the development, and that it makes iteration difficult. Alternative models attempt to resolve these problems.

The development will be carried out within the context of a specific *paradigm*, essentially a model or pattern of an application. The paradigm can be viewed as the *product model* rather than the process model. Typical hypermedia paradigms include scripting language (e.g. HyperTalk), iconic flow control (e.g. AuthorWare), cast or score scripting (e.g. Director) and hypermedia network linking (e.g. the Web). In each case, we have a different model of the underlying application. For example, with the iconic flow control paradigm we represent the application as a series of icons with the control flowing between them, such as in

Authorware Professional (shown in Figure 4-3a), and with the cast or score scripting paradigm we view the application as a musical score, such as in Macromind Director (shown in Figure 4-3b).

If we combine a process model and a product model (i.e. paradigm), then we have a general approach to be used in the development of a general type of hypermedia application. Within this context, we can create various *methodologies* which describe the specific approaches to be taken to the development. The approach will fit within the framework set by the process model, and involve the development of an application which has a form given by the product model. A methodology will provide the details of what *activities* are required, and how these should be carried out, and the *deliverables* required at various stages during the development.

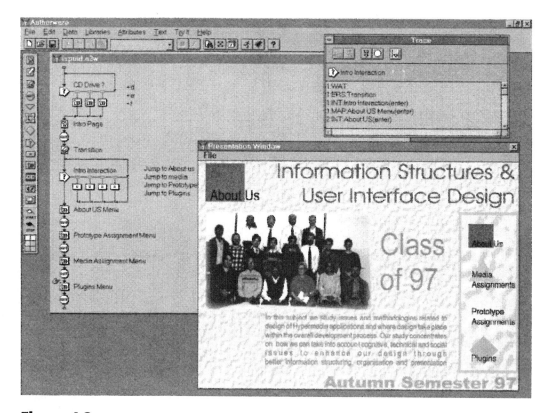

Figure 4-3a

Product models. (a) Iconic flow control paradigm used in Macromedia Authorware, and (b) the cast scripting paradigm used in Macromedia Director

As an example, the Relationship Management Methodology (RMM) (Isakowitz, Stohr and Balasubramanian, 1995) describes various activities, such as feasibility analysis, entity-relationship (E-R) design, navigation design and construction. Each activity is described in detail, and typically consists of a series of steps with detailed guidelines on how to approach that step. Each activity or step can have various deliverables (such as a feasibility document as a deliverable at the end of the feasibility analysis) which may have a required content and/or structure.

In practice, we may combine many methodologies (often from different paradigms) at different phases of the project. This can result from using established practices, because different methodologies suit a particular problem better, or because only certain resources are available. A good example of this may be the use of the iconic flow control paradigm during the initial mock-up of a prototype interface (for evaluation purposes) and

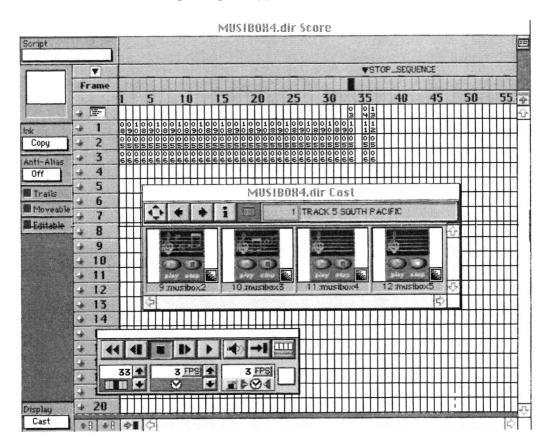

Figure 4-3b

then switching to a more general hypermedia linking model for the design and production phases of the development.

It is important to note that the field of hypermedia development is still very immature. Although every hypermedia application development involves some form of process and various activities, little work has yet been done on formalising process models, defining methodologies, or developing an understanding of what models and approaches are best suited to different types of application development.

Authoring, Design, Development and Engineering

One set of terminology which has resulted in much confusion are the terms authoring, design and development (and now we are adding engineering as well). These terms have been used in numerous ways, partly a result of the evolving view of what the development of hypermedia involves, and partly of the disparate perspectives of the different disciplines which contribute to the fields of hypermedia and multimedia.

In this book we use the term *hypermedia development* to refer to the process of creating and maintaining hypermedia applications (see Figure 4-4). In other words, development covers the entire hypermedia application lifecycle from conception to cessation. Hypermedia engineering refers to the application of an engineering approach to hypermedia development. Hence, hypermedia engineering also covers the entire application cycle, but in a way which is managed, practical, yet scientifically based.

There has been a growing interest in the field of hypermedia design (as demonstrated by the August 1995 special issue of the *Communications of the ACM* dedicated to this area (CACM, 1995)). Design, however, is only one small part of the overall lifecycle of hypermedia application (albeit a very important part). It covers the methods used for generating the structure and functionality of hypermedia applications, but does not typically extend to include consideration of aspects such as hypermedia application requirements elicitation, feasibility consideration, application maintenance, etc. (though some authors have used the term hypermedia design to cover some or all of these activities). We view hypermedia design as a subset of hypermedia development (and if carried out in an appropriate fashion, a subset of hypermedia engineering).

Hypermedia authoring covers an even tighter scope of activities than hypermedia design. Authoring is most typically used to refer to the use

Hypermedia development

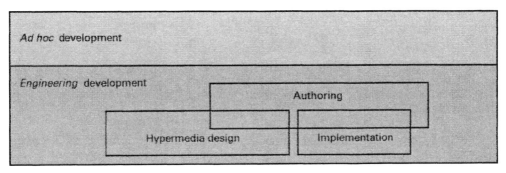

Figure 4-4

Hypermedia engineering is a specifically disciplined approach to hypermedia development. Within this approach we have hypermedia design and hypermedia authoring (which can overlap)

of suitable tools in the actual creation of the hypermedia application. Early development (and in many cases, current development) of hypermedia applications revolved around the use of specific 'authoring' tools to create, structure and present hypermedia content. This process often severely neglected activities beyond the immediate scope covered by the tool (such as analysis, design or maintenance). Unfortunately, this often led to the misunderstanding that the use of the authoring tool *was* hypermedia development, and hence as the scope of development activities broadened, the term authoring has often been used to refer to this broader range of activities.

We view authoring as encompassing those activities during which we manage the actual content and structure of the application and how it is presented, as distinct from the broader design of the application or the capture of the information. For example, authoring would include the design and creation of individual screen layouts or pages of information, but would not include broader design activities such as the design of global navigation structures.

4.3 Development Process Activities

Figure 4-2 illustrated the point that hypermedia development will typically contain a large number of activities. When combined in an appropriate manner into a cohesive methodology, these activities can result in an effective process for the development of hypermedia applications. As the first step in considering methodologies and processes at a broader level, we will look at the activities which can be used to construct methodologies, the relationships between these activities, how these activities can be managed, where effort should be distributed, etc.

Before looking at process activities, it is worth making a few comments about the historical context of hypermedia development. To a large extent, most existing and past development approaches have largely revolved around, and consequently been controlled by, the use of specific 'authoring' tools. Indeed, hypermedia development has to a large extent been seen as synonymous with use of these tools. There has been very little awareness of process, or any activities beyond the use of tools. This is particularly true of the class of tools such as NoteCards, Hyperties, Guide, KMS, Toolbook, Macromedia Director and Macromedia Authorware. This class of authoring tools encourages a process of development which focuses almost exclusively on low-level design and implementation. The same is largely true of the plethora of Web authoring tools that have appeared within the last few years. This results in applications which are unmaintainable, are cost-ineffective and have low quality in terms of structure and functionality. The situation is slightly better with the structured document approach (such as with the use of SGML). This approach:

- Encourages the structuring of documents independantly of the development of specific applications.
- Encourages a separation of information handling and application development.
- Helps ensure that the design becomes more visible, and hence more likely to be carried out effectively.

Alternative approaches based on representing and reasoning about knowledge have also been used. These include work based on semantic nets, knowledge-based approaches and concept maps. Systems worth looking at include Aquanet, StrathTutor, and Intermedia. These approaches are, however, more focused on the representation and utilisation of information, rather than considering the development of applications.

Process Activities

We have described the type of activities that historically have been included in the development process, and criticised this as inadequate. What activities should be included? As an initial step, we provide a comprehensive list of activities which have the potential to contribute to one or more of the hypermedia characteristics described earlier. This list does not presuppose any specific process or methodology within which these activities can fit.

We have decomposed the list of activities into a series of eight categories: management; investigation and specification; application design; component design; production; verification, validation and evaluation; maintenance; and documentation. These categories do not imply a relationship to a particular phase of a development process or methodology. Nor would we expect every development process and every methodology to incorporate every activity listed. In most cases, many of these activities will be irrelevant or unnecessary, or may be combined, decomposed or reorganised (for example, documenting the high-level design would typically require the documentation of interaction mechanisms, filter design, information structures, look and feel, etc.). The activities are given in Figure 4-5, and are considered in a little more detail below.

Management

Management activities are those which contribute to the overall supervision and organisation of the development process. These activities typically ensure the adequate progression of the development. Project initiation involves the concept development, selection of a process and methodologies to follow, and development process initiation. This will often occur in response to a perceived market niche, need or opportunity. Project planning, project management and budgeting cover organisation of activities, timing, work schedules, coordination of resource and skills allocation, specification of deliverables, cost analyses and predictions and expenditure management, and will often involve the use of conventional project management tools (such as project planners, and management tools such as GANTT charts).

Costing and resource management will often be particularly difficult. This is primary because the skills required for effective development are changing rapidly, and are typically on the cutting edge of the technology.

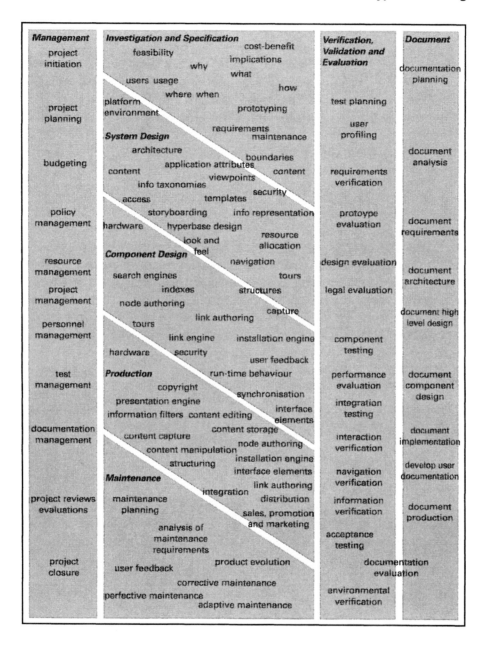

Figure 4-5

Activities which can be incorporated into a development process

This in turn means that the skills are in short supply and subject to wide variations in supply and cost. Personnel management involves the management of the human resources associated with the project, covering elements such as hiring personnel, evaluation of skills, assigning tasks, managing interactions, team management and building, etc. Analysis of skills requirements encompasses the determination of the skills required for successful completion of the project. For example, the development of a corporate Website aimed at promoting a corporation is likely to benefit from the involvement of advertising experts. Skills required could cover a potentially huge range, including programmers, design experts, user-interface experts, content experts, project managerial skills, legal experts, marketing experts, etc.

More technical aspects of the project management include project reviews, standardisation and style control, test and documentation management, and version control and configuration management. This last aspect can be particularly important for hypermedia, where the development is often a process of highly incremental and iterative development.

For all the management activities to be performed effectively requires an awareness of both the activities required for a successful development process and the resourcing required by specific activities. At present, this is often based only on experience or general heuristics (such as '1 hour of educational content typically requires 10 hours of authoring effort').

Investigation and Specification

We have grouped all those activities related to the gathering and understanding of information into the category of investigation and specification. These activities will typically revolve around the analysis of specific applications, issues, constraints, resources, etc. which are likely to affect the development in some way (such as a user's needs, resource costs, social constraints or content availability). These investigations should result in an understanding of the required application and knowledge regarding how to effectively develop the application. This knowledge may be as varied as an awareness of why the application is being developed, or a comprehensive specification of the required application functionality.

Activities within this category might include a feasibility study to develop an understanding of the financial, resource, functional, technical or cognitive feasibility, analysis of why the application is being used, the characteristics of potential users of the application, and analysis of the expected usage patterns, such as access mechanisms and navigation routes. The users and usage patterns will strongly affect the design of the application functionality. We also need to consider how and where the application will be made available, what information will underlie the application, the availability and constraints (such as legal, social or cost) on the use of information, and the boundary between the application being developed and other applications (this is especially relevant for Web applications).

Prototyping can often be used as a valuable aid in eliciting information for understanding the application to be developed. The information gained will depend upon the type of prototype developed, but can include user response to a specific look and feel, effectiveness of different interaction mechanisms, and examples of information structures. The prototype can cover anything from a simple mock-up of a screen layout to a detailed but simplified application used to demonstrate behaviour and interaction functionality. Other analysis tasks or activities can include an analysis of required application maintainability and intended lifespan.

The results of many of the above activities can be combined into the final specification of the application requirements. This would cover both functional requirements (such as the required support for interaction and information utilisation mechanisms) and non-functional requirements (such as performance and maintainability).

Application Design

A number of activities are related to the design of the overall application, or affect all or many parts of the application. For example, designing the overall application architecture will provide a form for the application, and designing an application look and feel will affect the presentation across all components. We have grouped these activities under the category of application design. Activities include:

- Selection of development and presentation platforms, environments and tools.

- Identification of an appropriate application paradigm and presentation metaphor.
- Development of the application architecture.
- Allocation of resources.
- Design of the application structure, content scope, depth and granularity.
- Design of information viewpoints and access mechanisms.

An important aspect of the development of information applications is the way in which we use them to retrieve information. As explained well by Urr (1991), our ability to retrieve information is influenced by our ability to conceptualise the structuring patterns being used, and these structuring patterns are dependant upon useful schemes of classification and information organisation, or information taxonomies. To ensure that the access mechanisms which are developed are effective, we need to design suitable information taxonomies. This means considering the overall information patterns, and then refining these into specific structures.

For example, consider a recent development of an educational case study which looked at the application of process to developing a specific software product (in this case it was an elevator control simulation application). The information space was separated into three distinct but parallel 'regions' with matching structures which were made explicit to the user, thereby facilitating the user's ability to effectively navigate. We developed the overall information structure shown in Figure 4-6, along with suitable navigation and tour structures within this framework. An example of a methodological approach to this activity is the use of Entity-Relationship modelling in RMM (Isakowitz, Stohr and Balasubramanian, 1995).

Other application design activities include design of the navigation structures, design of user-interface templates and the global look and feel, storyboarding to understand the flow of navigation or concepts, design of the underlying document management or hyperbase systems, design of the mechanisms for capturing and manipulating content for use in the application, design of navigation and contextualisation cues, and design of security and cost charging protocols.

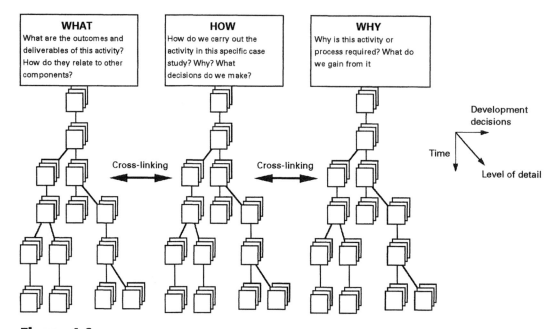

Figure 4-6

Overall information structure for a software development process case study

Component Design

Under the category of component design, we have grouped those activities which revolve around the design of specific low-level elements of the application. This can include detailed hardware design, detailed design of the specific information capture mechanisms, design of the individual information structures, and design of the search engine and support mechanisms.

Detailed design of the application structure includes aspects such as node design, which covers content allocation, screen layout and presentation design, and link design, which involves the creative design of the specific link anchors and trigger mechanisms consistent with the global information structure. We also need to undertake detailed design of the run-time behaviour, media synchronisation mechanisms, and tours and search engines.

Other aspects include design of the installation engine, if required, design of user feedback and evaluation mechanisms to be used for evaluation and refinement of the application, and design of the security and charging mechanisms.

Production

Having designed the application in detail, the various components can be implemented and integrated into a working, useable application. We have grouped all activities which produce items (other than just documentation, plans, ideas or understanding) into the production category.

Basic activities include hardware purchase and setup, organisation of copyright permissions, implementation or adaptation of the presentation engine and possibly the underlying linkbase or database for document handling, implementation of legacy information conversion filters, capture, creation, editing and/or manipulation of new data, implementation of data storage mechanisms, and the generation of interface elements. Creation of the actual information structures include node authoring aspects such as partitioning the information into nodes, and creation of anchors and links. Additional aspects also include the development of installation engines and integration of all the aspects into a final application.

There are a number of additional activities not directly related to the detailed implementation of the application, but which can still be considered part of the production. These are particularly relevant to mass-production items for commercial distribution, including the production of the release version of the applications (reproduction, packaging, etc.), distribution, sales and promotion. These activities are beyond the scope of this book, and are usually the domain of specialist publishers or related organisations.

Maintenance

It will be rare for a hypermedia application to be developed which does not require maintenance of some sort. At the most trivial level, this will involve simple corrective maintenance or refinements as feedback is obtained on the application usage. At a more significant level, in many cases the underlying information will evolve or expand. Whatever the case, we have grouped together in this category all those activities which typically occur after the 'release' of the application for use.

It is worth pointing out that many of the activities carried out during the development of an application will be similar to the activities carried out during its maintenance. Rather than reiterate these activities, we look at those which differ, or group them in different ways. These include

- Analysis of the maintenance requirements.
- Planning of the maintenance.
- Analysis of the effectiveness of the application to determine ongoing maintenance needs.
- Correction of errors or problems with an application which may be information errors, structuring errors or functionality errors.
- Adaptation of the system to a changing environment.
- Perfection of the application to better address requirements.
- Maintenance of the application documentation.

Verification, Validation and Evaluation

We have grouped all activities relating to testing and evaluation into a category of activities. In general, these are not aimed at producing the application itself, but at ensuring that the development occurs in an appropriate fashion. In many cases, the specific activities in this category will be dependant upon the specific development process adopted. We can, however, identify a representative list of activities:

- Test planning.
- Evaluation of prototypes.
- Evaluation of the requirements.
- Design of evaluation mechanisms.
- Testing of individual implemented elements of the application.
- Testing of the integrated system.
- Verification of the content, structure, and interaction and navigation mechanisms.
- Verification of the system under different platforms, environments and operating conditions.
- Final acceptance testing.

Documentation

Rather than providing a long list of documentation activities, it is sufficient to point out that most of the activities listed above will have a component associated with documenting the results of the activity. In many cases (except perhaps implementation activities), the documentation produced will be the main deliverable from each activity. The only additional activity worth mentioning is the planning of the documentation activities.

4.4 Process Modelling and Management

In Section 4.2 we considered the idea of processes and process models. Current practice is considerably varied with respect to the adoption of methodologies and formal processes. Small scale projects (which currently include most Websites) have tended to be developed *ad hoc*. The developers of larger applications have commonly developed their own process, adapting it on-the-fly as needs dictate.

The main difficulty with this approach is that there is no guarantee that certain critical factors have not been overlooked, or that the process is being timed and costed adequately. To-date, most projects have been small enough that an informal approach to the development is usually adequate (though probably not optimal). This will change (very significantly) as development projects grow in scope and/or complexity, and as we wish to gain increasingly high quality applications.

How then do we determine what is an appropriate process to use for a given development project? Unfortunately, there is not yet a significant body of experience relating to the use of a variety (of both appropriate and inappropriate) processes under differing conditions. Obviously, traditional applications engineering or software engineering process models can be (and have been) used (such as the waterfall process model and Boehm's spiral model (Boehm, 1988)). Although an effective starting point, these process models are not adapted for the particular considerations and idiosyncrasies of hypermedia applications. For example, with software applications (and most other applications) we wish to hide the complex interactions between program components behind a required application functionality. With hypermedia, the complex interactions are inherent in the information interrelationships, and rather than hide them from the user we wish to provide the user with mechanisms for handling them.

There is an already large (and still rapidly growing) body of literature providing methods for specific activities, particularly those relating to information creation and capturing and node and link authoring. However, work is only just beginning on developing hypermedia development process models and methodologies which cover the entire application lifecycle. Examples include the Relationship Management Methodology (RMM) (Isakowitz, Stohr and Balasubramanian, 1995) and the Object-Oriented Hypermedia Design Model (OOHDM) (Schwabe and Rossi, 1995a). However, even these do not yet extend to effectively consider aspects such as project management and application maintenance.

Having accepted that the field is still evolving and that we do not yet have access to a sufficient body of knowledge relating to process models, how do we proceed? The answer is relatively simple. We continue doing what has been done at present – improvising and adapting processes to specific projects, but we do it in the context of an understanding of what a quality process should incorporate, the issues we need to address during the process, and the range of activities from which we can build an effective process. So let us initially consider what the attributes of a quality process may be, and then look at several example process models from the software engineering domain.

Attributes of a Quality Process

What are the attributes of a quality process? If we return to the goal of hypermedia development given in Section 4.1, we can define a quality process as one which maximises our ability to achieve these goals – our ability to both develop a quality application, and to do this development in the most effective and efficient manner possible.

The most obvious characteristics of a quality process will be appropriateness and correctness. Each activity incorporated into the process needs to be appropriate, which means that we should be able to identify a mapping or correlation between the activities being carried out and the desired attributes of the resulting application. For example, a process would be inadequate if it did not contain an activity that considered issues associated with intellectual property rights (such as copyright).

Related to appropriateness is correctness: if the process is not correct then the resulting product will not be correct. For example, we need to ensure that in managing the process, we correctly estimate expected development efforts. A mistake could lead to inflated budgets, missed deadlines or poor quality applications. Similar observations apply to all or most other aspects of the development process.

The process should also focus the developer's attention. One of the main reasons for adopting a process of any type is that it guides us in understanding what is important and what is irrelevant in terms of distribution of effort. For example, the traditional waterfall model shows us that it is important to focus attention on analysis early in the development, as it ensures we have an adequate understanding of the application to be developed before we begin the design process. A process should not just be a collection of arbitrary activities; it should help us understand what is important in achieving our goals. Related to the above point is that a process also provides a context for the methodology or activities we are carrying out. It should assist us in organising these activities into a cohesive development effort.

A quality process will also ensure that we obtain feedback on the development progress at appropriate times. A common criticism of the basic waterfall model is that, while the discrete phases allow more straightforward project management, they result in the problem of not having an incremental delivery of products during the course of development (which is useful for ongoing application and progress evaluation – a common credo in software development is that when an application is 90% complete, about half the development time has passed!). The various alternatives proposed will usually avoid this problem by using an incremental approach to the development. This type of problem is likely to be even more pronounced with hypermedia, where we do not yet fully understand how hypermedia can be effectively developed to assist users in using information. A process model that provides consistent and regular feedback on development progress is particularly critical.

The process should be repeatable and measurable. If we are to individually and collectively improve our hypermedia development processes, then we need to be able to repeat a successful process and understand why it was successful (or unsuccessful). We need to ensure that the success of a given development project was the result of a suitable process rather then just fortuitous luck in overcoming an inadequate process.

Finally, the process should be flexible in adapting to different projects, and to the evolution of a project during the course of its lifecycle. A particularly important aspect is scalability in terms of adapting to a changing project scale.

Conventional Hypermedia Development Practice

It is useful here to take stock of conventional practice in hypermedia development. This practice often does not use an explicit process model at all. Indeed, the development often neglects many phases of the development. Figure 4-7 shows a possible simple model of the stages of the development process, with those stages which are the current focus of most hypermedia development practice shown highlighted. In other words, those few hypermedia development methodologies which do exist tend to focus only on the design and implementation of applications, neglecting both the early stages of the models as well as phases such as evaluation, risk analysis, determination of objectives and alternatives, and planning.

This trend is at its worst for many Web developments, where the focus is very squarely on implementation. It is worth pointing out, however, that in some cases, especially those involving only very small scale development, this may be justified. As with software development, a suitable development process only becomes important as the scope of a project

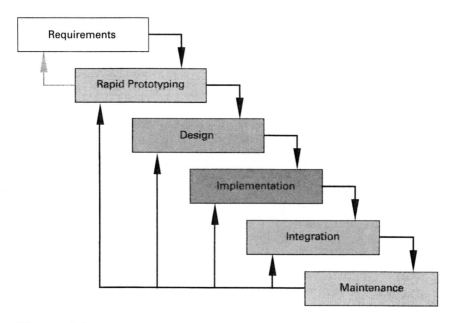

Figure 4-7

The shaded areas show the focus of current hypermedia development practice mapped onto an existing software development process model

increases, and even then formal models such as those described above can be adapted to suit the specific circumstances of the project.

Adapting a Process

In arriving at a suitable development process there are three different levels which must be identified: the first is to identify the process stages which are required; the second is to choose a development process framework within which these stages can be placed; and the third is to select the methods used to implement these stages.

The selection of development stages will be based upon the particular activities that must be carried out. Figure 4-5 showed a large number of different activities, broadly grouped into development stages. In practice, these can be adapted as appropriate and grouped into appropriate stages of development. In general, however, unless there is a specific reason for changing the stages, they will normally follow the pattern shown in the figure. For example, almost all processes will incorporate analysis, design, implementation, evaluation and management stages.

A much more difficult aspect is the identification of a suitable process framework for the development stages. Should they be carried out in a purely linear, once-through waterfall model? Should they all be carried out in parallel in a multi-pass incremental process? The specific choice will be dependant upon a number of factors. For example, as the size of the project increases, risk management becomes more important and so a spiral model becomes more attractive. If the requirements are likely to be poorly understood (for example, if the application is very speculative) then an incremental development approach based on prototyping becomes more suitable.

Finally, methods must be selected which allow implementation of each of the specific activities. Hypermedia design methods (such as OOHDM (Schwabe and Rossi, 1995a) and RMM (Isakowitz, Stohr and Balasubramanian, 1995) – described later in this book) can be used to support design activities. As yet, no hypermedia-specific requirements capture and analysis techniques have been developed, and so more conventional systems approaches must be adapted. Project management can use conventional approaches. Hypermedia evaluation techniques are beginning to appear which can be readily used or adapted as needed (CACM, 1995). In general the end result is that hypermedia development processes can only, at present, be carried out using an eclectic mix of different methods and approaches. One important warning is that this means care must be taken to ensure that differing assumptions built into the various methods do not result in conflicts and consequent development difficulties.

Process Management

Before finishing this chapter, it is worth commenting on how the development process can be managed. In general, this will be highly dependant upon the scale and type of application being developed, although there are a number of common requirements or practices which can be followed. The list of activities given in the management category in Figure 4-5 is a good starting point for consideration, and simply needs to be scaled for the particular project being managed.

Development of very large scale applications can be particularly difficult. In managing large projects we need to be particularly aware that many aspects of the development do not have a linear relationship between project size and required resources or effort. For example, the effort required for designing a consistent look and feel will certainly not double with each doubling in project size, whereas the effort in identifying link structures will grow at a much faster rate than project size. This is partially a result of the growing number of links and partially a result of the difficulty, for a developer, in comprehending the entire information structure as it grows. Indeed, as applications grow in size, the effort required for those activities related to information linking and structuring can come to dominate a project.

Most development projects of even a moderate size will require a broad range of skills and can involve a large development team. A typical team can contain project managers, content experts, application architects, user-interface specialists, programmers, application analysts, designers, creative experts (including artists and photographers) and technicians. Managing this team will require consideration of the balancing of skills and roles and hiring or retraining, where necessary. It is important to note that the field is changing very rapidly (look, for example, at the changing technology of the Web) This means that particular consideration needs to be given to how the skills base of a development team will be maintained.

Finally, a major aspect of the development of hypermedia applications is managing and understanding the cost of development. As skills and technology changes this can fluctuate wildly. For example, at the time of writing there was a substantial ongoing debate on the `alt.hypertext` Internet newsgroup revolving around the 'average' costs associated with Web development. Figures being discussed ranged from US$10 per hour (for simple HTML by inexperienced graduates) to US$200 per hour (for complex CGI, 3D graphics, database interfacing and hosting development).[3] One of the main causes of variation was the skill level of the developers. One of the more interesting exchanges was:

'*Developer 1* wrote: Yes I admit it, I charge by the Page!!! ... I do pages because it gives them (clients) a vague frame of reference they can understand (anyone can do a print preview and see how much area the page takes up).'

'*Developer 2* replied: The problem with this is that it's quite likely to break down if you're doing a very large site. Even assuming that you can define exactly what a 'page' is, the effort involved in creating a site usually won't scale up linearly: a 100-page site is almost always going to require more than 10 times as much work as a 10-page site. There are exceptions; if you're just chopping a big catalog into manageable pieces and linking straight to them with an index page, the amount of work is probably going to be linear in the size of the data, but if you have anything other than a simple, repetitive and stereotyped navigation structure, more of your time on a large site is going to be spent on creating and managing relationships between pages than on writing the pages themselves (if not, the site probably won't be very useful).'

If you charge purely by the 'page' without any other considerations, then you're going to either price yourself out of the market for small sites or take a bath on large sites (if you decide to specialize in a certain range of site sizes, this is less of a problem).

More information on the economics of Web development can be found at:

`http://www.homefair.com/homefair/moreread.html`

or by searching the Web for 'web site cost'.

---

[3] A number of contributors pointed out, quite validly, that this is a rather dubious way of specifying cost, since the scope, quality and content of a Web 'page' can vary considerably. A number of the more 'professional' contributors stated that when quoting on Web development projects, the quote was not a per hour rate, or a per page rate, but rather a project cost which was a composite of the overall project costs.

Tools to Support the Development Process

Strictly speaking, almost any development activity is a potential candidate for receiving support from an appropriate tool. This might include tools to assist in the analysis of users' needs and obtaining profiles of potential user characteristics, high-level structural and functional design tools, rapid prototyping tools, low-level design tools, information capture tools, interface design and implementation tools, testing and evaluation tools, project management tools and a variety of other miscellaneous activities. Unfortunately, many of these possible tools do not yet exist, either through a lack of awareness of the need for the tools, or an inability, at this stage, to create tools which are effective within the given activity. Let us briefly consider some of these.

Authoring tools

Most hypermedia tools currently available fall into the category of authoring tools – that is, they assist with low-level design and implementation of hypermedia applications.

These tools fall into a number of categories, the most common being tools which support a screen-based approach to development. These include development tools like Hypercard, AimTech's IconAuthor, and Macromedia Director and Macromedia Authorware. These development systems typically provide a combination of facilities aimed at creating the structure of the application (such as a flowchart made of icons representing various screens or actions affecting screens or responding to user actions) with a palette of user-interface design tools (such as drawing tools, image windows, animation editors, etc.). These tools typically result in applications encoded in proprietary formats which must be presented using specialised presentation engines.

A broad range of Web design tools have also recently become available in response to the rapid expansion of the Web. The tools can be WYSIWYG editors allowing design of the look and feel of individual Web pages, text editors supplemented with facilities to ease the creation of HTML, and tools to assist in the generation of Web interface elements such as image maps, CGI scripts and Java applets. At the most sophisticated level, full programming environments (such as Microsoft's Visual J++) are becoming available to assist in the creation of Java programs.

Data manipulation tools

A number of tools are available which are not specifically aimed at developing final applications, but which assist in preparing data for use within applications. The simplest examples are tools used to capture, create, edit and manipulate data in various media forms. Examples include image and video capture tools, image manipulation software, video editing programs, audio analysis and/or editing software, and programs designed to create animations.

Information management tools

A number of tools are aimed at managing information rather than data. For example, we use scanner software to read in large quantities of legacy documents and then perform Optical Character Recognition (OCR) to convert the images into the equivalent text. The next step would be to use information management tools to identify and record the structure of this text. The most common example of this style of tool are those aimed at managing SGML documents.

Analysis and design tools

An important focus of this book is the need for a suitable development process. Unfortunately, there are as yet few tools to assist with any development activities other than low-level design and implementation. In some cases, software engineering tools can be adapted for use (such as Entity Relationship Modeling tools), or tools from other related domains may be occasionally appropriate (such as concept mapping or semantic modelling tools). In a very few cases, specific hypermedia design tools exist (such as RM-CASE (Diaz *et al.*, 1995)) but these are not yet widely available.

Process management tools

At the time of writing, no process management tools exist which are specifically adapted for hypermedia development. In many cases, however, conventional project management tools are more than adequate.

5

Obtaining A Quality Product

... not picked from the leaves of any author,
but bred amongst the weeds and tares of mine own brain.
(Thomas Browne)

Chapter Goals

At this point, we have developed an understanding of the need for, and the basic elements of, *hypermedia engineering*. In this chapter, we begin to develop a detailed understanding of how the development process impacts on the quality of the applications we develop. The objectives of this chapter are to:

- Define the twin concepts of product issues (those in the development of applications which impact on the quality of the end result, such as navigability) and process issues (those which affect the quality of the process itself, such as development productivity).

- Define a comprehensive set of process and product issues, and then look at the product issues in detail.

- Look at application relevance as being the extent to which the application is pertinent to its intended goals. The relevance is affected by understanding the domain and suitable design methods.

- Examine the completeness and correctness of an application through suitable design techniques, as well as understanding the application goals.

- Consider the usability of an application through effective structural design, inclusion of appropriate navigation and searching mechanisms, and a good understanding of user-interface design.

- Address other issues, including supporting information utilisation and helping with user cognitive loads.

In the previous chapter we introduced the concept of hypermedia engineering. We viewed hypermedia engineering as being the formal and disciplined approach to the development of hypermedia application, and detailed a number of the activities which may be part of this process, and how the process itself may be structured.

What we did not consider, and what this chapter addresses, is what issues need to be addressed by these activities in order to obtain a quality hypermedia application. An important consideration in the development process of any hypermedia application will be an understanding of how certain process activities influence the quality of the resultant application, and what we can do to improve them. If we have such an understanding we will then be able to ensure that the activities are used and carried out in the most appropriate fashion.

5.1   Product and Process

In the previous chapter we refined our concept of hypermedia development to refer to the process by which we most effectively achieve the hypermedia application which has the attributes which we desire. If we look at this sentence, then we can effectively decompose it into two components: product and process. In each case, there will be various issues that we need to consider if we are to improve our development of quality applications.

Issues Related to Developing an Appropriate Product

> 'The process by which we most effectively achieve **the hypermedia application which has the attributes which we desire**'

As this indicates, we are aiming to develop a product with certain attributes. We need to consider what can be done during the development to guarantee that we are capable of consistently creating quality hypermedia applications (i.e. those with the desired attributes). We can view these as 'product issues', those issues which affect how we carry out the development to ensure the quality of the end product.

We can identify typical issues by returning to our list of hypermedia characteristics at the end of Chapter 2. From this, typical product issues (which we return to in detail shortly) are:

- How can the process be carried out so that we ensure the relevance of the application content?

- How can the process be carried out so that we ensure the completeness and correctness of the application content?

- How can the process be carried out so that we maximise the useability of the application (in terms of access and searching mechanisms, navigation support, guided tours, history mechanisms, etc.)?

- How can the process be carried out so that we maximise the ease of comprehension of the application content?

- How can the process be carried out so that we facilitate cognitive management during the use of the application?

- How can the process be carried out so that we ensure the effective contextualisation of information?

- How can the process be carried out so that we have an application with appropriate security and costing mechanisms?

- How can the process be carried out so that we have an application which makes appropriate use of resources?

- How can the process be carried out so that we develop an application which is politically and socially appropriate?

Each of these issues will be discussed during this chapter.

Issues Related to Developing an Effective Process

> 'The **process by which we most effectively achieve** the hypermedia application which has the attributes which we desire'

Completely independently of the quality of the final application, we wish to carry out the development itself in the most effective and efficient manner possible. For example, it is possible that we could carry out the development in such as way that we ended up with an application that had the desired quality attributes, but the cost of the development, or the use of resources, was completely unacceptable.

We need to consider how to carry out the development in a way which guarantees that the development itself is as effective as possible. If we are to consider this, then we need to begin by considering what 'effective' means? Possibilities include cost-effective, efficient, repeatable, manageable, scalable and measurable.

Once we understand what effectiveness implies, we can move on to considering the issues which impact on this:

- How can the process be carried out so that we manage the cognitive burden associated with authoring?

- How can the process be carried out so that we maximise the development productivity?

- How can the process be carried out so that we maximise reuse during the development?

- How can the process be carried out so that the resulting application is as simple and as flexible to maintain as possible?

- How can the process be carried out so that management of the process is facilitated?

- How can the process be carried out so that we are able to measure the process in a way which helps us improve the process? (i.e. process metrics).

These issues will be the focus of the next chapter.

Different Application Domains

Before we start looking at specific product issues, it is important to note that different application domains can place considerably different constraints on the application, and hence how the application is developed (i.e. the process). For example, reference works, educational material, edutainment, general information, databases, etc. all have very different sets of requirements. Where relevant in the following discussions, we will consider how different application domains influence our approach to the development.

The Linking Issue

Although we didn't explicitly raise linking as an issue in the previous section, it is something which impacts on almost all of the issues raised – both process and product – so we begin our discussion by briefly considering linking.

Theoretically, hypermedia can encompass a very broad range of link types, linking mechanisms and link activation and traversal functionality. Links can be uni- or bi-directional, single- or multi-source, and single- or multi-destination. As an example, links on the Web are uni-directional, single source, single-destination. Although typically development and presentation systems will place constraints on the types of links that can be supported, it is often possible to circumvent these constraints. For example, multiple destination links can be supported on the Web by using specialised browser plug-ins, intermediate pages which list the multiple destinations, or including multiple anchors instead of a single anchor.

One of the main difficulties which linking creates is the development effort required to create suitable link structures. As the information space grows and becomes more complex, there is a huge explosion in the number of possible or desirable links. This is exacerbated by the fact that, as the information space grows, creating each individual link (and especially identifying the link end points) becomes increasingly difficult. Many of the typical development activities are essentially focused on handling this explicit problem. One possible way of addressing this is to use *generic* links, defined by specifying the anchor a single time. The link then exists for any occurrence of the given anchor anywhere within the information space. This can significantly reduce the effort required for linking, but can lead to links which do not make sense in a given context. An example of a system which supports generic links is Microcosm (Hall, Davis and Hutchings, 1996).

Link activation functionality can also vary considerably. On the Web, links are activated through a simple mechanism of point-and-click on the link anchor. In Microcosm links are activated by selecting a section of data and explicitly requesting that any contained links be listed. This latter mechanism allows overlapping anchors – something which is not supported in the Web. The mechanism for traversing links also varies. The Web approach, when a link is followed, is to replace the current node or page with the destination of the link. An alternative approach, used by a number of systems, is to open a new window for each possible destination of the selected link. Whatever the mechanisms used for link activation and traversal, they will have a major impact on the types of functionality which are supported and the ways in which users interact with the system.

It is the link in hypermedia that provides the core functionality which differentiates hypermedia from other information management or access systems. In the next two chapters we will be discussing both process and product issues. Aspects of linking and link management affect both of these. With respect to product issues: the types of links which are supported, and the functionality used in managing and utilising these links, will affect the application in a fundamental way. The links provide the navigational structure which allow a user to manoeuvre within the information space. The completeness and correctness of the links will affect the overall correctness of the application and the ability to locate specific information. The links will also affect the mental model we build of the information space and the relationships between the information elements. With respect to process issues: creating the link structures will be a major activity in the development process, which will in turn be reflected in design and implementation of aspects such as the information space structure and navigation mechanisms. Consideration will need to be given to how this can be carried out in a way which promotes productivity and maintainability.

In the following two chapters on process and product issues, we consider aspects of linking in a large number of places, wherever relevant. Before we begin, however, one final aspect worth considering is that there is, to some extent, a belief that the current role of the link in hypermedia (or at least, the way it is typically associated with a statically anchored 'button') provides a constraint which is limiting the effectiveness of hypermedia systems (Hall, 1994). We need to widen our perception of what a link is and how it can be used to support navigation. One possible example is that we could consider hypermedia links to include dynamically generated links from any text selected during use of a system (a form of generic links).

Note on Holistics

Holistics can be interpreted to mean the 'interconnectedness of all things'. Nelson has stated that 'Everything is linked to everything else', and this is certainly true if we extend our contexts sufficiently. For example, Robertson (1997) uses the example of a semantic relationship between alarm clocks and alligators. These two concepts may at first appearance seem to have no connection, but within the context of the alligator in *Peter Pan* (the alligator swallowed an alarm clock) there is an obvious connection. Thus, it would seem that the link shown in Figure 5-1a would seem to be a valid connection.

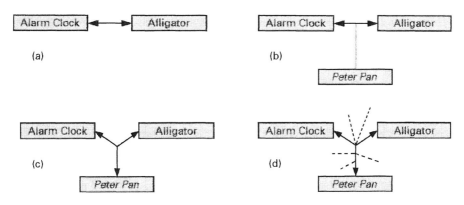

Figure 5-1

The relationship between two concepts is, in reality when we consider context, a complex relationship between many concepts which contribute to the context

This link is really only valid, however, within a particular context, and we could thus view that context as an element of the relationship, as shown in Figure 5-1b. We could go one step further, though, and recognise that the context is in itself just another concept. So what we really have is a three way relationship, as shown in Figure 5-1c, i.e. the link shown in Figure 5-1a is not a valid link – we do not have a relationship between alarm clocks and alligators, we have a relationship between alarm clocks, alligators and *Peter Pan*.

We could take this to the extreme and say that we have an even wider context for interpreting this relationship – such as the English language – and therefore the relationship is as shown in Figure 5-1d. However, this wider context is usually application wide (or even some broader domain), is therefore common across all links/relationships in the application, and can therefore be removed without destroying the context. Indeed, if in the example given above, the application (or even the local region within the application) was about *Peter Pan*, then the relationship shown in Figure 5-1a would be sufficient – though in reality this is a representation of the relationship shown in Figure 5-1d. What this tells us is that holistics is really just an illusion. We do not really have a relationship between alarm clocks and alligators, though we will have a relationship which includes these two elements (along with many others). Indeed, although we may not have a relationship which is solely between two given concepts, we will always be able to find a relationship that includes these two concepts along with others.

What are the implications for this in terms of how we approach the creation and management of links in the hypermedia development process? It means that we need to ensure the context of a link must be obvious. If it is not, then the link becomes meaningless (just as a link between alligators and alarm clocks would be meaningless in any context other than *Peter Pan*).

5.2   Making Applications Relevant

A hypermedia application is only going to be appropriate if the content (i.e. nodes) and structure (i.e. the way in which these nodes are inter-linked) are both relevant. By this we mean not just relevant to the topic of the application, but relevant to the broader goals of the application. For example, for a given educational application, the content may pertain to the topic, but may be irrelevant in the context of the specific learning objectives of the application, or worse still, they may inhibit the learning activity (often an educator will 'hide' from a student a perfectly valid relationship between several concepts until a student has developed a framework into which this relationship can be meaningfully integrated). What, then, does relevance mean?

Prior to answering this question, it is important to point out that there are two factors which will affect what we mean by the relevance of an application and how it can be achieved. First, in many situations the development will be open-ended. In other words, we will be developing a system which will not have a closure. For example, with a banking application that includes information on the current state of customers' accounts, additional information will be continually added to the application. In this case, we need to consider not only what is relevant at the time of the initial development, but also what material may become relevant or irrelevant in the future. In this type of development, the linking issues can become far more complex due to the constantly evolving structure. We need to keep a flexible structure which is capable of evolving and does not restrict the extensibility of the system. An ideal area of research in hypermedia – and one which has barely been recognised – is the design of hypermedia structures which are evolvable, or possibly even an understanding of what 'evolvable' means within a hypermedia context.

Secondly, the development of systems which use legacy data will impact on relevance. If we consider the banking application example from the previous paragraph, we are likely to have large amounts of legacy data which will be used in the initial creation of the application. This data will have a certain predetermined structure. We need to be careful about how this data is incorporated into a hypermedia application, and how the imposed hypermedia structure matches (or possibly contradicts) the previous structure.

Relevance

The following is a dictionary definition of relevance (from the *Oxford English Dictionary*, *2nd ed.*, Clarendon Press, 1989): 'relevance: in recent use, pertinency to important current' and 'relevant: *a*. 1. bearing upon, connected with, pertinent to'. We can interpret this to mean that if a hypermedia application is to be relevant, then it needs to be pertinent to the issues being addressed by the application, or connected to the application goals.

Thus, the concept of relevance will encompass three core aspects: providing content which is suitable, structuring the content in an appropriate fashion; and providing suitable functionality to use this content and structure. This is not a particularly enlightening definition, though – we need to consider what 'suitable' or 'appropriate' means in the particular context of the application under development. We shall look at some examples.

Educational applications typically provide a learning environment, or an experience which facilitates the learning process. Let us consider the three core elements in turn. Certain content may not be appropriate to the learning experience at certain stages, whereas other types of content (such as detailed explanation and justifications, case studies, support for feedback, questions and quizzes, educational hints, etc.) may be very relevant. We need to consider the types of content (and the presentation mechanisms) which facilitate the learning process. Many of these type of ideas are well developed in better textbooks which are used for educational purposes.

The structure that overlays the content provides the ability to navigate within the user space, and the visibility of this structure strongly influences the knowledge structures a student is likely to develop. An application might provide a structure which enables controlled exploration along certain paths that assist in the development of understanding. The development of the linking structure in such a circumstance will typically require considerable educational expertise. Unlike many other applications, in educational applications there will be certain links which may be correct but will not be relevant – simply because traversing that link (or even being aware of its existence) will colour the students' mental picture of the knowledge structures. Consider Figure 5-2. The way in which the concepts shown in this figure are structured can strongly affect the types of knowledge structures the application helps build. In the two cases given the concepts are the same, but the structures are subtly different. The first conceptual structure will tend to produce a perception of education as being about teaching, whereas the second will promote a perception of education as being about learning.

Finally, it is worth noting that the functionality supported by an educational application also needs to be relevant. This means that it should support student exploration (the student still needs to have a sense of ownership of their own learning – and this will not occur if they do not

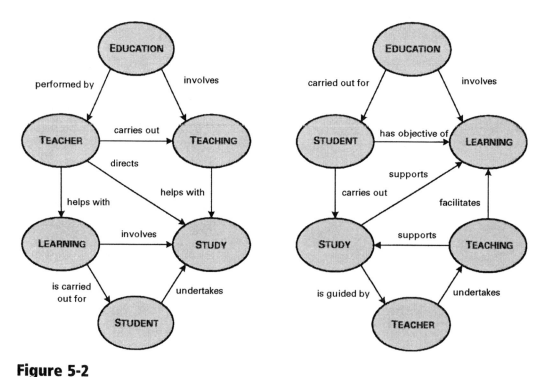

Figure 5-2

Different structures promoting different understanding – is education about teaching or learning?

feel as though they have control over their own learning). This exploration needs to occur within the controlled framework which maximises the educational effectiveness of the application. An advanced educational application will also provide functionality to support feedback to the student on their learning progress, and possibly adapt the navigation functionality based on this feedback. A useful example is cases where the functionality takes the form of games as a mechanism for encouraging the learners' interest and participation.

Reference applications (such as the Microsoft Encarta'95 CD-ROM encyclopaedia) are likely to be used to gain overviews of specific topics, rather than in-depth detailed understanding. This implies that relevant content is likely to include general overviews and structure is likely to imply detailed interlinking without the use of predetermined browsing paths. Powerful searching and indexing functionality is likely to be very important.

Online documentation will require a combination of explanations of concepts, user guidance and assistance with problems. The widest example with which most people are familiar are help files which are now part of most computer applications, especially on the PC and Macintosh platforms. The content will normally be aimed at a level suitable for the specific application, and will need to take into account the fact that most users will refer to the documentation only when they require assistance in achieving a specific goal. This means that content will need to be short and to the point, and that navigation trails will typically be quite short. This implies that searching and indexing mechanisms will dominate over general browsing, though browsing will still be important for explaining directly related concepts.

Catalogues and advertising material are for commercial objectives of promoting interest in given products, and therefore will have very specific impacts on what content and structure are relevant. The conventional ideas about how to effectively present advertising material (such as how to attract attention to a particular feature or product) will still be relevant. In addition to this, we would also need to consider how to structure the information to maximise the users' interest in wide browsing of the material. With advertising catalogues a user will often not be seeking a specific product (or even if they are, we want to entice them to browse more widely). As such, we need to ensure that the anchors are designed to create interest and encourage further browsing. A typical functionality which would be useful would be to track which nodes a user has visited and lead the user into new areas.

Interactive fiction will be structured by the story plot and the content will be delineated by the narrative. A user will typically not usually browse freely around the content of interactive fiction, nor want or expect searching functionality.

How to Achieve Relevance

What can be done during the development process to ensure that the application is relevant? An obvious first step is to develop an understanding of the goals of the application. We can then determine whether specific content, structure or functionality is consistent with these goals. Very few current methodologies or formal authoring approaches explicitly extract the application goals, though these will often be embedded implicitly in the identification of an application specification. The process should therefore provide some mechanism for facilitating an understanding of the application goals. Indeed, this should be extended to include an understanding (maybe through profiling) of the users and usage. In particular, prototyping can assist with these activities.

Once we understand our goals and users, how do we integrate this knowledge into the process whereby we capture/generate the content and structure? The obvious place to look is the process activities where the content and structure are created. In the activities we listed on page 100 the focus would be on activities such as design of content scope, depth and granularity, information representation design, information viewpoint design, design of access mechanisms and navigation structures, and design of information taxonomies and structures. In each case, we need to ensure that the design is consistent with the application goals.

An example of how consideration of relevance can be incorporated into a design process is given by RMM (Isakowitz, Stohr and Balasubramanian, 1995). In RMM, the E-R (Entity-Relationship) design step defines the information domain of the application (by identifying the entities in the application) and the relationships amongst the entities within this domain. Although Isakowitz *et al.* discuss the use of the E-R approach in identifying relationships to support navigation, we believe it is just as important for determining content and structure relevance. If we relate the entities and their relationships back to the goal of the applications, we can effectively ensure the global relevance of application. If we introduce errors at this stage, they will corrupt the ability of the entire application to achieve the desired goals, so great care needs to be taken.

The slice design step follows the E-R design and determines the detailed information structure and access mechanisms. This effectively ensures local relevance. Finally, the third design step is navigation design. It is during this step that we can ensure functional relevance.

Most other processes have similar stages which can be used or adapted to ensure application relevance. For example, navigation design and abstract interface design are (in one form or another) a part of many approaches to hypermedia application design (such as OOHDM (Schwabe and Rossi, 1995a)). Again, in this type of activity we can ensure relevance by tying the design elements back to the question of whether they support the application goals.

Within these activities, an understanding of content relevance will usually require the skills of a content expert. In contrast, the development of structural and functional relevance will require very specific design skills. For example, for an educational application these would include user-interface development expertise and an educationalist.

5.3   Making Applications Complete and Correct

Related to relevance is the completeness and correctness of the application content. As with relevance, we begin by considering exactly what we mean by completeness and correctness of an application (and why it is important).

Completeness

What is completeness? It is essentially the extent to which our application has included the material and the interlinking of this material which is required for the application to be effective. This includes both completeness of information content and completeness of information structure.

Information content: the content will be defined by the bounds of the information space we have constructed for use in the application under development. These bounds have essentially two elements: breadth and depth. The breadth of an application's information space is essentially the extent to which it has extended the bounds of concepts being covered. For example, if we have a hypermedia application on the history of the United States of America, should it include material on the how the USA was settled? On Christopher Columbus? On the ships (Nina, Pinta, Santa

Maria) used by Columbus? On the techniques used to construct the ships? Obviously, the breadth of material to include will be dependant upon the application, the goals and the users.

The depth of an application information space refers to the level of detail we include in an application. For example, having decided that it is appropriate to extend the breadth of an application on the history of the USA to include the trip of the Nina, Pinta and Santa Maria, we then need to decide what level of detail to include about this trip. Do we briefly describe the route followed? Do we include daily descriptions of the progress, with an animation showing the position on a map as time passes? Do we describe what daily life would have been like on these ships?

It is worth pointing out that in developing an application the user should be able to readily identify the bounds of the information space. This implies both suitable interface elements to support this, and a logical boundary which is both consistent and intuitive within the context of the application.

Information structure: completeness applies not only to content but also to how we organise the structure of the content. If appropriate links are missing from an application, then the ability to navigate around the information space will be compromised. For example, if a link which should exist is missing between node A and node B, then to a user at node A, the contents of node B will effectively not exist.

Even a small degree of missing content or links can severely damage the effectiveness of an application: a user will lose confidence in the application. Consider, for example, the situation of an online help application with missing content. Many users may find it more convenient to refer directly to paper-based user manuals than to refer initially to the online application and periodically have the search for information stymied – wasting considerable time in the search.

Let us look at several typical application domains. With educational applications completeness is particularly critical. The underlying goal in most educational applications is to assist students to develop understanding, and this typically involves the students building up appropriate knowledge structures (Figure 2-1 illustrated this process quite well). If content or structure is missing, we severely inhibit the building of the knowledge structures and hence the learning process.

In reference applications and online documentation, missing content or structure is not as likely to inhibit our understanding. Rather, it will decrease a user's ability and desire to rely on the application. If the expected content of an application is only partially complete, then we cannot be certain whether we are having difficulty finding material because it is missing, or just because we are using inadequate search mechanisms (which is in itself a significant problem). Almost everyone who has used the Web has experienced the frustration of searching for some specific content and not being able to find it, and then not knowing whether it is because the content is actually missing, or just simply difficult to locate. Such a situation dramatically reduces the usefulness of an application.

A final comment is worth making. In most cases, providing the user with an understanding of the content bounds (which requires having a logical schema for defining these bounds, and a method for conveying this to the user) is as important as the location of the information space boundary itself.

Completeness raises a series of questions. Where do we draw the line in including material (i.e. how do we determine the bounds of the information space)? How should this material be structured? How does the application domain affect our design? Before addressing these questions, let us consider the related challenges posed by correctness.

Correctness

What is correctness? Like completeness, correctness can be applied to both content and structure. Correctness of structure applies not only to the validity of the interlinking, but also to the validity of the way in which we have decomposed the information space into nodes or 'chunks' of information. Let us look at each of these ideas in turn.

Content correctness: at first glance, the issue of correctness of content would appear to be relatively straightforward – either the content is correct (e.g. '. . . Christopher Columbus sailed to America in 1492 . . .') or incorrect ('. . . Christopher Columbus sailed to Australia in 1498 . . .'). In many situations this black and white answer will be the case, and a content expert can readily provide appropriate guidance. Unfortunately, there are many situations where it is not quite this simple. Consider, for example, a history of the USA which contains 'Christopher Columbus discovered America'. At first glance this appears to be true, but many claim that it ignores the prior existence in the Americas of the native

Americans. We could go even further and give examples of opinions and analyses. In such cases, 'correctness' is a difficult concept to apply (and in some cases, either impossible or irrelevant).

How do we then handle the issue of correctness of content? One possibility is to ensure that the reader is fully aware of which components are considered to be 'fact' and which are opinions, fiction, etc. In some cases, even this may not be appropriate (such as advertising?) The way in which content correctness is handled will be highly dependant upon the particular application. Reference applications will almost certainly need to consider content correctness very carefully. For works of interactive fiction, correctness will be only peripheral (insofar as it affects the validity of the plot). Educational works are likely to contain both factual information (which needs to be absolutely correct) and analyses (which can provide viewpoints, perspectives or opinions, where correctness may be an irrelevant concept).

Decomposition correctness: decomposition correctness is a complex issue, relating to the way in which we decompose or 'chunk' the information into components. We need to consider what is the most 'correct' way to break the content into the blocks which form the basis of the information space. In one sense, we can view this as a form of information linking, since by combining specific material into a single node we are effectively providing a very tight coupling (which is just a form of linking) between this information. Indeed, the coupling is so tight (from an information perspective) that it warrants the use of physical proximity (in the same presentation page) rather than just associative proximity (using links). This is illustrated in Figure 5-3. The decision to group certain information elements into the same node will have implications for the way in which a reader interprets the information. (The decision will also impact on the usability – consider a single very long node as compared to a number of smaller nodes. This will be discussed below in the section on usability.)

What principles should we use for the decomposition or chunking process? Essentially, as the above comments indicate, it will be dependant upon the extent to which we wish to relate ideas, media, concepts or information. We need to consider the degree of coupling we wish to imply, and the likelihood that the various elements being combined need to be used together to make sense. There is considerable debate in the literature about how the chunking process should be carried out. For example, Kreitzberg and Shneiderman (1988) carried out an experiment where a given information space was partitioned in significantly different ways (46 small nodes versus five large nodes). The results of their survey was that users appeared to obtain a better understanding of the topic when many small nodes were used (this may have been a result of the environment they were using – Hyperties – which does not support linking into the middle of a node of information). We believe that the single most important design guideline that can be used is that each node should capture (and hence be based around) a single concept. This ensures suitable cohesion and improves the ability of a user to understand the information and its structure more readily.

Linking correctness: related to decomposition correctness is linking correctness. As with the other forms of correctness, this is not a simple issue. The most basic idea of correctness in linking is simply whether the link connects two appropriately related ideas. If we take this a step further, though, we realise that the connection between ideas is not a binary characteristic (i.e. they are not just related or unrelated, but have a 'strength of relatedness') and is highly context dependant (Christopher

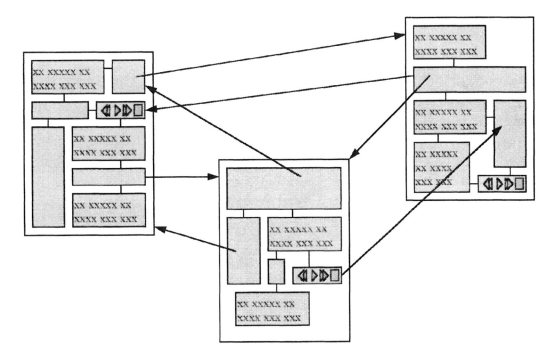

Figure 5-3

Physical proximity (in the same presentation page) can be seen as a form of very tight linking

Columbus and Cats may not appear to be related, but consider the situation where we are teaching children about the letter 'C').

As Nelson has stated, (1993a) we can take the position that everything is connected to everything else (see the note on holistics at the beginning of the chapter). Although this is true in one sense, it is not particularly helpful in terms of assisting in information navigation and utilisation. As we discussed, for connections to be useful, understandable and relevant, they need to exist within an appropriate context. In identifying the validity of a link structure within a particular application, we need to do so within the context of the application and its specific goals. In other words, in generating the structure of an application (i.e. creating links) either statically or dynamically, we need to consider not only the actual inter-relationships, but also the relevance of these inter-relationships to assisting us in the process of information navigation and retrieval.

Robertson (1997) has categorised link errors into three classes: under-linking; over-linking; and links that connect concepts which are not associated. Many researchers include a fourth category, dangling links, though this may be viewed as a special case of incorrectly connected links. Under-linking implies that we have links that have been omitted, but if included would have improved the users' ability to navigate and identify desired information. Similarly, we can view over-linking as the case where, if certain links were removed, the overall usability of the application would be increased. We can view this as a typical case of improving the signal (highly relevant links) to noise (irrelevant or less relevant links) ratio.

Inaccurate links are those where the concepts being connected do not have a valid association in the current context. This will often be the most damaging type of link error. If a user loses confidence in the validity of the links, not only does the readability suffer, but studies have shown that the reader will abandon the use of the link structure (Parunak, 1989; Raskin, 1987).

Achieving Completeness and Correctness

What can we do within the development process to ensure the highest possible level of application completeness and correctness? As with the consideration of relevance, the logical place to start is by ensuring that we understand both the application objectives and the problem domain. The context set by these will ensure we have a good grasp of the context within which we are performing our development. Beyond this, though, we can identify activities within the application design that have the greatest impact on application completeness and correctness. In particular, this will include the design of content scope, depth and granularity, the design of information taxonomies and structures, and the design of navigation structures (though these activities may be embedded into some other stage or phase of development, depending upon the particular methodology being adopted).

First, let us consider the process whereby we actually design the bounds of the information space. Unfortunately, in many processes this is only performed implicitly, i.e. we consider information elements we wish to include (often by considering the information sources to which we have direct access), rather than those which we *should* include given the application objectives. Often it will not be possible to identify the boundary of the information space directly, due predominantly to its complex shape. A more fruitful approach may be to adopt a technique such as brainstorming, where a large concept base is identified and then the concepts are considered as possible candidates for inclusion. Robertson (1997) proposes an approach based on concept mapping, where a brainstorming session is followed by a series of stages of progressive refinement and concept merging.

Where the application content is being sourced from another location (such as existing paper-based documents), great care needs to be taken that the existing material does not unduly control the bounds of the content. Problems can often arise because content which is appropriate to include is embedded within content which is not. For example, in developing an application on the history of the United States of America we wish to include material on the Nina, Pinta and Santa Maria. We may have access to source material on these three ships which is part of a broader collection of material on 15th century ships. We would need to be careful which material we use from within this broader collection.

When we come to consider the actual correctness of the content itself, we need to consider the veracity of the source from which we obtain the content. For example, is the content being obtained from a reputable source (encyclopaedias, refereed journals, bureau of statistics, etc.), a less reputable source (the media, books, etc.), or a totally unreliable source (personal opinion, etc.). In each case, the content may be appropriate – we simply need to be aware of the implications of obtaining material from that source.

Once we know which concepts we wish to include and what content is correct and appropriate within the information space, we can begin the process of allocating these concepts to particular nodes. This process (usually referred to as chunking) will also significantly impact on the correctness of the application. The information chunks need to be designed as a compromise between navigability and readability. If the chunks are too small, then the information loses cohesiveness and the user spends proportionally too great an amount of time navigating. If the chunks are too large, then we lose the ability to create flexible navigation structures.

A number of quite simplistic hypermedia design principles relate very specifically to this problem. For example, a common 'hint' is to ensure that each page of information contains, or focuses on, a single clear concept. Implementing this hint may not, however, always be straightforward. We first need to identify which concepts are appropriate.

The approach by Robertson (1997) mentioned above includes a mechanism whereby content experts provide indications of the degree of 'relatedness' of the various concepts which is then used to generate a measure of semantic distance, which is in turn used to group concepts together. There is a significant body of literature on semantic distance which is useful within this context.

RMM (Isakowitz, Komis and Koufaris, 1996) uses slice design to split each identified entity (the entities effectively define the information bounds) into meaningful 'slices', where each slice is effectively a concept. Isakowitz *et al.* use the example of a 'faculty' entity being split into biography, video clip, general and research area slices. Slice design guidelines emphasise that each slice represents a *whole* for the user, and is based around domain analysis.

Creating a correct and complete structure amongst the information nodes or pages is one of the activities which is typically very poorly carried out. In many cases, much of the cross-linking is performed automatically or semi-automatically. Current analysis tools are sophisticated enough to be useful in this process, but not yet adequate enough to be able to carry out the cross-linking completely effectively. As a result, many applications which have used automatic or semi-automatic cross-linking exhibit a very poor link structure. To be effective, such an approach needs to be used only to support humans, who can intervene and correct the process where necessary. As an example, consider the case where we have the following fragments of text.

```
. . . the Santa Maria valley, in California, was
settled in . . .
. . . The Nina, Pinta and Santa Maria were the
ships which Columbus used on his travels when he
discovered the Americas . . .
```

If we used an automated filter to search the text database for references to 'Santa Maria' and insert links from the identified text to a page of information on the history of the Santa Maria Valley, then we would obviously end up with incorrect links.

Robertson (1997) asserts that the development process must assist the author to identify links which are not only semantically correct, but valuable or important *within the context* of the application and its usage. Most existing hypermedia design approaches include some form of linking stage, though this is often integrated into some form of 'navigation design'. We would claim that design of linking networks and design of navigation structures can benefit from being treated as two separate activities. Linking networks are the underlying structures which identify what inter-relationships exist. Navigation structures are the structures which we place on top of these linking networks , allowing them to be used to manoeuvre within the information space. The navigation structures can only be developed effectively if the underlying linking network is correct and complete. By combining these two stages, we are forced to split our attention between the creation of suitable links and a consideration of how these links will be utilised.

5.4 Making Applications Usable

Probably the single most evident characteristic of any hypermedia application, and the one which is most likely to affect the ability of an application to achieve its goals, is the usability of the application. A very broad range of factors affect the usability of an application: examples include information access mechanisms, support for browsing and searching, and the style of the user interface. If we return to our original discussion regarding hypermedia, we gave the following definition:

> **Definition**
>
> **Hypermedia** An application which uses associative relationships among information contained within multiple media data for the purpose of facilitating access to, and manipulation of, the information encapsulated by the data.

This tells us that for an application to be usable it needs to *'facilitate access to, and manipulation of'* information. The supported functionality must begin by allowing us to access information. Within hypermedia this implies active support for both manoeuvring around the information space, and for understanding where we are within the space relative to other information elements. Beyond this, however, the application should support appropriate manipulation of the information.

Information access within hypermedia relies on a variety of mechanisms, including searching, browsing, general navigation, understanding of context and understanding of information structure. Let us look at these in reverse order.

Information Structure

In an excellent article by Clifford Urr, ('Will the real hypertext please stand up?' (Urr, 1991)) the importance of an information structure or taxonomy was discussed. The essence of this argument is captured in the following extract:

> 'Accumulate enough knowledge – whatever its form – and you need an application, a taxonomy, a structure of how that information is organized so that you can intuitively find information – as you would using a card catalog searching for a book – in a complicated hypertext network. Those constructing quality classification structures make a pattern of access consistent and predictable. When classifications are well conceived, such structures are virtually invisible to the user; they stay out of his or her way.'

In other words, if users are to be able to readily find desired information, they should be able to understand the way in which the information space is organised. This understanding should not, however, be something that requires considerable effort (this would, after all, distract the user from the task of accessing and understanding the information itself). The structure should be intuitive to the user. This is where considerable skill is required (and, as Urr points out, why cataloguing skills form such an important part of librarianship). If the structure is not intuitive or does not organise the information in a way which places specific items of information in suitable locations within the information space, then the resulting hypermedia application will be next to unusable.

> '. . . if a given hypertext application lacks in quality classifications of the information it contains, then almost all other features a supposed hypertext application contains are irrelevant or are merely distractions. If a jet cannot fly, well . . . so what if its wings are aesthetic or if the jet's paint finish is attractive or if it is able to run on less fuel than other jets? . . . If a hypertext application or knowledge base lacks good classifications, it will not fly as an information access application, at least not in accordance to the vast potential inherent to genuine hypertext. This will remain true regardless of how many "bells and whistles" the application contains, regardless of how pretty the interface it offers. Style is no substitute for substance in hypertext, as in most anything truly valuable.'

What can we do to develop a suitable structure? This is not a question which can be readily answered. The effort and skill required of a developer to create the access structures (especially for a large complex application) can be very advanced. A valuable person to include on a large development team would be a librarian (or someone with librarianship skills). The process followed will be to carefully analyse the content to be included in the hypermedia information space, and in doing so, identify the key terms and concepts that best represent the information. Even more importantly, the developer must identify significant connections which occur between the many separate units of information, and then create an overarching information taxonomy. One of the best examples of this style of approach is the E-R design step within RMM (Isakowitz, Stohr and Balasubramanian, 1995).

Another mechanism which can be used to support an understanding of the information structure within an application is to explicitly provide the user with an overview of the information space. The simplest way to achieve this is to use a map of the information space. If a map is used correctly, it can provide not only an understanding of a hypermedia applications structure at varying levels of detail, but also orient the user within this structure (i.e. 'you are here'). Many tools exist which will generate maps of information spaces automatically. However, these map generators tend to be purely mechanistic and cannot take into consideration the underlying taxonomy which was used to generate the structure. Nevertheless, automatically generated maps can serve a useful purpose as a navigation aid.

Local Contextualisation

Having a taxonomy within which the hypermedia information is organised is critical, but it will lose effectiveness if the local context does not provide feedback to the user as to their location within the information space. We can almost view the information taxonomy described above as a global context. The way in which specific information elements are presented provides a local context. If we return to our original definition of information given in Chapter 2:

Definition

Information   The interpretation of data within a context set by *a priori* knowledge and the current environment.

Looking at this definition we see that the context allows us to interpret data in order to extract information. If the context is inadequate, then our ability to interpret the data is damaged, and consequently we are unable to extract information as effectively. What, then, sets our context? As indicated by the definition, it effectively consists of two elements – our *a priori* knowledge and the current environment.

A priori knowledge will be a function of the users' history, both long-term (what is the background of the users of the application?) and short-term (where have they already been within the application?). This indicates that an understanding of the users is critical. We would need to consider their expertise, knowledge, maturity, social context, etc. Consider, for example, the difference in how we would present information on cooking recipes, if the intended audience was young children as compared to an audience of chefs. The content and goals may be the same, but knowledge of the users will greatly affect the ability to interpret the information. A development process should therefore include an analysis of the users and their needs, and then during the application design, a review of the design in the context of this analysis. An example of an activity which may be beneficial would be a walkthrough of a prototype by a sample of expected users, and a subsequent analysis of how they coped.

The short-term history of users also affects the *a priori* knowledge of the users, and hence their context. When creating individual pages, we should consider the regions within the information space which we can guarantee the users must have visited. For example, if the application is an education application, and users are following a specific learning pattern, then we may be able to guarantee that immediately prior to arriving at a specific page of information, the user was viewing some other known page, which provides us with a very explicit context. In other cases, we will have little or no control of the local context. Consider, for example, the case where we have Web pages that anyone can link to from anywhere – we cannot control the context, and therefore need to be more careful in designing Web pages[4] (a common occurrence when browsing the Web is to find a page which does not appear to make sense – because we are missing the local context of that page).

Ensuring that each page of a hypermedia application is valid within the context of the users' short-term history is usually very difficult. This is a result of the complexity of the possible navigation paths within an application. Typically, the solution is to assume that a page can be accessed from anywhere (and therefore we cannot make any assumptions about the short-term history of the users' navigation) unless we can explicitly show that a page can only be reached by travelling along one of a known set of paths. This will typically require a navigation map of the information space. Indeed, drawing a navigation map (or a link network) is often listed as a useful design step (particularly in lists of hints on designing for the Web).

The last factor to consider when looking at context is the local environment. Consider the situation where we have a page of information on the effects of pollutants on natural waterways. We could include as the background to the text an image of pristine natural rivers, an image of dead salt flats, or an image of fields of wheat crops. Each image will

---

[4] The authors are currently working on a modification to a Web server which attempts to look at the history of a Web browser which is requesting a page. The server will only return the requested page if the browser has recently been used to look at one of a given set of 'context-setting' pages. This would enable development of Web pages to more actively take into account the local context of a user.

significantly affect the way we interpret the text which is the core of the page of information.

Navigation and Browsing

The functionality provided to support general navigation and browsing within the information space will be critical to the usability of an application. If we are to develop appropriate functionality, we need to be aware of why and when the user navigates around the information space. As with most of the issues discussed in this section, the form of browsing/navigating will vary from application to application. For example, in an encyclopaedia or on-line reference work the navigation is likely to be highly directed. In a shopping catalogue or online magazine, the navigation may well be more random.

The core functionality of moving within the information space is likely to be set by the environment being used. For example, with the Web the linking mechanism and the process of selecting a link will be determined by the browser (such as 'clicking' a highlighted anchor). We can, however, augment this functionality to improve the navigation. For example, various tools allow a user to browse a Website structure and select specific pages for loading. Similarly, browser plug-ins can provide more complex forms of interaction. A typical example is the development of a three-dimensional space (using the 3D modelling language VRML) within which the user can manoeuvre and select items. We can also add other forms of functionality, such as removing the concept of 'selecting' an item of information, and having the traversal of links triggered by other types of actions (timers, the results of user queries, the browsing history of the user, etc.).

A word of warning is appropriate at this point. Many existing hypermedia applications, especially on the Web, have over-complex interfaces. There is a strong temptation to use a very broad array of approaches to interact with an application in order to make the application appear sophisticated. Although appropriate in some circumstances, this often leads to an application where the users' ability to retrieve information is actually hampered, either by the necessity to understand the interaction mechanisms, or because the interaction mechanisms are interesting enough to divert the users' attention. As with all components of an application, the interaction functionality should be developed with the goals of the application in mind. This implies that in almost all cases, the interaction mechanisms should be intuitive and as transparent to the user as possible. The users' attention should be able to focus on the task at hand, not on how to interact with the application.

What all of this tells us is that we need to determine how the user is most likely to want to use the information, and how they are likely to move within the information space. We can then use this knowledge in developing forms of interaction that most proactively support the user, without having the mechanisms themselves impinge upon the users' awareness. In many cases, the most obvious way of developing a suitable understanding of the appropriate functionality will be to use prototypes and user experiments. Often, users will be familiar with an existing application and a suitable metaphor can be adopted. For example, many applications have adopted a book metaphor where the users can turn pages, or move to a table of contents or index.

Searching and Indexing

Most hypermedia applications will incorporate searching and indexing mechanisms. Searching is basically a mechanism which allows a user to bypass the imposed link structure and identify possible destinations anywhere within a given information space. This is analogous to the use of indexes in paper books. The use of searching mechanisms raises several important issues: How do we support searching? When is it appropriate to search? What are the consequences of searching? Let us begin by considering common practice.

It is relatively standard practice, especially with Websites, to attach a search engine onto an application once the site has been designed and implemented. A search engine is built (often using a commercial or public domain search engine or indexer such as wwwwais[5] or Harvest[6]), and a link to the search engine is added to some or all of the Web pages in the site. Although this does provide a useful search mechanism, it fails in several ways. First, it does not consider which components of the application should typically be indexed, and the implications of allowing a user to effectively wander the information space unconstrained. It also means that the searching functionality is not truly an integrated component of the overall application.

---

[5] http://www.eit.com/software/wwwwais/wwwwais.html
[6] http://harvest.cs.colorado.edu/

Figure 5-4 gives an example of how we may better integrate a search engine into an application. In this case, the search engine can often be more profitably used by constraining its scope to act as an access mechanism onto a region of the information space which does not contain a highly structured linking network. Consider the case where we have a Website which contains a large amount of information about a particular organisation. Much of this information may be highly structured, such as organisational descriptions or company work practices and guidelines. Other regions of the information space will be less structured (at least on a global scale, though the individual pages or records may still be highly structured), such as the collection of information on each employee. As shown in Figure 5-4, we can use a search engine as the interface between the unstructured region of the information space and the appropriate area within the structured region. In one respect, we can almost view the search engine as a multi-destination, automatically maintained link.

This is, of course, not to say that search engines cannot be effectively used globally across an entire Website – just that this style of use is only one of the possibilities for effective use of searching mechanisms. Even when using a search engine on an application such as an encyclopaedia, we may not want a completely unconstrained search, as it will often only make sense to link to the beginning of the encyclopaedia articles. The

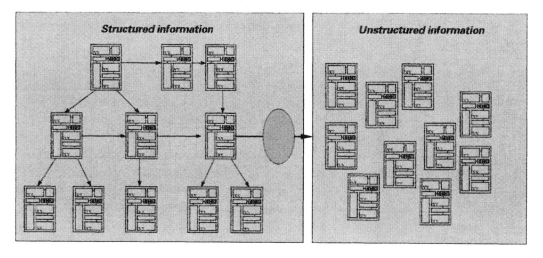

Figure 5-4

Using a search engine in a controlled fashion

appropriate use of a search engine can be understood by considering, during the design phase, the types of usage patterns which are likely, and the types of information structures which will exist. Given these two factors, the suitability of a search engine and the scope of its operation can be determined.

Apart from the scope of a search engine, we must also design the specific functionality. The sophistication of the search functionality which is provided varies considerably. At its very simplest, a trivial keyword match on page titles can be used. At the opposite extreme we have context-dependant searches involving complex search criteria. Additional search functionality is not always desirable. Often we will have a relatively simple style of search which needs to be supported, and making the search engine more complex may serve only to distract the user. As with the design of the search scope, the search functionality should be designed early in the development process and integrated into the overall application, being based on the predicted usage patterns.

The usefulness of a search engine will be heavily dependant upon the quality of the indexed information which is the basis of the search. Many existing search engines for Websites have simply used an automatic indexer to index the entire contents of the site. While this can be useful if the site is suitably focused (so that users are able to specify suitably focused search criteria), it can cause problems if the site is very large in content or broad in focus. Also, using an automatic indexer does not give any control over what material (and what destinations) should be included. In most circumstances the effort required to manually build an index (or manually construct the constraints to place on the indexing) is not warranted. There will, however, be some circumstances where this can be very important. It is also important to bear in mind in selecting the application environment that some environments are capable of providing better support for indexing and searching. For example, if our data is stored using SGML, as in Figure 5-5, we can more readily provide constraints on the types of searches which we allow, such as searching by movie title.

A number of other factors need to be considered in search engine design. These include the mechanism and/or frequency of update of the underlying indexes, information gathering processes and the efficiency (especially for large indexes). These will typically not affect the search functionality (except where performance constraints place restrictions), and are often relegated to the component design stage of development.

```
<title Maltin 4 Mystery PG C>Sleuth

<length>138 <year>1972

<Director>Joseph L. Mankiewicz

<Cast>Laurence Olivier Michael Caine

<Review>Lighthearted mystery tour de force for two stars, adapted by Anthony
Shaffer from his hit play about games-playing mystery writer Oliver his wife's lover
(Caine) into diabolical trap. But who gets the last on whom? Delicious from start to
finish; remarkable production design Ken Adam. Mankiewicz's last film to date.

<Nomination Actor Director Score>
```

Figure 5-5

The SGML mark-up language facilitates controlled searching

A final factor which should be mentioned before leaving the discussion on search engines is the consequences of providing search mechanisms on user orientation. As mentioned previously, a search engine will bypass the link structure and identify possible destinations anywhere within a given region of the information space. This introduces two possible problems: the first is related to the possibility that the link structure was imposed so that the user would follow a certain logical sequence through the information. Breaking this sequence (by using the link engine to jump outside the link structure) may destroy the logical flow of concepts and ideas, and hence damage the effectiveness of the application. The severity of this problem will be dependant upon the particular class of application (for example, this is likely to be a much greater problem for educational applications than reference applications). The solution is to exercise care in generating the indexes and allowable destinations for the results of searches.

The second problem with 'unconstrained' jumping which searching facilitates is user disorientation. This can be partly a result of the discontinuity (moving a long 'conceptual' distance very quickly), and partly of the sudden change in context. Again, the only reasonable solution is to carefully design both the search engine (so that only reasonable jumps are allowed) and the context of each page or node which is likely to be the destination of a search-based jump (so that the context facilitates user re-orientation).

User Interfaces

User interfaces provide the mechanism by which users interact with an application and make use of the underlying functionality. User interface design is a very complex field. In designing a user interface, consideration will need to be given to artistic and creative aspects, cognitive issues (such as how to present information in a way which makes it as easy as possible to interpret), technical constraints (such as how to manage the various media), hypermedia specific aspects (such as how to present link anchors to the user) and interaction aspects. To effectively create a suitable interface, a developer will also need to be aware of the effect of the interface on information contextualisation and the mechanisms for ensuring seamlessness with other applications.

Typical elements which can be used in the construction of hypermedia interfaces include maps, search engines, presentation metaphors, windowing mechanisms, interface elements, etc. Information space maps (such as hierarchical diagrams, graphs, fish-eye lenses, concept maps) can be used to support an understanding of the overall structure of the information space and the users' location and orientation within this space. Search engines can be used to support identification of unstructured information. The interface to search engines will usually require entry and submission of the search criteria, and so will often be based on the use of forms. Presentation metaphors (such as a book, shop, office, desktop, filing cabinet or stack of cards) provides a context for the application, and will often be supported by templates provided with the development tools.

The use of different types of window can provide feedback to users to allow them to orient themselves. For example, Microsoft Encarta'95, shown in Figure 5-6, uses a variety of different windows for such things as presenting the main information, searching, general navigation, and providing additional functionality such as a dictionary. Each window can incorporate different panes for related components (such as the text and image panes in the main window).

Interaction mechanisms include the use of special cursors, menus (such as those across the top of the main window in the background of Figure 5-6), lists (in the pinpointer window), keyboard interaction via forms (such as the entry of a word in the dictionary window), buttons (such as the navigation panel at the bottom left of Figure 5-6), and the usual variety of other interface elements (such as check boxes, sliders, toolbars and scroll bars).

Figure 5-6

Screen dump from the Microsoft Encarta'95 CD-ROM encyclopaedia, depicting multiple windows and panes

Many current Websites which contain good content fail badly because the user interface is poorly designed. User interface design is a sophisticated enough process to require specific skills, especially for a large complex application. Appendix 1 provides a comprehensive list of design tips and hints which will assist in developing effective interfaces. It is important to remember, however, that arbitrarily applying a series of design principles will not necessarily result in an effective interface. A solid understanding of user interface design is very important.

Apart from the interface design itself, activities which can be important for the creation of an effective interface during the development process include observing and evaluating user interactions and iterative refinement of the interface. Several published studies exist where the utilisation of hypermedia applications has been monitored. This monitoring can either be unobtrusive (as in Egan *et al.*, 1989 and Shneiderman *et al.*, 1989, where the application was designed so that it was able to log the user behaviour), or intrusive (as in Hardman (1989), where the users were asked to think aloud as they used the application). This latter approach can provide valuable feedback on both the effectiveness of (or problems with) elements of the user interface, or more deep-seated problems with the structural design. For example, Hardman (1989), in an evaluation of *Glasgow Online*, found user interface problems such as the readability of parts of the screen and design problems such as a confused linking structure.

Iterative refinement of interfaces can also be a valuable tool. It is generally accepted that user-interfaces can rarely be initially implemented ideally (Nielsen, 1993b), and so progressive refinement based on user feedback is important. The evaluation by Hardman (1989) mentioned above included obtaining feedback from users on specific interface elements (such as the icons used for link anchors), how they interpreted the interface element (such as determining what an icon might signify), and whether the interface element was intuitive. This information was then used to refine the interface. Another good example of iterative development is given by Nielson and Sano (1994), where a series of interface icons were developed and then shown to users (without labels) who were asked to interpret the icons. The feedback from the users was used in the refinement of the icons. It also pointed out where problems existed with the overall metaphor being used, and where specific elements were designed correctly but had too dominant a concept, colouring the users' perceptions of other elements.

5.5 Supporting Use of Information

Early in this book we discussed our conception of hypermedia as extending beyond simple information retrieval to include information utilisation. Most of the discussion within the section has so far concentrated on the information retrieval aspects of hypermedia. Let us now consider how we may provide support for the effective utilisation and manipulation of information within hypermedia applications.

Having developed mechanisms to locate and (where relevant) retrieve information, we can consider the ways in which we can utilise the information. We can break this into several distinct forms of use: sharing, analysis and interpretation, augmentation, reorganisation and adaptation. We consider each of these in turn.

Analysis and Interpretation

Obviously, one of the main reasons for using hypermedia applications is because of the access to information which it provides. However, we can look at how we intend to use the information to which we have gained access. In many cases, the hypermedia application should be able to assist in the process of analysing or interpreting the data.

As an example, we have developed a Web-based hypermedia application which teaches students about the software development process, using a case study built around the design and implementation of an elevator control application. This application incorporates a considerable body of material related to the justification for the time and effort spent on various stages of the development process. We have also included a simulation engine which models the development process and allows the user to change various parameters (such as the time allocated to the various activities). The model then provides feedback to the user on the effects on the process and the resulting software application. This approach helps a student analyse the implications of changes and interpret the information which is being presented.

We can consider two different categories of tool for supporting analysis and interpretation. The first are tools that affect the information we retrieve. A good example of this is given by Microcosm (Hall, Davis and Hutchings, 1996), where additional filters can be readily added to the application to allow specialised functionality for aiding in interpretation (such as incorporating a filter which only shows links that were created by a specific author or sorting links by their creation date prior to presentation).

The second category of tools are those that actually perform some form of information analysis for us. A trivial example might be where we have access to a large collection of documents detailing specific criminal legal cases, and we wish to know the ratio of guilty verdicts to not-guilty verdicts for each judge mentioned. This information may be present in the information implicitly, but nowhere made explicit. Rather than manually generating the information ourselves, we could use a suitable tool to analyse the information for us and extract the relevant information.

This style of tool is almost non-existent in most hypermedia applications, predominantly due to the difficulties in predicting what forms of analysis are likely to be required. One alternative may be to provide a flexible 'analysis' language in which users could formulate and develop analysis requests.

Augmentation, Reorganisation and Adaptation

Rather than perceive the information space as being fixed, we can view it as a dynamic entity and allow the user to manipulate the information space as appropriate. This type of manipulation can be by adding new material (i.e. augmenting the information) to extend the information space, or reorganising and/or restructuring the information space to reflect the users changing perception of the structure. Also, these changes can be either manual (i.e. managed by the user) or automatic (i.e. triggered by the user but transparent to them).

The simplest form of information space augmentation, incorporated into many applications is to allow the user to add their own annotations and notes. These are then linked to the appropriate pages or nodes, and provide the user with a permanent record. This can then be used by the user to assist in later interpretation. Unfortunately, the ways in which this is typically implemented means that the added information remains as an annotation to the given page, and is rarely fully integrated into the information structure. To achieve this type of functionality would require that the annotations were stored using the same representation as the original information, and the user could add linking information in addition to the node information – in other words, having an environment in which the user is effectively given (possibly limited) authoring functionality.

The simplest example of information space reorganisation is the ability which most Web browsers provide for bookmarking. We can view a collection of bookmarks as a users' own personal collection of links into an information space. Unfortunately, this is extremely limited. A better approach may be to allow the user to add not just bookmarks into the information space, but to layer new links between elements within the information space. This type of functionality is impossible to provide given the current architecture of the Web (except where the Web pages are directly under the control of the user). Applications such as Hyper-G (Andrews and Kappe, 1994) and Microcosm (Hall, Davis and

Hutchings, 1996) allow this approach to occur. For example, in Microcosm the links are stored separately from the data ,and so users can add new links to the link base.

The process of restructuring the information space can occur automatically as well. An example of how this might occur is that, whenever a user accesses two different nodes in a related way (which may mean related in time, related in context, etc.), a link is created between those two nodes for later use. In a multi-user application the 'strength' of this link may be adjusted depending upon its frequency of use – so that commonly used links gain in strength. What we would then have is a hypermedia network structure which 'learns'.

Groupware: Sharing of Information

In many cases, hypermedia applications will be used within the context of group activities. For example:

- CASE (Computer Aided Software Engineering): tools such as the Dynamic Design project (Bigelow, 1988) at Tektronix can benefit from the ability of hypermedia applications to organise the management of, and access to, the large volume of documentation which is typically associated with software development projects.

- Issue analysis: gIBIS (graphical Issue Based Information Application) (Conklin and Begeman, 1988) (developed by MCC) is an application which supports multiple users in a design process revolving around the contribution of issues, positions (a particular stance on an issue) and arguments (in support of, or contradictory to, various positions). The various elements were linked together in a hypermedia-like structure. Each user can browse and edit the structure independently of the other users.

- Idea organisation: hypermedia provides a mechanism for organising and relating ideas in a way which many claim is the most naturally suited to our own mechanisms for organising ideas. Although this is valid for single user applications, hypermedia can be especially valuable when applied to multi-user applications, providing a common framework for organising the disparate ideas from different sources. For example, SEPIA (Streitz et al., 1992) is a hypermedia development tool which supports both asynchronous and synchronous collaboration by a distributed group of authors during the different activities of the hypermedia authoring process (such as planning, content acquisition and documentation). The application supports individual work, a loosely coupled mode (where each user works independently, but can see the results of the other users' operations) and a tightly coupled mode (where each user sees the same thing and acts together).

- Games: many recent games allow multiple users who interact with each other. Specific variants of this style of game can incorporate, or benefit from, hypermedia. Alternatively, hypermedia can benefit from the use of games. Many of this style of hypermedia games are based on a 'shared universe' concept.

- Education: there is a very large potential for the use of groupware in educational hypermedia. We can visualise the situation where students using an educational hypermedia application interact not only with the application, but with a teacher who can guide them through the application, or answer questions.

In all these cases, the underlying functionality supported by the group-ware nature of the application (as distinct from a single-user application) is the exchange of information. This information exchange may be multiple users contributing to the construction of an information base of some form, or one user sharing their knowledge with other users. The essence is, however, that by exchanging information we are able to make more effective use of the information. If the information is to be shared then it needs to be represented in a way which allows it to be interpreted equally by all those involved. This implies that user customisation of either the information or the environment in which the information is viewed does not prohibit other users from using the information. (Two trivial examples are the use of browser-specific HTML code in Web pages which are going to be used by users with a variety of different browsers, and the transmission of video data at a rate which is incompatible with some of the other users' hardware).

The types of activities given above are, to a large extent, a combination of hypermedia and CSCW (Computer Supported Cooperative Work). In developing these applications, we need to consider such things as whether we wish to support synchronous or asynchronous communication and cooperation, the communication mechanisms which will be used, what types of information will be exchanged, how consistency between different users will be maintained, and how access and privileges will be controlled.

For groupware elements to be integrated into the application in a seamless manner, the underlying support will need to be factored into the architectural design of the application at a very early stage. For example, the feasibility of incorporating a video connection between users of the application will only be possible if the application has been designed to incorporate suitably high bandwidth network connections. The development of the conventional hypermedia elements will also need to consider the effect of multiple users, e.g. will having multiple users allow the context of a user to be changed unexpectedly, and how can the application be designed to minimise the impacts of this?

5.6   Cognitive Management

One of the most widely discussed issues in hypermedia is how we can (or should) manage the cognitive burden which is placed on a user (the parallel issue of how to handle the developers' cognitive burden is discussed in the next chapter). Essentially, cognitive management will cover two main areas: presenting concepts in a way which facilitates their interpretation in the intended way, and minimising the cognitive effort required by a user in managing the information space. One of the better examples of problems related to the latter, is the 'lost in hyperspace' syndrome. This results from the user having too many links and too complex a structure to be able to manage effectively, raising a range of broader issues related to the development process, such as how do we assist the user in understanding the structure? How do we delineate development roles (such as content expert versus presentation expert versus cognitive expert) in a way which is consistent with achieving an appropriate structure while ensuring suitable access to content? Let us begin by considering the 'lost in hyperspace' problem.

Lost in Hyperspace

The idea of being lost in hyperspace is essentially about the user losing an understanding of either their local context or where they are in the information space. If we take being 'lost in physical space' as an analogy – we can see that the interpretation of 'lost' can be quite relative. If we are travelling and arrive in a new city, then we may have no idea of the 'local space' in which we currently exist. This will only be a problem if we need to be able navigate and are unable to do so. For example, if we are catching a cab then we do not need to understand the local space – the cab driver is effectively able to take us wherever we wish to go – whereas if we are driving then we will need a much better understanding.

In an analogous way, if we arrive in a new region of 'hyperspace' which we have not visited previously, then problems may arise which affect our ability to navigate within this local space. We can circumvent these problems either by making use of some form of guide (such as a linking substructure which provides a guided tour or is able to take us directly to the information we require, i.e. a bus or taxi driver). Alternatively, we could use a map to show us the 'terrain' or layout of our local space. Additional aids would include road signs (this way to further information on X) or index pages (possibly the equivalent of a central rail or bus terminal?) which help us correlate our current specific surroundings to the structure of the map.

Being lost in hyperspace is a significant problem for several reasons. First, it impedes our ability to navigate further. If we do not know where we currently are, then we will have great difficulty finding out how to get elsewhere. It is common to see users consistently navigating by repeatedly returning to a home page and navigating outwards from that point rather than moving around within the space (see Figure 5-7). This will often be the result of the combination of the user not being familiar with the overall information structure, and not being aware of where they are within this structure.

We shouldn't extend the physical space/information space analogy too far. There are several significant differences between these two spaces which will affect how we behave and navigate in each. The first is that, unlike in a physical space, in a hyperspace the distance to move (i.e. conceptual distance) is not correlated to the time it takes to make that move (i.e. I can type in a new URL in my Web browser, and move a great conceptual distance very quickly). This alone is often sufficient to make re-orienting particularly difficult. An implication of this is that each node of information (at least each node which is a prospective link destination – which in many applications is essentially every node) should provide some form of facility for orienting the user if required. One mechanism that we have experimented with is to provide a map of the information space (which can be scaled in a suitable fashion) with a marker showing the current location. The user then has access to this map from every page in the application or Website. Such a tool (even if only used occasionally) allows the user to build up a much better picture of the information space within which they are navigating.

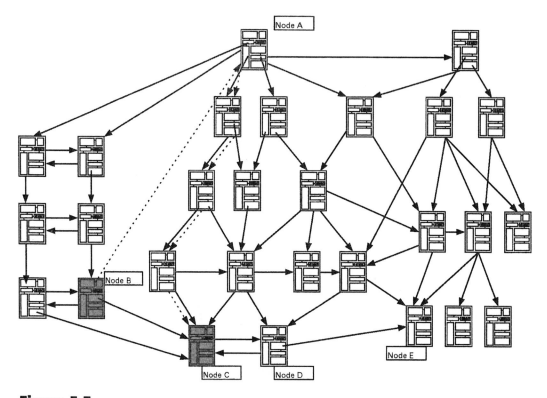

Figure 5-7

Example of inefficient navigation due to a non obvious information structure

In a previous section on contextualisation we also mentioned a number of additional factors which can be used to help with the lost in hyperspace problem. The page contexts themselves can be used to provide the user with feedback. We can use different colours, window shapes, background patterns or other presentation styles for different types or levels of information. For example, if we have a hierarchical structure to our information, then each layer of the hierarchy can use a different background, and incorporate the titles from the higher level nodes to provide a context. The image shown in Figure 5-8 is an example of this from a course which we run on the use of image data within multimedia and hypermedia.

What can we do within the development process to minimise the 'lost in hyperspace' phenomenon? There are two obvious answers:

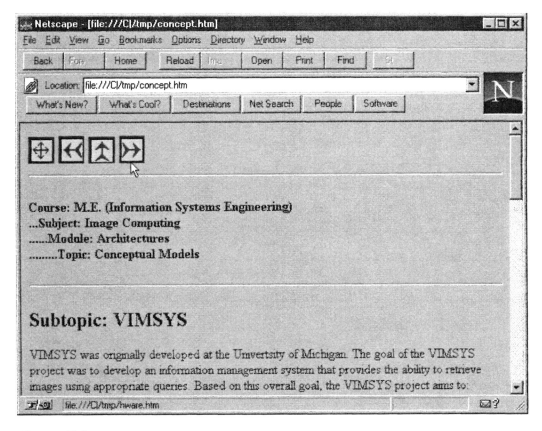

Figure 5-8

An example of providing contextualisation details within a page of information which exists within an information hierarchy – to assist with avoiding becoming lost within hyperspace

- *Structure schema*: as we design the structure of the information space we need to ensure that it is relatively straightforward and self-consistent. For example, the structure shown in Figure 5-7 is quite poor insofar as it is not obviously intuitive (several different types of structure can be identified – but no overall schema). The design of the schema for the structure will need to be carried out relatively early in the process and adhered to during the remainder of the development. Any material which is added or additions to the structure, should be consistent with this schema.

- *Presentation schema for contextualisation and orientation*: an overall schema needs to be developed which ensures that the presentation of all pages fits within a schema designed to ensure ease of contextual-isation. For example, the Website from which the page in Figure 5-8 was taken uses a schema which enforces the inclusion in all pages of the location within the information hierarchy. Again, the develop-ment of this style of schema should precede the development of any specific user interfaces, presentation templates, and especially the implementation of any material. Indeed, a useful design exercise would be to evaluate a presentation schema through prototyping.

In addition to the above global mechanisms, we can also add specific additional tools to assist users in orienting themselves. Examples include the use of a map tool (such as that discussed previously) and 'road signs' at appropriate places within the structure.

Cognitive Overload During Use

Concept management

Even if users are able to understand exactly where they are within a given information space, and the content is presented in an appropriate fashion, they can still have difficulties interpreting the data which is presented. In particular, the ability of a user to utilise information may be inhibited by the cognitive effort required to manage the information space. For example, there is a well documented (though still open to some debate) level of 7 ± 2 ideas or concepts which we are typically able to manage at a single time. If an information hierarchy requires the traversal through more than four or five levels, then the ability of the user to manage navigation, focus on the goal of the navigation and interpret each layer of information which is presented will be severely hampered.

This implies that, during the development, we need to consider how to ensure the user does not need to manage more than four or five levels of concepts or information at any one time. At a page level this is related to an ability to understand structure. For example, consider Figure 5-7. If the user navigated from node A to node B and then across to node E (via nodes C and D, rather than going back up to node A), then we need to ensure that the user is able to relate node E to node A via the true structure, rather than the actual path taken. In the case shown this will not be easy, because the structure is relatively complex. This again points to the need for an effective structural schema to be developed early in the process and then adhered to during the structural design. Even within individual nodes difficulties can arise if the node contains too many concepts which must be managed together. This reflects back on the need for suitable design of the contents of individual nodes, and appropriate partitioning of the information spaces.

Related to both of the above is the concept of 'releasing' an idea, as we move on. In the example given above of navigating from node A to node B and then to node E, once we reach node E, the ideas or concepts presented in node B can be 'released' from our immediate focus (though the knowledge gained may well have been integrated into our own knowledge structures). We do not need to keep a mental handle on node B to understand the position in the information space or the context of node E. If, in moving from B to E, we had backtracked to A, the backtracking process would have provided a mental trigger to 'release' the intermediate nodes. However, if we move directly from B to E, then this mental trigger is not provided by the action of backtracking, and needs to be supported in some other way. Unfortunately, there has not yet been any significant research within the hypermedia field of the implications of this, or how it may be achieved.

Functionality

A users' ability to navigate effectively and understand and interpret the information presented can also be inhibited by the functionality which is provided. This can be because the functionality is either inadequate or intrusive. If the functionality provided is either inadequate or obscure then the user can spend a considerable amount of time focusing on how to operate the hypermedia application – how to navigate, search, reconfigure the application, etc. The more mental effort which is expended on this style of activity, the less mental effort will be available for understanding and interpreting the data provided.

Similarly, too much functionality can be inappropriate. Problems can arise either because the functionality provided is either obtrusive or distracting. For example, consider an application which constantly provides (incorrect) suggestions for where you may want to navigate to next. Another common failure with many applications is to provide so many gimmicks and tricks that the user is forever being distracted by trying out new elements of functionality.

It is critically important during the development process to bear in mind that the purpose of the functionality which is provided is to *facilitate* access to, and utilisation of, information: the functionality is not the end goal. In a well designed application the functionality will be unobtrusive, intuitive and yet sufficient.

5.7 Effect of the Development Approach

Different approaches to the development of hypermedia applications will impact in different ways on our ability to address the issues discussed in this chapter. This will cover the process and methodology which is adopted, the product paradigm selected, the tools used and the resources applied to the development.

Probably most obvious in terms of the impact on the resulting application is the tools used in authoring activities. Indeed, for much conventional development, the use of the tools encompasses almost the entirety of the development effort. These tools can vary from conventional multimedia authoring tools, such as Macromedia Director, to SGML management tools, such as OmniMark to Web authoring tools such as HotDog. In each case, the tool typically implies a specific development paradigm, and possibly even a presentation platform or environment. This in turn places considerable constraints on what can and cannot be achieved in terms of application characteristics and functionality, and thus how these various development issues are addressed.

For example, Macromedia Director assumes a timeline-based paradigm or metaphor for the presentation. This will subsequently colour the way in which a developer views the application design. Similarly, most Web authoring tools are bound by the simple client-server node-link paradigm used by the Web. For example, the Web only provides support for single source, single destination, uni-directional links. Although it is possible to work around this constraint, few tools allow a more generic model of links and nodes to be adopted during the design and implementation of Websites.

An additional problem with most development tools, and possibly one which is more fundamental and far-reaching, is the scope of development activities which they support. Most development tools in common use only cover low-level design and implementation. Although this is not an indictment of these tools – after all, these activities must still be carried out – it does mean that much current development is led towards focusing only on these later stage activities at the expense of the earlier analysis of the application goals and high level design of the application structure and functionality. Tools which address these earlier stages of the development are only just beginning to appear as prototypes. A typical example is RM-CASE (Diaz *et al.*, 1995) – a tool designed to support the RMM design methodology (see the chapter on RMM later in this book).

The use of specific tools draws the development focus towards implementation aspects and away from high-level design. As has been stated at numerous stages in this chapter, important aspects in addressing all of the issues raised are a thorough understanding of the goals of the application and the users who will be using the application, and the development of a design which is based on this understanding. If we focus only on the implementation of an application using a specific tool, then we are much less likely to have a resulting information structures which is relevant, correct and complete. Similarly, if we do not understand our users, then we are not likely to develop an application which has the most effective usability possible.

What we are implying here is that, although the use of suitable tools is important, these tools must be selected and used within the context of an appropriate process, and not *vice versa*. The tools shouldn't control the process, except where we know the process is appropriate and the tool is simply providing procedural guidance.

It is worth finishing this chapter with a few observations about much current practice and its effect on relevance, completeness, correctness, usability and information utilisation. Most Web authoring tools focus squarely on the design of individual Web pages. In general, they provide very little (if any) support for the design of information structures. This means that aspects such as the completeness and correctness of the link structures is overlooked almost entirely, being left up to the author to consider independently of the tools. The design of the structure is therefore performed separately from any consideration of Web page design and implementation, and the design of the interfaces and interface functionality occurs during the page implementation. This means that often the application structure is disjoint from the application functionality.

One strong point with many Web authoring tools is that they provide a strong suite of tools to assist in the design of interfaces and operational functionality, such as design tools for images maps and icons, CGI scripting tools, interfaces to databases, etc. This means that applications often have a high level of usability. The down-side of this is that there is a strong temptation to focus design effort on interface aspects at the expense of the core structure and functionality – resulting in a usability which is unfocused or inappropriate. This trend, which is common to much hypermedia development but is at its worst with Web development, has often been described as the triumph of presentation over content.

Many existing multimedia authoring tools (which have usually incorporated a degree of hypermedia linking functionality) are founded on a screen-based approach where every screen is handcrafted and manually linked together. The structuring is usually based around either a control-flow (such as in IconAuthor) or a timeline (such as in Macromedia Director). In either case, as with most Web authoring tools, the focus is largely on the design and implementation of individual screens.

The situation with regard to the structure of the information space is not quite so bad as with most Web authoring tools, since these at least provide a mechanism for supporting an inherent structure (be it a timeline or control flow). This means the developer must at least provide a minimal degree of structuring design. Unfortunately, the design is typically focused on a linear presentation, and often will not adequately represent the complexities of a hypermedia information structure. As a result, this needs to be handled outside the scope of the tool, and therefore often becomes rather *ad hoc*. As with Web authoring, screen-based approaches provide the tools to address the design, and especially implementation, of suitable functionality and hence usability, but this is not suitably guided or integrated into a useful whole.

Finally, it is worth pointing out that current practice with respect to large scale development typically adopts a broad range of *ad hoc* practices. Analysis of the needs of an application and high-level design is often carried out, but without an understanding of how to integrate these activities into the constraints imposed by both the development tools and the final presentation environment. For example, how do we undertake the design in a way which results in a design which can be readily implemented with the tools we have available, yet satisfy our requirements as effectively as possible – and how do we know that we have achieved this?

6

Obtaining A Quality Process

Action to be effective must be directed to clearly conceived ends.

(Jawaharlal Nehru)

Chapter Goals

In the previous chapter we looked at factors in the development which impact on the quality of the applications which we develop. In this chapter we develop a strong understanding of the factors in the development which impact on the quality of the process itself – in other words, how we achieve an effective, productive, high-quality process. The objectives of this chapter are to show that:

- Development productivity is impacted by both the productivity achieved in individual activities (such as content generation), and the ways in which these activities are inter-related.

- Managing the cognitive burden of the developer is critically important.

- Reuse of media is common. Reuse of information and processes is extremely uncommon. This is a major problem!

- Maintenance of hypermedia applications tends to be very fine-grained and very poorly managed.

- Managing the development process for hypermedia development is currently something of an art which requires further work to achieve reasonable levels of understanding.

- Hypermedia process measurement is almost non-existent, but potentially extremely important in improving current practice.

In the previous chapter we considered a broad range of product issues which need to be addressed during the development process. These issues were those which relate to the quality of the application being developed, its ability to achieve the goals of hypermedia applications. Let is revisit the definition we provided on the goals of hypermedia development:

Definition

Goals of Hypermedia Development   The goals of hypermedia development are:

- to develop high quality hypermedia applications which have the optimal balance of desired characteristics;

- to carry out the development in the most effective and efficient manner possible consistent with achieving the desired application.

The first of these is related to the product issues described in the previous chapter. In this chapter, we address the second goal – carrying out the development in *the most effective and efficient manner possible*. In other words, we consider process issues – those considerations which do not impinge on the quality of the application (at least not directly), but rather affect how cost-effectively we are able to carry out the development (and continue to carry it out).

6.1   Productivity Issues

One of the most obvious factors which affects the cost-effectiveness of the development process is the productivity we are able to achieve. There are many things which can be done during the development process that lead to significant productivity improvements, including process support, automation or semi-automation of development activities and techniques for helping an author handle or manage data, information and knowledge. Robertson, Merkus and Ginige (1994) describe a development approach (using a tool called HART) which is based around providing both procedural guidance and intelligent assistance. Procedural guidance is where the application guides the developers or authors through the development process (such as providing tools which are used in a given sequence in order to achieve all or part of the development. Intelligent assistance is where the tools attempt to assist the developer during the process. For example in HART, suggestions are provided to the author on possible link anchors and destinations.

If we are to improve productivity through techniques such as these, we need to consider where time is spent during the process, and focus our attention on these activities (reducing by half the time spent on an activity which only consumes 1% of the time resources will not, after all, have a significant overall impact). At present, the activities which are most time consuming (often by a considerable margin) in typical hypermedia development applications include media capture (such as scanning paper documents and digitising images), media manipulation (such as touching up images and performing OCR on documents, along with cross-checking the results of the OCR), media structuring (decomposing the captured content into nodes and identifying appropriate links), and user-interface development (such as screen creation or Web page authoring).

We need to consider what we can do during each of these activities to improve the development productivity. Before doing so, however, it is worth pointing out that the balance of effort varies considerably between different applications and environments. For example, in small applications or applications which have a very well defined structure, the linking effort may be relatively small. In large applications, or applications with complex interlinking, the linking process can be very time-consuming. Similarly, if we have an application using information which is already highly structured in a paper form (such as legal documentation), then the process of digitising and structuring the information can be to a large extent automated, and the effort can be minimised.

Media Capture and Structuring

A major factor which limits the productivity during the development process is the effort currently required to capture or generate the underlying data, and then to convert this into an appropriate form. In many current hypermedia development projects (especially for large projects) the data to be used in the application comes largely from a legacy application. Examples include paper-based documentation or manuals, encyclopaedias and dictionaries, image, video and audio archives, and legal or financial data. In all these cases, the existing data needs to be digitised and then put into an appropriate form for use in a hypermedia application.

Even when the data to be used is being created rather than adapted from an existing source, it will often be created in an analogue format and require capturing and structuring. For example, image and video will be recorded using appropriate cameras and then captured and stored digitally.

This process typically involves several activities. The first is to obtain the raw data to be used – either from legacy applications or records, or by new recording of information. This process requires considerable judgement as to what data is appropriate, and is effectively impossible to automate. Once we have the data we need to digitise it. This can involve scanning in text and images, digitising images or video using frame or video grabbers, capturing audio using sound cards, etc. Again, this process is difficult to automate, though it is a relatively mechanical task which does not require a specialised skill level. Much of the data that has been captured will need to be manipulated in some form. The obvious example is textual data which has been scanned in; suitable Optical Character Recognition will need to be applied to the scanned pages. Similarly, we may often want to adjust the quality of images, crop them, adjust the size, etc.

Having obtained suitable data, we then need to structure the data. This effectively involves two primary steps: the first is to identify the internal structure of the information and partition it appropriately. For example, with a trouble-shooting procedures manual we can identify the internal structure (such as each procedure and the components which make up the procedure – observed problem and symptoms, cause, corrective action, required parts, etc.), and then partition the data into separate pages or nodes for each procedure. The second structuring step is to introduce the appropriate linking mechanisms which provide the overall application structure. As discussed in the previous chapter, this will have to occur within the context of the schema developed for the application structure. An example of these processes are shown in Figure 6-1.

Automating the Structuring Process

Given the above description of the types of information capturing and structuring activities which typically occur, we need to consider the extent to which we can increase productivity during these activities. As already mentioned, the information capturing processes are typically difficult to automate, but the structuring activities are quite different. In many cases,

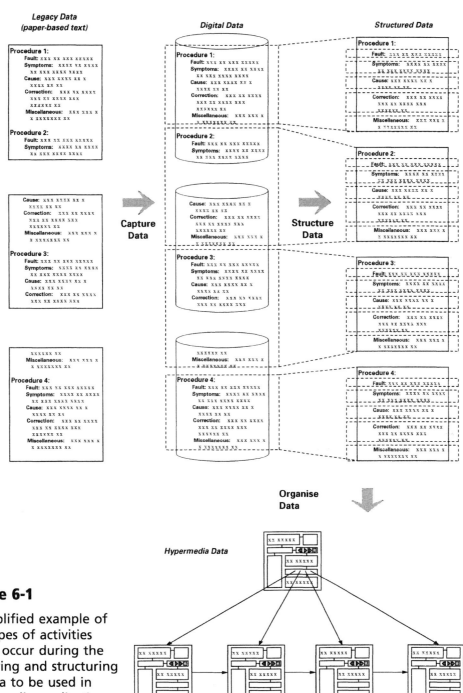

Figure 6-1

A simplified example of the types of activities which occur during the capturing and structuring of data to be used in hypermedia applications the structuring activities can be improved to a certain extent by developing appropriate 'filters'. For example, a common practice is to develop programs or filters which accept textual documents that have a well know and consistent format, and output suitably structured documents (such as SGML). There is a wide variety of tools available for this type of processing, one of the leading examples of which is OmniMark, which can be used to develop and use filters that allow the conversion of legacy data (such as raw text documents with a known structure) into an appropriately structured format (SGML) for use in a hypermedia application (http://www.omnimark.com/).

This type of filter will typically only work if the information being structured has a consistent format that can be parsed and analysed by the filter. This will typically be the case with well-structured paper documents. However, if the legacy data is poorly structured then the structuring process will be extremely difficult or impossible to automate, and will typically need to be performed by hand – though appropriate tools can even assist in making this process more straightforward.

Where data is semi-structured, the ability to automate the structuring process will be dependant upon the intelligence which we are able to build into the filters. There will be a trade-off between the sophistication of the filters developed and the need to manually check the results of the structuring process (i.e. a form of proof reading) for problems which the filters were unable to detect or manage. Indeed, this latter activity will often be a major cost associated with a project.

Early in the initial application design the developers we will need to consider the sources of data available. From this it should be possible to determine the extent to which it is possible to automate the information structuring. Indeed, an initial estimate of this should be performed early enough to be able to be used as input into the planning and budgeting stages of the project, even if the specific filter design and information conversion does not occur until much later in the development process.

Structuring non-textual information

Most of the above description has been particular to textual data. Non-textual data is also an important aspect of many hypermedia applications, yet in most current hypermedia applications the interactivity is predominantly derived from the textual information, rather than other media such as images, video or audio (with the exception, to a limited extent, of the use of clickable image maps). In fact, most existing hypermedia applications would be more appropriately called *multiple media hypertext applications*. Hypermedia is unlikely to achieve its full potential until all media can actively support the full level of functionality expected. They tend to be hypertext applications (i.e. the textual information provides the interactivity), with the additional media acting as annotations, but not truly integrated into the application.

The few minor exceptions to the lack of visual information interactivity predominantly revolve around hand-crafted, small-scale applications. These, however, are sufficient to illustrate the significantly enhanced functionality which can be achieved with active visual information. For a good example of this, look at the map images in the *Virtual Tourist* on the WWW. These small-scale applications have tended to be hand-crafted using low-level tools (such as MapEdit – a shareware Unix tool), and contain hard-coded static syntactic descriptions of the image data. We are not truly interacting with the visual information here, but with an underlying syntactic description of the image (which provides us with the illusion of interaction with the visual information).

We can better understand the poor use made of visual information by considering the above description of the structuring of textual data (an area that has received, and continues to receive, considerable research and development attention). Text can be analysed and structured relatively easily because of its precise lexicon and syntax, e.g. we can readily detect word and sentence boundaries and then perform simple pattern matching on these lexical elements. It is this which enables tools such as OmniMark to work so effectively with text.

The evolution of non-textual data is still at a much lower level, and is predominantly treated as a passive media or structured almost entirely by hand. Audio and visual information, in its raw form, is highly unstructured and yet very commonplace (documentary video tapes, audio clips, sound bites, image and photographic collections and databases, etc.). Many visual information applications (such as medical imaging, robotics and interactive multimedia) make use of the visual information in a highly structured format. Conceptually, non-textual media should be able to be treated in the same way as text; consisting of discrete entities which obey certain syntactic rules, and hence can be used in the structuring process. For example, just as we might automate the process of extracting the titles from the list of procedures shown in Figure 6-1 to include in an index page, we might wish to extract a central element from each of a collection of images, turn this element into a thumbnail image, and include it in an index page.

The primary difficulty in automating the structuring of non-textual media lies in identifying the components within non-textual media. A study by Lowe and Ginige (1995) investigated the use of computer vision in assisting in the authoring process through the use of a model-based computer vision application (which in this particular study was used to identify, and subsequently create, anchors from grocery items in a series of images in a hypermedia application on groceries). The study showed that, whilst the approach was a success and saved considerable authoring effort, the computer vision techniques used were not yet mature enough to be widely applicable to anything except very constrained data sets. In addition, the effort required to implement the vision application was still excessive.

Despite these current technical limitations, there is every reason to believe that in future, analysis tools will be developed which can be applied to non-textual media in as an effective a fashion as current text analysis tools. In the meantime, there are still some analysis operations which are technically feasible and can be readily used in specific cases. Two such cases are worth mentioning because of their widespread applicability. First, video segmentation, while not able to reliably identify specific objects, can still perform low level tasks, e.g. video scene segmentation is becoming progressively more reliable, and can now be successfully used to segment long video sequences into the component shots and scenes (which can then be manually indexed if necessary). The second example is the use of voice recognition, which can perform a similar task with audio that optical character recognition performs with text – taking audio samples and sound bites and either segmenting the audio clip by identifying the breaks, or generating a textual version of the audio (which can then be used for various tasks such as indexing and cross-referencing).

Managing the Information Interface

One of the greatest consumers of development time with many hypermedia applications is the design and implementation of user interfaces. This is particularly true of many Websites, where the rapidly expanding array of user interface devices and mechanisms is expanding at a phenomenal rate. The user interface will be the component of the application with which a user has (by definition) the most obvious direct contact, and so to a large extent will influence their initial perception of an application (first impressions *do* count!).

What can be done to most effectively manage the cost and improve the productivity when developing user interfaces? Possibilities include reuse, using templates, using prototyping and other rapid development tools, effective management of the development process, and avoiding WYSIWYG development. Before looking at these in more detail, it is important to mention that there has been a growing trend (especially with respect to many Website development projects) to unnecessarily waste considerable effort on interface development. It is tempting to put a lot of effort into adding as many sophisticated elements as possible into a Website in the belief that it will make the site look 'professional'. This can often have the reverse affect, making the site cluttered and cumbersome to use, and frustrating users. Careful consideration needs to be given to why a user will visit the site, and how best both their goals in visiting the site, and your goals in having them visit the site, can best be accomplished. Similar comments also apply to other forms of hypermedia.

Within this context, we can point out that a common trap in hypermedia development is often to use WYSIWYG development tools in creating the application. This can lead to very significant problems, especially with respect to focusing the attention of a developer on interface rather than information and usability issues. A more effective approach, in terms of both application quality and development productivity, is to explicitly separate the interface design and implementation from the content and structure design and implementation. The latter should be performed using non-WYSIWYG tools. The interface design can most effectively be carried out using WYSIWYG tools. A good approach is to develop, using suitable tools, interface templates which can then be overlayed on content. This circumvents the problem of hand-crafting each individual page, and ensures application consistency. These templates may be implemented as an HTML page which is dynamically populated with data by a suitable CGI script when data is requested, or it may be something as simple as a screen layout or skeleton HTML page which can have content added as necessary by the application authors.

Prototyping tools can be especially effective in developing user interfaces. Given that user interface design will often involve a certain degree of creativity, and hence iterative development, prototyping can be especially effective. This is discussed in more detail below. Similarly, effective use of reuse (through the incorporation of interface components developed previously) can increase productivity substantially. A common example is the use of component libraries. Again, this will be discussed shortly.

Probably the best single way of reducing user interface development costs is to effectively manage the process of developing user interfaces. In particular, it is critical to avoid the temptation to dive in and start building interfaces (such as developing Web pages) before the requirements are understood and a design has been created. It is very important to ensure that a solid understanding of the requirements of the interface precedes any design or implementation work. Similarly, before the implementation of the interface begins, a consistent design should exist. Prototyping can be effectively used as part of the design process, but it should not replace it, i.e. prototyping itself is *not* design. Without an effective design process to give the prototyping a context, the prototyping can easily become directionless. During the design and implementation, suitable coordination of the various skills involved needs to occur. This may incorporate graphic designers, user-interface experts, content experts and project management.

Rapid Prototyping

Rapid prototyping is a well established development tool in a number of fields. Essentially, it involves the creation of an incomplete application or application which can be used for evaluation purposes prior to the development or implementation of a final application. This incomplete application can take a large variety of forms – a simple paper-based mock up of the expected interface, a cut-down application implemented using a specific prototyping tool, or an application 'front end' implemented in the same environment as the final application, but lacking any of the underlying functionality.

Prototyping can be particularly effective in assisting with improving development productivity. We consider a number of examples. Simple paper-based mock-ups allow an application interface, or an overall information structure, to be evaluated. They can be useful for both assisting in capturing requirements (allowing both the user and the information provider to provide feedback), and for performing an initial design (largely because of their flexibility). This approach can provide rapid feedback at an early stage of the development.

Prototypes which incorporate a degree of functionality can be rapidly built using various tools. Many commercial multimedia authoring tools, such as Macromedia Director and Macromedia Authorware, are not well suited to the development of very large complex applications, but can be used very effectively to develop prototypes. For Web-based development, non-Web-based tools (such as those mentioned) can still be used for developing prototypes. Alternatively, a scaled down version of the final application can be built on the Web, but without including substantial content or functionality. Such an approach is most effectively used during the design process to evaluate possible application architectures and structures.

Procedural Guidance

One of the largest causes of problems within hypermedia development is the lack of suitable process management and the subsequent problems this can cause with productivity. One of the partial cures which has been suggested for this is the use of tools to provide procedural guidance (Robertson, Merkus and Ginige, 1994). In this approach, the authoring tool (or possibly a separate hypermedia project management tool) provides guidance on what activities (or procedures) should be carried out at various stages of the development process. This is aimed at ensuring that the development activities stay focused.

This raises the question as to how much guidance is appropriate. For example, we could select a process with a defined set of steps (media capture, content analysis, structural design, etc.) and then guide the author through these steps. However, each individual development project will be quite different, and a rigidly defined set of steps may not always be appropriate (in fact few projects, if any, would be expected to adhere to a rigidly defined process). The guidance will indeed need to depend upon context, expertise and application domain.

Intelligent Assistance

We discussed previously the use of automation to improve productivity. In many cases, however, we will not have access to algorithms that are sophisticated enough to be reliably used for automation. In circumstances such as these, an alternative would be to use assistance rather than automation.

We consider an example. In many cases we can automate the process of partitioning textual data (such as breaking a text document into nodes containing sections or chapters). To achieve a similar degree of automation is not particularly feasible with image maps due to the complex nature of image data. In cases where we need to identify the components of an image, such as when we use image maps in Web pages (i.e. images where a user can click part of the image and get an appropriate response), the author will typically be required to manually outline each region in the image. Tools such as HoTMetal and MapThis for the PC and WebMap for the Macintosh will typically support the user in using the mouse to draw round each region and then store the results in a map file. Although computer vision schemes are not yet sophisticated enough to reliably identify the objects in images (except under very constrained circumstances), lower level image segmentation schemes can be used effectively. Although this has not yet occurred, a typical use of intelligent assistance would be to use an image segmentation scheme to identify possible object edges in an image and then provide a list of suggestions to the author, who can select from these the desired (or correct) object boundaries.

In a similar way, intelligent assistance can be used to improve productivity in the information structuring activities. HART (Robertson, Merkus and Ginige, 1994) is a research application which has incorporated an ability to suggest to the user possible link destinations during the linking process. The author can accept the suggestion or manually identify the link destination. The work has shown that such an approach can substantially improve the information structuring productivity. Unfortunately, support such as this is yet to be built into commercially available tools, and the effort required to construct one-off customised tools is likely to be prohibitive, except in extreme circumstances. Finally, it is worth mentioning that this approach will only be worthwhile if the analysis engine underlying the tool is sophisticated enough to provide accurate suggestions for a relatively high proportion of the time.

6.2 Cognitive Management

In the previous chapter, the cognitive burden which is placed on the user of an application was discussed. The burden placed on an author is likely, in many cases, to be even worse. There are many causes of this problem, but the two most critical which we discuss here are management of the information and information space during development, and process management.

Cognitive Overload during Information Management

Typically, if an application is well developed then effective use of an application by a user does not require the user to understand the entire information space. To navigate, a user should only need to understand their local context and the schema used to structure the information (which should be intuitive) – much as to drive from New York to Washington DC I would only need to know the local streets in New York and Washington, and the major connecting routes, but not every single road on the US eastern seaboard.

However, consider a typical scenario in the development of a hypermedia application. The developer has created a large collection of Web pages and is adding cross-linking to provide an information structure for the application to support appropriate navigation. The developer identifies an appropriate link within the content of a page, and then attempts to determine the appropriate destination of the link. How can this be done? If the application is small enough the developer may understand the entirety of the information space, and be able to locate a suitable link destination. As the application size grows this becomes impossible, and the author will need to search through the information space to find the appropriate destination. Bear in mind that this searching will incur a significantly greater cognitive overhead than occurs for users of the final application, as during the development the information space will be unstructured, or only semi-structured. Indeed,what will often occur is that the developer will insert a link to the location in the information space which she/he understands or can readily find – without any guarantee whether the link destination is indeed the most appropriate. This problem is demonstrated in Figure 6-2.

How, then, can we manage the cognitive burden which is placed on an author by the requirement to deal with, and possibly manage, a large information space at a time when it is very unstructured? There are a number of mechanisms which can be adopted. First, as with a user navigating an information space, a developer will be able cope better if a suitable schema has been developed to provide an overall structure for the information space. If such a schema exists, the develop should be able to identify whereabouts, within an information space, a certain component ought to exist, even if the structure to support this does not yet exist. An analogy we have found useful is the jigsaw puzzle. When a person is trying to solve a jigsaw puzzle, if they have access to a completed picture then the location of a given piece can often

Complexity: Manageable   Complexity: Overwhelming

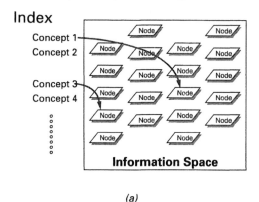

(a)

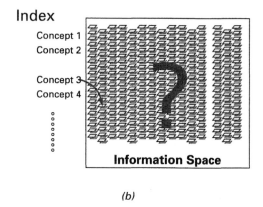

(b)

Figure 6-2

The authoring of links in hypermedia can rapidly become overwhelming as the size of the information space grows. This is partially due to the difficulties inherent in the management of an initially unstructured information space which is very large

be identified, even if the surrounding pieces are not yet in place (Figure 6-3).

We can go one step further. As we create the structure, we can place items in approximately the right location, and then as the structure is built up the specific locations (of both information nodes and the anchors and destinations of the links between them) can be iteratively refined (analogous to putting a jigsaw puzzle piece on the puzzle at roughly the right location and then moving it to the precise location as other pieces are added).

As an example of how the cognitive burden associated with handling the information space can be further handled, consider the following example. The development effort could be partitioned so that responsibility for different sections of the information space (and hence content, structure, etc.) would lie with different developers. Each developer would have an in-depth understanding of their local area of information space and an overview of the other areas and the way in which they fit together. When undertaking the structuring of the information space, the developers can integrate their efforts. A developer could anchor a link in their own space and then identify the region where the link destination will lie – and pass the responsibility for the specific location of the link destination to the developer who has an in-depth knowledge of that area.

Figure 6-3

With a jigsaw puzzle, we can often locate the correct location for pieces, even if we don't have any of the related structure in place, by using an image of the completed picture (which need not show the entire puzzle detail). Similarly, when initially creating the information structure for a hypermedia application, a schema for the information space allows us to identify the location of information, even if the information space itself is incomplete

Such an approach would require that a consistent overall schema for the information structure be developed at an early stage, and adhered to during the development.

An alternative approach (or possibly one which could be used in conjunction with the above ideas) would be to adopt a top-down development approach, so that the overall structure is developed initially, and then the detail within this structure is progressively refined. Link destinations could be inserted at a high level of abstraction in the design, and then refined as the detail is inserted.

A top-down approach would be more straightforward if supported by a suitable hypermedia model which supports browsing and editing in a semi-structured information space. An example of this is the graph model used within Matilda (MGraph) (Lowe and Sifer, 1996). As shown in Figure 6-4a (a simple example based around the markup of Shakespeare's *Macbeth*), we can initially create a high level structure containing just the *PlayImage* and *PlayText* nodes, and then insert a link showing that there is a semantic relationship between these nodes. We can then expand each of these nodes (or possibly just one), as shown in Figure 6-4b with the link being progressively refined until we reach the ultimate link between leaf nodes, as shown in Figure 6-4c. At no point have we lost context, or shown more information than was required. This process can work in reverse as well, allowing us to hide information during the authoring process, whilst maintaining the global structure and local contexts. MGraphs also uses link summarisation, so that we did not end up with unmanageably large numbers of derived links at high levels in the hierarchy.

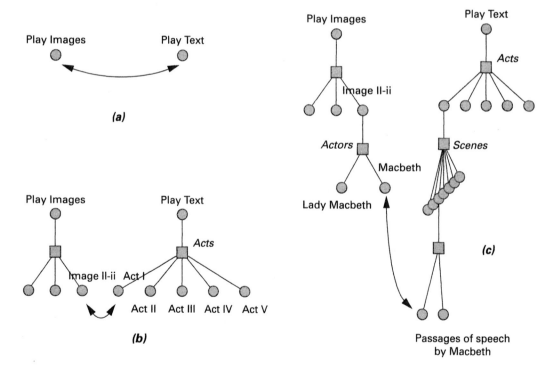

Figure 6-4

In this top-down authoring example using MGraphs (Lowe and Sifer, 1996) the highest level is initially created (a) and then progressively refined (b) and (c). This style of approach facilitates the management of the cognitive burden associated with creation of a structured information space

It is worth noting that, while the above discussions have focused on managing information during the development from a productivity perspective, they will also have significant ramifications for the correctness and completeness of the resulting information space. For example, if we are able to create a structure more productively, then we are much more likely to undertake a more comprehensive development (and hence have a more complete information space).

Process Management

As with any development process, the development activities can become quite complex. Managing the process can distract the developers from the actual development itself. In addition, the delineation of roles defined for managing the process can, in some cases, result in a worsened cognitive burden. For instance, for large projects (and even for many small projects), the content expert(s) are likely to know little about presentation, structuring or 'authoring', yet a developer or author may not understand the content well enough to realise the implications of particular structures. How do we bridge this gulf? We certainly can't expect the developer to become a content expert, or *vice versa*.

What this implies is that we need procedures in place to manage this specific problem. The content experts, user interface designers, application analysts, information specialists, programmers and authors need to be able interact and use each others' expertise without incurring significant cognitive overheads. To a large extent, this simply requires suitable project management.

6.3   Reuse in Hypermedia

Reuse during hypermedia development has the potential to offer substantial benefits. Reuse of data and interface elements (such as Java applets) is increasingly common, yet reuse can extend way beyond this. We can reuse data, information, knowledge, experience, interfaces and interface components, templates and designs, information structures, application architectures and designs, whole applications, process models, and numerous other outcomes of the development process. Benefits which reuse can potentially provide include:

- *Improved productivity*: in all the cases of reuse mentioned above, reuse allows us to use the results of previous development, thereby minimising the amount of new development effort required. One caveat to the above is that reuse will often require a degree of adaptation – we need to be careful that the effort required to adapt does not exceed the effort required to develop from scratch.

- *Improved reliability and maintainability*: components or elements which have been used previously are more likely to have had any problems, errors or difficulties dealt with. This becomes increasingly true as elements are reused more widely. Again, there is a caveat to this. If an element which is reused has not been appropriately adapted, then it can introduce errors which may not have occurred had the element been specifically developed for the application. This is particularly true of interfaces and information structures.

- *Improved quality*: reuse of elements across a number of applications or within an application can improve the quality of an application by ensuring a more consistent look and feel and a greater degree of robustness. The caveat to this is that care needs to be taken that any interface metaphor or information structure schema which is reused is suitably matched to the application.

Given the above benefits, we need to consider what we can do during the development process to improve reuse. We consider a number of different categories of reuse: media reuse, information reuse, application reuse (including aspects such as information filters, interfaces, functional components) and process reuse.

Media Reuse

At present, the two most common types of reuse within hypermedia development are media reuse and application component reuse. Most media which underlies hypermedia applications exists as either raw data or marked up data, and is stored as either raw files or in a database or hyperbase (an exception is when data is dynamically generated as required). Whichever mechanism is used for storing the data, it is possible to reuse the raw data. It is quite common to be able to cut and paste data from one source to another.

In promoting the reuse of media, what issues do we need to consider? First, it is important to remember the definition of information we gave earlier in the book – that information is the interpretation of data within a context (where the context is a combination of the current environment and the *a priori* knowledge). What this implies is that the same data can result in quite different information if the context changes, which is both advantageous and disadvantageous. It is good because it implies that a given data set can be used quite widely for applications requiring very different information by adapting the context appropriately. The disadvantage is that it becomes easy to incorporate data which provides incorrect or inappropriate information, since we can see the (valid) information it provides in one context, and then move it to another context where the information provided is no longer valid.

Obviously, reuse of media elements developed outside the organisation for whom the development is being performed raises issues of copyright, trademarks and intellectual property rights. In many cases, even where royalties must be paid, the ability to reuse specific information can be readily justified. In other cases, the effort required to redevelop data may cost less than the royalties which may have to be paid on a reused component.

Another issue to consider is the mechanisms which can be used to find the data to reuse. This is part of the broader consideration of what can be done to improve data reuse? In software engineering, software component repositories are becoming increasingly widely used (especially for object-oriented development, where software components are more self-contained). This process is only just beginning to occur in hypermedia development. We will consider repositories (and how they can be used to assist in the identification of appropriate reuse elements) in more detail at the end of this section.

Another important aspect in promoting reuse of media is the consideration given to reuse during the initial capture or generation of the data. This has two primary elements: use of suitable representations; and development for generality. What is a suitable representation for media files in terms of promoting reuse? Consider the situation where a given image is required for an icon for a specified application. A suitable scene is located and photographed, the photograph is scanned in, and the scanned image is then scaled (by subsampling using an appropriate image processing tool) down to the size of an icon before being saved for use in the application. At a later date, and for a different development project, a similar image is desired to be included in a new application. The image from the original application is not appropriate for reuse because it has been saved only as a small icon, whereas the larger original scanned image, which was discarded, would have been appropriate.

As this example indicates, one of the characteristics of media representations which is suited to reuse is scalability, which can be spatial or temporal. The case given above is an example of spatial scalability. Another example would be saving a graphic as a vector image rather than a bitmap or pixel mapped image. An example of temporal scalability is the specification of movements in an animation, rather than specifying a series of frames. Another characteristic of media representations suited to reuse is the use of widely available and supported data formats. A bitmap stored as a GIF or JPEG image is more likely to be reused than the same image stored as an ILBM file (an Amiga specific format). Certain formats are platform specific; others have support only in a limited range of tools.

The second consideration for reuse during initial information capture or generation of data is more subjective – generality of application. Again, let us consider an example. If we are developing an astronomy application which uses sections of the dialogue between Neil Armstrong and Houston ground control, rather than just digitise and store those fragments we want to use directly, it would make considerably more sense to digitise the entire dialogue (this is, after all, unlikely to require any additional effort, as once the process has been started it is essentially automatic). The entire audio track could then be stored into a reuse repository, and those fragments required for the current application could be extracted and used.

We can take the concept of generality one step further and recognise that in identifying sources of information, we can attempt to ensure that the data we capture or create is as general in applicability as possible. This requires an awareness of how information can be used at a later date. A simple example would be using a wider angle lens when photographing a scene so that the image that was captured would contain more possible information (the image could be cropped back to the desired size for the original application). The obvious trade-off in this approach is the additional memory required (memory is, however, typically much cheaper than labour costs – at the time of writing the cost of 1 MByte of hard disk space costs about the same as about five minutes of a hypermedia developers time[7]), and the labour costs associated with performing the additional processing (such as cropping an image, though often this

---

[7] A 1 Gigabyte hard disk drive can now be bought for around US$300, or about US$3.33 per Megabyte. Assuming a mid-range contract rate for hypermedia development of US$40 per hour, US$3.33 corresponds to five minutes.

will only be a minor part of any media manipulation which must occur anyway).

Information Reuse

Although claims of information reuse in hypermedia are often made, this is usually referring to media reuse. True information reuse is much less common. What exactly do we mean by information reuse? To answer this, let us again go back to our definition of information – that information is the interpretation of data within a context. So to reuse information implies that we are reusing some of the interpretation of the data which has occurred. For example, we may have identified the objects within an image (and possibly stored this information in some form of image map). This identification of objects is information which should be able to be reused (i.e. we have interpreted the image in the context of what we understand to be relevant objects in the image).

In a way, this almost implies a contradiction. Surely the application sets the context, and according to our definition, information requires a context – how then can we share or reuse information across applications? The answer to this is that some of the context is set by the application, but not all. For example, in an English language text document, groups of symbols can be understood as words within the context of all English language applications, and understood as carrying useful information within the context of all applications related to a specific topic, i.e context is not an all or nothing. Rather, it progressively narrows as we extract more sophisticated forms of information. As this indicates, different applications will have overlapping contexts, and can therefore share information. For example, almost all applications will interpret the identification of objects within images in the same way. Reusing information related to the identification of lexical elements (image objects, words, etc.) is straightforward. Reusing semantic relationships can become progressively more difficult.

What can we do to promote information reuse? The most obvious aid is to ensure that the information we extract during the development process is captured, made explicit and stored in a way which is accessible. This does not occur with many current development approaches (especially the Web). One of the reasons why information reuse is uncommon is that often the information is embedded into the application structure, and never made explicit. For example, with Web pages the same mechanism

(HTML) is used for representing content, structure and presentation. The information, along with the data, is typically embedded into the HTML code, and is therefore difficult to extract and reuse. It is usually easier to go back to the original data and re-identify the information than to try to extract the information from the HTML.

This would imply that for information to be effectively reused would require the information representation be independent of the application representation. A common example of this is the use of SGML, where the information is represented in an application independent way, and appropriate mechanisms are used to map the information into the application when required (though the information is still embedded directly into the data, making various forms of data reuse difficult). Indeed, we can interpret the application as simply being a viewpoint onto the underlying information, rather than being the container of the information itself. We can then effectively reuse the underlying layer of information by simply providing different viewpoints onto the information for each application.

Where HTML or proprietary applications must be used, there are still several mechanisms which can assist with information reuse. One approach is to store the information using a representation which encourages reuse (such as SGML) and provide filters which can rebuild the application (such as the HTML pages) when required (either statically after a change, or dynamically as the pages are required). Another less effective approach (though still useful) is to ensure that all information which is extracted is suitably identified. A trivial Web-based example serves to illustrate this quite well – consider the case where we analyse several media files and extract sections of these which are appropriate to our application. The identification of these sections is in itself information. Rather than simply combining the sections into a single Web page and losing access to this information, we can write our HTML in a way which includes bookmarks (i.e. `<a name='test'></a>`) at the beginning of each of the sections so that it can readily identified at a later stage. Activities such as this require negligible overhead, but can assist in improving information reuse at a later date.

Finally, it is worth mentioning a parallel perspective on information reuse – Nelson's (1995) concept of transclusion. Indeed, Nelson defines transclusion as 'reuse with original context available' (very similar to the idea of information being interpretation of data within a *context*). What Nelson means by transclusion is the existence of the same information within different conceptual threads. Information is really the intersection of these threads, each of which contributes part of a context. In this approach, reuse simply implies the addition of another thread which intersects the underlying information element – which is not copied, but made available through embedded shared instancing – much like the idea of an information layer with different viewpoints (or threads) which are overlaid onto the underlying information.

Component Reuse

Many hypermedia applications incorporate a large number of both development components and application components which can be reused. Examples of development components include information conversion filters, information analysis tools (such as a text segmenter), and a variety of other tools developed specifically for use during the development process. Examples of application components include search engines, interface elements (such as Java applets) and functional components (such as CGI scripts).

In a number of cases, reuse is already common. For example, a large number of applets created for use on the Web are being widely reused. Indeed, libraries of reusable interface and functional components are becoming available for Web development, e.g. Java applets, Java developers kits and browser plug-ins are all becoming increasingly widely available, and all actively support reuse to varying extents. Similarly, a number of tools or libraries exist for other hypermedia platforms. As an example, Macromedia make available various template libraries and components for use with Macromedia Authorware, as do most other developers of hypermedia and multimedia authoring tools.

If we wish to reuse those components we are developing in house, we need to consider how the components may be used in a wider context than just the current application. For example, if we are developing a Web applet to scroll a message continuously across a window, it is more likely to be reused if various operation parameters are configurable, such as the message text, the message format, the scrolling speed, etc. In other words, where possible, it is always good practice to develop for a wider context.

Process Reuse

Up to this point we have primarily been discussing the reuse of development artifacts, such as media, information, interface components, etc.

We can also reuse less tangible elements of the development. There is a broad range of items which can be reused from the development process itself: specific outcomes (such as analysis and design results); development experience; and knowledge and expertise about the process.

Specific outcomes of a given application development process which can be reused include feasibility studies, budget analyses, user requirement analysis results, designs, user models and usage pattern studies, prototypes, information structure and information access schemas, resource studies, application architectures, storyboards, project plans, policy studies and project management guidelines. In almost all of these cases, what we are actually wishing to reuse is the knowledge which has been gained during these activities. If we are to reuse this knowledge, then it needs to be documented appropriately.

Although reuse of this type of knowledge does occur, it is often constrained to individuals being aware of the results of their own earlier efforts. If we are to reuse application knowledge gained during a development process in other development projects, and with other development teams, then we need a mechanism for handling this knowledge and cataloguing it is a suitable way. A good basis for such a scheme would be to cross-reference the information based on development activity and development context. Indeed, a hypermedia application would itself be of considerable benefit in documenting the results of hypermedia development. Although applications specifically for hypermedia do not yet exist, those which exist in other application domains may be adapted. For example, RDD100 produced by Ascent Logic Corp. is a requirements capture tool which uses a hypermedia application to cross-reference the various documentation components.

In addition to application specific knowledge gained during the development process, knowledge relating to the process itself will also be gained. Examples of this include an understanding of what aspects of the development process were problematic, the costs (especially labour costs) associated with various activities, which tools were useful in the development process, and the relationship between various activities. This type of knowledge is important in that it allows the development process to be refined over time, resulting in a progressively better development process. Again, this type of knowledge will often be very personalised. For example, a project manager will be aware of many aspects of the development which may not be part of the project documentation (such as 'we didn't start the prototype development early enough – it should have been started during the initial requirements capture rather than being delayed to the commencement of the application architectural design'). Although the individuals involved increase their knowledge, this may not lead to an increase in the team or corporate knowledge (after all, individuals can easily leave projects or organisations). It is worth developing procedures for capturing the process knowledge which is gained in a form that makes it readily accessible. In particular, the following items provide an initial indication of the types of process knowledge which should be captured:

- Time estimates and actual time required for all project activities, as well as the synchronisation of the various development activities.

- All project budgets and actual costs, including labour costs, information costs, hardware costs, etc.

- Processes and sources used in obtaining authority to utilise information (such as copyright permission, etc.).

- Approach to project management, and specifically any difficulties which were encountered.

- Tools which were used and reflections on their appropriateness and limitations.

General Considerations

There are a number of general considerations with respect to reuse in hypermedia that we have not yet discussed. The first is a consideration of the cost of reuse compared to the potential gain which can be obtained. Reuse typically does not come from free: as has already been alluded to, there is an effort required during the initial development projects in supporting reuse. For example, components need to be designed more flexibly, process knowledge needs to be documented, etc. This cost can be difficult to justify in the light of project time constraints, deadlines and budgets, and is one of the main reasons why reuse is relatively limited. For reuse (in any of the above cases) to expand, a conscious decision must be made to bear the initial costs in the expectation of later (and greater) gains. This implies that reuse requires support from appropriate management, as it represents an investment in the future rather than an immediate gain, and the question of who should pay for the initial overheads arises.

One of the mechanisms that has been widely adopted for promoting reuse in the software field has been to create a role (either full- or part-time) for a 'reuse engineer' or 'reuse librarian' (Norman, 1995). Such a role would involve a person who is nominally independent from any specific project (and therefore not likely to be limited by the project constraints), but is responsible for monitoring ongoing projects and maintaining a reuse repository. Such a person could identify possible sources of reuse (either elements of the projects that should be included into the repository for later reuse, or elements in the repository that can be of benefit to the current project).

6.4 Maintenance in Hypermedia

As both the number and size of hypermedia applications continues to expand, there will be an increasing need to take the maintainability of applications into account. Applications will be increasingly dynamic, in that they will tend to evolve over time (this trend is increasingly evident in the World Wide Web even now). As a result, we need to develop applications in such a way that allows them to be easily maintained.

Let us look at software applications as an analogy. In 1994 European Commission statistics indicated that, for the first time, software costs accounted for greater than 50% of the cost of all manufactured goods worldwide. At the same time, estimates indicate that maintenance costs associated with commercial software applications typically account for between 60% and 80% of all software lifecycle costs. There is no reason to believe that a similar situation will not develop in hypermedia applications. Indeed, the complex structures inherent in information relationships and the evolutionary nature of hypermedia applications tend to indicate that maintenance may be even more significant in hypermedia than in software (though to-date the field is not mature enough to have produced reasonably indicative data to confirm this).

This implies that, to ensure acceptable levels of ongoing development productivity and application relevance, we initially need to develop applications in such a way that not only allows maintenance, but actively addresses issues related to maintainability. This is an area requiring considerable research. We need to begin by considering exactly what we mean by the maintainability of hypermedia applications, and then look at how we can manage application maintenance.

What is Hypermedia Maintenance and Maintainability?

If we consider a dictionary definition of maintenance, we typically come across words and phrases such as 'support', 'correct', 'rectify', 'update' and 'improve'. The common thread can be viewed as being activities revolving around a 'working' application – in other words, the application is usable (and has probably been put into operation) but is still undergoing modification. Within this framework, we can identify three core categories of application maintenance.

- **Corrective maintenance:** involves the correction of errors or problems with an application that were introduced during earlier development. In hypermedia applications, typical errors will include invalid or incorrect information, incorrect information structures (including incorrect links) or errors in functionality (such as an applet with a 'bug' which causes the application, or part of the application, to 'crash' under certain circumstances). It is worth pointing out that with distributed applications such as the Web, these errors may have been introduced by a part of the 'development' beyond our direct control. The classic example of this is dangling links on the Web.

- **Adaptive maintenance:** involves the modification of an application to adapt to a changing environment or conditions. A good example of this is the adaption of a Website to take advantage of changes which occur (such as incorporating suitable applets into an application developed before Java became widely used). Other examples include the use of resources which were unavailable during the original development, or the migration of an application to a new environment (such as developing a Macintosh version of the application in addition to the original Windows version).

- **Perfective maintenance:** involves functional enhancement of an application. With hypermedia applications this could involve changes (usually an increase) to the scope or structure of the information space, or increased or enhanced functionality (such as providing a more flexible to powerful search engine).

Why do we maintain hypermedia applications? The simple answer is that they are invariably imperfect and exist within a changing environment. For any application to retain applicability and relevance, it will need to be constantly maintained.

This gives a reasonable indication of what hypermedia maintenance involves, but it does not give us a definition of maintainability. A simple definition of hypermedia maintainability is the extent to which a hypermedia application provides support for maintenance activities. A trivial example of a trait which enhances the maintainability of an application is the level of documentation provided for the application. Before looking at characteristics of maintainable applications in more detail, let us consider a few of the more common problems with maintaining hypermedia applications.

Spaghetti Linking

The term 'spaghetti linking' has gained increased popularity within the last few years. This term alludes to the complex (and often poorly structured) 'spaghetti-like' interlinking which can occur in hypermedia applications. Such a complex structure makes an application inherently difficult to maintain, for a number of reasons. First, since the structure of the information space is incredibly complex, we find that it is difficult to evaluate the consequences of changing some part of the information space. This means that in modifying (i.e. maintaining) an application, we typically need to consistently cross-check (and possibly correct) the side-effects of any change. Having a complex structure also makes it difficult to identify the elements of an application that need to be modified to achieve a desired result. Finally, a complex structure will obviously place a much greater cognitive burden on someone maintaining an application, thereby reducing productivity and possibly an increased error rate in the development.

If we look again at the software analogy, we find that a very similar term (spaghetti-code) has been widely used in software development – gaining currency around 30 years ago – and referring to similar, poorly structured control flows within computer code. We need to be careful about stretching the software analogy too far (after all, if we take a holistic view where everything is related to everything else within some context, information by its very nature has a very complex spaghetti-like structure). Nevertheless, we can gain some insights into how we might manage the maintainability of complex information spaces by looking at how software applications manage complex control flows.

Software development primarily addressed the problem of spaghetti-code by introducing a modularised coding structure. Only specified control constructs were considered appropriate, and the 'GOTO' statement found in many languages was considered a major flaw. In addition, the concepts of coupling and cohesion were used to guide development (these are discussed in much greater detail in the next subsection). The idea of imposing a structure in hypermedia is inappropriate; in software the structure is only a means to an end, whereas in hypermedia the structure is inherent in the information inter-relationships (and cannot, therefore, be modified at will for the sake of improving the 'structure' of the application).

What we can do, however, to manage the complex (spaghetti-like) relationships is to only make explicit within our application those elements of the implicit structure which fit within the guidelines or structural schema adopted to improve understandability. There will obviously be a trade-off between expressing the true richness of the structure (and hence providing flexibility of navigation), and limiting the structure (through the use of an appropriate schema) for understandability. Essentially, during the development process, we can identify that structural schema that provides the best compromise.

Coupling and Cohesion in Hypermedia

Another concept borrowed from software engineering is the idea of coupling and cohesion. In software, coupling refers to the extent and complexity of the interconnections between separate software modules (such as functions or modules). Cohesion refers to the extent of the self-consistency within modules. Typically, we will wish to minimise coupling (resulting in modules which are more reusable and more readily adapted or modified – 'I can change this with minimal effects on other components . . .') and maximise cohesion (resulting in modules which are more understandable – 'I know precisely what this component does, therefore I can reuse it more readily, and understand the implications of change more easily').

What are the implications of these concepts for hypermedia, and in particular, maintenance of hypermedia applications? Cohesion is related to the process of chunking or breaking information into nodes. If the chunking process is done well (i.e. the nodes are cohesive), then we have both a high level of reusability and an improved understanding of each node, and hence the implications of change. What makes a node cohesive? Essentially, to be cohesive, the various contents of a node should all relate to a single primary concept or theme which is highly visible. A common design guideline in hypermedia development which reflects this idea is that each node should be based on a single concept. (This guideline is typically aimed at improving the understandability of the application from a users' perspective, but it is just as valid from a maintenance perspective.)

What about coupling? This is a fundamental part of hypermedia insofar as hypermedia is about the associative coupling of information, and yet in software applications the goal is to minimise coupling. In hypermedia, we wish to control rather than minimise coupling. If a given region of an information space is highly coupled to another region, then it will be difficult to make changes to the first region without it affecting the second. A common example of this problem is when there are two tightly coupled Websites being separately managed. In such a situation, avoiding problems such as dangling or incorrect links can be extremely difficult. One possible way to avoid this is to structure the information space so that the coupling (i.e. linking) within a region has the richness required for flexible browsing and navigation, but the coupling between regions is constrained to well-defined avenues of navigation. One mechanism for achieving this would be to ensure that each region of the information space has a very limited number of well defined entry points.

Analysis and Design Maintenance

In many respects, this is one of the least well understood areas of hypermedia maintenance. Very little formal work has been undertaken in looking at the maintenance of the outcomes of any of the development activities, other than the implementation of the application itself. However, several quick comments can be made.

Experience in other applications development domains indicates that one of the most significant factors which affect the maintainability of analysis and design outcomes is the level of documentation that exists and the traceability of aspects of the development through the development process. For example, with a hypermedia application for an airline fare and ticketing application, we may discover early in the initial investigations that a typical user area of interest is how far ahead of the expected date of departure that a given flight ought to be booked. This can result in a requirement for the application to include statistics on when given flights have been booked out in the past. This is then included into the design and subsequent implementation. The documentation should make explicit development threads such as this, so that if a re-evaluation of the users indicates, for example, that the users are more interested in immediate flight availability than how far ahead they need to book, the whole thread of development which is affected can be readily identified and adapted.

Another observation is that one of the factors which strongly affects the maintainability of process elements, such as requirements and designs in traditional applications development, is the extent to which the various elements are kept synchronised. For example, a common problem with software applications is that after commissioning, minor changes are made directly to the implementation and are not propagated back to the earlier stages of the development (such as the design or application requirements). A series of such changes results in an application which can often bare little resemblance to the original documented application – thereby greatly compromising the ability to undertake effective ongoing maintenance.

Improving Maintainability

Apart from the various factors mentioned so far, there are additional aspects worth considering, with respect to making applications maintainable. The first point to emphasise is the importance of planning for maintenance. In a large number of existing hypermedia development projects, the future of an application beyond its immediate commissioning is overlooked. The maintenance of applications is often left as something of an afterthought. This can create significant problems for several reasons. First, the maintainability of an application needs to be built into the application during the original development. It is typically not something which can be added into the application after it is ostensibly completed. Also, the effort required for maintenance can be quite significant, and this needs to be considered during the original budgeting and planning. The maintenance of an application should be carefully planned and managed.

Secondly, during the original development the requirements for maintenance should be carefully considered. This will cover aspects such as the currency of the information being used (how long before information becomes 'stale' – consider, for example, changing tax laws), changes in the user population (such as changes in users' familiarity with the Web), possible ongoing evolution of the application (such as progressive refinement as the need arises), and prospective changes in hypermedia technology (consider, for example, the rapid changes underway in the Internet). This last point is particularly significant. For example, Websites which appeared cutting edge even 12 months ago often already appear dated. We need to be clear about our requirements for how the application needs to be maintained from an early stage of the development.

Another important aspect of maintainability is the mechanisms used to evaluate the ongoing need for maintenance. For example, progressive improvement of an application will be heavily dependant upon how effectively the application has achieved its goals, and whether it continues to do so over time. To determine this we need to obtain ongoing feedback from users and monitor how they have been using the application. This information can be analysed to evaluate the application's effectiveness. This process of evaluation needs to be planned and organised using a consistent approach.

6.5   Process Management

Most of the previous discussions in this chapter have been about aspects of the process, and what can be added to, or refined about, a process to improve the resultant application. However, what about the process itself? How can we manage the process? How can we control and improve the process? Indeed, what exactly is a process, and what type of process is appropriate? In short, we need to consider what issues need to be addressed in any application if we are to have the best possible process. These issues will typically cover the spectrum of skills, roles and responsibilities, activities to be carried out, deliverables from these activities, and timing and planning of the process.

Process Activities and Process Planning

Figure 4-5 listed a large number of possible activities which may occur during a development process, and these were described in some detail. Providing a list of activities is not sufficient, however: we need to be able to understand how to identify that subset of activities which is appropriate to the development project, and how these activities should be integrated into a cohesive co-ordinated process.

In general, we simply need to consider the application we are developing and identify those development activities which will be included. Unfortunately, at the beginning of the development when planning the process, we may not understand the project well enough to adequately identify those activities required and those which are not relevant.

In many cases, components of the development process will be controlled by a particular methodology. For example, RMM provides a basis for the design stages of the development process – covering information and navigation design, conversion protocol design, user interface design, and run-time behaviour design. It does not, however, explicitly cover earlier aspects such as application requirements analysis and feasibility studies, or broader aspects such as process management, verification and validation, documentation and application maintenance.

Unfortunately, no complete lifecycle process models yet exist. Indeed, it may turn out that it is not appropriate for them to exist at all, as the variations in projects may mean that the processes themselves are too varied. Nevertheless, we can still provide some guidelines that are worth following.

One option is to select an existing methodology (such as RMM or OOHDM) and use this as the foundation for a wider process model developed specifically for the development project in question. For example with RMM we know that an input into the design activities is a requirements document, and so we can build around the RMM methodology a process which includes user requirements analysis and user evaluations. If we know that the development is going to be solely Web-based, then we can include an evaluation of related applications on the Web (to evaluate potential useful sources of information or competition). If the application being developed is an educational application, we could include an evaluation stage where the learning objectives are evaluated. In addition, until we better understand the needs of hypermedia development processes, we should ensure that our planned process is as flexible as possible.

Process Roles and Responsibilities

Hypermedia development, including development on the Web, is very eclectic in terms of the skills required. Many existing Websites and CD-ROMs fail badly because some aspect of the development has been overlooked, or has been undertaken by someone with inappropriate skills. For example, the content and structure of an application or Website may be excellent, but fail because of a poor interface (a lack of user-interface development skills), or an educational application may contain appropriate content and a well designed interface but fail because of a lack of awareness of educational techniques.

Typical skills which are required (or may be required) for development projects include:

- **Project management**: the ability to organise a development project and ensure appropriate progress and coordination of activities and resources is a complex skill requiring a knowledge of most aspects of the development process, including the ability to predict and manage development effort.

- **Content expert**: in most cases, the content of an application will be sufficiently complex so that those with appropriate development skills will not have a detailed understanding of the content. This in turn implies that those undertaking the design and implementation of the application may not understand many of the subtleties of the content. Remember our definition of information: interpretation of data within a context. A content expert will be able to understand what data is necessary and the context that is required for this data to be interpreted correctly. They will therefore need to work together with the application designers to ensure that the content is conveyed appropriately.

- **Media skills**: managing media in many cases requires specific skills. This will be particularly true during the capture and manipulation of data. This might include the specific skills of photographers, audio and video engineers, animation experts and musicians and composers. In these cases the skills are essentially based around knowledge of what media elements are worth capturing, and how best to use technology in capturing the information. For example, a photographic expert will understand aspects such as lighting, scene geometry and perspective.

- **Information design**: although media specialists can typically handle individual media, understanding how to effectively combine these into a cohesive structure is a separate skill. This will involve the ability to understand how to develop and apply a schema for providing an information structure, how different media elements can best be used, and how these elements inter-relate. To a certain extent, this understanding will be used to drive the work of the media experts. It can also be viewed as involving librarianship-style skills.

- **Educationalist**: where an application is intended as an educational tool, an understanding of principles of learning will be important. This will include aspects such as different learning style, how to support the learning process, and possibly methods of evaluation or assessment (both formative and summative) both within the application and of the application. As a result of a poor understanding of what the learning process involves, many early (and indeed current) 'educational' applications are really no more than information sources, and do not actively support the learning process.

- **User-interface and functional design**: the user interface and the associated underlying functionality in an application is critically important to the effectiveness of the application. User interface design is a very explicit skill. Unfortunately, because the tools used to generate user interfaces are often relatively simple to use, the design of interfaces is often treated as a relatively trivial task. The result is commonly poorly designed interfaces (overly complex, counter-intuitive, favouring presentation over content). User-interface design skills include the ability to understand and manage the complexity of the cognitive response, and an understanding of the way in which people and machines interact. Similarly, the types of functionality used to support an application are critical to the way in which the application is used. Indeed, this area is the basis of the large Computer-Human Interaction (CHI) research community. A good book which focuses on user interface design is *Multimedia Interface Design Studio* (Malcolm, Poltrock and Schuler, 1991).

- **Hardware design**: the hardware in an application falls into two categories: development hardware (such as scanners, digitisers, etc.); and application support hardware (such as hardware Web servers). In both cases, an understanding of the different types of hardware available, and the relationship between the hardware and software, is important.

- **Legal**: the legal aspects of managing and using information is particularly difficult, and will typically require very specific legal skills. As a simple example, at the time of writing there was an ongoing court case between Curtis Management Group Worldwide and American Legends relating to the rights to certain information contained on two Websites related to James Dean (the dispute is over protection on Dean's signature and certain photos). As with many legal technicalities, the protection of information and the way it can be used (and, in the case of sensitive material such as pornography or commercial secrets, disseminated) is a difficult legal problem which is rapidly changing.

- **Implementation (programming, etc.)**: implementation skills include aspects such as HTML, Java or CGI programming, the use of authoring tools (such as Macromedia Director and Macromedia Authorware), and management of Web servers. In most cases, these are quite specific skills. In addition they are, in most cases, evolving quite quickly.

- **Evaluation**: a significant factor in much development is the evaluation and testing of an application under development. Testing can involve quite specialised skills, e.g. as with testing execution paths in software development, testing all possible combinations of navigation paths in hypermedia is usually not a possibility. Instead, we can use a series of techniques (such as thread testing) which evaluate representative aspects of the development. Another aspect worth considering is the fact that the developers of an application or Website will often be too intimately involved with the content and structure to reliably evaluate the application.

- **Marketing**: the techniques used in presenting information in a way which is appropriate from a marketing perspective are quite specialised. Typically, this may involve aspects of advertising, sales, presentation, etc. As an example, in designing a Websites homepage, piquing a users interest and encouraging them to browse further may be more important than immediately providing useful information.

- **Publishing**: publishing involves skills in production and dissemination of the hypermedia application. If the development is based on a CD-ROM, this may involve an understanding of the mechanics of producing and distributing the physical CD-ROM. With a Website this may involve disseminating information on the existence of the site to potential clients and search engines.

- **Documentation**: documenting a hypermedia application can involve specialised skills, depending upon the type of documentation being produced. For user documentation, an understanding of how to guide a user through the use of an application can be important (this is much more than just providing a description of the application). For the development, understanding how to record development decisions in a way which is understandable is important for future evolution of the application.

It is worth noting that, due to the rapidly changing nature of the hypermedia and multimedia fields, many of the above skills are in short supply (or alternatively, it is difficult to evaluate the depth of an individuals skills). This is exacerbated for some of the skills in that, where they do exist, it is often in isolation from a hypermedia context. For example, although many people have reasonable educational skills, this is often not in the context of hypermedia (which can place a greatly different perspective on how the skills are applied).

Another consideration is that skills and roles are very different. A given individual will often have a number of the above skills, but their role will be strongly determined by the particular combination of skills and how they can best be used. For example, although a developer may have skills both in structuring information and evaluating a structure, the use of the first skill will typically preclude the use (within the same project) of the second, since a developer cannot evaluate (in an unbiased fashion) an information structure which they themselves have developed.

Managing personnel, skills and roles will typically require a solid understanding of the skills required, the skills available, and the stages of development where these skills will be used. Typical project management and time management tools can be used for this process quite effectively.

6.6 Process and Product Measurement

Why Do We Measure?

'We can't improve something unless we can measure it' is an age-old dictum. If we are to improve both hypermedia applications and the processes we use to develop these applications then we need to be able to measure the appropriate characteristics of both the applications and the processes.

If we can make suitable measurements, we will be able to identify where the application and the process of developing the application is failing. This can then be used as feedback to correct the application or improve the process. For example, we may have a measurement capable of telling us the relevance of the link structures we are developing. If we find that the relevance is low, we can look at aspects of the process where we do our information structuring. Of course, this relies on having accurate measurements.

Essentially, we have two levels of measurements: heuristics and metrics. A metric is a measurement which results in a absolute figure on some scale, i.e. it is quantitative rather than qualitative. Metrics can include things like the average number of links in each page of information, or the hours spent on developing each page of information. A heuristic can be viewed as a rule-of-thumb, something which is qualitative rather than quantitative, and which can often be used to provide an indication of how to interpret a metric. A typical heuristic might be: 'if a Website has a structure which goes to a depth of greater than five layers then it will be very difficult for a user to locate information'.

At present, very few reliable metrics exist in hypermedia, and for those that do exist we do not have the experience (captured as heuristics) to effectively interpret them. In many cases, heuristics are built up from personal experience and are never made more widely available.

Product Measurements

Product measurements can take two forms: those aimed at detecting errors, and those for measuring application quality. Very few metrics currently exist with respect to either of these forms of measurement for hypermedia applications, and those that do exist are often difficult to interpret. As Johnson (1995) points out, 'hypertext construction, assembling often thousands of nodes and tens of thousands of links, has a dramatic potential for error'. He proposes an approach based on the analysis of both structure and connections by comparing an application's design and actual implementation.

Common structure errors include missing nodes, invalid types of nodes and nodes with incorrect properties. Connection errors include incorrect link destinations, dangling links, too many links with a common destination, and nodes (or groups of nodes) which are unreachable (i.e. do not form the destination of any links).

Very few techniques exist which have been specifically developed for assessing link correctness, apart from manually assessing each link to evaluate whether it is consistent with the application design. Mechanical aspects, such as checking for dangling links, can be checked using various automated tools, though these do not evaluate consistency with a hypermedia design. Structural aspects, such as average node size and variations from this average size, can also be determined automatically or semi-automatically, but must still be interpreted to be useful.

Botafogo, Rivlin and Shneiderman (1992) provide a list of possible types of structural analysis which can help with this process, examples being centrality, compactness and stratum. All of these metrics use the converted distance matrix – a matrix of the number of links required to move from one node to another (with infinite distances, i.e. unreachable, replaced by some selected constant K, often set to the number of nodes in the application). An example is given in Figure 6-5. In this figure the centrality measures how central a node is within the structure, and is calculated as the sum of the distances from the given node divided by the sum of all distances. Note that, in the given figure, despite initial appearances, node 4 is actually the most 'central' node.

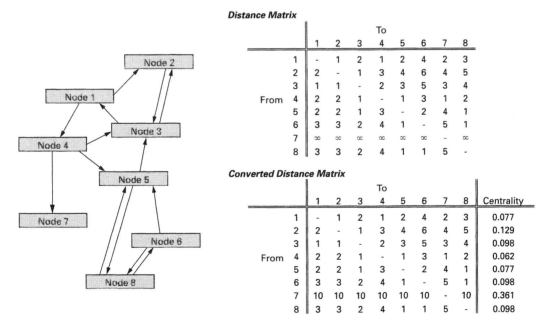

Distance Matrix

From \ To	1	2	3	4	5	6	7	8
1	-	1	2	1	2	4	2	3
2	2	-	1	3	4	6	4	5
3	1	1	-	2	3	5	3	4
4	2	2	1	-	1	3	1	2
5	2	2	1	3	-	2	4	1
6	3	3	2	4	1	-	5	1
7	∞	∞	∞	∞	∞	∞	-	∞
8	3	3	2	4	1	1	5	-

Converted Distance Matrix

From \ To	1	2	3	4	5	6	7	8	Centrality
1	-	1	2	1	2	4	2	3	0.077
2	2	-	1	3	4	6	4	5	0.129
3	1	1	-	2	3	5	3	4	0.098
4	2	2	1	-	1	3	1	2	0.062
5	2	2	1	3	-	2	4	1	0.077
6	3	3	2	4	1	-	5	1	0.098
7	10	10	10	10	10	10	-	10	0.361
8	3	3	2	4	1	1	5	-	0.098

Figure 6-5

A simple example of a hypermedia graph and its related distance matrices. Note with a converted distance matrix, infinite distances are replaced by some selected constant (in this case 10)

Compactness refers to the extent of the interconnectedness of a hypermedia structure, and can be viewed as a normalised measure of the average distance (i.e. hypermedia links) between any two nodes in the structure. Compactness is defined mathematically as:

$$compactness = \frac{max - sum}{max - min}$$

where max is the sum of all converted distances for a completely unconnected structure, min is the sum of all converted distances for a completely connected structure, and sum is the actual sum of distances for the given structure. A fully connected structure (i.e. every node connected to every other node) has a compactness of 1.0. A highly connected structure can provide too many links and hence damage navigation by separating useful navigation paths from the numerous possibilities. A totally unconnected structure (i.e. no links at all) has a compactness of 0.0. A poorly connected structure does not provide sufficient linking to be useful in moving about a structure. For the example in Figure 6-5 (with K set to 10), max is 490, min is 49 and sum is 194. This gives a compactness of approximately 0.67.

Botafogo, Rivlin and Shneiderman (1992) suggest that a compactness of 0.5 may be a reasonable target value at which authors can aim. However, the actual target value will be dependant upon the style and size of the application being developed. For example, it would be expected that a reference application would have more comprehensive cross-linking than an educational application (where we may wish to constrain the possible navigation paths). As yet, no heuristics exist which allow us to determine a suitable value under given circumstances. In addition, the compactness metric is based purely on link quantity, and does not attempt to address link quality in any way.

Stratum is a measure of the ordering of an application, and can be used to indicate whether there is an inherent order (such as a linear or hierarchical structure) for reading an application. The calculation is based on the *absolute prestige* of the application relative to the *absolute prestige* of an linearly ordered application with the same number of nodes. The stratum of the example in Figure 6-5 is approximately 0.51. Again, as with compactness, the stratum metric provides a figure which can be used as an indication, but heuristics are still missing to help us interpret the metric effectively.

Possible additional product metrics

To give an indication of what metrics may be useful (but which do not yet exist), we need to return to the list of desirable hypermedia characteristics and look at possible ways of evaluating each of these characteristics. As a very brief example, we shall consider a few typical possibilities.

- **Navigability**: is strongly affected by two aspects – the existence of an appropriate path between two desired points, and the ease with which this path can be located. Metrics such as compactness focus mainly on the first of these two aspects. The higher the compactness, the more likely it is that there is a short path between any two points. One possibility would be to weight the distances by the likelihood that a path will be required between two points – possibly using something such as comparing the existing path navigation distance to the theoretical semantic distance between two concepts (which is in turn exceedingly difficult to measure).

  The second aspect, the ability to identify a path which does exist, might be based on an analysis, for each possible navigation path between two nodes, of the number of alternatives presented at each stage of the path (as shown in Figure 6-6). Other navigability metrics will need to consider how simple it is to identify anchors (which is, at least to a certain extent, dependant on the user inter-

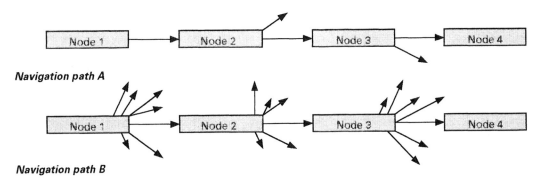

Navigation path A

Navigation path B

Figure 6-6

Moving from node 1 to node 4 will be much simpler for path A than path B, as the user does not need to sift between as many competing possible directions at each stage of navigation. Path A will be more navigable then path B (but only for this particular desired path)

face) and the validity of the structuring metaphor which has been used.

A useful navigation metric may be to measure the number of navigation steps it typically takes users to move between two nodes, as compared to the actual minimum possible navigation distance. Other, similar measures would include how often given links are followed and the delay in a user locating a desired anchor within an intermediate node.

- **Link validity**: link validity can be measured in a large number of ways, depending upon what aspect of validity is being measured. If we wish to evaluate correctness, we need to determine what are correct links (often rather arguable). A simple metric (though not a particularly accurate one) may be to measure the number of links which have a source and destination with a correlation above some threshold (where correlation is based on, say, a pure textual comparison – how often the same words appear in both nodes). A more accurate metric may be to require a content 'expert' to evaluate the correctness of each link.

- **Concept organisation**: the structure of an information space is dependant not only on the linking, but also on the way in which the information has been partitioned. Simple partitioning metrics could include aspects such as the average amount of content per node, the balance between different media (such as proportion of screen space devoted to each media type), and the proportion of links originating in each media type.

More sophisticated metrics may address factors such as the coupling and cohesion within an application. For example, a metric for the localised cohesion of an application could be the average of the ratios between the maximum semantic or conceptual distance within a node, and the minimum conceptual distance between nodes (as shown in Figure 6-7) – though measuring conceptual distance presents an obvious problem.

Process Measurements

Measurement of process characteristics within hypermedia development is currently almost nonexistent. Metrics are usually limited to aspects such as quantity and balance of development time. No widely accepted metrics yet exist for evaluating aspects such as quality of development

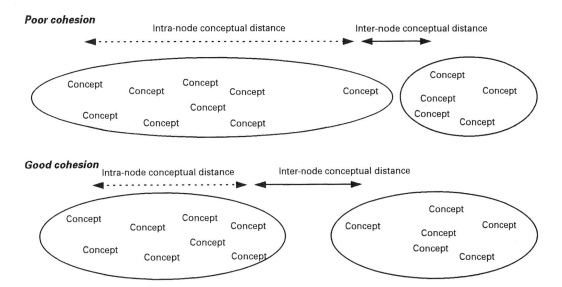

Figure 6-7

A given set of concepts can be partitioned into nodes in different ways. One possible metric for the cohesion of a set of nodes could be based on the ratio between intra-node conceptual distance and inter-node conceptual distance

documentation, extent of reuse, effectiveness or quality of project management, or proportion of the development which is completed. One of the biggest gaps is in metrics which can be used to evaluate the potential development scope of a project. Without this style of metric it is very difficult to reliably determine the resources which a project will require (or even the feasibility of a proposed development project). This is obviously an area which still requires considerable ongoing research.

6.7 Effect of Approaches on Issues

At the end of the previous chapter, we finished by pointing out that different approaches to the development of hypermedia applications impact on our ability to develop applications which have the characteristics we desire in the final applications. Different approaches also impact on the various process issues raised in this chapter. Let us consider each of the issues raised in turn.

The development productivity is a difficult issue to effectively consider. When undertaking small scale development, the earlier stages of the process – analysis and high-level design – tend to be almost intuitive, and the later stages of the development require most effort. As a result, the use of authoring tools can result in significant increases in development productivity. This can give the impression that authoring tools, be they Web design or multimedia tools, are all that are required to dramatically improve productivity. This is not true. One of the major lessons learnt from software engineering is that development effort and productivity is not directly scalable with the size of the application.

As the application size grows, both the importance of understanding an application, and the difficulty of achieving this understanding grow significantly. Development techniques which give high levels of productivity for small-scale applications will not do so for large-scale applications, largely because of this failure to understand the application and its needs. What this means in practice is that, whereas authoring tools may be sufficient for small-scale development, they are invariably inadequate (on their own) for large-scale development. They need to be used in conjunction with (or rather, as part of) a more comprehensive suite of techniques which explicitly address all stages of the development process.

Typical authoring tools also fail to deliver adequate levels of productivity for large-scale development for a number of additional reasons. As the scope of applications grow, so does the difficulty of understanding the complexity of the application structure and functionality. Few tools provide any inherent mechanism for dealing with this growing complexity, and so the author will typically spend increasing amounts of time trying to deal with this complexity and less time using the tool. Indeed, many tools (such as Web authoring tools) exacerbate this problem by obfuscating exactly those elements (such as anchors and links) which contribute to the complexity. If these tools must be used, then the development should introduce mechanisms or procedures aimed at circumventing these problems.

Related to difficulties with productivity during the development is cognitive management. Most existing tools focus on providing the necessary functionality to allow an author to implement the desired elements. They typically do not attempt to ease the burden on an author in terms of understanding what elements are required or how they should be used. There are two principle ways in which the cognitive burden can be eased: procedural guidance and directed assistance (Robertson, Merkus and Ginige, 1994). With procedural guidance the developer is given assistance in understanding what steps she/he must take, and in what order, to complete some aspect of the development. This may be in the form of a full lifecycle methodology providing step-by-step guidelines for the entire development, or it may simply be an addition or modification to an authoring tool which guides the author through the low-level design and implementation of some part of the application. For example HART (Robertson, Merkus and Ginige, 1994) guides an author in the identification of content, and then the links among this content. Procedural guidance removes the burden of requiring a develop or author to not only focus on the application, but also on the development process for the application.

Directed assistance goes one step further and provides active help to the developer or author. Although this could theoretically be provided at any stage of the development, the only practical examples to-date have been at the authoring level. For example, HART will make suggestions to an author regarding possible links, which the author can then accept or reject. The cognitive effort required to ascertain the validity of a prospective link is usually much less than that required to manually locate the link. An example (as yet unrealised) of directed assistance at an earlier stage of the development process would be a process management tool which uses the requirements of an application to make suggestions to a developer regarding the most appropriate development tools and environments, and how development resources could best be used.

Reuse and maintenance are also strongly affected by the approach taken to development. Probably the most significant aspect affecting both of these issues is the way in which the various types of information are treated. The simplest way of demonstrating this is to look at the basic level of Web development. If we create a static set of Web pages, then these pages encapsulate both the content and the presentation structure. Indeed, the result is that they have a tendency to cloud the distinction between raw data and the information represented by that data, between the data content, the structure of the data, and the inter-relationships between the data, and between the data structure and the way in which the data is to be presented within the context of the application. If we wish to change the content, or we wish to change the presentation, then we need to manipulate the same page of information. The result is that Web pages are typically extremely difficult to either reuse (in whole or in part) and maintain.

The main mechanism used by most approaches to improve reuse and maintainability is to store the information and the information structure (e.g. the actual data and the way in which it is structured) separately from the presentation structure (i.e. the way in which this information and structure is presented). This can be done in numerous ways and to varying levels of sophistication. This is discussed in much more detail in the next part of the book, but to give an indication of the possible approaches, several examples are valuable.

One simple possibility is to store the document and document structure separately and generate the Web pages as required. For example, we were involved in the development of a prototype application used to store course notes (Ginige, Witana and Yourlo, 1996). This application stored the documents as standard HTML files. However, the hierarchical structure into which these pages were arranged was stored in a separate custom-designed database. When a Web page was requested, the appropriate HTML file was appended (using suitable CGI scripts) with appropriate navigation buttons (such as *previous*, *next*, etc.) based on the structure stored in the database. This meant that the entire structure of the application could be reorganised without changing a single Web page – only the structure database needed to be updated. A more sophisticated version of this involves storing all the data as customised documents (such as SGML documents) and combining these with presentation templates dynamically as requested. This means that the presentation of the application can be adapted as needed without affecting the content being presented.

The two most difficult issues to comment on, with respect to current approaches, are process management and measurement. In general, these are carried out in either an *ad hoc* manner, or using a custom-developed in-house approach, which is usually proprietary and adapted for a specific application domain. Very little work has been published or made available on suitable process management techniques or process measurements for hypermedia development. Current authoring tools and available methodologies do not yet address these areas, and this is an active area of ongoing development.

Part Two

Hypermedia Development Practice

Dr David Lowe
University of Technology, Sydney, Australia

Professor Athula Ginige
University of Western Sydney, Australia

Professor Wendy Hall
University of Southampton, UK

Part One of this book focused on developing an understanding of the underlying principles and issues in developing hypermedia applications. Part Two will focus on how to carry out practical development in a way consistent with this understanding. We look at best practices within the constraints of current understanding and technology, and provide a basis for developing an approach to the engineering of quality hypermedia applications. We also identify the (many) problems and issues which even best practice has yet to adequately address.

We begin Part Two by developing (in Chapter 7) a framework within which we can discuss practical approaches to the development of hypermedia applications. We also consider issues which impact on the overall approach to the development: especially product and process models and planning the development process. In Chapter 8 we look in general at the development process, and consider each of the development phases. Chapter 9 then considers specific issues and techniques which can contribute to the hypermedia-specific aspects of the development process.

7

Development Process

Plans get you into things but you got to work your way out
(The autobiography of Will Rogers (1949))

Chapter Goals

Part One of this book focused on the fundamentals of hypermedia engineering; Part Two will focus on practical development. In this chapter we provide a framework for the overall development process. The objectives of the chapter are to consider the following:

- Hypermedia development is incredibly diverse; no single process will be uniformly appropriate. Indeed, very few processes currently yet even exist. Furthermore, there is currently only a poor understanding of what aspects are required in these processes.

- To develop an effective process, we need to understand the project! We should begin this by undertaking some form of domain analysis.

- A domain analysis includes understanding the problem, understanding potential solutions, and understanding any constraints on the development process.

- Based on our domain understanding, we need to identify appropriate product models. A product model defines the architecture of our solution.

- Based on our domain understanding and our product model, we need to identify or adapt a suitable process model. The process model defines the approach which we take to development.

- Different process models are suited to different conditions. Risk is handled well by a spiral model; uncertainty is handled well by prototyping and incremental development.

- We can use our process model to plan the appropriate activities and outcomes of the development.

In earlier chapters, we considered what is meant by the term 'development', and looked at factors and issues which affect how we carry out development. We now wish to look at the specifics of how we carry out development, i.e. what should be occurring in current practice. In this chapter we look at the broad issue of how the development process can be identified and managed, and what types of development processes are appropriate.

7.1 Introduction

As both a maturing formal academic discipline and a set of evolving practical commercial activities, hypermedia development is only just beginning to be understood. In particular, we are only just beginning to appreciate the issues related to the development of large hypermedia applications.

At present, most large scale hypermedia applications are developed for either the World Wide Web or CD-ROM. Often these applications start at a relatively small scale and evolve over a period of time. Current practices tend to consist largely of a piecemeal approach to this development. These practices tend to not so much fail to provide useful techniques, as to fail to provide an overall development approach (analogous to programming being only one small part of the software development process). Current practices are usually valid to be used under certain circumstances – they simply need to be placed in an appropriate context, and supported by a suitable process.

Experience is progressively (and often dramatically, in financial terms) demonstrating that failure to provide this process for development of large applications is leading to significant problems, at least in terms of what *should* have been achievable, and at what cost. With current approaches, the cost of development increases at a much faster rate than increases in the scale of applications. We have yet to obtain economies of scale in development. Further, we now have many unmaintainable applications due to the *ad hoc* development approaches that were adopted. Some guidelines are beginning to appear to help practitioners identify suitable, and practical, techniques (the book by West and Norris (1997) is a particularly good example), but these are still limited in scope and rarely address broader process issues.

When developing hypermedia applications various sets of activities are undertaken. Typical examples of activities include:

- *Specification*: we need to define the hypermedia application we are going to develop. This includes such issues as information content and how this information is to be accessed, intended audiences, purpose of the application, etc.

- *Design*: we should address issues such as what is the optimal information structure for the given content and purpose, a basis for generating the Hyperlinks, what is a suitable user interface, etc.

- *Content generation*: we must capture, extract from other sources or generate the raw information (text, audio, video, images, animation, etc.).

- *Authoring*: during the authoring phase, content that has been generated is structured, hyperlinked and formatted based on the design that was developed earlier. Sometimes people refer to the whole process of developing an application as authoring. In this book we limit the term authoring to refer only to the process of organising content into a hypermedia application.

The order in which these activities (and the many others) take place, the interaction between the activities, the outcomes of the activities, the resources required and the amount of effort spent on each phase of the process depends upon numerous factors, including the scale, scope and characteristics of the hypermedia application. These activities also require varied skills and a team approach to development.

The main reason for the failure of current practices used for developing large-scale hypermedia applications is, as with development in many other domains (such as software development), lack of planning of the development activities, not properly understanding all the issues, and use of inappropriate processes, methodologies and techniques. The methodologies and techniques typically used for development of small-scale applications won't scale up to handle the complexities of large-scale applications (Ginige and Lowe, 1995). The development of large-scale applications needs a significantly more disciplined approach supported by appropriate methodologies, techniques and tools than is currently typical. In this chapter, we develop a framework within which we discuss the development process. In the next chapter we begin the process of demonstrating in practical terms how a disciplined approach can be achieved. We consider the project commencement, domain analysis, the selection of suitable product and process models, and the project planning. In the chapter which follows, we look at the carrying out of specific development activities such as problem analysis, system design, implementation, etc.

7.2   Understanding the Project

The Development Process

We begin our consideration of hypermedia development practices by looking at the overall project. We can consider the starting point of a hypermedia development project as either when a client provides an initial problem statement or project tender, or when a market need is identified. From this point we need to consider how the project proceeds. If the project is for a large-scale hypermedia development, we need to ensure that the process adopted is both appropriate to the scale of the development and properly managed. This goes beyond simply adopting a development process from a different domain (such as software engineering). We need to consider how the issues raised in the first part of this book impact on the development process, and particularly what hypermedia-specific activities should be carried out.

Before we can identify a suitable process and develop a plan for this process, we need to understand the factors which impact on the process. This should occur as close to the start of the development project as possible, though it is recognised that the plan will often (indeed, almost always) be refined, adapted or modified as the project progresses and a better understanding of the project develops.

We can view the plan for the project as an instantiation of (among other things) the development process to be used (this point is discussed further in Section 7.4). To be able to undertake the initial planning of the development process, we need to ensure we understand the project adequately. This involves understanding the problem being addressed, the solution we are targeting, and the development issues, technologies (especially hypermedia technologies) and techniques we can use. The specifics of developing this understanding, what we refer to as 'domain analysis', is explained in more detail in the following section.

Once we have developed an understanding of the project, we can make suitably informed decisions regarding the hypermedia product model to use for the application (e.g. will we develop an information-centred application? A screen-based application? etc.), and the process model to use for the development (e.g. shall we utilise a waterfall approach to development? incremental development? iterative development? or some form of hybrid approach?). These models can then be formalised in the creation of a project

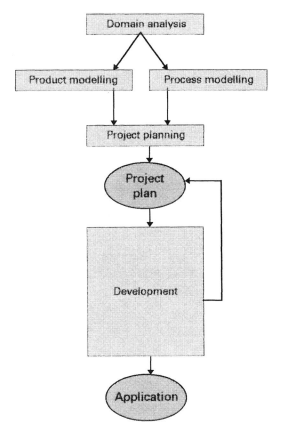

Figure 7-1

Abstract view of the hypermedia development process

plan which details the approach to be adopted, the development phases, timings, budgets, resources, etc. This plan will be used to guide the project development. In other words, at the most abstract level, the initial steps of the development process are shown in Figure 7-1.

It is worth pointing out that substantial information exists regarding development process models. In this book we do not go into great detail regarding elements covered extensively elsewhere. Rather, we look at those aspects of the development process which are specific to hypermedia.

Domain Analysis

For effective planning of a hypermedia development, the developers must have an appropriate understanding of the product and process models used. These will in turn be influenced by our understanding of the domain within which the project exists. We can consider this domain as having three main elements: the problem domain; the development domain; and the solution domain. An understanding of each of these domains is important to understanding the development process.

The problem domain defines the pre-existing context for the application. In other words, understanding the problem domain allows us to understand why we are developing the hypermedia application. As a brief example, if we consider the *HyperBank* case study (see Appendix 4), then understanding the problem domain would encompass an understanding of the context within which banks in general, and the *Archaic Banking Organisation (ABO)* in particular, currently operate. For example, we would need to understand that the *ABO* currently has multiple branches, with tens of thousands of customers (with the expectation that this will continue to grow), and a large number of staff with varying levels of computer literacy. All these aspects may influence how we undertake the development or the form that the final application may take. In particular, these aspects will affect how we structure the information space – and hence how we perform the information interlinking. Understanding the problem domain is also important from a hypermedia perspective, in that it will allow us to understand the types and structure of information we wish to model in hypermedia structures, and the types of behaviour and functionality that may be appropriate.

The solution domain defines the bounds of the solution that we wish to develop. There will be certain factors which will either tightly constrain or actively encourage the application to have a certain form. With the *HyperBank* application, for example, we have been constrained to a solution that uses the World Wide Web as a result of a managerial recognition of the growing ubiquity of the Web and the bank's competitors' increasing presence on the Web. The solution domain is also constrained by what hypermedia technology is currently capable of achieving. For example, irrespective of what the requirements of the *HyperBank* application may be, our final solution will be constrained by what is technically feasible given current Web technologies (such as currently available charging and security techniques).

The development domain defines the bounds of the development process, those factors which exist solely because of the development activities themselves, rather than either the problem or solution domains. In other words, both the development process and the final application developed will be influenced by the certain developmental constraints. With the *HyperBank* application, for example, the development process will be constrained by specific timeframes we may wish to support, budgets which are considered reasonable, and development skills and knowledge which are available within the *HyperBank* organisation or obtainable through outsourcing.

Domain analysis overall provides us with an understanding of these three domains, and this should be sufficient to allow us to identify the hypermedia product model to use for the application and the process model to use for the development. From this point we can also plan the development. However, if we are to do so, we need to understand those factors which influence the planning. Without this understanding we would be unable to be confident that our models or plans reflect the application to be developed or the most appropriate process to use in the development.

Domain Parameters?

The domain analysis needs to consider various parameters which will influence the selection of product and process models and the subsequent project plan. We should also consider the implications of each of the above parameters.

Problem domain parameters

- **Current information, information sources, and information structure**: an understanding of the types of information currently used or available, the sources, and structure of this information can be important to an understanding of how the development may be carried out. As a simple example, where we have large quantities of highly structured information that changes regularly, it is probably appropriate to adopt an information-centred product model (considered in more detail in Section 7.3). Other aspects related to information are security, legal and ethical considerations. For example, if the information raises privacy considerations, then the development process will need to consider how privacy is handled in the design and implementation.

- **Stakeholders**: any existing system will have numerous categories of people who have a stake in the system and are performing different functions. Possible categories include clients (those who have responsibility for the existing systems and require the new system), users, content providers, etc. An understanding of the different stakeholders allows us to understand the way in which information is used. For example, if the clients are highly literate in hypermedia systems, it may appropriate to involve them more actively in the development process. Aspects of the stakeholders which could be considered include responsibilities, roles and current access to and generation of information sources.

- **Current applications**: in many cases, hypermedia applications to be developed are a replacement for an existing application (or collection of applications). Understanding these applications will help us develop an understanding of the scope of the new applications, and possible approaches to supporting stakeholders and information. For example, we should consider what problems the current applications address, what issues they fail to address, activities they carry out, and what are the goals of the applications.

- **Current constraints**: the existing problem domain (and hence the domain within which the application(s) to be developed must exist) will impose certain constraints which are inherent in the problem domain. Examples include desired availability of access, commercial considerations, etc.

In all the above cases, it will be important to consider not only applications which are immediately familiar (especially the applications belonging to the clients), but also other applications within the problem domain. These would include applications belonging to competitors.

Solution domain parameters

- **Project goals**: the project will have certain specific goals which, apart from the detailed requirements, will influence the development process. In particular, these might include features such as reliability, compatibility, robustness, evolvability, maintainability and reusability of information. Several examples might be useful.

First, if we have an application where we do not understand the solution domain well (if, for example, we are not confident how users may react to a specific solution), this would indicate that it is appropriate for the development process to incorporate iterative development including multiple evolving prototypes, so we can obtain early feedback on user reaction. Secondly, we may have a system where compatibility with existing applications is critically important. This would imply that the development process needs to incorporate an analysis of these existing applications, and how compatibility affects the design.

- **Client and user literacy**: the level of client and user familiarity with possible solution domain technologies and issues will influence the product model and the development approach. For example, if the client is familiar with possible solution technologies, it may be appropriate for them to be more actively involved in the development process. If clients are unfamiliar with a possible solution technology (such as CD-ROMs, as opposed to the WWW), then it makes that technology less suitable.

- **Solution domain constraints**: in many cases, clients may have specific reasons for imposing specific constraints on the solution domain. Examples include compatibility with existing applications or a response to functionality offered by competitors (this is commonly seen with companies seeing a need to develop a Web 'presence').

- **Technological limitations**: these include factors which constrain the possible solutions that may be possible or appropriate. Limitations include processing power, bandwidths, storage capacity, equipment costs and equipment reliability. As an example of the significance, a system which requires reliable access to information (such as access to customer account information by bank tellers in the *HyperBank* system) probably cannot afford a solution which relies on Web technologies (which often suffer from unreliable access).

Development domain parameters

- **Budgeting**: the expected or allowable budget will strongly influence the development approach adopted. However, further, consideration needs to be given not just to expected budgeting for the immediate development, but to ongoing maintenance.

- **Development resources**: these include personnel (and their expertise), development tools, time, information and development hardware. These resources will strongly influence both the product model and process model selected. For example, if the development team has no expertise with specific tools (which support a given product model), then consideration will need to be given to whether the cost and time associated with retraining in those tools is warranted.

- **Development expertise**: expertise includes factors such as an understanding of and familiarity with different development processes (such as incremental development) and the relationships between processes and attributes of final applications. As an example of the significance of these aspects in terms of planning a project, if we recognise that the developers' level of expertise is lacking, then we can identify that there is likely to be a high risk associated with the development, and therefore a spiral model of the development process (which specifically addresses risk) may be most appropriate.

- **Development domain constraints**: in many cases the client will place certain constraints on the development process which need to be considered during the development. These constraints might include the client's need for managerial feedback or involvement during development (e.g. the need for defined regular development milestones), required documentation, reporting or auditing standards or formats, awareness of and response to acknowledged client uncertainty with regard to application requirements (which would indicate the need for prototyping or iterative development).

Performing Domain Analysis

As discussed above, domain analysis allows us to understand the project, how it should be carried out, and is essential in gaining sufficient knowledge to begin planning the development process. This in turn indicates that domain analysis will be carried out at a point when the project is still ill-formed and often poorly understood. It will often be carried out by the project management (indeed, at this stage, it is likely that the project manager will be the only person associated with the project).

Domain analysis will incorporate collection and analysis of information related to the problem, solution and development domains. The specific mechanisms used in domain analysis will vary greatly. The activities will depend upon the possible sources of information which can provide the required insights. In general, we need to identify these sources of information and then use them as effectively as possible. Existing documentation is likely to provide an insight into the scope and cost of applications; this documentation might include application descriptions, training manuals, procedures manuals, publicity material and reviews of applications.

Interviews with stakeholders can also provide a valuable source of information. Users of existing systems can provide feedback related to current applications, including why current applications are used and the functionality which is provided, and where current applications fail to provide desired characteristics. Interviews with clients can provide important information related to the consideration of budgets, timeframes, development constraints, etc.

Evaluation of the developers' own capabilities within the context of the problem domain is also important. This includes what resources are available, familiarity with the problem domain and the extent of development expertise.

The primary outcome of domain analysis is a thorough understanding of the domains affecting the development, which will either be documented as a separate report, or more commonly, as elements in the project plan. In particular, the project plan will usually incorporate a number of sections that rely explicitly on the understanding gained during the domain analysis. This includes sections related to project scope and description, domain-specific terminology and notation, justification for the selection of product and process models, available resources, risk and project management, and required standards and procedures. This is discussed in greater detail in Section 7.4.

7.3   Selecting a Product Model

What is a Product Model?

A critical aspect of developing hypermedia applications is being able to identify and then represent the information underlying the application, the structure of this information, and the application behaviour and functionality which supports this information. We can identify different models for supporting these elements of applications – what we refer to as 'product models' or 'hypermedia paradigms'.

The model we adopt for a given application will have a major impact on both the final solution and how we carry out the development process for this solution. In particular, if we look at existing hypermedia tools, we find they are based around a very specific model of the structure of hypermedia applications. Systems such as HyperCard (Goodman, 1987) and Hyperties (Shneiderman, 1987; Shneiderman *et al.*, 1989), or even the Web are good examples of systems relying on specific models of information interlinking. Let us begin by consider some of the more common hypermedia product models.

Programming language-based model

In this model applications are coded from scratch using a programming language such as C, or a scripting language. In this case the information and information structure (and in particular, the interlinking) is embedded into the programming structure. As such, the information model is extremely flexible, being constrained primarily by the ability to develop suitable code, and the coding effort required. Having information embedded into a program structure implies that it is typically very difficult to visualise the information structure during the development. This in turn makes it difficult to update and maintain both the information and information structure.

In hypermedia applications the overall screen layout and the presentation aspects also play a very important role in terms of usability, navigability and comprehension of the information. In a programming language-based model, one does not explicitly design the screen layout and interactions, though this situation has changed somewhat due to the introduction of visual programming languages and environments (such as Microsoft Visual Basic).

Though early computer-based training systems used this model, this was mainly due to the lack of any other sophisticated model. Use of this model is now limited primarily to very specialised sub-components of a larger system, a good example being the use of Java applets to do specific tasks in a Web-based information application.

Specialised programming skills are typically required to support this model, but it is rare to find those with these skills also having both detailed knowledge of the problem domain and skills in visual communication.

We thus have a severe mismatch which can make the relevance of this model very limited.

Screen-based model

In the screen-based model, every screen is handcrafted and manually linked together to represent a hypermedia application. Each screen tends to convey a single theme (a chunk of information) such as a particular topic or sub-topic. Some systems that support applications based on this model use fixed-size screens, while others allow scrolling screens. These chunks of information are known as *nodes* in hypermedia, *cards* in NoteCard and HyperCard, *frames* in KMS, *documents* in Augment and Intermedia, or *articles* in Hyperties. Strong emphasis is placed on the screen layout. The information model essentially revolves around information nodes (with the information being embedded into the screen layouts) and links embedded directly into the nodes/screens.

Many commercial authoring systems such as IconAuthor, Authorware Professional, Macromedia Director, Hypercard, and Linkway Live, use this approach to develop hypermedia applications. Variations in model constraints include allowable nodes sizes (from single fixed screen sizes to large scrolling windows) and link structures.

With the increase in application size, the representation of the structure of information nodes became a problem. Thus, the screen-based model is further extended to include visual representation of the structure of the information nodes. This representation can be based around a number of presentation metaphors, including the following common metaphors (as well as various other minor alternatives and hybrids):

- Iconic / flow control: this approach uses a metaphor of a flowchart to present the flow of control among the various pages, or possibly the control showing how each page is manipulated or changed as events occur. A typical example of a tool supporting this approach is Macromedia Authorware Professional.

- Cast / score: this approach treats the screen as a stage, and various activities can occur on the stage. This is coupled with a timeline so that the various activities can be effectively coordinated. A typical example of this approach is Macromedia Director.

- Card hierarchy: this approach treats the application as a hierarchical collection of information which can be navigated. The simplest version of this has no concept of time. A simple early example of this approach on the Internet was Gopher.

This model helps the developer visualise the information structure, thus making it simpler (with respect to applications using the programming language model) to perform maintenance and updating of the information and application and structure. One significant limitation is that if the same information needs to appear in multiple places (though possibly organised differently), then it will have to be physically included separately in each place. This makes changes to the underlying information very cumbersome, time-consuming and error-prone.

Also, as the information is embedded within the screen layout, it is very difficult to reuse this information from another application in a different context (and with a different screen layout). These limitations, together with the high resource requirements for hand-crafting screens, restricts the usefulness of the screen-based model for large-scale applications. It is most useful for small, highly visual applications that do not require substantial maintenance. A particularly good example of where a screen-based model may be suitable is in the rapid development of initial prototypes in order to gain user feedback.

Information-centred model

In this model the information and its structure, rather than the presentation, becomes paramount. Rather than representing a presentation, the focus is on the structure of the information. This 'structured' information is then coupled with a suitable presentation specification to create an application. The required content is structured and stored in a separate database. A good example is a simple Web application; authors first create text and other media and then structure these using a HTML (Hypertext Markup Language) editor. The links to other relevant documents are embedded into the document during this markup process, though the documents do not usually contain explicit presentation information. The presentation system consists of a Web server and a Web client (browser), and the information is stored separately from both of these as a set of HTML files (see Figure 7-2).

This is a very powerful concept, as it allows us to maintain the information independant of the storage, delivery and presentation mechanisms. This is similar to the evolution of database management systems in the early 1960s.

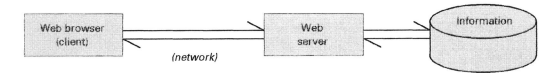

Figure 7-2

Use of a separate database for storing application content

We can now start to further divide the information into different components, such as content, structural information and presentation information. Links could be further divided into structural, associative and referential. If we store these different types of information separately, then we devise individual management and maintenance schemes for these, which are optimised for the particular type of information.

The structuring of the information typically involves aspects such as dividing information into nodes and identifying key concepts. A good example of a technology supporting this type of product model is SGML, where the information can be marked up and the structure identified, and the specific application is only generated dynamically as required. Multimedia Viewer from Microsoft is another example of an authoring and a presentation system which supports an information-centred product model. As these systems separate the development of content from the screen layout design; the author can quickly develop the content and use a set of standard screen layouts to present this information to the user, through a presentation system.

Selecting and Adapting a Product Model

An important step in the initiation of a hypermedia development project is the selection of a suitable product model (or models) for the application to be developed. The model will influence the entire structure of the application, and thus the approach we take to the development.

How do we decide what is an appropriate product model for the application to be developed? The simplest approach is to consider the characteristics of the application to be developed and map these to characteristics of the different types of product models we can use. As a rough guide, a programming language model is suited to small-scale, but very high performance applications. A screen-based model is useful for medium-scale, rapidly developed applications. Information-centred models are suitable for large-scale applications, and applications requiring a high degree of maintenance.

Finally, it is worth pointing out that we are by no means constrained to a single model for a given application. In many cases, it will be appropriate to use different models for differing components of the application. As an example, we may have an application which contains both a large amount of structured but highly dynamic information which must be maintained on a regular basis, and some specific information based around a demonstration which is very resource intensive. We could implement the dynamic data using a database-oriented, information-centred model, with a defined interface to the demonstration component of the application which is implemented using a programming-language approach so that it is suitably optimised.

Example

To demonstrate the appropriate selection of a product, let us briefly consider the *HyperBank* application described in Appendix 4 (note, however, that a full coverage of all aspects of *HyperBank* would take considerably more room than we have available here).

Let us begin by considering the problem domain. This covers the existing environment within which the need or desire for the *HyperBank* has arisen. This context is defined by existing banking practices, customer expectations, government regulations, etc., and raises a number of relevant considerations. First, we are constrained in our development by the client's focus (whether appropriate or not) on the use of Web-based technologies. This means that any product model we adopt must be consistent with that which underlies the Web. In particular, the Web actively encourages separation of information and presentation (though this can be circumvented to a limited degree through mechanisms like designing interface elements as Java applets).

Next, when we consider the current sources and types of information and the prospective users of any application we might develop, we note that there is a huge diversity within the domain – both in terms of types of information and the way this information is currently used. This in turn means that the application(s) we aim to develop will need to address a broad spectrum of needs, indicating that a single hypermedia application product model (or even a single application) may not be appropriate.

Indeed, we can identify different classes of user (such as current bank customers and bank tellers) that will need different types of interfaces, but which access and use identical information (such as customer account details) – though this information may be structured in different ways for the different users. This indicates that it is likely to be appropriate to separate the underlying data from the way in which this data is structured and presented, i.e. a form of information-centred model.

In addition, much (but not all) of the underlying data will be very dynamic in nature (such as customer account information, advertising material, bank administrative information). This implies that we need a product model which actively supports maintainability. An information-centred model which separates data and information structure will assist with this, but separation of the structure and the presentation will also be a significant advantage for those applications where the presentation remains the same but the information structure changes. A good example of this would be legal documents where the presentation of the information remains consistent, but the information and structure evolves as laws change, legal rulings become available, etc.

Another important observation is that the applications being developed will need to coexist with existing systems. Many of the existing systems (and current operating procedures) are such that they cannot be readily supplanted by the new hypermedia applications (either for procedural reasons, or for financial reasons such as the cost of replacing existing teller terminals). These existing applications and systems will have certain data formats (and possible specific access mechanisms). For example, the customer account information may be stored in an large centralised database, and accessed through a database management system. Any new applications will have to be developed in a way which is consistent with existing formats and access mechanisms – another reason why our product model is based around the separation of data, information structure and presentation. A major part of the development of the new applications will involve an analysis of which components of the existing systems and applications can (or should be) replaced.

Finally, another useful observation is that the same information (and possibly structure, and even presentation) will be used with different functionality in different applications for different classes of users. A good example of this will be security. For example, the same information may be made available to both current and prospective customers, but only current customers may be allowed to use the search engine, or access specific areas of the information space.

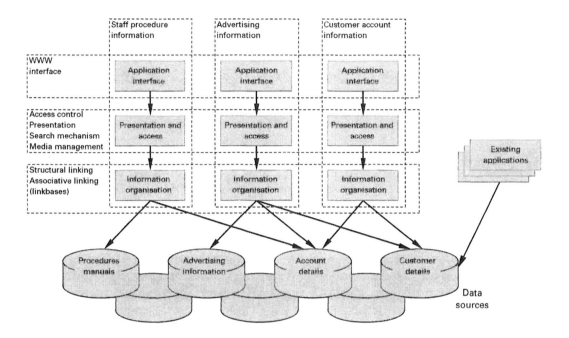

Figure 7-3

A possible structure for a product model which allows disparate applications to access disparate underlying information sources

The above observations result in the selection of a layered product model which supports multiple disparate applications accessing the same underlying information. The structure of this product model is given in Figure 7-3. Note that the individual applications shown will still be integrated within an overarching framework for the *HyperBank* system.

Note that the product model shown is not an architectural model of the applications to be developed (though it will be used in guiding the development of the architecture). Rather, it shows the elements of information and the way in which they are combined to create final applications. The specific architecture for the applications (which in this case will be based on the Web) will be developed as part of the high level design activities.

7.4   Selecting a Process Model

What is a Process Model?

A hypermedia application will have a lifecycle – the entire period of existence of the application from conception, through development, delivery and maintenance to final application cessation or retirement. Within this lifecycle the development processes, activities and deliverables can be modelled in various ways, resulting in assorted process models. The models capture the essential elements of the process, and allow us to reason about the process and plan for it to be carried out.

A process model will contain a number of different elements, including subprojects, resources (physical resources, knowledge, skills, time, etc.), actors (those individuals or organisations involved in the project in some way), activities (things we can do) and artifacts (things which exist as a result of the project). A process model essentially considers the development phases or stages of development and how these are integrated into an overall development process. It does not describe the specific techniques used to carry out development activities (these are left to specific methodologies), but provides a framework in which we can understand and plan the development process. Indeed, this framework is usually instantiated as a project plan early in the development (see the example of a typical application development plan given in Appendix 3).

We can design different process models to suit different types of development (and development issues), which will in turn be suited to different types of applications. For example, a model incorporating iterative refinement of an initial prototype may be best suited to small-scale trial applications. A competent hypermedia engineer would be aware of the models available, and would use the most appropriate model for each problem, adapting it in a way which takes into account the limitations and strengths of the model chosen, and the application being developed.

Process phases and activities

To manage the complexities associated with the development of large-scale hypermedia applications, we carry out various development activities. As an aid in managing these activities, we will combine them into manageable groups called subprocesses or phases, which combine to form the overall development process. There are several reasons for considering groups of activities together. First is the simple issue of cognitive management of the process. By merging activities into phases, it allows us to better conceptualise what needs to occur and the relationships between the various development activities.

A second, and in many cases much more important, reason for combining phases is as a project management aid. Effective management of the development process will require that development progress can be evaluated. This in turn requires both intermediate deliverables in the development and suitable development milestones. The completion of development phases (or the movement from one phase into another) act as these milestones – thereby providing valuable project management aids.

The grouping of activities into phases can be undertaken in various ways, though this will usually be guided by conventional engineering principles (such as grouping activities in such a way as to minimise the coupling among subprocesses). One possible (simple) grouping is: planning and management, analysis, design, production, delivery, maintenance. Appendix 2 gives a detailed list of possible activities which may contribute to the development phases.

Process structure

The order in which these development phases (and activities within these phases) take place along a time line, the amount of effort required to carry out each activity, and types of coupling between phases varies from application to application, based on the nature of the application. We need to consider aspects such as the inter-relationships between phases and the extent to which we can iterate the development.

For example, when developing a small application consisting of only a few Web pages, it may be sufficient to follow a reasonably linear development sequence, starting with analysis followed by design, production and delivery (i.e. putting the Web pages into a Web server with appropriate access control) and maintenance. However if we are developing a large, complex application in a relatively unknown application domain (and using technologies which are unfamiliar), we may well discover when in the production phase that a change to the design can make the production process much more cost-effective. In such a situation, we would have to re-visit the design phase and check whether these changes can be accommodated. A process model which facilitates iteration would therefore be very beneficial (such iteration can, for example, be accommodated by techniques such as appropriate partitioning of the design and suitable documentation of the individual phases).

In other words, different domains, application scales and other factors will all influence not only the activities we are carrying out, but also the way in which these activities are combined and undertaken – the process structure.

Factors Influencing the Process

A number of factors influence the choice and/or adaptation of a process to use for the development. These factors include the scale of the application, the need to publish to the same information in non-hypermedia formats, the level of developer expertise, and the risk or uncertainty associated with the project. We will consider the implications of each of these factors in turn.

Development timeframes

One of the most significant issues affecting the development process is the rapid rate of change of technologies associated with hypermedia (such as the Web), and (in some cases) commercial imperatives to rapidly develop hypermedia applications (such as obtaining a Web presence). This will often mean that the development process must be such that outcomes are achieved particularly rapidly (unfortunately, even at the expense of application quality, functionality, or completeness).

Application scale

With small-scale applications a formal development process will be unnecessary, as it is possible for a single developer to understand all aspects of the development and manage them informally. However as the project scale increases, the ability to manage the project effectively without some form of formal guidance diminishes. An important question is thus at what point does a formal development process become necessary? A useful benchmark is that, once a project involves more than a few people, it is certain to be large enough to benefit from a formal development process. This will ensure that each person involved has defined responsibilities, and that all appropriate elements of the development are considered.

This last point provides us with a guideline for determining the scope of the formal process adopted (as distinct form leaving elements of the process informal). Where it is evident that aspects of development can be handled informally, these can be removed from the formal process. As a simple example, a very large scale, full lifecycle process would incorporate a comprehensive analysis of expected development costs. In a smaller project (which is still sufficiently complex to warrant a formal process), in a well established area with which the developers have significant experience, the costing may be sufficiently obvious as to be undertaken informally. Nevertheless, it is important to bear in mind that considerable care needs to be taken in assuming that aspects of the process are sufficiently obvious or simple to not require formalism.

In practice, the scope of the formal process model adopted will be a trade-off between the cost of formalising the process and the risk of problems arising in the development as a result of aspects which have been overlooked.

Provision of information in multiple forms

In many cases, the development of a hypermedia application (or applications) will exist in parallel with the need to deliver the information in other forms. As an example, with the *HyperBank* system, it is proposed to provide advertising information to potential customers via a Web interface. The provision of this information through the Web will not remove the need for this information to also be distributed in more conventional forms (such as paper-based advertising brochures). Where we must deliver material in multiple forms, our development process must consider the requirements or constraints imposed by these various forms. As a trivial case in point, standard practice for producing conventional advertising material may require storyboarding and iterative refinement of these storyboards. The development of the advertising material for the Web applications must either work within this framework or adapt it in a way which is still acceptable.

Level of developer expertise

The level of developer expertise will have a major impact on the development process adopted. The most obvious example is where the developer expertise is limited (either in terms of general development experience or familiarity with the specific problem domain); then there is an increased risk associated with the development, and as a result, a formal development process to guide the development becomes more important.

Project uncertainty

In many cases, a project will have an inherent risk or uncertainty associated with it, perhaps because it is in a domain which is unusual or not well understood, because the user reaction to the new technology or approach is uncertain, because the potential benefits have not yet become apparent, or because the requirements are fluid (often due to the level of the client's unfamiliarity with what is possible or desirable). In each of these cases, we can identify specific ways of adapting the process to handle the risk or uncertainty. For example, if we are uncertain of the system requirements (and aware that they are likely to evolve as we become more familiar with the systems), then we can adopt a process which supports iterative development of the application.

Waterfall Model of Development

Having provided the above background on issues and factors which impact on the development process, we can now begin by looking at the specific practicalities of selection and/or adaptation of a development process. Obviously, in beginning a hypermedia development project, we must select a suitable process to give form to the development. The simplest hypermedia development process model is the waterfall model. We can begin by considering this as a template for a possible development process, and then look at how it fails to address certain aspects, and how we might modify it to better suit given projects.

The waterfall model is a simple process model widely used in software engineering. It is called the waterfall model because it is like water falling from top to the bottom without any feedback from the lower phases to phases that took place earlier (Figure 7-4). Although this is not a specifically hypermedia-focused model it does provide an indication of the typical phases of development which may be appropriate.

The overall structure of the waterfall model is a single sequence of phases with minimal (if any) recognised feedback between the processes. It is assumed that each phase of the development is carried out in a way which ensures that the outcomes of each phase are complete and correct, and will not be affected by information or insights gained later in the development process. The actual phases describe the broad intention of a large group of activities. However, the specific activities will depend upon the actual application being developed. Having identified a process

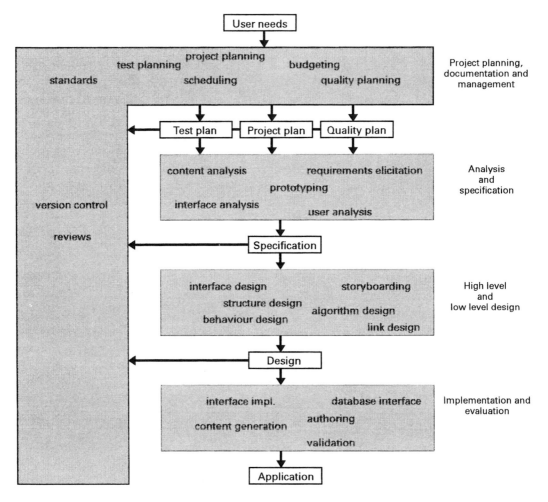

Figure 7-4

Basic structure of the waterfall model of the hypermedia development process with typical activities for each phase

model, we can then 'populate' the phases of this process with appropriate activities (Appendix 2 gives a collection of typical activities).

Waterfall model phases, activities and deliverables

If we use the waterfall model, development of a hypermedia application starts with a concept or an initial user problem statement which is then analysed to establish a detailed application specification. The technical and economical feasibility of the application should also be analysed and established during this analysis phase. The specification will include an outline of the information required, intended audiences, purpose of the application, and specific functional and non-functional requirements (an example of the contents and structure of a requirements specification, in the form of a document template, is given in Appendix 3).

The next development phase is the application design. The input to this phase is the system specification, and the output is a detailed design, including aspects such as detailed information content and structure, the application architecture and required hardware/software components and interfaces, access, indexing and searching mechanisms, application user interfaces and both general and specific look and feel, etc. The output may be presented as diagrams showing the information linking structure, reports describing various access mechanisms, storyboards or prototypes showing overall look and feel, and user interfaces, guidelines and house styles, in terms of a report and examples on content creation.

Production covers the conversion of the application from a design specification into an actual product. We can identify various activities within the production development phase, including content generation, authoring, publishing, and final production and delivery.

Content generation involves the capture or creation of the underlying data to be used within the application. This data will be in a variety of media (including text, audio, music, speech, graphics, animations, images, video, etc.). For new content we either need to capture this in an analogue form (such as video recording scenes) and then digitise the data, or generate the information directly in a suitable digital form (such as using animation software). Either case requires specific activities and skills. For example, generating analogue video might (depending on the desired quality) require the full range of skills normally associated with video production. If we are converting existing legacy data into a suitable format, we might need to look at the use of tools which can parse the legacy data and convert it into a suitable format for use within the application. Also, with both new and legacy data, we may need to undertake appropriate editing or reformatting of the content. For example, we may wish to edit image files to modify the background or analyse audio files to segment them into specific sequences.

Authoring covers those aspects of the development process where the content is mapped into the desired structure and the actual application is constructed. The information needs to be structured in a way that supports the forms of interaction and access needed for the application as strongly as possible. Publishing covers the development of the presentation techniques for the structured information (such as user interfaces, functional components, system integration, etc.), and results in a final system. Authoring and publishing are the two activities directly involved in manipulating the information. Final production and/or delivery covers those elements required for commercial utilisation of the system (such as mastering, advertising and distributing CD-ROMs).

To demonstrate the above phases, consider a scenario where we have an architectural firm which provides small scale services to private home builders. This company wishes to add to their existing Website a system to allow registered customers to 'build' and investigate three dimensional models of houses (using architectural information on house structures, furniture, etc. in an existing database), while allowing the user to follow automatic links from any element of the model to related information. We can identify a number of appropriate activities to include in our waterfall model. First, the structure of the information is relatively simple: most of the complexity of the application arises from the underlying functionality rather than the information structure. Other useful points to note (most of which would have become apparent from the initial domain analysis) are: the interface design is critical, but constrained by the existing application; the interfaces to existing systems (such as the modelling database) are important; the users are likely to already be well understood; the requirements of the system are quite straightforward and are unlikely to evolve significantly; maintenance of the system is quite simple and will mainly involve modifications and updates to the modelling database (which already occurs as part of the normal company operating procedure, and therefore does not need to be considered within the scope of this project). If we adopt a waterfall process model, we can select suitable activities based on the above considerations.

Problems with the waterfall model

While the waterfall model is a useful starting point in terms of developing a process model, it has a number of significant deficiencies which limit its appropriateness. We usually have to modify or adapt it to make a process that is more suitable to specific hypermedia development projects.

The most significant limitation is that it does not take into account the fact that we often gain insights later in the development process which impact on earlier phases. As a simple example, if we make a mistake in analysing the information the application requires, but do not identify this mistake until we start capturing content, then the waterfall model gives us no indication of how we can handle this situation. In other words, we need to explicitly consider the need for feedback between the development phases, or iteration around them.

Another problem with the waterfall model is that no usable application is produced until very late in the development process. Unfortunately, with projects which are ill-defined or poorly understood (which includes most hypermedia applications – at least during the initial problem formulation), the use of a working product in evaluating needs is often an important step. With the waterfall model this does not occur until very late in the development process.

Other problems with the waterfall model include general inflexibility, lack of consideration of the concurrent nature of much of the development, lack of consideration of risk, and poor involvement of the client and/or user in the process.

We have recognised that we can use the basic waterfall model as a starting point, but that it has limitations which mean that it needs to be adapted. From here we can look at how these limitations can be handled in terms of alternative or adapted processes. To do this, we shall look at each of the main problems given above, and then consider the implications of that problem and how it might be addressed.

Process Feedback

The waterfall model provides a useful structure, but one which is very inflexible. It provides no indication of how to handle unusual or unexpected situations (such as the loss of key development personnel). Similarly, if it is discovered that the process is not providing the required results (such as a schedule over-run), then the waterfall model provides no guidance on how this can be addressed. Indeed, the basic waterfall model simply assumes that the development process always progresses in an orderly fashion from project initiation to project completion with *no* deviation from the standard pattern.

The simplest way to address the inflexibility of the waterfall model is to explicitly introduce various feedback paths into the development process, and to recognise the need for these paths. This implies more than just adding a few lines indicating feedback paths to the waterfall process model; it needs to include an understanding of the implications of these feedback paths, when feedback is appropriate, and how it should be managed. This feedback mechanism will often be formalised using some form of change management, a simple example of which would be to allow iteration through the process only in response to documented problems. The documentation should include analysis of the problem, identification of the causes, and consideration of the implications for the project plan.

Systems and software engineering process models use the concepts of *problem/change reports* (which document identified problems that cannot be handled within the basic process framework) and *engineering change proposals* which document the need for changes that require a return to an earlier development stage. The development plan can identify specific formats for these documents and procedures for handling them.

It is also worth pointing out, that once we have introduced feedback and iteration into the process, we will run into the problem of configuration management. We may obtain many different versions of the various artifacts generated during the development process; we need to consider how these versions are managed, and ensure that we have suitable procedures in place for ensuring consistency within related documents and other deliverables.

The extent to which we need to model feedback within our identified process will depend upon the extent to which we are likely to be able manage the feedback informally. If we have a small scale project involving few developers, and in particular a single layer of project management (i.e. a single person who understands the entire development project and its activities and status, and has relatively direct control of the entire process), then formal modelling of the feedback mechanism and procedures for managing it may be unnecessary. Indeed, the cost of this is likely to be completely inappropriate.

However, when a development project grows beyond the level of a single person having a day-to-day understanding of the total project status and management, then formal procedures for managing the feedback within the process become more important. This will be especially true where the communication channels between various members of the development team are awkward, uncertain or blurred. For example, consider the situation where a programmer discovers a problem during the implementation of a search engine, which means that a particular requirement (such as the speed of searching) cannot be met. This may require a return to the requirements analysis, and a subsequent change in the application specification. If care is not taken, other members of the development team may not be made aware of these changes, and their implications not adequately considered.

Prototyping and Incremental Development

A significant problem with the conventional waterfall model is that the linearity of the development results in a failure to provide early feedback on the development. This has two main implications: first, hypermedia development projects are often carried out in circumstances of a lack of expertise, rapidly changing technology, and uncertain goals, which means that the feasibility of the overall project, or certain aspects of the application (such as given requirements, or a particular design approach) cannot be reliably ascertained without progressing further along the development path. In such a situation we will often find a need to backtrack a substantial distance in the development, because of insights gained later in the development.

The second implication is related to the first. Many hypermedia applications have uncertain initial requirements (for a variety of reasons, but including a lack of familiarity with both what is technically possible and with what users are likely to accept or desire). This understanding of requirements can often only be improved by providing example applications or sample solutions to the clients or users, and evaluating their response to these systems. Unfortunately, the linearity of the waterfall model means that demonstrable applications only appear very late in the development process, when it may be difficult (because of cost or time constraints) to make major application changes.

The most obvious solution to the above problems is to modify the process model so that we either develop the application incrementally or use prototyping. Incremental development essentially implies the development of successive components (or increments) of the system. Each iteration of the development can be carried out using a waterfall-like process, with possible variations as discussed in the following sections. This also implies an activity within the project planning which identifies suitable product increments (Figure 7-5). At the beginning of each increment, both the system plan and system requirements specification can be refined based on the feedback from previous increments.

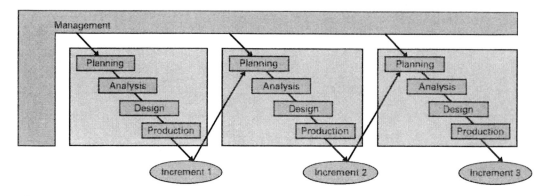

Figure 7-5

Incremental development process model

With prototyping we rapidly develop minimalist applications as a vehicle for enabling developers, clients or users to evaluate aspects of potential solution applications (see Figure 7-6). The prototypes can be developed using specific prototyping tools or tools which are effective for small-scale systems such as screen-based tools. The building of the prototypes will involve aspects of design and production based on initial (possibly ambiguous or incomplete requirements), and then subsequent evaluation of the prototype to assist in refinement of the specification or design approach. Although superficially similar to an incremental development, this is fundamentally quite different. In this process we have a number of development iterations, but each iteration produces a final (possibly incomplete) product which can be evaluated to gain further insights for the next level of refinement.

Typically, a prototype will be used to ensure that the developer understands the requirements developed at the beginning of the project. The prototype will be superficially equivalent to the final product, but is likely to lack aspects such as valid underlying functionality, error checking, comprehensive documentation, etc. Results from the prototype can be used to refine or correct requirements, and in this respect it is particularly useful for evaluating user interfaces. With both prototyping and iterative refinement, care needs to be taken that each iteration does indeed move the project towards closure. A common problem with many current hypermedia development projects is ongoing and unbounded modifications resulting from an inability to determine the true nature of an application.

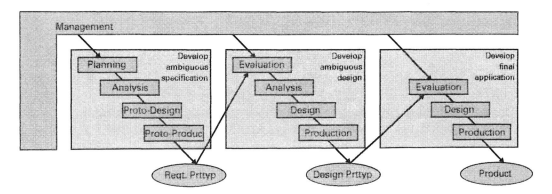

Figure 7-6

Prototyping process model

Incremental development and prototyping will often be most appropriate where the requirements of the application are not initially well understood, and especially where similar applications or applications in a similar domain do not exist. In these circumstances, it will be particularly difficult to ensure that initial understanding of the problem and subsequent application requirements specification will correctly reflect a valid solution. Prototyping ensures that we have a mechanism for understanding the problem and possible solutions before we have committed unnecessary resources to an unprofitable development path.

An incremental development approach is particularly appropriate in a situation where clients (or project management) require a regular indication of development progress. The delivery of project increments provides a valuable (though often abused) mechanism for measuring development progress, and possibly provides a basis for progress-based development contract payments.

Handling of Risk

Hypermedia development projects will regularly need to address issues of risk. Hypermedia technologies are changing rapidly, skills are often lacking or inappropriate, tools are ineffective or inappropriate, problem domains are often poorly understood, and budgets may be uncertain. All of these factors can contribute to potential problems in the development process, including both financial (either timescale or budget overruns) and technical failures. An effective process should acknowledge that these risks exist, and take steps to manage the risks appropriately.

Certain risks can be handled relatively simply within existing process models by the introduction of activities aimed at identifying and containing risks. As a simple example, risks associated with a lack of development skills can be minimised through the introduction of suitable training schemes. Risks associated with changing technologies can be minimised by using designs which are flexible and evolvable. Section 6 of Appendix 3 provides a list of a number of possible risks, and the strategies which can be introduced to manage these risks.

Apart from the introduction of specific risk management activities, we can also adapt the process as a whole in a way which facilitates risk management. Some of the process modifications or variations discussed above (such as prototyping and iterative development) can contribute significantly to managing risks. Another approach which has been widely adopted within the software engineering discipline is to use a process model which explicitly incorporates risk management.

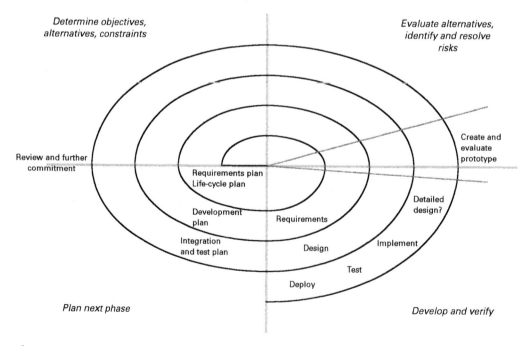

Figure 7-7

The spiral development process

The Spiral model, shown in Figure 7-7, was originally proposed by Barry Boehm (1988). The motivation was the lack of any substantial form of risk analysis in conventional software development process models. In the spiral model there are four distinct cycles of development: concept, requirements, design and implementation. Each cycle involves essentially the same four activities (though performed in a progressively more complete and detailed way). These activities (shown as the four quadrants of the figure) cover determination of objectives and constraints, evaluation of alternatives and resolution of possible risks, development and verification, and planning for the next cycle.

In the first development cycle, the concept cycle, the overall objectives of the project are identified, and then possible alternative approaches to generating a solution are proposed and evaluated as a mechanism for ascertaining the risks associated with the development. The second cycle focuses on generating a complete specification of the system. Initially, the objectives are re-evaluated and another risk analysis is performed, which can be supported by the creation of suitable prototypes, simulations, etc. The third stage of development performs the design of the system. Again, the objectives, alternatives and constraints are evaluated, and all risks again addressed. A high-level design is then generated and validated, followed by planning for the last cycle of development. The final cycle covers the detailed design, implementation and validation of the actual product.

Although the Spiral model provides a process which actively addresses risk analysis, it suffers from two main problems. First, for small projects it introduces large and unnecessary overheads, though this can be addressed by appropriate adaptation of the model. Secondly, the project does not handle the issues of maintenance well. It is not handled explicitly by the model, and it is not simple to determine where the model should be entered if a modification is to be made.

In general, because of the rapidly changing and poorly understood nature of much of hypermedia and the issues which affect it, hypermedia development projects are particularly susceptible to significant risks. Managing these risks can be an expensive process, especially in a commercial environment which has not yet developed effective mechanisms for allowing clients to evaluate developers processes. The risk management strategy is built into the spiral model at a fundamental level, making it appropriate for high-risk or critical projects. Examples of projects where risk management is likely to be critically important include commercial systems where the application provides a key element of a company's strategy, especially in comparison to possible competition. For example, a bank which is using hypermedia technology in migrating its business from a physical, branch-based customer interface to electronic business has the potential to damage its entire business if possible applications do not provide the desired quality.

Example

Let us briefly look at what might be an appropriate process model for the development of the *HyperBank* system. The project management team begin by considering factors which affect the development process. First, and most obviously, the project is very large scale. The scope of the application(s) being developed is significant. As such, the project is likely to require a comprehensive process (and associated planning and project management). Secondly, commercial imperatives mean that the *Hyper-Bank* system needs to be developed and launched as rapidly as possibly. The most obvious implication of this for the development process is that an incremental approach which rapidly creates a minimalist system and then progressively expands this is likely to be most effective. Thirdly, a number of factors impact on the risks associated with the project. Our analysis of the solution domain indicates that the underlying technologies (the Web and associated technologies such as Java and security mechanisms) are evolving rapidly. It is also uncertain as to the extent to which security requirements can be met by current technology. The analysis of the development domain indicates that the *Archaic Banking Organisation* has a severe lack of skills in the development (and in particular, project management) of large hypermedia information systems. There is also concern over possible customer reaction to such a radically different approach to the provision of information and services in the banking industry. All of these factors contribute to a significant degree of risk associated with the project, implying that a development process which manages the risk effectively is required.

Another point is that the requirements of the system are likely to be poorly understood, partly because the technology (and especially its potential in this domain) is not well understood. It is also a result of a lack of understanding with respect to the potential user response to the applications. As a result, prototyping as a mechanism for refining requirements is desirable. The process model we adopt should be able to incorporate some form of prototyping of the specific applications to be developed.

The product model described in the previous section indicates that the development of multiple applications (which may be integrated in some form) which use common information sources is an appropriate product model. This has several significant implications for the process model that we adopt. First, we can view the requirements of the applications we are developing as existing at two levels; the first level will be the overall requirements of the whole system (for example, we may see several requirements as being that from a bank customer's perspective, the applications are seen as an integrated whole, and that security issues are completely transparent). The second level of requirements will be those relating to specific applications such as bank employee access to operating procedures and customer access to account information. These two levels of requirements do not necessarily need to be captured at the same time. However, it is recognised that there is likely to be a large degree if interaction between the different applications, and so that if they are to be developed separately, then mechanisms need to be in place to revisit and refine previously developed sections of the overall system, i.e. a degree of iterative development.

Another aspect related to the product model and its use of individual applications is that this implies that an incremental development approach is possible. In other words, the application structure shown in Figure 7-3 allows individual components of the system to be developed almost independently once the broad structure is developed. For example, the initial development could focus on the overall requirements of the project, then the development of the high level architecture, and then creation of an *ABO* Website which provides both basic customer information and a starting point for a number of other system components. This could be followed by the development of those elements required for customer access to account information, then interactive customer operations (such as payments, account transfers, etc.), then support for tellers in their daily operations, etc.

At this point, the above observations may appear to indicate that we have simply said that the process model should manage risk, include prototyping, and be incremental and iterative, i.e. almost all possible process model combinations! However, careful consideration shows that even though we are incorporating numerous process model structures, they are being combined (indeed, need to be combined) in a very deliberate way.

Figure 7-8 demonstrates the high level structure of the process model being developed. Note the incorporation of two levels of process – the top level is the development of the overall system (the base Web appli-

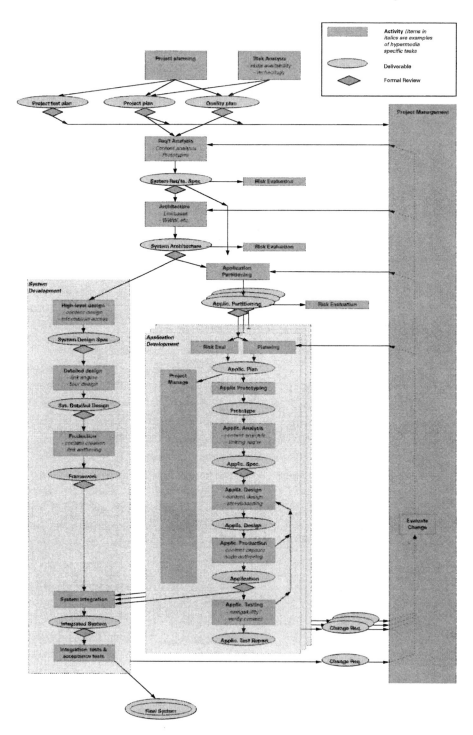

cation framework, which might, for example, involve the development of the basic information management structures, and the basic *HyperBank* homepages). The top level of process incorporates suitable risk management, within which we have a second level focusing on the incremental development of specific applications that fit within the higher level architecture (such as the development of an account access application for use by bank account holders).

It is important to note that the process shown in Figure 7-8 is only the initial consideration of the process. In practice, we need to refine this to a much greater level of detail, determining the specific detailed activities, outcomes and deliverables, etc.

7.5   Project Planning and Management

Project Planning

The above discussions on product models (or hypermedia paradigms) and process models provide us with a framework for visualising the application and its development. However, this will only be useful if we have a mechanism for actually guiding the development. This is provided by the development plan (or plans): we can visualise the development plan as an instantiation of the process which we are adopting.

The purpose of project planning is to provide guidance and control of the development project. It should assist the project managers in understanding what needs to be performed in order for the project to achieve the desired results. The plan, in essence, is a baseline which is used to control the project, and as such, the plan will be used as a working document which will evolve with the project. It will tell the development team what must be done, when it must be done by, and who is responsible for various activities.

For the plan to be effective it needs to cover a broad range of material, obviously including specific activities (and explanations and justifications of these activities). It will also include the process framework within which

Figure 7-8

An example process model for the development of the HyperBank applications these activities exist. It is this framework which lets us understand how the various activities interact and interrelate. The plan will also cover general project management aspects of the development such as roles and levels of responsibilities. Other aspects include time, budget and resource estimates to be used in allocation of resources for the process. Identification of risks is also important, allowing these risks to be managed or addressed. A plan will also cover formats or standards which should be adhered to, and procedures for handling aspects of the development (such as managing different versions of the applications to be developed).

All of the above aspects should usually be formalised as a project plan document. An example of the structure (and hence the content) of a typical application development plan is given in Appendix 3. In many cases (including the example given in the appendix), we will choose to partition the plan to make it simpler to handle. This will be dependant largely on the specific scope of the project, and the people involved. A common example is the separation of the quality aspects of the development, resulting in the separate development of a quality management plan covering aspects such as reviews and audits, traceability of the development process, and reporting procedures and standards.

It is important to remember that the development plan is intended to be an aid and not a constraint. As such, it may be appropriate for the plan to evolve with the development process. This is not an excuse to ignore aspects of the development in the initial planning, simply a recognition of the dynamic nature of development practices.

Hypermedia-specific aspects of planning

A significant point is that the hypermedia-specific aspects of the planning (such as planning activities like identification of content, information structuring, design of link handling mechanisms, etc.) are particularly critical. Whereas conventional aspects such as project and personnel management are typically well understood, expertise with the hypermedia specific aspects of projects are usually much lower, they warrant special attention.

Examples of hypermedia-specific activities and issues include:

- Selection of a suitable hypermedia product model.
- Requirements analysis activities such as required information content, relationships with existing systems (and hence linking to these), and required navigation and searching behaviour.

- Design activities such as the creation of a system architecture, design of suitable information management strategies, design of the link structure and navigation behaviour.

- Production activities such as capturing and manipulation of content, development of user interfaces, and especially mechanisms for interacting with the information structure (such as how anchors are presented to the user and how the user differentiates between different link types).

- Mechanisms for managing the cognitive burden associated with the development process, such as partitioning of the information space.

- Mechanisms for handling ongoing changes in the underlying information base.

Project Management

What is project management? It is those activities which are not focused so much on the application development as on those activities which ensure that the project proceeds appropriately. This might include things like planning itself, guiding the development, assigning resources, controlling the development pace, evaluating progress and results, refining the procedures, etc.

The project management activities will often be carried out by the project manager. Again, this is not intended to be a trite observation; many development projects (in all domains, not just hypermedia) fail because there is not a clear indication of who is responsible for managing various aspects of the project. Project management typically requires the most sophisticated skills (though in one sense less obviously technical) of any aspect of the development. It requires a deep understanding of development costs and resources, project sizing, personnel management, and techniques for evaluating progress.

There are a few tools which can be effectively used in project management. The most common, tools such as GANTT charts, are simply used for documenting activities, resources, critical paths through given activities, etc. These tools are well established and well understood within other domains, though little attention has been focused on their application to hypermedia development.

Work Breakdown and Scheduling

One of the most difficult aspects of managing a development project is identifying the activities which must be performed, and how these activities are combined and managed. This is often represented as a Work Breakdown Structure (WBS). In developing a WBS, we are in essence trying to achieve three things: first, we need to know what actual elements of work must be carried out; secondly, we need to estimate the effort and resources required for each of these elements of work; and thirdly, we need to consider the structuring of these activities or work elements into a cohesive pattern.

Identifying tasks

The main sources of information for identifying tasks which must be carried out include the results from our domain analysis and the selection of process and product models, lists of possible activities which might need to be considered (such as that in Appendix 2), and experience. There are many approaches which can be used to formalise the identification of tasks, but one of the most common is to use a hierarchical decomposition of the activities, guided at the highest level by the process model that has been selected. For example, if we have adopted a basic waterfall approach, we will decompose or work into analysis, design, etc. Design may be decomposed into interface design, link design, database design, etc. Link design may incorporate information structuring, associative link design, link databased design, etc.

The result is a (well documented) hierarchical set of activities to be carried out. The depth of the hierarchy will depend upon the scope of the project and the experience of those who will be carrying out the activities. For each task we usually need to consider the purpose, inputs, outputs, skills and resources, and it may be considered appropriate (depending on the scale and scope of the project) to document this using a standard template. Care needs to be exercised that unfamiliarity with hypermedia development (and familiarity with other domains) does not skew the planning process.

Estimating effort

Having identified the specific activities which need to be carried out, we can effectively plan them to be carried out only if reasonably reliable estimates of the effort each will require can be made. This can be incredibly difficult without considerable experience, and is often one of the main risks associated with planning a hypermedia development project. With hypermedia development, the largest development cost will usually be time (i.e. personnel) costs. If labour is such as large part of the cost, and so important in being able to plan the process, then we need to consider mechanisms for estimating effort required for various activities.

Although tools, techniques and metrics have begin to evolve in other domains, these have not yet appeared in a mature or reliable form for hypermedia. For example, in software engineering, techniques such as function point analysis allow reasonably reliable estimates of the size of a project to be obtained (based on consideration of the expected system functionality in conjunction with other project specific information), from which effort estimates can then be derived. Similar metrics do not exist for hypermedia development aspects such as information generation, information structuring, link authoring, application maintenance, etc.

Insufficient research and experience exists within hypermedia for these types of tools to have yet been developed. Indeed, we would see this as a particularly valuable area of ongoing commercially relevant research. In the absence of effective guidelines or effort metrics, great care needs to be exercised. Measures such as the expected amount of content and the number of pages which we *expect* the application to contain can be *very* misleading (and often cannot be reliably known until design time).

Without further research and work in this area, the best we can reliably say at this stage is several of our own observations. First, in the planning for any development project we need to recognise that our effort estimates are likely to have wild fluctuations, and that this should be taken into account in considering the task scheduling (especially with respect to critical paths through the development) and budgeting. Secondly, in adopting a process model, we can select those models which best handle risks associated with poor effort estimates. Thirdly, where possible when estimating efforts, we should always attempt to use multiple independent methods as a cross-check, and do our best to validate the efforts with technical or domain experts (such as checking video editing time estimates with those who will be carrying out the editing).

Finally, we should try to ensure that we have in place procedures to learn from experience – such as documenting development efforts correlated against appropriate project characteristics. Possible sources of correlation might include the number of clients, number of users, sophistication of clients and users, breadth of information, domain of the problem, level of desired functionality, and the underlying technologies.

Task scheduling

Once we have a list of activities and effort estimates for these activities, we can consider task scheduling. The specific structure (and flexibility) of this scheduling will depend upon the particular process model used.

We can use conventional project scheduling tools (such as GANTT charts or PERT diagrams) to schedule the tasks. Other factors we may need to consider will be the identification of important milestones (such as completion of critical activities or delivery of a given outcome), checking of the critical development path, and the balance of resources (including personnel) between parallel tasks.

Risk Management

Within the current environment of rapid changing technologies and lack of hypermedia development expertise, most (if not all) large scale hypermedia development projects will be inherently risky. As such, it is important that we plan to acknowledge and manage these risks. In a previous section we considered the role that a process model can play in contributing to providing a framework for handling risks. Beyond this, however, there will be a number of other areas worth considering.

First, if we are to manage the risks, we need to begin by identifying possible risks. Examples include loss of critical personnel and skills, unrealistic schedules, unrealistic budgets, development of incorrect content, structure, functionality or presentation, constantly changing requirements, failure of external components or subcontractors, changing technology and performance shortfalls. Specific details of these possible risks are given in Appendix 3. The actual risks (and the severity of the risk) will very much be project-specific. In identifying the potential risks, we need to consider the impacts of the risk on the project.

Once we know what our risks are, we can plan to manage them. This planning can take two forms: planning to avoid the risk, and planning for risk contingency. In the first case, we identify ways to minimise the likelihood of the risk occurring, e.g. we can reduce the risk of losing key personnel by using team building or putting in place appropriate personnel agreements. In the second case, we look at what happens if the risk occurs and how we can manage the situation. As an example, if we are contracting for a project we could include a caveat to the contract which enables delivery extensions to be negotiated if key personnel are lost during the development. Appendix 3 also includes possible techniques for managing the more common risks.

In general, with our planning we wish to explicitly identify the risks, and document the procedures for handling these risks at a stage when we are in a position to be able to do something effective.

Quality Assurance

A final aspect of project planning is those elements which relate to the overall process and application quality. Let us begin by considering the issue of 'quality'. What exactly is 'quality'? In Section 4.1 we considered this question, and stated that we could consider a 'quality' application to be one which has the optimal combination of desired attributes balanced against the cost of achieving these attributes. Similarly, in Chapter 4 we defined a quality process as one which maximises our ability to achieve these goals – our ability to both develop a quality application and to do this development in the most effective and efficient manner possible.

Some aspects of a quality process considered in Chapter 4 were appropriateness and correctness, the ability to focus the attention of the development effort, ensuring that we obtain feedback on the development progress at appropriate times, and that the process should be repeatable, measurable and flexible.

In planning the overall development process, we ideally wish to consider all of these aspects, and how we can effectively embed them into the process we are carrying out. Often, this will be achieved through the creation of a separate quality plan (or possibly a section of the main project plan) which is aimed at ensuring quality in the process.

Such a plan will cover aspects such as roles, activities, standards, guidelines and checklists – all of which contribute to the characteristics mentioned above. In Appendix 3 we have given a template for a quality plan, showing the typical coverage of such a plan. Essentially, what we are trying to achieve is guidelines and procedures for ensuring that quality is embedded into the process (rather than being tacked on as an afterthought).

To a large extent, the example structure of the quality plan speaks for itself. The only substantial point worth making is that an effective approach to managing the quality of the development process will often rely on an appropriate evaluation of the process. This can in turn be achieved through suitable audits and reviews of procedures and documents associated with the process (such as the development plan), and the adherence to the procedures and documents during the course of the development.

Example

In previous sections we developed specific product and process models for the *HyperBank* system. The plan for the development of *HyperBank* will effectively be the formalisation and instantiation of these models. The full development plans for a system as large as *HyperBank* would normally be expected to be large documents in their own right, and it is impractical to demonstrate full plans here. Nevertheless, we can consider certain aspects of them. It is worth noting that the process model for the development of *HyperBank* involved the development of the main application structure, and then the incremental development of specific sub-applications within this structure. As such, the development plan shown here is only for the overall application structure.

First, given the scope and size of the project, it is deemed appropriate to develop both a project development plan and a quality management plan for the project. The project management plan should provide the basis for guiding the overall development process. If we adopt a structure as shown by the template in Appendix 3, then the document might begin as follows:

Section 1: Scope

Section 1.1: Identification
This document defines the project management planning for the system to be known as *HyperBank* being developed for the *Archaic Banking Organisation*. This is document number *ABO-HB-PMP* version 0.0a (pre-release draft).

Section 1.2: Background
The *ABO* management has been influenced by the current hype about the Internet, Intranets, the information superhighway and the World Wide Web, and a fear that they might be left behind in the race to adopt these technologies. An internal report (reference ABO-IR-97/065a) had two major

recommendations. The first is that Web technologies . . . [*more details providing the overall context*]

Section 1.3: Scope
This documents defines the project management planning for the entire *HyperBank* system. This extends from initial planning to final delivery, training and maintenance. . . . [*more details on the specific scope of this document*]
Section 2 of the plan would detail specific references, terminology and abbreviations. This information provides a reference point for standardising the language used within the document, and the related sources of information.

Section 2: References, Terminology, Abbreviations

Section 2.1: References
This document references the following information. Where there is a conflict, this document should take precedence:
Ref ABO-SBOP) (version 3.7.8b, 4/May/1997): *ABO* Standard Branch Operating Procedures (this document details . . . }
. . . [*more details on all referenced documents*]

Section 2.2: Terminology
. . .

Section 2.3: Abbreviations
ABO: *Archaic Banking Organisation*
. . .

The third section of the plan provides an English language description of the system to be developed. In essence, this is an extended version of the problem statement provided by the client, and provides the detailed context for the development plan. Sections 4 and 5 of this plan would detail the outcomes and justifications of the product and process models selected. These will both need to be quite detailed.

The core of the plan are sections 6 (work breakdown), 7 (scheduling), 8 (resourcing) and 9 (risk management). In section 6 of the plan we identify, based on our detailed process model, the specific activities to be carried out and the procedures to be used. For example:

Section 6: Work Breakdown

Section 6.1: Overview

...

Section 6.7: Application Design

...

Section 6.7.8: Task: Content Design – Sub-task: High-Level Content Structuring
> 6.7.8.1: Task description
>> This activity involves the creation of the top-level structure to be used to organise the information contained within the *HyperBank* applications. The purpose of this task is to ...
>> The scope covers ...
>
> 6.7.8.1: Task inputs:
>> The inputs to this task are the user profiles (reference ABO-SBOP), the expected information content (reference ABO-HBIC), the ...
>
> 6.7.8.3: Task outputs:
>> The sole output from this task is a documented structure of the information space. This will take the form of a RMM Entity Relationship diagram ...
>
> 6.7.8.4: Task reviews:
>> ...
>
> 6.7.8.5: Task method and plan:
>> This task shall be carried out using RMM Entity-Relationship Design. This shall be modified to incorporate ...
>
> 6.7.8.6: Task resources:
>> This task will requires the following resources:
>> Personnel: Two hypermedia designers with the following skills: ... Time required: 70 hours for initial design, 10 hours for reviews, 40 hours for refinement, 40 hours for documentation.
>> Client: No time
>> Equipment: Document preparation facilities – 40 hours. Design tools – none currently suitable.
>
> ...

An important point worth noting is that the process model adopted is such that the development of the individual applications within the *HyperBank* system will have their own planning and project management activities which fit within the broader context of the *HyperBank* development plan. The *HyperBank* development plan will, however, include a framework for these sub-plans, including the overall timeframes to which they must adhere.

Section 7 of the plan details the scheduling of the project, which to a large extent, will be a GANTT chart detailing timings, deadlines, milestones and dates for deliverables. Section 8 covers resourcing, and will detail what resources are required, when they are required, whether they are currently available, and procedures for ensuring that they can be procured when necessary. Section 9 of the plan details risk management. In particular, risks are identified and strategies and procedures for managing the risks are specified. For example:

Section 9: Risk Management

. . .

Section 9.4.3: Risk: Potential Loss of Key Personnel
    9.4.3.1: Description:
        A primary major risk is the potential loss of key personnel during the project. These key personnel include . . . Two major strategies for combating this risk is to ensure adequate documentation of the process at all time, and to put in place incentives to retain staff, and ensure that all contracts include appropriate penalty clauses . . .
    9.4.3.2: Procedures
        Procedure 1: The project manager will (during final reviews prior to signing) ensure that all contracts with external parties include a penalty clause aimed at minimising potential loss of key personnel. This clause shall cover the following elements: . . .

Finally, section 10 of the plan covers general project management procedures and guidelines. As mentioned previously, much of this is generic to most development processes.

7.6 Framework for Documentation

Before finishing this chapter it is worth focusing briefly on the issue of documentation. What exactly is 'documentation'? We can view it as both a formal record of outcomes and knowledge, and as a mechanism for communicating these outcomes and knowledge. In both cases, for the documentation to be effective it needs to be comprehensive and precise.

The effort required to produce effective documentation can be considerable. We need to consider whether this effort is justified, and the simplest way to do this is by looking at what we gain from effective documentation, and what we lose by having ineffective or absent documentation. Effective documentation provides us with a way of ensuring that the process is open and understood, and that we understand the process and the results of this process. Documentation provides a record which can be referred to, both to learn from and, more significantly, as a benchmarked and accepted milestone in the development. If this is missing then we risk misinterpreting or losing information gained in the process (such as our own understanding of the requirements of the application being developed).

To manage documentation effectively we need to plan the level and form of the documentation – we need a framework for governing the production of documentation. This framework may be as simple as guidelines (as part of the project plan and/or quality plan) for the production of the documentation and what standards it will adhere to. The guidelines should, as a minimum, cover aspects such as a list of the documents to be produced, expected dates (or as outcomes of certain activities which themselves have specified timeframes), formats, content, scope and responsibilities. Consideration should also be given to configuration management with respect to the documentation (though this is a broader issue which covers all artifacts resulting from the development process).

Requirements documentation is typically aimed at specifying 'what we want' rather than 'how we will create it', and providing sufficient information to the developers so that they can understand unambiguously what is required. This documentation can include aspects such as: context and scope for the project, an analysis of the users, specific constraints on the development process, required content, functional and non-functional requirements of the system to be developed, and project acceptance criteria. The design documentation covers the specifics of *how* the application will be created, including aspects such as the application architecture and structure, specification of the specific content and how it will be organised and accessed, and design of the functional components. Implementation documentation can include aspects such as user guides, installation documentation, and will generally be related to the final implementation. Evaluation documentation will cover aspects such as test plans and procedures, test cases and the results of testing and evaluation.

Example

Very briefly, the following is a minimal list of documents which might be expected to be generated by the *HyperBank* project:

DA   Domain analysis report

PMP   Project management plan

PQP   Project quality plan

HRS   Hypermedia requirements specification

HDS   Hypermedia design specification

HAP   Hypermedia application partitioning

HDD Hypermedia detailed design

And for each application

AMP   Application management plan

ARR   Application risk review

APE   Application prototype evaluation

ARS   Application requirement specification

ADS   Application design specification

ATE   Application evaluation

Review and test documents

RRE   Requirements risk evaluation

SRE   System requirements evaluation

SDE   System design evaluation

STR   System implementation test report

SAT   System acceptance testing

For each of the above documents, the *ABO* development team will have defined the scope, the activities where the document is generated, expected dates of delivery, formats, content and responsibilities. Each document will require an appropriate work standard defining the scope and format of the document. A useful place to start for a number of these standards might be relevant ISO and IEEE software engineering standards. For example, consider the following IEEE standards:

730–1989 IEEE Standard for Software Quality Assurance Plans (ANSI) together with 730.1–1995 IEEE Guide for Software Quality Assurance Planning (ANSI)

828–1990 IEEE Standard for Software Configuration Management Plans (ANSI)

829–1983 (R1991) IEEE Standard for Software Test Documentation (ANSI)

830–1993 IEEE Recommended Practice for Software Requirements Specifications (ANSI)

1008–1987 (R1993) IEEE Standard for Software Unit Testing (ANSI)

1012–1986 (R1992) IEEE Standard for Software Verification and Validation Plans (ANSI)

1016–1987 (R1993) IEEE Recommended Practice for Software Design Descriptions (ANSI)

1016.1–1993 IEEE Guide to Software Design Descriptions (ANSI)

1028–1988 (R1993) IEEE Standard for Software Reviews and Audits

1042–1987 (R1993) IEEE Guide to Software Configuration Management (ANSI)

1058.1–1987 (R1993) IEEE Standard for Software Project Management Plans (ANSI)

1059–1993 IEEE Guide for Software Verification and Validation Plans (ANSI)

1063–1987 (R1993) IEEE Standard for Software User Documentation (ANSI)

1074–1995 IEEE Standard for Developing Software Life Cycle Processes together with 1074.1–1995 IEEE Guide for Developing Software Life Cycle Processes

1219–1992 IEEE Standard for Software Maintenance (ANSI) (1–55937-279–6)

1228–1994 IEEE Standard for Software Safety Plans (ANSI)

1233–1996 IEEE Guide for Developing System Requirements Specifications

We have now shown how a project can be initiated, planned and managed. The next step is to consider the specific development phases for hypermedia applications.

8

Development Methods

'All I know about method is that when I am not working I sometimes think I know something, but when I am working , it is quite clear I know nothing.'

(John Cage, "Lecture on Nothing", Silence (1961))

Chapter Goals

In the previous chapter we looked at the development process in a somewhat abstract sense. In this chapter, we provide an understanding of those activities which can form the components of these processes. The objectives of this chapter are to show that:

- The development stages are not necessarily linear, or even distinct.

- Analysis aims to help us understand the problem, the users, the content, the context, the structure, etc.

- Design takes a set of requirements and converts these into a description of an application which can be created. The critical aspects of design are the information structuring and creation of access mechanisms. Design often makes extensive use of prototyping.

- Application production is typically a relatively mechanistic task (apart from the graphic design elements) but is usually very time consuming.

- Verification of applications is exceedingly important, but poorly understood and often overlooked.

- Maintenance is very important for hypermedia development, but is often ignored during the initial development, resulting in applications which become stale very quickly and are extremely difficult to maintain.

8.1   Introduction

In the previous chapter we looked at how the development process can be planned and managed. The process often begins with some form of domain analysis (involving consideration of the problem, solution and development domains), and the outcome of this analysis is a suitable product model (or a high level architecture for the hypermedia system), a process model, and an instantiation of these into a project management plan and a framework for documentation.

In this chapter we look at the process in general, and various activities that need to be carried out within each phase of the process. Although the specific activities and the arrangement of these activities into a suitable process will vary (depending on aspects such as project scale, risk, timeframes, expertise, etc.), we can still look at how these activities themselves can be carried out. In the previous chapter, the activities in a process model were broadly categorised into system analysis, design and production, as well as verification and testing, delivery and maintenance.

Throughout this chapter we continue to use this organisation, though it should be remembered that this is not a definitive taxonomy, and in many cases, the activities described in this chapter will be arranged into completely different phases, with different dependencies. For example, it is possible for some of these activities to repeat or spread throughout the process model. Verification is a good case in point – often happening at the end of many phases. Also, not all activities need to be in a given process model. During our domain analysis and planning, we only select those activities required to achieve the goals of the hypermedia application that is under construction.

Some of the tasks we have to perform when developing hypermedia applications are similar to tasks in other engineering disciplines, such as systems engineering and software engineering. This is especially true for tasks in the categories of systems analysis, implementation, verification and validation and project management. Thus, we can borrow various well-developed methodologies from these disciplines, and adapt them to suit hypermedia development processes. We begin by considering those activities which typically form part of the analysis phase.

8.2   Analysis

In the previous chapter we discussed domain analysis, which provides us with an understanding of the context within which we will be performing the application development. It does not, however, provide us with an unambiguous (and documented) understanding of the specific application(s) we wish to develop. Without this understanding, we will be unable to undertake the development reliably. The focus of the analysis phase (or analysis activities, where we do not have a defined 'phase' for analysis) is to develop this understanding, and to record the results in a clear, unambiguous, understandable form – typically, some form of application specification.

The specification is a very important document as it describes the client's requirements in detail, and will form the basis for designing the application. The specification forms an important part of any contract document which the developer has with the client. A specification may include (among other things) an overall context for the application, profiles of the users, information requirements, functional and non-functional requirements, development requirements and acceptance criteria. To develop these requirement specifications, we have to carry out activities such as requirements elicitation and analysis, implication analysis, user analysis, boundary analysis, content analysis and constraint analysis.

The specification which results from the analysis activities should cover both the functional and non-functional requirements of the application. Once we have a deeper understanding of the application, we will be able to refine the process model and the project management plan, identify resource requirements more suitably and develop a much more accurate cost estimate.

A failure to carry out the analysis activities or to develop an appropriate specification will have a number of significant ramifications. First, a failure to adequately understand and document the requirements of our application will mean that we are developing an application which may be incorrect, inappropriate, unnecessary, or simply irrelevant. Whichever the case, we are likely to end up with an application which is not what we wanted – having wasted considerable time, money and other resources.

When we try to formulate the requirements for the application which needs to be developed we face many difficulties. A common problem is that the client is not aware of the full capabilities of the hypermedia technology which supports the application. The client may therefore often find it difficult to clearly articulate (or even conceptualise) the requirements.

Another difficulty is that requirements are often derived from an existing environment. When a new application is introduced into this environment the environment itself changes, which in turn changes the requirements. (This can be viewed as a systems development perspective on Heisenberg's uncertainty principle!) Thus, we often find that we cannot come up with the final application requirements in a single monolithic iteration of the analysis phase. We may have to do an initial requirement analysis, develop a prototype, evaluate it together with the client and the users, get their feedback and refine the requirements. We may have to repeat this process within available resources until the client accepts the application described in the requirements document.

Activities

When developing a specification for a hypermedia application we begin by finding out about client requirements. These will be influenced by elements such as available information and the form of this information. The ultimate test for any hypermedia information system is its acceptance by the users. Thus, it is very important during the analysis stage to find out about the users who are going to use the application: user profiles will have a significant influence on the design of the information system. The client requirements analysis, content analysis and user profile analysis may lead us into investigating issues such as implication analysis, cost benefit trade-offs, etc.

We can consider different categories of information which influence the specification of an application (such as information about users, about desired content, etc.). On this basis, we can identify a set of major activities which we may carry out during the analysis:

- Clients requirement analysis.
- Content analysis.
- User analysis.
- Boundary analysis.
- Implication analysis.
- Constraint analysis.
- Feasibility analysis.

It is worth noting that, in many cases, these activities may overlap, or cover similar aspects of the development

Client requirements analysis

The purpose of the client requirements analysis is to fully understand the clients' requirements. This information also forms the basis for other types of analysis that need to be performed. During the clients requirements analysis the developer should aim to find answers to the following questions:

- What is the purpose of the application?
- What is the scope?
- How will it be used?
- Who are the users?
- What content is already available and in what form?
- What content needs to de developed?
- Who can provide the contents?
- What is the available budget?
- What is the envisaged time frame to develop this application?
- What hardware and software resources are available for development and delivery?
- What level of security is required?
- Any other critical factors?

Content and boundary analysis

The purpose of content analysis is to identify what content is required, what content is available, and who are the content experts that can provide any new content that is required. Also, it is useful to establish the structure of the existing content. In boundary analysis we wish to establish the breadth and depth of the information content required for the application. In other words, we need to determine the extent of the information to include.

For example, consider a situation where are developing a WWW-based hypermedia system for a hospital, which supports access to information for patients, visitors, medical staff, etc. The system may interface to an existing hospital database which records current ward and bed numbers for patients, their medical condition, prognosis, etc. We would need to determine what information we wish to provide to each class of user (or possibly what information we are able to provide). For example, it would be unethical to include information on a patient's prognosis on an open-access system, but it may be reasonable to provide information on their room number. Or another example: if we have are developing a hyper-text fiction title, then we may wish to determine the extent of the character development we wish to provide, or the extent and type of information available for each character.

In many cases, the information scope (and structure) will be partially limited by existing content. This content can be available in different forms such as print documents, images, video sound clips, etc. It is important to identify all of these, catalogue them in a structured way, and establish what is required for the application being developed and what can be discarded.

User analysis

The purpose of user analysis is to establish a profile of the users who will be using the application. Irrespective of the quality of certain aspects of the application (such as the resultant system interface or quality of the content), if the users at the end find it difficult to use the application, then the application will not meet its intended goal. Thus, it is very important to accurately profile the user community at the specification stage.

During user analysis, we should determine aspects about the users such as:

- Computer literacy level.
- Language literacy level (i.e. what are their first and second languages?).
- Past experience in using similar applications.
- Cultural background.
- Expectations as to what the application will be doing for them.
- Age range of user population.

Implication analysis

The purpose of the implication analysis is to establish what the implications are when the application is introduced into the environment where it is to be used. For example, to introduce the application it may become necessary to make changes to the existing infrastructure, procedures, management structure, etc. There may be situations where the introduction of a new information application might have a negative impact on some employees in the organisation. For example, if the system is going to result in loss of jobs then it will be very hard to obtain information from this group of employees.

Constraint analysis

The purpose of constraints analysis is to establish any limits that may exist within which the application development should take place. These limits can be in the form of:

- Policy.
- Adherence to particular set of standards.
- Organisational rules and procedures.
- Limitations based on delivery platforms.

Technical feasibility analysis

The purpose of technical feasibility analysis is to establish the technical feasibility of the application requirements. For example, if there is a requirement that the time to get information should be less than 12 seconds and during content analysis it was found that the application will have a number of large video clips, then it may not be possible to meet this requirement using commercially available technology. In such cases, it becomes necessary to revisit the original requirement and consider its appropriateness.

The Application Requirements Specification

The primary outcome of the various analysis activities will be some form of requirements specification. As shown in Figure 8-1, the requirements specification will typically contain:

- A general description of the hypermedia information system.
- Information requirements.
- User profiles.

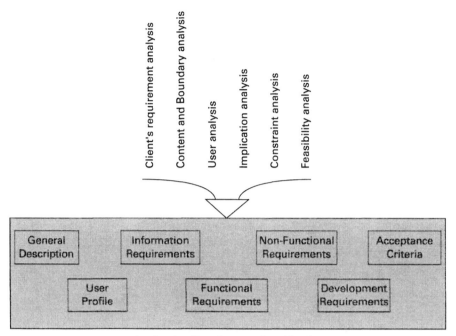

Application Requirement Specification

Figure 8-1

The activity space for the analysis phase covers the elicitation, formulation and validation of requirements from a number of different Information sources

- Functional requirements, such as types of interactivity, search mechanisms, etc.

- Non-functional requirements, such as need to conform to specified standards, etc.

- Acceptance criteria.

The specific structure used to document requirements will vary depending upon the particular type of application being developed. Section A3.3 in Appendix 3 gives an example of the form in which requirements may be formally documented. Irrespective of the specific document form, the final specification should have a number of attributes. These include:

- Correct: we can consider the specification to be correct if it specifies every true requirement for the application to be developed.

- Precise: any requirements given in the specification should be precise, i.e. they need to be quantifiable (such as 'no page of information should take longer than 10 seconds to access' rather than 'access should be quick').

- Unambiguous: every requirement given in the specification should be interpretable in only one way. For example, consider the following specification statement:

  If the user has been using the system for less than 10 minutes and they attempt to access the search engine or they attempt to access the advanced information database then they should be given the following warning . . .

  It is unclear from this statement whether the warning should be provided for a user who has been using the system for longer than 10 minutes and attempts to access the advanced information database. Either interpretation is possible from the above statement – which could be giving the logic *(A and B) or C* or the logic *A and (B or C)*.

- Complete: the specification will be complete if it covers everything pertaining to the application to be developed. Completeness is likely to be one of the most difficult attributes to adequately evaluate.

- Verifiable: every aspect of the specification should be verifiable. There is no point in including a requirement in the specification if we are unable to ascertain whether that requirement exists within the final applcication.

- Consistent: the specification should not contain any internal inconsistencies.

- Modifiable: requirements are notoriously fickle, and are likely to change regularly. The specification should be formulated in a way which allows changes to be made (at least when these changes are appropriate).

- Traceable: a specification can be considered to be traceable if the origin of each requirement is clear (so that we can understand the implications of any proposed changes to the requirements) and expressed in a way which allows us to reference and utilise it appropriately in later documentation or development.

- Version control: a significant difficulty associated with most hypermedia development projects is the evolutionary nature of the hypermedia application. The main elements of this include changes in the users (such as users becoming more familiar with the technology), changes in the requirements (especially a progressive refinement of the current information sources and expansion in the scope which is covered), and changes in the supporting technology (such as the progressive improvement in Web technology). All of these impact regularly on the underlying requirements. Maintaining a consistent set of requirements (which are both self-consistent and consistent with the design and the actual application) is a major difficulty and requires a thorough and careful approach to be adopted.

Example

In developing a specification for the *HyperBank* system we would begin by analysing current practices, interviewing staff, looking at competitors systems, etc. As a starting point, the *HyperBank* client statement identifies two core objectives: to provide a cohesive integrated information management strategy which incorporates a significance presence on the Web; and to use this to support access and use of the *HyperBank*'s diverse information resources.

During the requirements analysis phase, the developer should fully understand these core objectives and expand on them so that when the product is built, it should be possible to trace the requirements to particular features in the product. The first activity within the analysis phase is to interview management to find out more details about these objectives, and to develop them into specific requirements. For example, if you take the first requirement, the developer will need to identify the specific range of information which is needed in the system, how this information is to be utilised, who has access, and who has responsibility for managing the information. It will also include aspects such as detailed profiles of users and any constraints on the system development.

Often in a large organisation, management may not be able to provide answers to all the questions. They may provide an overview and list of people who can provide specific details. The developer then has to obtain the specific information from these people. For this, the developer can use interviews, questionnaires and brainstorming sessions. The information that is obtained needs to be organised into a list of requirements and checked for consistency. Using this information, a requirement specification can be developed.

As an example of the type of material which might be included in the specification, consider the following typical extracts of the *HyperBank* Web Requirements Specification:

Section 1: Introduction
. . .

Section 2: General Description
. . .

Section 3: Users
Section 3.1: The following are the potential users of the *HyperBank* Web
. . .

Section 4: Application Information Requirements

Section 4.1: General Information Access

4.1.1   The primary homepage for the *HyperBank* Web (http://www.hyperbank.com/) shall be targeted at existing and potential users. It shall make no reference to the information specific to internal bank users. Access to this information shall be provided only through a separate . . .

4.1.2   When accessing information through the *HyperBank* Web, all information shall be structured in a way which ensures that it is accessible by following a maximum of 4 hyperlinks.
. . .

Section 4.2: Current Customers
4.2.1   When accessing information through the *HyperBank* Web, current customers shall not be aware of the information sources to which they do not have access. For example, the existence of the online internal bank operating procedures shall not be made evident.
. . .

4.2.5:   Accessible Information: Every current user shall have direct access to the following information:
  – Current Account Information:
  – current account balance
  – previous 12 months of transactions
  – . . .
  – Terms and Conditions of all accounts:
. . .

Section 5: Application Functional Requirements

Section 5.1: Security mechanisms

    5.1.1   All information shall be provided with a security rating, as follows:
- Level 0a: Information access – freely available to all users
- Level 0m: Information modification – freely available to all users
- Level 1a: Information access – freely available to specified user classes
- Level 1m: Information modification – freely available to specified user classes
- Level 2a: Information access – freely available to specified users
- Level 2m: Information modification – freely available to specified users
- Level 3a: Information access – available to registered users
- Level 3m: Information modification– available to registered users
- Level 4a: Information access – available to registered users with authentication
- Level 4m: Information modification – available to registered users with authentication
- Level 5: Not appropriate for transfer across Internet

    5.1.2   To gain access to secure or sensitive information, *HyperBank* customers shall be able to register with *HyperBank*. The registration process shall require the customer to specify the following details:

    – . . .

    5.1.1   Whenever access to secure information is attempted, this access shall be verified by requiring . . .

    . . .

Section 6: Non-Functional Requirements

Section 6.1: Reliability and Availability

    6.1.1   The *HyperBank* Web must be very reliable. It shall have an availability in excess of 99.99% (i.e. less than 1 minute per week downtime) and a mean time between failure (MTBF) of 100 weeks.

Section 6.2: Load

    6.2.1:   The *HyperBank* Web shall incorporate an architecture which enables straightforward extensions to cope with increases in accesses.

    6.2.2:   The *HyperBank* Web shall be able to manage an average load of 2 million accesses per day, and a peak load of 10,000 accesses per minute, with a maximum delay of 10 seconds.

    . . .

8.3   Design

In the design phase the hypermedia application specification gets converted into a description of how to create an application that will meet the specification. The word 'design' in a narrow sense will refer to the specific design of elements of the application, such as designing the link model which we will be using, or the structure of the information database.

If we interpret 'design' in a broader sense then, in addition to the above specific components of the application, design will also cover components not directly impacting on the user's operation of the final application. This could include activities such as platform and environment design, design of installation engines, design of user authentication and activity logging system, and the design of search engines.

It is important to bear in mind that design is a creative process. For any given set of requirements, there will be no single correct solution. For a given specification of an application, different designers will come up with different designs that meet the same specifications. This is similar to designing a house. If we give our requirements to different architects, they will come up with different plans for the house.

Typically, design comes after analysis, but often it may become necessary to do a design based on some initial specification and develop a prototype in order to fully understand the application requirements. As mentioned earlier, clients are often not fully aware of the possibilities and limitations of hypermedia information systems. In such situations, a prototype can greatly assist in addressing this problem.

Prototyping is extensively used within the design activities, as this can help the designers (and clients and users) to visualise different elements and functionalities of the application (such as screen layout), and also to obtain feedback from the clients and users. Figure 8-2 below shows a possible iteration cycle that can be used when designing the application.

The design process itself will encompass two broad areas: application design and design of associated components and systems. Application design encompasses the design of the actual hypermedia application itself (content, access mechanisms, presentation interfaces, etc,). Design of the non-application components includes elements such as design of the hardware used to support the application, design of the installation engine used to install the application, and design of the logging system used to obtain feedback on how the application is used.

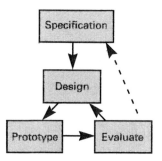

Figure 8-2

Example of iteration of the design activity to include prototyping

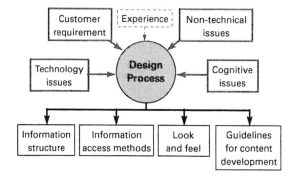

Figure 8-3

Typical inputs to, and output from, the hypermedia design process

As designing is a creative process, previous experience will have a major influence on the final outcome. Figure 8-3 shows various inputs to the application design process and the outcomes from this process. The output of the design phase will typically be a design specification, which will usually consist of components such as reports, prototypes and/or storyboards, and detail the information structure, information access mechanisms, the application's look and feel, and guidelines for development of the content.

There are many other factors (apart from design creativity) which influence the design. These can be broadly classified into:

- Technical issues.
- Cognitive issues.

- Non-technical issues.

The designer should take these factors into consideration (in a creative way!) when developing the design specification based on the system specification.

Technical issues

Currently available technology provides limits as to what can be achieved, and a designer needs to be aware of these limitations. For example, available bandwidth may put a limit to file size that can be accessed within an acceptable time when developing an online system. This in turn may impose limitations on the type of graphics, video and sound which can be used in the application. If the application is to be distributed using a storage medium such as CD ROM or a DVD, then this in turn will enforce a limit to the overall file size.

Another limitation is related to the processing power and capabilities available at the user end. For example, if the computers which the user is going to use to access the information does not have sound capabilities or processing power to decompress and play back a video at the required frame rate, then there is no point using these media type in the application (or scalability needs to be built into the application).

The designer should also be aware of the available tools which can be used to assist during the design and implementation processes, and the capabilities of these tools. These include various authoring tools available for developing a quick prototype during the design phase, databases and search engines which can be used during the implementation phase, etc.

Cognitive issues

Cognitive issues play a very important part in designing hypermedia information systems. The designer should have a good idea about how users will perceive, comprehend and organise information. The designer should also be aware of the specific characteristics of the digital medium and its strengths and weakness. These aspects were discussed in detail in Part One of the book.

Non-technical issues

The designer should be aware of non-technical issues that are appropriate within the overall design context, including issues such as legal, moral, security and authenticity issues. Overall context will include the relevant laws in countries where the application will be used, what is culturally acceptable, implications of a security breach (e.g. sensitive information stored in the application being read by an unauthorised person), etc.

Design Activities

The application design can cover a broad range of tasks (many of which are listed in Appendix 2). However, many of these can be grouped together. We will consider the following activities in some detail:

- Platform and environmental design.
- Content design.
- Information database design.
- Design of access and navigation mechanisms.
- Design of the overall look and feel.
- Developing guidelines for content development.
- Installation engine design.
- Authentication and user activity logging system design.

Platform and environmental design

The development and use of hypermedia applications will require the use of specific development and delivery platforms and associated environments (operating systems, windowing mechanisms, etc.) on these platforms. The specific platforms will be dependant on the particular application domain and the type of solution being developed. Let us consider two extreme examples.

At one end of the spectrum we have a standalone kiosk style application. Such an application will have no keyboard or mouse, a touch-sensitive screen, be rack mounted to hide the hardware from the user (except, of course, for the screen), and will run no applications other than the hypermedia application being developed. At the other end of the spectrum, we have a Web-based application. This type of application will operate via the Internet from a Web server, and must be able to viewed by users having an incredibly diverse range of platforms and operating systems.

In addition to the delivery platform, we also need to consider the platforms used to develop the application. This will include elements such as the media capture hardware (including cameras, microphones, scanners, frame grabbers or video digitisers, video editing tools, etc.), and development tools (such as software development environments).

Though the detailed design and construction of such an environment comes under mechanical, electronic and computer systems engineering, the initial design specification arises within the hypermedia engineering process. Examples of typical knowledge which might be required of someone undertaking specific platform design would include:

- Knowledge of comparative performance of different hardware platforms.
- Skills in hardware and software installation and configuration.
- Skills in network setup and configuration.

Consideration of these elements is beyond the scope of this book. Numerous guides exist on the selection, installation and operation of hardware platforms and environments for these platforms.

Information structure and content design

In this activity we fully specify the required information content and organise it into an appropriate content structure (by 'content structure' we are referring to the organisation of the stored data, not the presentation structure which the user will see). What is important in this stage is to select or develop a structure that will help the developer in capturing the information, and highlight any missing information. The structure should be free of redundancies (i.e. the same information should not appear in more than one place, though it may be *presented* in more than one place). This aspect is very important, especially from an information maintenance viewpoint.

It is important to recognise that at this stage, how users are likely to want to access the information (user viewpoints) is not a consideration. Once all the information has been captured, we will create different sets of navigational structures (and possible presentation structures), one set for each user viewpoint.

The main purpose of content design is to fully capture the data and organise it into a maintainable structure. The granularity of the information nodes in this structure should be such that, when we create different user viewpoints, we should be able to use the information in the nodes without further need for partitioning.

For example, if the information application we develop is about an organisation, then a suitable structure to capture and store the information could be its organisation structure. This will ensure that information about all its divisions and departments gets captured without redundancy. The users may want to access this information, for example, based on various services provided by the organisation. For this, we have to separately develop the various user view points.

Information database design

For any large application it makes sense to store the same types of information together, as this makes it easier to maintain. For example, if one is developing an information system for a university, we can group all staff details together, all course details together, all subject details together, etc. In the information database design, we have to look at an efficient way of storing, accessing and maintaining this information.

There are many types of information database. A simple information database can consist of a set of marked up files, such as a set of HTML files in a Web server. A more complex information database can be a specially designed hypermedia database which supports complex information interlinking. If the information is highly structured, it may be possible to use a relational database to store the information. For a certain type of information structure, object-oriented databases may be more appropriate.

Once we decide how we are going to store the information required for the application, then we have to map the information structure developed earlier into a structure effectively supported by the information database, i.e. which is suited to the storage and maintenance requirements. By now, as we have fully identified the information that needs to be in the application, we can use this as a check list when developing the information database.

There are currently few techniques available to assist in designing the information database, depending on whether information is highly structured, semi-structured or unstructured. The techniques which are applicable are discussed in the next chapter.

Design of access and navigation mechanisms

The success of a hypermedia application finally depends upon its degree of acceptance by the intended users. Thus, during the access and navigation design phase, we have to pay special attention to users' information needs and provide access and navigation mechanisms that will enable different users to quickly and easily find the information for which they are looking.

The design of the mechanisms used to support access to information, and navigation within an information space, can involve a large range of different types of activities. Examples include the design of navigation structures, linking mechanisms, anchor styles, searching mechanisms, etc. We shall look at each of the more significant elements in detail in the next chapter.

Design of the overall look and feel

Design of the 'look and feel' of an application includes aspects such as overall screen layout, interface elements, navigation aids, fonts and colour, and individual screen layout. A very important aspect that needs to be considered when designing the look and feel is the usability of the application. Users will use a hypermedia application to achieve some goal, which could be in a customer support centre to help a customer, or in an education environment to learn about some theory. To achieve the goal we want to minimise the cognitive burden required to learn how to utilise the application. The design of layout and navigational aids should make it as straightforward as possible for a user to identify how specific operations (such as link following) are performed, and what the result of the operation will be (such as where a specific link will lead).

A very common problem is that designers make certain assumptions which they think are obvious, but which are not obvious to the target audience. Getting initial feedback from the target user group at this stage of the design process is vital. A designer must know what looks good and what does not. Also, it is useful to maintain a folder full of examples to inspire further design ideas.

Developing guidelines for content development

Often in large projects, most of the content is created by a team of people during the production stage. Therefore, it is important that the design team develops suitable guidelines for content creation, and this is used by the people who will be creating the content.

These guidelines should include aspects such as how to work out what should be included in a node, the size of the nodes, what labelling and indexing terms need to be added to contents, and information about individual screen layouts. Specific details of approaches will be considered in the next chapter.

Installation engine design

An activity which is often overlooked is the design of suitable installation mechanisms. Although more relevant for standalone applications (such as CD-ROMs) rather than online information systems, it will nevertheless be important in online systems which require the installation of suitable client components (for example, the installation of plug-ins for Web browsers).

Although often only undertaken as a one-off activity, installation is nevertheless very important. It can often be difficult to determine the appropriate installation options given the variability in operating environments, system configurations and other installed software. Typical issues the developer should consider include:

- What form of assistance needs to be provided to the user during the installation process?
- What customisation options to include?
- How to avoid applications from being pirated?
- Whether to provide online help and upgrades.

Design of authentication and logging systems

Some applications may have a requirement that only those users with necessary approval can access the application (or certain parts of the application). Similarly, in some applications it may be necessary or beneficial to keep a track of various activities users carry out when using the application (primarily for security or evaluation purposes). This information can then be used to provide feedback in educational applications, or gather marketing information, etc. Two issues that warrant particular attention are the design of an architecture to support authentication or logging, and obtaining feedback on the application usage.

Design of a suitable architecture which supports appropriate authentication or logging is critical. For example, the World Wide Web typically only supports stateless communications, i.e. a Web server cannot typically find out information from a client. Mechanisms (such as cookies) can be used to circumvent this, but put constraints on the Web clients that can be used. A possible alternative would be to use an architecture which requires a user to download and install dedicated authentication or logging software which operates in conjunction with Web technologies.

Design of user and usage evaluation mechanisms allows the developers to improve and effectively maintain an application. For example, with a Website, monitoring the navigation paths and time spent browsing different pages can provide insights into what structures and interfaces may be most effective. This feedback can often be obtained during normal use of the application.

8.4 Production

During the production phase, various components required for the application will be produced, obtained or modified as per the design specification. These components will then be integrated to create a prototype or the final application. The overall production process is shown in Figure 8-4.

The typical components that need to be produced are:

- Media components (text, images, video, audio and animation),
- User interface components (windows, frames, buttons, banners and logos, forms),

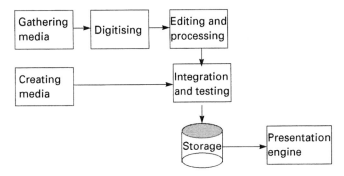

Figure 8-4

Overall production process

- Search engines,
- Server extensions (CGI scripts, user activity tracking system),
- Databases (relational, files with mark-up),
- Interfaces to dynamic data sources.

In addition to these, there can be other tasks that needs to be carried out which are not directly related to the production of the application. Typical examples include:

- Sorting out outstanding copyright,
- Creation of installation engines,
- Production of physical environment, if required.

Once all the components have been produced, they need to be integrated and packaged to create the prototype or final application.

The production and integration of various components can take place at different magnitudes. At one end of the spectrum it may be that we only have to produce a few screens (as in the case of a very small application or a prototype for a large application). At the other end of the spectrum could be the production of a final version of a very large system. It is important to select an appropriate production method and tools based on the size of the hypermedia application being produced.

The product model selected will have a major influence on how we integrate the components to make the product. For example, if we have decided to use a screen-based product model then we will have to use a manual authoring scheme for integration. If we are using an information-centred product model, we have a choice of manual authoring or automating the production process by using information filters and scripts. The choice will also depend upon the size of the application and how often the information needs to be updated.

Typically, the production phase comes after the design phase, but often it may be necessary to produce prototypes during the analysis and design phases to represent and to communicate various concepts and ideas, and to obtain feedback from clients and users.

Component Production Activities

This includes the production of media components, production of user interface components, creation of search engines, creation of server extensions, creation of information databases and creation of interfaces to dynamic data sources.

Production of media components

This would involve obtaining or creating the media required for the application, converting any non-digital media into a digital format, and editing or processing these as required. This is a very labour-intensive activity as very little can be automated.

Once the media is in a digital form, these media elements needs to be chunked into smaller units to meet the granularity requirement of the hypermedia information system. For example, in a video clip we use for the application we may need to access different scenes. To achieve this after we have captured the video clip, we will have to chunk it into different scenes.

Capturing and processing media

Table 8-1 shows some activities that can be used for capturing or creation and processing media components required for the hypermedia information system.

An important aspect of media production is to identify the various operations required and select the appropriate tool(s) to carry out these operations. Another important aspect is to select the appropriate file format for the media type. There have been many books (Andleigh and Thakrar, 1996; Steinmetz and Nahrstedt, 1995) written on this topic, thus we will not go into any further details on production of media components in this book.

Processing and chunking of information

The captured information will often need to processed and then broken into suitable chunks based on the guidelines for content development created during the design phase. Some of the typical processing activities are converting scanned text into ASCII format using Optical Charter Recognition (OCR) software and touching up scanned images.

Table 8-1

Activities for media capturing and processing

Media type	Common input format	Capture/Conversion	Typical creation and processing activities	Typical digital file formats
Text	Printed text	Scanning Direct input using a word processor or text editor	OCR, Word processing, text analysis tools	ASCII, RTF, HTML, SGML
Graphics		Direct input using a drawing package	Drawing, Colouring, Rotating, sizing	Proprietary vector graphic formats (CDR, etc.)
Images	Photographs	Scanning, capturing using digital cameras, generation by rendering	Drawing, painting, compositing, filtering, resizing, cropping, transforming, etc.	TIFF, GIF, JPEG, PNG
Video	Video tape	Capturing and compression	Compression, segmentation, sequencing, sound dubbing, synchronisation, etc.	AVI, MOV, MPEG
Audio	Audio tapes, direct speech, CDs	Capturing and compression	Compression, filtering, tonal or pitch adjustment, normalisation, special sound effects, etc.	WAV, AU
Animation	Sequence of images	Scanning	Cel animation, flip book animation, sprite, path and vector animation	AVI, FLI, GIF

Information chunking can either be done manually or automated. If manually, one has to go through the captured information and break it into different chunks. When the information volume that has to be processed is very large, this can be a very time consuming process, yet very little of the media production activities can be automated, though some progress has been shown in the automated structuring of text.

Most documents have an inherent structure: for example, if you take a book it will have a title, authors, foreword, table of contents and chapters. Each chapter will usually consist of a chapter title, paragraphs, lists and images. We can mark up the contents using a mark-up language such as SGML, and write routines using a text processing language such as Perl or OmniMark® to chunk and restructure the information as required for hypermedia applications.

Production of user interface components

Some typical user interface components are windows, frames, buttons, banners, icons, logos and forms. During the production stage, these need to be produced using appropriate tools. Some authoring tools have the facility to create windows, frames and forms. Typically, the buttons, banners and logos are created using appropriate drawing or paint programs.

Creation of search engines

Some authoring tools such as Macromedia Authorware Professional and Multimedia Viewer have built in search engines, which can perform full text search or keyword search. If you are developing a Web-based hyper-media information system, you can either link to an existing search engine that allows external Websites to use this facility, or obtain an existing search engine such as 'Harvest' (http://harvest.transarc.com/).

Creation of server extensions

If the application requires server capabilities beyond what is readily available, we have to create server extensions. In the case of a World Wide Web server, its capabilities can be extended by using CGI scripts or Java servlets.

Creation of information databases

If an information-centred product model has been selected for the application, it is likely to require information to be stored in a database independent of the presentation engine (in the case of a standalone application) or the server software (in the case of a client server application). The information can be stored in a relational database or a marked-up file system organised into a hierarchical structure in some logical way.

Often the structure of the relational database or the way to perform the mark-up is specified at the design stage. What should happen during the production phase is to physically create the required storage structure and populate it with the data. In a large project this would involve creating procedures for date entry operators to carry out this task.

Creation of interfaces to dynamic data sources

If the dynamic information is originating from a sensor, this would involve creating a software routine to read the sensor either at regular intervals or when requested by a user. If the information is coming from an external database, the typical activities would be to develop ways of querying the database to capture the required information. This can include activities such as developing SQL queries or CGI scripts in the case of a WWW-based application.

Integration of Components

Once we create the required components, we have to integrate them to create the application. How the integration is carried out depends very much upon the product model selected.

Programming language-based approach

If we are using a programming language-based product model, then component integration will mainly involve coding of the various modules to integrate the media types according to the design specification. We can make use of various methods available in software engineering to carry out these coding activities.

Screen-based approach and simple information-centred approach

If we are using a screen-based product model or a simple information-centred product model, the central activity during the production phase is authoring. Authoring is the process of structuring and combining different media types and formatting the screens according to the design specification. As a result of various WYSIWYG authoring tools such as Microsoft FrontPage™ and Netfusion™, the distinction between authoring a screen-based application and an information-centred application has blurred. The main differences between the two authoring approaches lies in the format and extensibility of the information representation. In a screen-based approach, the authored information is typically stored in a proprietary format and no further partitioning or processing of authored information using other software tools is possible. In the information-centred approach, the authored information is stored in a standard or *de facto* standard format such as SGML, HTML, RTF, etc. This enable us to develop specialised software tools and routines to create and maintain information in a effective and efficient way without using authoring tools.

How authoring is carried out very much depends upon the tool selected to carry out the authoring. Most tools rely on a specific authoring metaphor (such as a timeline, script or cast): these are discussed in detail in the next chapter.

Information-centred approach for large applications

The use of authoring tools to develop large applications is often unproductive, as a considerable amount of time can be spent on manually structuring the information, linking and formatting each screen. Since in the information-centred product model information is de-coupled from any specific authoring tool or presentation engine, we can develop software tools and routines to enhance the productivity of information capturing, structuring, linking and formatting activities based on the design specification.

If we are producing a large hypermedia application using an information-centred product model, we will not usually carry out authoring in the conventional multimedia sense. Instead, we might capture the information into a database or set of files marked-up using SGML. We could then develop a set of programs to automatically structure, link and output sets of files that will include appropriate presentation tags to suit the selected presentation engine. This process is shown in Figure 8-5.

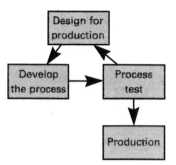

Figure 8-5

Overall production process for large hypermedia applications based on an information-centred product model

In this approach, the first step is to redesign for production. We have to take the design specification and redesign it to suit this type of production, which would include analysing different screen layouts specified in the design specification and developing a set of standard layout templates. We would also analyse the guidelines for content development and create a suitable set of Document Type Definitions (DTD) which define the information structure.

The next step is to develop the production process. If the information is coming from a legacy system, we have to identify the existing format and develop software routines using a text processing language such as Perl or OmniMark™ to automatically mark up the information based on the selected DTDs. Often, SGML is used as the mark-up language. The process of converting some existing document structure into a structure specified by a DTD and marking-up using a language such as SGML is called *up translation*.

The marked-up legacy data has to be reorganised as specified in the design specification to form the nodes. As with SGML you can capture the document content rather than document format, it is now possible to identify different parts of the document by parsing the document. The next step is to create a new document combining various parts to form the nodes, as per the design specification. Also, the links are embedded into the document using the algorithms developed earlier. There are commercial tools available to carry out this process, which include elements such as a built-in parser. You can write a program and load that into the parser specifying what the output should be. This process of generating a SGML document from another SGML document is known as *cross translation*.

Finally, the document mark-up needs to be converted back to a format that is understood by the presentation engine. In the case of the World Wide Web, this format is HTML. As before, one has to now write a program using a text processing language to convert the SGML mark-up to an appropriate HTML mark-up. Some tools allow a developer to specify a style sheet and perform this conversion based on this style sheet. This process of converting an SGML document to a non-SGML format required by a presentation engine is called *down translation*, (shown in Figure 8-6).

Once the production process and routines have been developed, we can run the process with some data to check the correctness of the routines. We can then extend this to the production of the whole application. If the information is stored in databases, then the production process would include creating the databases, developing input forms to enter data, populating the databases, and creating output reports which can be viewed by users or generate files that can be viewed using some presentation engine.

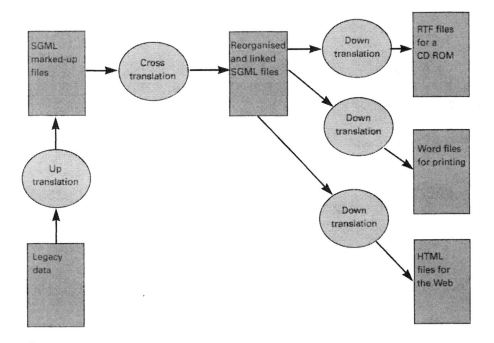

Figure 8-6

Detailed production process for large hypermedia applications based on legacy data

Other Supporting Activities

Copyright resolution

An important activity within the overall process is to resolve any copyright issues. This is carried out in the production stage, as by then the developers will know exactly what content will be used in the application. Often the procedure is to find the copyright owner and write to the person asking permission to use the relevant information in the hypermedia application, and negotiating a royalty agreement if applicable.

Construction of presentation engine

We often use a commercially available presentation engine such as a Web browser or Multimedia Viewer(to present the information to the user. However, in some cases (especially where we require very specific features not supported by the presentation engines available) we may have to consider the implementation of a specific presentation engine.

Production of a physical environment

This is applicable to applications such as kiosks or tourist information systems, etc. which will be located in public places. In such cases, it is necessary to produce a physical environment in which to house the information system.

8.5   Verification and Testing

Throughout the development process for a hypermedia application, we should be asking two very important questions: Are we building the right product? Are we building the product right? Verification and validation focus on addressing these two questions.

To understand what verification and validation mean in the context of developing hypermedia applications, first we look at how these terms are defined in a different (but analogous) domain: software engineering. These definitions come from the IEEE Standard Glossary of Software Engineering Terminology (IEEE Std 729, 1983).

> **Definition**
>
> **Verification** is the process of determining whether the product conforms to the requirements specified in the previous phase. Thus, verification tries to answer the question, Have we built the system correctly?
>
> **Validation** is the process at the end of the software lifecycle in which it is tested whether the software conforms to the requirements specification. Thus, validation tries to answer the question, Have we built the right system?

It has been pointed out that when developing software, the cost of correcting a mistake later in the development process can be orders of magnitude greater than finding and fixing it early in the development process (Boehm, 1981). This is equally applicable to the development of hypermedia applications. One should not wait until late in the development to validate the results of the development activities. It is very important to carry out the necessary verification and validation activities at least at the end of the major specification, design and production phases. Typically, verification and validation activities are distributed throughout the development process.

We can use different activities to perform verification and validation during the process of developing a hypermedia application. Some typical activities are walk-throughs, audits, prototyping and testing.

Walk-throughs

This involves a group of people other than the original designers going through the analysis, design and production together with the original designers. During walk-throughs, the goal is to evaluate the extent to which the results of the development activities are consistent with the application intention.

Audits

Audits involve checking the output at the end of a development phase against a check list or input specification for that phase.

Prototyping

Prototyping consists of making a scale model of the application and using this to validate various aspects of the design. These aspects may include functionality of the system and user interface design.

Prototyping assists in determining whether the developer is making the right product by showing a 'scale model' with reduced content and/or functionality to the client and users.

Testing

Testing is a process of checking the correctness by exercising or running a system. When developing a hypermedia application, we have to carry out different types of tests:

- *Functionality tests:* to verify if the application is functioning as specified. For example, after we create links in an application we have to verify whether all of the links lead to the correct destination, that there are no dangling links, and also that from every node in the application there is a way of moving onto another part of the application (i.e. no dead ends).

- *Performance test:* to verify whether the application is running at an acceptable speed, and that the response time is acceptable. This test needs to be carried out on the different platforms on which the application is intended to be used.

- *Compatibility test:* this is to verify that the application is running effectively on all platforms on which it is intended to run.

- *Reliability test:* this is to verify whether the application is running reliably. Are the actions repeatable? Are links taking the user to the correct destination, etc?

- *Installability test:* this verifies whether a new user can install the application easily and reliably.

- *Useability test:* this test is aimed at identifying the difficulties a user may experience when trying to use the information system as a result of the design.

8.6 Maintenance

From the point at which users begin to user a hypermedia application it has to be maintained, an attribute hypermedia applications share with software. In software it is estimated that the proportion of the total life-cycle costs for commercial software systems spent on system maintenance after commissioning is typically between 60–80%. There is no reason to believe that a similar situation will not develop for hypermedia.

We need to develop applications in such a way that not only allows maintenance, but actively addresses issues related to maintainability. This is an area requiring ongoing research, but issues which may prove fruitful include making the structure of the underlying information as visible as possible (at least to the author, if not the user), and avoiding embedding structure directly into the underlying information.

When developing hypermedia applications it is very important to take into account the maintainability needs earlier in the process. Maintainability is not something that can be added on later. Some typical categories of maintenanability are:

- *Corrective maintenance*: this includes fixing errors that are found once the users start using the hypermedia application.

- *Adaptive maintenance*: is carried out to modify a hypermedia application as a result of changes to the environment. Some of these are changes to the information being used (for example, in a legal information system, changes to legislation), changes in the user population and changes in hypermedia technology. Adaptive maintenance is usually driven by external factors.

- *Perfective maintenance*: no system is perfect when it is first developed, and will undergo enhancements when the developers, users and clients get a deeper insight into various aspects of the system. This type of change is known as *perfective* maintenance.

It is worth pointing out that maintenance of hypermedia systems is still a very poorly understood area. Although it is the focus of considerable research, at present little of this has filtered through into current commercial practice. A typical example of the types of practices which can be adopted is to separate links from the underlying content. For example, Microcosm uses a linkbase and the concept of generic links (these aspects will be discussed in more detail in Part Three of the book). Even where there is no inherent support for advanced maintanence mechanisms, there are still techniques which can be adopted, and these will be discussed in the following chapter.

9

Development Techniques

There is always a best way of doing everything, if it be to boil an egg
(Emerson, 'Behaviour', The conduct of life (1860))

Chapter Goals

Chapter 8 looked at the stages of development and how they are combined. In this chapter, we go deeper into the practicalities of how the development might be carried out. Although we cannot provide a cohesive methodology (it will be different for every project, and the field is still not mature enough to be able to be so prescriptive), we can provide certain guidelines. The objectives of this chapter are to show that:

- The important activities in analysis are elicitation of information and formulation of the requirements. Techniques such as interviews, questionnaires, brainstorming, scenarios and proto-typing are all useful.

- Structuring of information is one of the few activities where formal methods are beginning to appear. The use of these depends upon the type of information and whether legacy data exists.

- Designing associative links can be incredibly time consuming, and is currently difficult to manage other than manually.

- Design of searching and indexing methods can use well established techniques from database systems and information science.

- Design of an application's look and feel is still largely an art rather than a science.

9.1   Introduction

In the last chapter, we looked at the development process in general and the various activities we have to carry out within the development process. In this chapter we look in detail at how to carry out some of the hypermedia-specific activities.

We have already mentioned that some of the activities we have to perform are common to other disciplines of engineering, such as software or systems engineering. These activities are in the areas of analysis, planning and coding (in the case of a programming language-based product model). We do not discuss these activities further here.

When considering the practicalities of selecting and/or adapting an activity, we should also consider the cost associated with that activity. The most significant element of cost-effectiveness will be the development productivity. Two aspects which strongly influence productivity are the structuring and linking of information, and reuse and maintenance issues. The activities we are going to use when developing a hypermedia application should allow us to address these aspects in a systematic way.

9.2   Requirements Analysis

To carry out the analysis activities we can perform various tasks, including elicitation of required information, formulation of this information into a logical structure and validating the information against client or user requirements, or for internal consistency. These activities are shown in Figure 9-1.

Elicitation

Elicitation is the task of gathering all of the information that we think is relevant to the type of analysis needed. Rather than overlooking some important information, it is better to collect all the information we think may be relevant and then eliminate those sections that we find are not. As knowledge elicitation from humans is inherently very difficult, this task can be very labour-intensive.

Techniques which are commonly used to elicit information include:

- Interviews with both the clients and prospective users of the application to determine what their requirements or expectations may

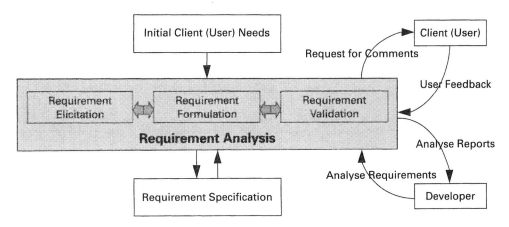

Figure 9-1

Activities associated with requirements analysis (reprinted by permission of Vithanage (1997))

be. This can include aspects such as a discussion on possible information sources, ways in which this information might be used, the different information relationships which might exist, the types of metaphors which are familiar to users, etc.

- Questionnaires and surveys can address similar aspects to interviews, but can provide a much wider coverage.

- Brainstorming can be used to identify possible alternatives, approaches, requirements, information sources, etc. Brainstorming is a useful technique in ensuring that aspects of the requirements have not been overlooked.

- Scenario analysis can be used to obtain a better understanding of how an application might be used, and therefore what functionality and information may be appropriate. For example, a scenario for the *HyperBank* application might be as follows:

  Customer X connects to the *HyperBank* main World Wide Web homepage using their favourite Web browser. From this homepage they navigate to a page providing access to personal account information. They enter their name and account number and the application provides their account balance. They follow a link to a page providing a detailed listing of their account details for the last month. They then request that all transactions in the last year relating to interest paid be totalled, and the application responds with the requested total.

The above scenario provides us with a wealth of ideas regarding requirements for the inclusion of specific types of information (such as account balances and transaction histories), functionality (such as an ability to calculate totals for specific types of transactions) and behaviour (such as the application being accessible using common WWW browsers).

- Analysis of existing documents, systems, or applications can be used to gain an improved understanding of both possible requirements, and the domain within which the application will be used.

- Prototypes can be used to assist users in understanding the implications of various forms of information and functionality. In particular, users are often unaware of the potential and limitations of new technologies such as hypermedia, and therefore are not able to adequately identify or articulate their requirements. Once a prototype has been seen, a user is often able to better understand what is feasible. Prototyping can require considerable effort, but has the potential to elicit detailed feedback.

- Literature searches can provide information related to similar systems, technological or other constraints, and other types of knowledge which might impact on the application requirements.

Formulation

This involves organising information that was obtained into some logical structure and eliminating redundant information. Hierarchical organisations are quite common when organising information.

Validation

The requirements identified need to be validated against the client's intention, if they originated from the client. Similarly, if the requirement originated from a user, it needs to be validated against the user's intention. Also, these requirements needs to be validated against the goals of the application, and for consistency, e.g. there cannot be two requirements that contradict one another.

9.3   Information Structuring

In Section 2.1 we discussed the different types of links, and provided one categorisation: structural, associative and referential. Structural links reflect the underlying organisation of the information, whereas associative and referential links provide navigation support based on the semantic associations between the underlying concepts. In each case, we need to consider specific techniques for generating both the information relationships and the links which implement these relationships. Let us begin by considering structural links – as it is these that provide the form of the information space within which the user will be moving and navigating.

Information Structuring Methodologies

There are currently few methodologies which can be used to guide developers during information structuring. The type of approach adopted for content structuring will depend very much upon the nature of the data being used in the application, as different applications will have different information models.

West and Norris (1997) describe an approach for managing the design of small to medium scale applications. Their approach addresses the design of the document or page structure within an application particularly well (i.e. structural links as distinct from associative links). For example, they consider the development and appropriateness of alternatives such as guided tours, hierarchical structures, menu and index pages, and storyboarding. They also provide a very good overview of the management aspects of the development of the information structure. What they fail to consider, however, is the effective design and authoring of the complex associative linking that occurs in large-scale applications.

An alternative (though complementary) approach is the Relationship Management Methodology (RMM) (Isakowitz, Stohr and Balasubramanian, 1995). This is suitable for applications that have highly structured information models with a lot of information in a collection of related classes (the types of applications which have traditionally been suitable for database applications). These types of application are often based on a physical system (such as an information system for library loans, or for details on personnel in an organisation).

There is another class of large information applications based on legacy data which are not readily class-based, including applications such as those which include a large amount of information on organisational procedures. For such applications, a diagramming technique can be used. In this formal technique, the designer attempts to organise the information into a hierarchical structure. The approach is also very useful in the production stage, as it allows us to partially automate the information structuring based on the information model developed at the design stage. Figure 9-2 illustrates the use of the diagramming technique for a simple example (a manual), but it can just as easily be applied to a large complex information set which has a well defined structure (Figure 9-3). Table 9-1 explains the various symbols used in the diagramming technique.

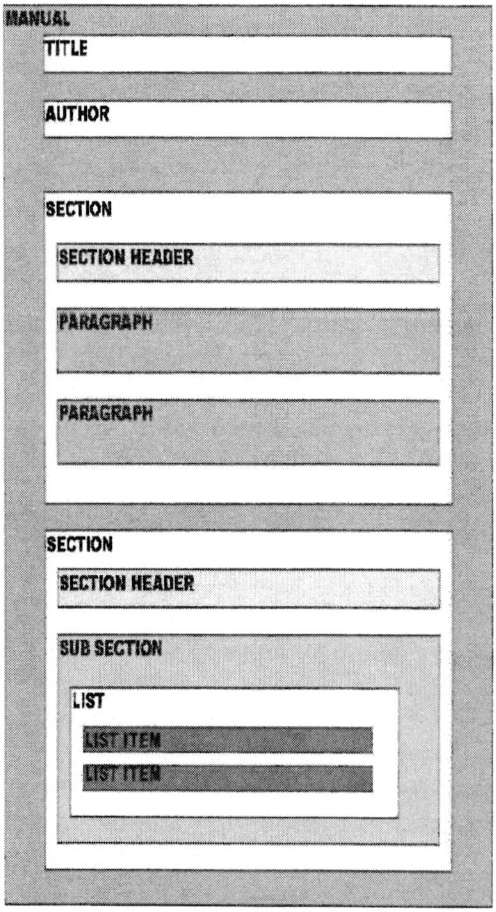

Figure 9-2

Example elements of a manual

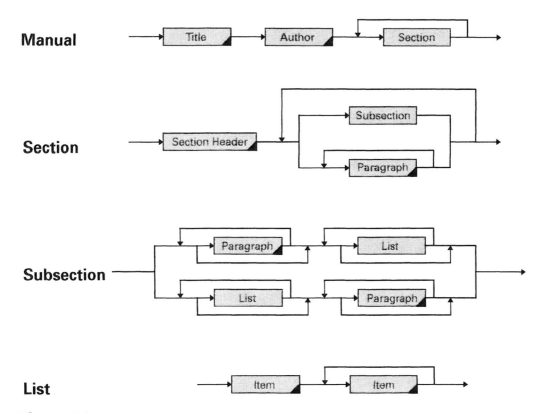

Figure 9-3

Example of the diagramming technique

Where we start content design varies depending on what information is available. There can be three broad possibilities:

1. Legacy data is available (for example, if we are developing a legal information system, the relevant legislation and case histories are available in print form).

2. No legacy data is available, but a physical structure exists (for example, if we are developing an information system for an organisation there may not be legacy data to cover all aspects of the operation of that organisation, but a management or an organisational structure exists that can be used as the starting point for content design).

3. A new application where no legacy data or physical structure exists (for example, an information system for a new education module in a distance learning application).

Table 9-1

Symbols used in the diagramming technique

Symbol	Description	Content Model
A	A component in a document called "A". (e.g. a paragraph).	A
A	A component which can not be decomposed further.	#PCDATA
A	0 (A) 1 Element A is optional or can occur once.	A?
A	1 (A) n A is repeated 1 to n times where n can be any integer.	A+
A B	A and B in series (B after A).	A, B
A A	1 (A) 2 Consists of one or two As. ie the second A can be bypassed.	A, A?
A A	2 (A) n Two or more components of A.	A, A+
A	A can be bypasses or repeated – similar to 0 (A) n.	A*
A A A A	A or B or C or D Selection.	A|B|C|D
A B C	Parallel components with repetition.	A, (B+|C) Note: A, B+ |C is incorrect
X A B C D	A and B and C and D in any order.	X, (A&B&C&D)

Let us look at each of these three cases in some detail.

Legacy data available

In this case the starting point of content design is obtaining all the relevant legacy data, which we then analyse. Often, legacy data tends to have a hierarchical structure, so one can use a diagramming technique as described above to capture and manipulate this structure. This approach is especially helpful if, during the implementation phase, the information is going to be marked up using SGML (Goldfarb, 1990).

No legacy data, but a physical structure exists

In this case the starting point is to model the physical structure. These applications tend to have a highly structured information model. The Relationship Management Methodology (RMM) (Isakowitz, Stohr and Balasubramanian, 1995) is a useful approach for applications that have a highly structured information model. This is because RMM uses an approach based on entity relationship modelling, and hence it can model highly structured information well.

A new application with no legacy data or obvious physical structure

If we are developing such an application, we have to use domain-dependent theories to develop the initial information structure. An example of this is the use of learning theories for educational applications. For this purpose, we can classify the different domains as shown in Table 9-2.

A final question relevant to all three of the above cases is the question of how to eliminate redundancy from the data sources. Once the existing structure of the information has been identified, it has to be refined, and any redundancies in information needs to be identified and removed. For example, it is quite common at this stage to find the name of a person and some associated details being repeated in many places within the information space. From a maintenance point of view, it is important to keep this information in one place and create links from other locations to this single location.

Another option is to identify the basic information elements and how these are combined to create various user views, store the basic information elements in some form of a database and generate the user views using a suitable script.

Table 9-2

Example application domains where learning theories can be applied

Task-specific	Training	Learning		User-specific
Assists to perform a task	Tells how to perform a procedure	Provide expert view point	Provide resource material for learning on demand	Provide information on demand
Example: air line reservations	Example: procedure manuals	Example: Text books, scientific papers	Example: virtual museums, reference books, encyclopedias	Example: video, news, weather, tourist info. etc. on demand

Information Database Design

In information structuring we design the logical structure of information and the relationships among different information units. In information database design we design the physical structure in which to store the data. This information database can consist of set of mark up files and other files containing various non-text media elements such as images, video and audio clips. Other possibilities are that we may decide to use a relational database or an object-oriented database to physically store the information required for the application.

Many conventional databases and database tools have been modified to incorporate the ability to work with hypermedia systems (and in particular, Web applications). An example of this is the development of Java APIs to allow Java applications to interface (through ODBC and/or JDBC) to databases. Similarly, tools such as Microsoft Frontpage incorporate the ability to interface to databases such as Microsoft Access.

Currently, no specialised tools or techniques exist for designing the database structure specifically for hypermedia applications. Conventional database design techniques, however, will still largely be relevant, especially when used in conjunction with mechanisms such as RMM's entity-relationship design methods, which can provide an indication of the information structure.

A main consideration when developing the information database structure is the maintenance requirements. With respect to maintainability, as both the number and size of applications expand, there will be an increasing need to take these into account. Applications will no longer be static: they will increasingly tend to evolve over time (this trend is evident in the World Wide Web even now). As a result, we need to develop applications in such a way that allows them to be easily maintained.

For adaptive maintenance it is essential to store similar information, such as names of people in an organisation and their details, physically together in a single file or database table. Then when there is a change in the physical organisation in terms of people, it is easy to change the corresponding information in the information system by just modifying a single file or database table.

9.4   Associative Linking

Whereas structural linking looks at the physical organisation of the information space, associative linking provides the ability to navigate across this structure based on conceptual or semantic associations. It is these links which provide the real strength of hypermedia systems.

The linking of related information is in most cases still done based purely on location – an anchor in a specified media item is linked to a fixed location in another media item. This is typically a constraint imposed either by the development tool or the underlying information model, implying that the author will need to know the location of associated information to create a link. When developing large hypermedia systems, the need to remember the locations becomes a major cognitive burden on the author, affecting both the quality and productivity.

Probably the most challenging aspect of the linking process is the need to mentally manage all the existing nodes within a set of information. This problem of finding relevant destination nodes for a given concept is shown graphically in Figure 9-4. When the number of information nodes in the system is small, the user can remember the information associated with a particular concept and create the links. Almost all authoring tools commercially available at present support this type of manual linking. When the information space is large (over 500 nodes is a typical figure), it becomes increasingly difficult for the author to remember information contained in all the nodes. If the system is developed by many authors

Complexity: Manageable   Complexity: Overwhelming

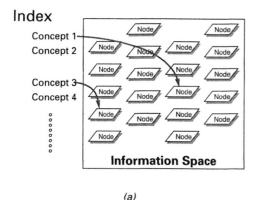   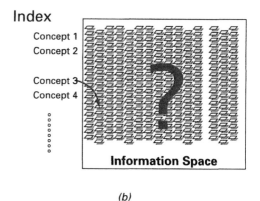

(a)   (b)

Figure 9-4

As the application size increases, managing the information space from a developer's perspective becomes increasingly difficult. The complexity involved in creating meaningful structure increases rapidly with application size

this adds to the problem. Thus, with increasing size the cognitive overload becomes unmanageable.

Techniques for managing the burden associated with linking is still an open research issue. In practical terms, however, the use of tools which can parse text (usually based on templates that have been developed for specific application domains) provides a reasonable starting point. For example, many SGML tools (such as OmniMark) provide pattern matching languages which can be used to specify the structure of legacy information, thereby semi-automating the structuring and linking process.

Designing Associative Links

In designing associative links, probably the most useful current technique is to begin by identifying a suitable basis for the creation of associative and referential links. Often, these are expressed as a set of rules. For example, with referential links we can have a rule such that if a word exists in a glossary used for the application, then there should be a link from this word anywhere in the application to the entry in the glossary.

Defining a basis for creating associative links is yet more complex. The developer first has to decide on a relevant set of associations, which could be:

- A thing and its application (e.g. in a legal information system, a law and its interpretation or case history).

- A cause and an effect (e.g. in a history information system, a war or a revolution and its social impact).

- Thing and a strongly associated property (e.g. in a store catalogue, a product and its financing plan).

- A raw material and a product.

- Two complementary and concurrent activities.

- an activity and an agent of that activity (e.g. in a history, the apartheid struggle and Nelson Mandela, a lecturer and subjects taught by the lecturer).

- whole and part (e.g. in a science application, a diagram of a car and how each part works, a university degree program and a subject description).

From a practical perspective, a number of guidelines exist to assist in ensuring effective links. These include aspects such as ensuring consistency in associative linking, and ensuring that the link anchor provides as obvious indication of the link destination as possible. For example, consider the text:

> In designing *associative links*, probably the most useful current technique is to begin by identifying a suitable basis for the creation of associative and referential links.

In this text it is not clear what information would be contained in the destination for the link from the text 'associative links'. It may be a definition of associative links, it may be an essay on how to design associative links, or it may be information on how different hypermedia systems (such as the WWW) implement associative links. If the latter was the case, then a more informative anchor may be:

> In designing associative links (more information is available on how they are *implemented in different systems*), probably the most useful current technique is to begin by identifying a suitable basis for the creation of associative and referential links.

Beyond these relatively simple observations there are a number of much more complex approaches, such as the use of generic and dynamic links.

These are still not widely used, and will be discussed in detail in the final part of this book (especially in the chapters on Microcosm, Hyper-G, and the final concluding chapter).

9.5 Example of Link Design

As a simple example of how we may design specific link structures, let us consider a small subset of the *HyperBank* case study. We shall look at three levels of structure within this application: the high-level application structure; the detailed structural linking of one section of the application; and the associative linking within this section.

High level structure

First, let us consider the high-level structure of the *HyperBank* application. We can begin by considering both the potential users, and the sources of information. The potential users vary incredibly, from current and prospective customers to internal users (staff) and external users (bank suppliers and regulatory agencies). Each of these system users will have differing levels of expertise and different requirements. However, the information they will be accessing will in many cases be the same (such as both staff and customers accessing customer transaction records).

This implies that the structure of the information space should be organised in a way which allows different users to be presented with different structures for the underlying information space. Indeed, different users must be able to visualise the information space in very different ways (much as a commuter who uses a subway system will visualise the layout of a city differently from a commuter who always drives).

This indicates that at the very top level of the information space, we have a demarcation between the different potential users. Note that this does not imply that when the final Website if completed, the homepage would reflect this partitioning. It is likely that it would be considered appropriate (from a customer relations standpoint) that the perspective seen by the customer when first entering the Website is only a reflection of their viewpoint on the information space, and not the total range of different perspectives.

Having identified that the top-level structure should reflect the fact that the underlying information is organised in different ways for different users, we can look at the structure for a single user – current customers.

Given the variable level of expertise and knowledge of customers, a very simple structure to visualise is most desirable – a standard hierarchy (though we may determine that certain information belongs in numerous places within this hierarchy).

To determine the specific details of the structure, we need to consider the information we wish to provide to the customers, and their expectations of how this information is organised. This could be achieved by interviewing a range of current customers; investigating both current information to which they have access, and future potential information sources; analysing the current structure and content of information sources; developing and analysing typical customer scenarios; analysing competitors' Websites; and possibly developing prototypes. A typical resultant high-level structure of the *HyperBank* information space, as seen by a customer, is shown in Figure 9-5.

Detailed structure

Once we have a top level structure we can start to develop the detailed structure of specific information components. To demonstrate this, let us consider the information provided by the bank on the conditions of use of a specific type of bank account – say, a personal cheque account. This information already exists in a conventional document form, and is mailed out to new customers along with account details, or mailed to existing customers whenever details change.

This implies we use can the existing structure of the document to assist in defining the structural links. For example, the existing document may have the following (partial) form:

Terms and Conditions for *HyperBank* Personal Cheque Account
Deposits . . .
Interest . . .
Bank Fees and Charges . . .
    Fee types: account servicing fee, excess withdrawal fee, . . .
    Current fees
    Exemptions and Fee rebates
Provision of credit
Termination
Error and Dispute resolution
  . . . etc.

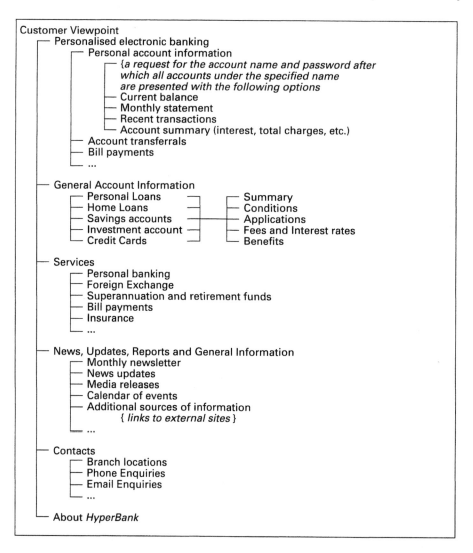

Figure 9-5

Structure of the *HyperBank* information space as seen by a customer

We could immediately treat this as a suitable structure for the electronic form of the information, and simply migrate the information directly onto the WWW. Indeed, much information on the WWW (and other hyper-media applications) simply provides what is essentially access to existing documents. This case would have two disadvantages: first, it would not be making the most effective use of the hypermedia functionality available; secondly, it it does not acknowledge that many of the related documents (on conditions for other types of accounts) will have a similar structure. This second point should indicate that we ought to identify a common structure and then map the information into this structure. The headings listed in the example above would be common for most types of bank account. The main difference may be specialised fee types for different accounts, and conditions on account balances and transaction types, etc.

We would end up with a set of terms and conditions for each account type. This could be viewed as a matrix structure (the account type, and conditions forming the two axes). This information could be mapped into a suitable SGML structure, thereby minimising the effort required to both maintain the information and to present it in different forms (the paper version of the information will still be required!) A suitable SGML Data Type Definition could be developed to define the structure of the information to be presented. Figure 9-6 shows how this could be mapped to a specific Web page design in order to present the information to the

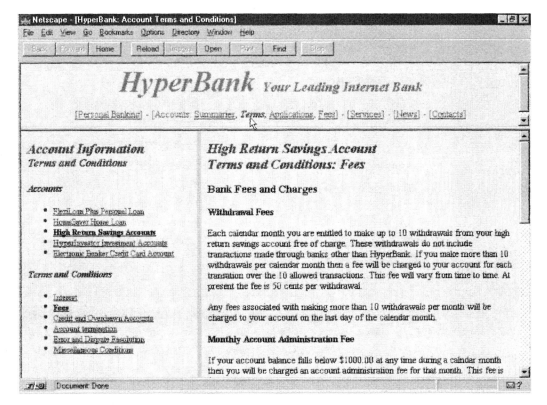

Figure 9-6

High-level presentation format of the *HyperBank* Web

user. These pages could be created dynamically from the SGML information by using a suitable filter.

Associative linking

Once we have a structure for the information space we are creating, we need to consider the support we provide for navigation within this space using associative links. There are numerous ways this could be managed, depending upon the types of associative links we wish to develop. The first step in developing suitable associative links would be to identify the types of relationships we wish to support. To facilitate, this we analyse the information sources and develop the following association types:

- A concept and it's definition

You are entitled to make up to 10 _withdrawals_ from your high return savings account	links to	**Withdrawal:** A withdrawal is defined as a . . .

- An entity (such as a customers personal account) and the conditions on that entity.

When using your _account_ you must always . . .	links to	**Savings Acount Terms and Conditions** The terms of usage of a . . .

- An organisation and details of that organisation

HyperBank has for many years had a strong association with _Electronic Investments Incorporated_. This . . .	links to	Website homepage for _Electronic Investments Incorporated_

- etc.

The difficulty, of course, lies in knowing when to use an appropriate link type. This will particularly be the case where a given anchor could have several different interpretations. For example, consider the following link anchor:

Your current _account_ balance is available from . . .	links to	**Savings Acount Terms and Conditions** The terms of usage of a . . .

| | or links to | Defn: **Account:** An account is defined as a . . . |
| | or links to | The *HyperBank* offers many different types of accounts. In order to determine which is the best type of account for you needs . . . |

In this example, if a user encountered the anchor *account*, the user would be uncertain as what information this anchor was linked to. Three possible solutions might be to:

- Modify the anchor to make it more expressive (such as 'Your current account balance (which has various *terms and conditions*) is available from . . .')

- Provide a mechanism for selecting a link and obtaining more detailed information on the destination prior to activating the link.

- Provide a mechanism for having anchors link to multiple destinations.

Advanced hypermedia systems allow links to have multiple destinations (and the user is able to select the appropriate destination from a list of choices). This mechanism is not supported on the Web, and so we are forced to simply rely on design guidelines. These should be developed to be consistent. For example, the following are a typical set of guidelines for use with the *HyperBank* system:

- Any single words (or composites) which are part of standard text (e.g. 'When using your *HyperSaver Account* you must . . .') will be linked only to a glossary of terms which provides a definition of the term.

- Any bullet points or list items which incorporate links (e.g.

    - Automatic teller machines
    - Electronic Funds Transfer Point of Sale . . .'

will link only to detailed information on the given item.

- Any other associative links will utilise full anchors which make the link context and destination obvious (e.g. 'All *HyperBank* accounts are required by Law to incorporate a standard transaction tax. More information on this tax is available from the *Government Taxation Office* homepage.')

9.6 Access and Navigation Support

The design of access and navigation mechanisms includes the design of navigation structures based on user viewpoints, establishing a basis for anchor selection and link traversal and, if applicable, selecting an indexing approach for searching the information.

Design of Navigation Structures and Viewpoints

When structuring content the aim is largely to develop a data structure that will assist in fully identifying the required content, and also help to eliminate redundancies in the information. Often (indeed, most of the time) this will not be the structure a user wants to follow when accessing and utilising the information. During viewpoint design, we try to identify how users are going to access the information, and then superimpose multiple user viewpoints on top of the original information structure.

A common technique used to determine user viewpoints is to write the various headings on a set of index cards and ask a sample of users to group these based on how they would like to navigate the information space. Once we get this information from a number of users, we can do a cluster analysis to determine the dominant user viewpoints and provide hyperlinks to support them.

Design of Searching and Indexing Mechanisms

Another important activity that needs to be carried out at the design phase is to decide whether to use a search engine and, if so, what type of searching mechanism to use.

Before discussing specific approaches, it is important to understand several basic concepts related to measuring the effectiveness of searching mechanisms. When an end-user begins searching there will be certain information in the information space which will be highly relevant to their information needs some which will be useful, some marginally

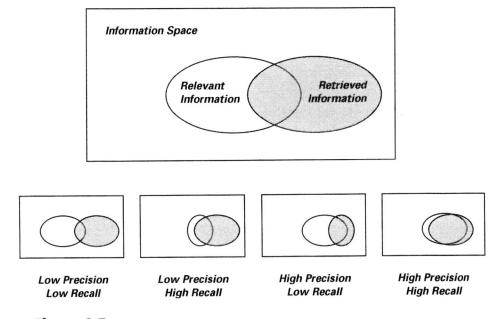

Figure 9-7

Precision and recall in searching

relevant and some not relevant at all. Only some of this information will be returned by a search engine. We measure the performance of a searching mechanism using two ratios: recall ratio and precision ratio.

Precision is the ratio of the number of *relevant* documents (or nodes, pages, etc.) retrieved, to the total number of documents retrieved, i.e. the proportion of returned 'hits' which are relevant. Recall is the ratio of the number of relevant documents (or nodes, pages, etc.) *retrieved*, to the total number of relevant documents, i.e. the proportion of relevant documents which are returned as 'hits'. This is illustrated in Figure 9-7.

It is also worth noting that, with most search engines, we have the ability to trade off precision against recall. As shown in Figure 9-8, if we increase the number of documents retrieved, then we are more likely to retrieve more of the relevant documents, and hence increase recall. At the same time, however, we will typically retrieve more inappropriate documents and hence decrease our precision.

In developing search engines we can either have a full text search or search using a selected subset of words. There are two main ways of selecting this subset: one is to use a statistical mechanism to select the words from

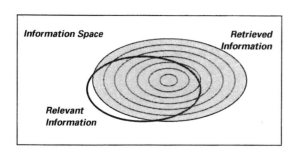

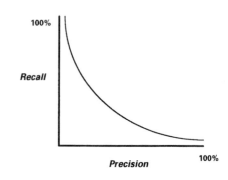

Figure 9-8

Trading off precision against recall

the text, an approach commonly known as keyword searching; the other is to use a control vocabulary to select the indexing terms.

- **Keyword searching:** for large sets of documents it is economical to assign keywords using a statistical algorithm based on the frequency of occurrence of certain words. In this approach, the keywords are automatically extracted from the document. This has the advantage that the whole process can be readily automated, making it economical for very large document sets. However, if during searching the user uses a synonym (for example, the keyword in the document is 'compact disk' and the user typed CD ROM), the application may fail to find the information. Therefore, this approach may not produce results as good as manual indexing based on control and entry vocabularies.

- **Searching using a control vocabulary:** in this approach we first develop or select an existing vocabulary for the subject domain. Generally, these vocabularies are hierarchically organised.

Once a user selects a vocabulary, you have to select what level of granularity is required and decide what index terms to use. For example, for an article we can assign the index term '*Mammals*' or be more specific and say '*Dog*'. This type of indexing system will use a much larger entry vocabulary that will have pointers from synonyms to words used to index the document. For example, if a user typed CD ROM it will then point the user to compact disk.

This approach tends to give much better results in terms of precision and recall, but is very time consuming as all documents need to be manually indexed. During the design phase, one has to weigh the advantages and disadvantages between the two methods within the application context and select a suitable indexing approach.

Design of the Overall Look and Feel

Overall screen layout

The overall screen layout should provide an appropriate visual impact, but most importantly, should make it easy for people to use the application. The designer can enhance the usability of the application in many ways with respect to look and feel. Examples include the use of metaphors, appropriate labelling of information nodes, and use of split-screens.

- **Use of metaphors:** if the designer knows about the user's background and experience, then he can select a suitable metaphor, by which we mean the application of some form of schema to provide a basis for understanding the applications' structure, functionality, behaviour or interface by analogy.

  Metaphors are used to relate the task being performed to something with which the user is likely to be familiar (often something from the domain or environment described by the application). A very common example is the use of a book metaphor – so that the display appears as a book to the user. The user will then readily be able to relate to concepts such as turning pages, using tables of contents and indexes, etc. Another example might be laying out the main application interface to look like a kitchen, for a cooking application. Proper use of metaphors can greatly reduce the cognitive burden associated with learning how to use the application.

  A designer can use a metaphor for the overall application, or for individual parts of the application. A good example at the overall application level is the common desktop metaphor used by many computer operating systems. Another example is the use of a card index metaphor for a hypermedia telephone directory. Often, users use a card index to keep a record of telephone numbers and they know how to find a telephone number quickly. When you use a card index metaphor and provide similar functionality to conventional card indexes, users can intuitively start using the application more effectively.

  Use of icons such as filing cabinets and trashcans are examples of using metaphors for the individual components of an application to enhance the usability. Appropriate metaphors can help a user understand the functionality and operation of an application. They can also assist in helping a user understand where they are within the information structure (thereby avoiding the 'lost in hyperspace' problem). For example, if we support a cooking application with a presentation metaphor of a kitchen, it can become obvious whether we are discussing ingredients (the display shows a cupboard), preparation (the display shows a workbench), cooking (the display shows a stove), etc. We can also use other mechanisms to also support a user in understanding their location within the information space. Examples include appropriate labelling, use of split screens, and information maps.

- **Appropriate labelling:** support for orientation of a user within the information space can be supported by appropriate labelling of information which is presented. A simple example is the use of structured labels within a hierarchical application – which might take the form:

    chapter_title – section_title – node_title

    For example, we might have a node labelled

    Cooking 'chicken kiev' – preparation – selecting ingredients

    Labels such as these provide valuable information to locate and contextualise the user.

- **Use of split screen:** another technique that can be used to show the user the overall information context is the use of split screens. Here the screen is divided into two or more parts, and some parts are used to provide the location and the other part for the content. An example of this approach is shown in Figure 9-9.

Such an approach allows the user to always have access to a single, well-understood mechanism for navigating. In a more advanced form, the fixed component used for navigation can change to indicate the location within the information space. Taken even further, this navigation mechanism can take the form of an explicit map of the information space.

Figure 9-9

Examples of split screens designed to facilitate navigation

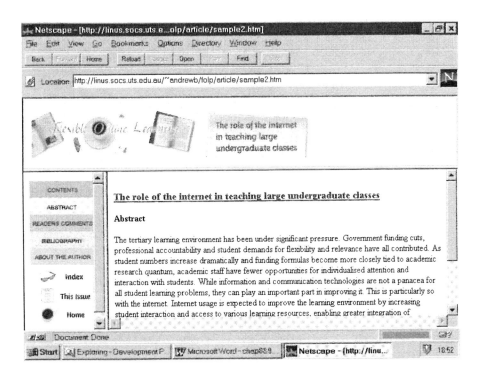

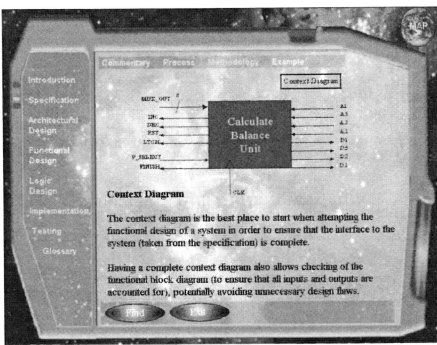

Design of interface screen elements

Once we decide on the overall screen layout, then we have to design each component of the interface. This can include the design of elements such as:

- Forms.
- Menus and Labels.
- Buttons.
- Windows/Frames.
- Icons.
- Tool bars.
- Dialogue boxes.
- Status lists.

In using these interface elements there are a number of important considerations, including how to most effectively select and group navigational buttons, making sure that the meaning of interface elements is obvious (this is related to the above discussion on the use of a suitable metaphor), minimising screen clutter and visual distractions, the suitable layout of the interface elements, etc. These aspects are well covered in most texts on user interface design.

- **Colours:** different colours convey different meanings, and this will often vary with context, culture, gender, etc. For example, red can mean danger, green can mean freshness.
- **Fonts:** most popular fonts can be classified into five categories: these are Oldstyle, Modern, Sans Serif, Script and Decorative. The general rule is that one should not use more than two categories of font types in a design – one category for labels and headings and another for the main body text.

Developing Guidelines for Content Development

There are various principles we can use to determine the guidelines for developing content. The following principles were developed by Horn (1989), based on various cognitive and user research. Four principles of node construction are:

- **Chunking principle:** whenever groups of information, concepts or choices are presented (such as lists of information, buttons across a toolbar, items in a menu), the information should be grouped (i.e. 'chunked') into manageable units. The number of units in a group will usually be defined by the number that humans can handle within their short-term memory limitations. A good rule of thumb is to provide a limit of 5 ± 1.

- **Relevance principle:** each node should be based on a single primary point or concept, which is readily conveyed to the reader. This improves understandability.

- **Consistency principle:** for similar subject matters, use similar words, labels, format, organisations and sequences.

- **Labelling principle:** label every node and group of nodes, and other interface elements such as buttons and links, according to specific and appropriate criteria. Proper labelling helps users understand their context, as well as understanding the consequences of specific operations (see Figure 9-10).

Horn also identified that most information we come across can be classified into one of seven major categories (Horn, 1989), shown in Table 9-3. This information type classification becomes very helpful when applying the chunking and relevance principals mentioned above. We can identify a consistent chunk of information as information describing a concept, classification, process, procedure, etc.

Table 9-3

Categories of information

Concept:	What is it?
Classification:	Can we group or divide based on some property?
Process:	What happens or How it works?
Procedure:	How to carry out a task?
Structure:	What are the sub parts?
Fact:	Statement of data without supporting information
Principle:	A rule that describes a relationship or what should or should not be done.

Plan		Plan for the Human Resource handbook
First Cut		Handbook First Draft
Reactions		Employee Task Force Comments

Figure 9-10

Labelling information chunks. Which is more informative?

Individual screen layouts

The digital medium supports a wide range of media forms, and by properly combining these we can enhance the communication of the message in our hypermedia applications. We can develop guidelines for individual screen layout based in the information types described above. For example:

- *Classification*: always specify the basis used for classification. Keep the number of items in the classification list to about 5 ± 1, in keeping with our short-term memory capacity.

- *Structure*: use of visual representation and hyperlinks to explain the parts using text and/or audio.

- *Process*: visual representations of process (such as flowcharts, dataflow diagram, etc.) can be important. Use of animation and video can be especially effective.

- *Procedure*: step-by-step guide generally formatted using a table or flowchart. Methods for performing each step can be enhanced using other media forms (such as a video clip of the procedure being performed).

- *Other information types*: mainly presented as text.

9.7 Production Techniques

The main emphasis during the production process is on productivity. We can enhance productivity through automation, use of appropriate tools where automation is not possible and information reuse.

When developing large hypermedia information systems there are certain areas of the production process which are most amenable to automation. Most of this is in structuring (based on syntactic structure of legacy data) and algorithmic linking (creating links based on some algorithm) of textual information.

Certain production activities require decisions based on the semantics of information being processed, including structuring of mostly non-textual data and certain types of associative linking. To carry out this type of production operation, we need to use tools that will minimise the cognitive burden on the author and assist the author to increase productivity.

Information reuse is another factor that impacts heavily on productivity. It will become increasingly impractical to recreate the underlying information structures for every new application. Where possible, authoring productivity (and productivity of the overall process) can be greatly improved by reusing information structures which have already been developed for other hypermedia applications (or even applications such as databases, archives, etc.). This can be actively promoted by leaving those aspects of the information structuring which impose a specific viewpoint on the information to as late in the development process as possible (see the description of the Matilda project later in this book). Other factors which will help promote reuse include the development of suitable repositories and data models, browsing tools, standards interoperability, etc. For example, it may be appropriate to include, as part of the process, planning for a dedicated role of 'reuse engineer'.

Information Organisation

Capturing information (such as entering text, digitising and editing images, etc.), structuring this information (such as partitioning of the content into specific nodes), and linking the information (creating the logical structure and semantic relationships) is very time consuming. Indeed, these activities often take most of the time spent in producing hypermedia applications. Non-textual information (such as images, video and sound) can be particularly time-consuming, as these are still predominantly structured manually. We need to consider the extent to which the process helps manage these activities.

Organising the information involves activities such as breaking the information into nodes, identifying key concepts that best describe the information contained in that node, and marking anchor points. As a general rule, information within a node should be focused on a single theme. The key concepts identified during the structuring process will assist later when searching for specific information.

Various researchers have looked at automating these activities (Furuta, Plaisant and Shneiderman, 1989; Niblett and van Hoff, 1989; Rearick,

1991). A common strategy for automating the identification of nodes within paper based information is to use existing structural information. Keying on markup languages such as SGML or undertaking layout analysis of the text (Furuta, Plaisant and Shneiderman, 1989) are popular approaches. These approaches can be effective if the information is uniform in structure or has been previously marked up, but otherwise these approaches break down quickly.

Also, researchers have used information retrieval algorithms to produce key phrases and/or anchors. Although this is a step in the right direction, this approach introduces the problem of missing relevant anchors and key phrases, plus creating key phrases and anchors which are not relevant (recall and precision) (Bernstein, 1990). These projects have demonstrated that if the information contains non-structured documents or a document set with divergent structures within it, total automation is not possible. Further, we have a major problem if we try to extend these methods to non-textual media such as images, video and sound, as these do not have a well-modelled syntax.

Information Integration

Depending on the scale and the structure of the application the integration of various components to produce the application can either be done manually or automated. If the information has a relatively consistent structure, the various links that needs to be created can be expressed using an appropriate algorithm, and if the size of the application justifies the extra effort required to automate the process, then an automated approach can be used to integrate the various components and create the links.

If these characteristics are not present, then we have to use a manual approach to integration. This process of physically creating the application is known as authoring. Authoring involves the development of the macro structure as well as the micro structure of the application. Creation of a micro structure involves developing and formatting individual nodes. Many authoring tools have page editors to assist in creating the micro structure. The support available for creating the macro structure varies greatly from tool to tool.

Creation of the macro structure involves the integration of nodes, windows, forms, etc. into a cohesive application. This integration happens through the linking of nodes, windows, forms, etc. together. The non-linear information structure of the hypermedia applications make this

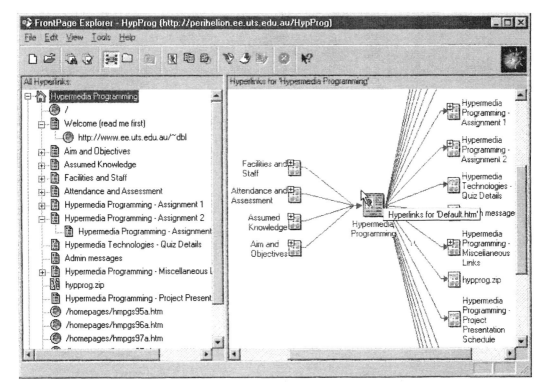

Figure 9-11

Microsoft Frontpage can be used to visualise the Web pages which are
linked to, or from, given pages

linking process very complex and demanding for the author. A common
result is to find many errors occurring during manual linking, thus if
manual linking is to be used for economic reasons, it is important to use
a tool such as Macromedia Authorware which allows the creation and
editing of the overall structure, or Microsoft FrontPage which shows a
graphical view of the structure (Figure 9-11).

9.8   Conclusions

At the conclusion to Part Two of the book, we should revisit the concept
of process. It is important to bear in mind the necessity of a suitable
process, a process which is neither easy nor straightforward. Lehmann
states:

'Only by a miracle can the quality of (a) software product be better than the process that produced it ...'

This is just as true for hypermedia development. Unless we can get the process right, and then the activities within this process right, we will be unable to develop quality hypermedia applications. In general, there are no easy solutions or 'silver bullets' for the difficulties inherent in hypermedia development. Although we have discussed various techniques and methods in the last three chapters, these are still far from providing a comprehensive approach which guarantees success. Such an approach does not exist: indeed, it is unlikely that such an approach will ever exist due to the huge variation in problem, solution and development domains. Our initial aim should therefore be to develop an understanding which allows us to maximise the application quality and development productivity and minimise the risks of development.

Although the technologies to support hypermedia are changing constantly, this should not stop us from developing effective processes. To do this we need to ensure we have an understanding of not only current techniques, but where and why these techniques might be inadequate. One way of developing an improved understanding of these aspects is to consider current research and how it is approaching the development of solutions to particular problems. This is the focus of Part Three of this book.

Part Three

Hypermedia Research Developments

Many of the issues raised in the first two parts of this book are still open research questions. Hypermedia development is still a young and evolving discipline, and as such there are many areas in which we do not yet have a sufficient understanding. There are numerous research groups around the world undertaking cutting edge research into many of these areas.

In this final part of the book, we provide an overview of a number of current hypermedia research projects. In particular, we look at how these research projects provide insights into how many of the issues raised in this book are likely to be addressed in future systems, development tools and development approaches.

10

Current Research

'Research serves to make building stones out of stumbling blocks.'
(Arthur D. Little)

Chapter Goals

In this part of the book we look at development projects which provide an insight into some aspect of hypermedia development. We explain why this is important, provide a set of criteria which can be used to guide our analysis of cutting-edge projects, and begin the process of considering various research and development projects. The objectives of this chapter are to:

- Look at cutting-edge research and development to provide us with valuable insights into how to improve hypermedia development practices, and how these practices may change in the future.

- Show that there is very little research currently being carried out on improving hypermedia development practices. Indeed, there is often an attitude (misguided, in our opinion) that this is unnecessary.

- Demonstrate that we have defined various important questions which can guide our consideration of cutting-edge research and development.

In this part of the book we look at a number of research and development projects. It may seem strange to be considering research projects in a book which is trying to discuss and promote best *practice* in hypermedia development, but there are several very good reasons for this.

First, the hypermedia field (and especially the Web) is changing so rapidly that what is research now can quickly become practice tomorrow. In such a dynamic field, it is important to be aware of the potential evolutionary (and possibly revolutionary) changes which may occur in even a short time frame. Secondly, although specific research projects may not become mainstream, they are still able to provide indications of how the field is likely to develop. Alternatively, they may provide useful hints or concepts which can be adapted for specific practice, or provide a more thorough understanding of specific development problems or issues and how to handle them.

10.1 Research Directions

Hypermedia is an extremely active research area, and it would be impractical to provide a comprehensive overview of all the research in this area. However, we can provide an indication of the directions of hypermedia research, and in particular, work on hypermedia development and/or process.

To provide an indication of the changing focus of hypertext and hypermedia research, we can look at the conferences in the area and consider what has been published. The most significant conferences on hypermedia are the ACM series of conferences:

- Hypertext '87 [Chapel Hill, NC, USA]
- Hypertext '89 [Pittsburgh, PA, USA]
- Hypertext '91 [San Antonio, TX, USA]
- ECHT '92 [European Conference on Hypertext] [Milan, Italy]
- Hypertext '93 [Seattle, WA, USA]
- ECHT '94 [European Conference on Hypermedia Technology] [Edinburgh, UK]
- Hypertext '96 [Washington DC, USA]
- Hypertext '97 [Southampton, UK]
- Hypertext '98 [Pittsburgh, USA]

- Hypertext '99 [Darmstadt, Germany]

If we look at a selection of these conferences, and the focus of the papers included in each, we can identify trends and see how the field is evolving. Let us begin with the Hypertext '91 conference. This included 25 technical papers, of which:

- Seven discussed applications and use of hypermedia (including evaluations).
- Six discussed authoring of structure.
- Six discussed presentation issues.
- Six discussed mechanisms for navigation, and
- Five discussed structural models or hypermedia architectures.

The focus was obviously quite strongly on implementation aspects such as presentation and structure generation (but not structure design). There was only a single paper which could be said to have attempted to address process issues in any form. This paper, 'HDM – A model for the design of hypertext applications', describes an approach to 'authoring-in-the-large', and considers the definition of the topology of a hypermedia. It does not, however, consider process in a broader sense.

There was not a single paper at Hypertext '91 which considered (except possibly at a very trivial level in passing) development process models, developing for maintenance, reuse (except for structure templates and data reuse), process measurement, etc. If we look at the 19 papers from Hypertext '93, two years later, we find that:

- Seven discussed navigation and access mechanisms.
- Five discussed applications and use of hypermedia (including evaluations), and
- Five discussed link and/or anchor generation or analysis.

The focus is still strongly on implementations and hypermedia structure, but one of the more apparent trends is a move towards recognising the need to consider how hypermedia is used and what forms of support (i.e. navigation and information access) are effective.

Again, however, there was only a single paper, 'Designing Dexter-based cooperative hypermedia applications', which addressed broader process issues. This paper considered, in particular, issues of collaborative work and development responsibilities. Again, there was not a single paper which considered broader process issues. Hypertext '96 included 24 papers:

- Six discussed navigation.
- Five discussed applications and use of hypermedia (including evaluations), and
- Four discussed link generation, analysis or typing.

Although this indicates a continuing focus on navigation and hypermedia structures, an important observation is that there were three papers (and indeed, a dedicated session) on models of hypermedia design and evaluation. The need to consider process issues and the whole hypermedia development lifecycle is gradually becoming increasingly recognised.

10.2 Example Research Projects

For most of the remainder of this last part of the book, we will be looking at a selection of research and/or development projects. These have been selected as representing a broad cross-section of the technical research and development currently being undertaken on hypermedia. The purpose was not to select working applications or systems which can be chosen as possible development applications or approaches (though for some of the descriptions this is the case), but to demonstrate possible approaches to addressing many of the issues described during the first two parts of the book.

Selected Projects

- **Matilda**: Matilda is a hypermedia framework developed within the HyVIS (Hypermedia and Visual Information Applications) research group at the University of Technology, Sydney. Matilda is based around a novel scalable information representation which supports browsing on information abstractions and promotes information reuse, as well as providing a framework within which the development process can be guided. The project is still at a relatively early stage of development, but encapsulates a number of interesting ideas and concepts which are worth investigating.

- **Microcosm:** Microcosm is an open and extensible hypermedia architecture that has been under development by the Multimedia Research Group within the Department of Electronic and Computer Science at the University of Southampton since 1989. Microcosm is essentially an open document and link management system which supports large-scale development through the use of a separate linkbase, which manages various link types (including generic links) overlaid on arbitrary document types. Microcosm is available as a commercial hypermedia development application.

- **Hyper-G:** the Hyper-G project began at the Institute for Information Processing and Computer Supported New Media (IICM) of Graz University of Technology, Austria. Hyper-G (and the commercial system into which it has evolved, Hyperwave) is a client-server Internet-based hypermedia application which provides session support, access control and a data model that is much richer than that provided by the WWW.

- **AHM:** the Amsterdam Hypermedia Model (AHM), developed at CWI in Amsterdam, is an amalgamation of basic principles from both the hypertext and multimedia domains. It draws together the Dexter hypertext model with the CMIF (van Rossum *et al.*, 1993) multimedia model to produce a useful model of the hypermedia domain. AHM extends upon the Dexter Model by adding a conceptual framework for the inclusion and management of temporal data, the addition of high level presentation attributes, and the incorporation of link context into the model.

- **RMM:** the Relationship Management Methodology (RMM) was developed predominantly at New York University's Stern School of Business, and is a hypermedia design approach. RMM focuses on the design and construction phases of development, and describes various design activities and procedures for carrying out these activities.

Questions to be Addressed for Each Project

For each of the applications or approaches we consider, we focus the discussion (and comparisons, where appropriate) by addressing a series of 12 focused questions. These are intended to highlight those aspects of the projects which address many of the issues raised in the first two parts of the book.

It is important to remember that the applications we discuss expressly address given domains of interest. In many cases, the projects or applications to be discussed will not explicitly address some or many of the questions given below. This is often not because of a failing in the application, but simply because that particularly area was not the intended focus of the research project.

Product questions

1. *How is effective navigation and browsing addressed?* Obviously, a major consideration is the mechanisms which either directly provide support for effective navigation and browsing, or facilitate the development of this support.

2. *How is the issue of cognitive management during browsing addressed?* Many, if not most, hypermedia applications will involve complex information structures. We wish to consider possible alternatives for handling the cognitive burden imposed on a user associated with managing these complex structures.

2. *How is information contextualisation addressed?* As described early in the book, information can be understood as the interpretation of data within some context. It is therefore important that we can place data that is provided to users in some appropriate context (both a global context of the entire application or Website, and a local context of the specific concepts being presented and their immediate neighbourhood). We wish to look at mechanisms for providing or developing these contexts.

4. *How are issues of link and content validity addressed?* Aspects such as correctness, completeness and relevance of the individual content, the partitioning of the content into nodes or pages, and the links between the nodes are important to the overall effectiveness of the application.

5. *How are issues of information structure addressed?* Whereas the issue of link and content validity raised in the previous question is a 'local' issue, the 'global' issue of overall information structure is just as important. Hypermedia is, after all, to a very large extent about organising information. It is thus important to consider how this organisation is created in a way which ensures an understandable and effective structure.

6. *How is the use of different media managed?* Finally, hypermedia is about the use not just of text, but of a range of additional media. We need to consider mechanisms for handling these other media.

Process questions

1. *How is the issue of application maintenance addressed?* It is likely that maintenance of hypermedia information applications will become increasingly important as the size and scope of applications continues to evolve. We need to consider possible avenues for improving both the maintainability of applications and the maintenance procedures which are carried out.

2. *How is the issue of reuse addressed?* Development costs can be significantly affected by reuse, which can include not just the reuse of raw data (which is reasonably common), but also the reuse of a much broader range of application and process elements, such as information, knowledge, frameworks, presentation templates, functional components, documentation, designs, information structures, etc. We will consider different approaches to reuse.

3. *How is the full development lifecycle supported?* Obviously, any given hypermedia application must have a lifecycle. Many of the stages of this lifecycle are often overlooked when considering the development of hypermedia. We want to consider possible mechanisms for handling a broader range of lifecycle activities.

4. *How is process management supported or promoted?* We look at how each of the projects described either addresses process management directly, or provides support which assists with project management. For example, a development framework which describes (or even supports) specific development activities will provide an inherent management guideline based on these activities.

5. *How is the issue of cognitive management during development addressed?* The information, structure and functionality must be managed not only during use of an application, but also during development. Indeed, during development the application will be incomplete and therefore more likely to be difficult to manage. We shall consider how each project addresses this particular problem.

6. *In what ways is support for enhancing development productivity provided?* Finally, we look at how each project addresses the broad issue of improving the productivity of the development process.

10.3 Other Research Work

Although the projects we discuss in the next five chapters demonstrate a cross section of awareness (or lack of awareness) of development process considerations, there are various projects which address process issues to which we haven't dedicated an entire chapter[8]. Although not comprehensive, the following research projects and areas provide an indication of the types of issues being addressed by various researchers and research groups.

Open Hypermedia Systems

It is clear that authoring effort and the management of links are major issues in the development of large hypermedia applications. This has led to the design of systems which separate the link data from the document data which enables the information about links to be processed and maintained like any other data, rather than being embedded in the document data. Research effort has also been concentrated on the development of link services that enable hypermedia functionality to be integrated into the general computing environment, and allow linking from all tools on the desktop. The hypermedia management system then becomes much more of a back-end process than a user interface technology. Such systems are usually referred to as 'open hypermedia systems', although much use and abuse has been made of the term 'open' in this context. There are those who use the term to mean that the application runs on an open system such as UNIX: in this sense, the World Wide Web is an open system. However, this is not what is meant in the context of open hypermedia. Various definitions have been proposed: we discuss these and the development of open hypermedia systems below.

The paper by Malcolm, Polbrock and Schuler (1991) is an excellent summary of user requirements for open hypermedia systems, although the authors do not directly refer to their proposed system as such. The

---

[8] Mainly through lack of space – we are, after all, simply trying to illustrate various approaches and not provide a comprehensive discussion of research projects. Our selection of projects to consider in more detail is based purely on trying to demonstrate a broad cross-section of approaches, and does not imply that we consider those systems which we haven't discussed any less worthy. A good introduction to much of the research work in this area can be found in the August 1995 special issue of the *Communications of the ACM*.

paper argues for the development of *industrial strength* hypermedia systems which provide an adaptable environment for the integration of data tools and services that do not confine users to a particular suite of editors and specialised software packages, are platform independent and distributed across platforms, make it easy for users to find, update, annotate and exchange information, and in which all forms of data and media are treated in a conceptually similar manner.

In the early 1990s, the hypermedia systems commercially available were all, in the main, closed systems. A closed hypermedia system is defined as one that provides a fixed set of encapsulated applications which are normally tightly integrated with the hypermedia linking mechanisms (Legget *et al.*, 1993). The hypermedia links are generally embedded in the data which is stored in a proprietary document format. It is therefore not possible to access the data or the links from outside the hypermedia system. In contrast, an open hypermedia system provides a protocol that allows any application to participate in the hypermedia service. The applications are loosely integrated with the hypermedia linking mechanisms, but the degree of openness can vary considerably according to the restrictions that the protocol imposes on the applications, ranging from complete control to none at all. A hypermedia link service and an associated protocol is therefore an essential part of any open hypermedia system.

Sun's Link Service (Pearl, 1989) was a ground-breaking project that was probably the first truly open system. Running on Sun workstations in a distributed environment, it consisted of a link database service integrated with registered applications through a library and an associated communication protocol. It therefore provided a link service to existing applications, and dedicated applications for editing and processing information were not required. However, an application had to be aware of the link service and be registered with it in order to make use of the service. It had to be able to send information to the link service that identified the element in the document from which a link is to be followed.

The Intermedia project was a pioneering project with respect to the development of open hypermedia systems (Haan *et al.*, 1992), though it may best be described as a partially open system. Document and link information was held in a central database, but dedicated Intermedia applications were needed to access the database in order to make use of the hypermedia services. Applications were required to place link markers in the documents, thus creating problems when accessing information with external tools. Hyper-G (Maurer, 1996) works in a similar way, except that the link markers are only placed in the documents when they are being viewed through the Hyper-G system, and in the latest versions of Hyperwave, access to the hypermedia functionality is available through standard Web browsers rather than specialised clients (see Chapter 13 for a more detailed description).

Davis *et al.* (1992) published their criteria for referring to a hypermedia system as open as follows:

1. *The hypertext link service should be available across the entire range of applications available on the desktop.* This implies that, since applications would not normally be capable of manipulating anchor identifiers, as required by the Dexter model, it would be necessary to design a system that held links and their anchors externally from the node content.

2. *The link service must work across a network on heterogeneous platforms.* This implies that hypertext functionality must be provided by a number of communicating processes – a framework for routing messages between the various components.

3. *The architecture should be such that the functionality of the system can be extended.* This implies that the design should be modular so that new components may be written to a specified API then added to the system. The API should be kept as simple as possible so that applications may be adapted to conform to the API.

4. *There should be no artificial distinction between author and reader.* Many systems have an authoring mode and a reader mode: such a system is not open from the reader's point of view. Removing this distinction implies that all users should have access to all parts of the system. This is not to say that one user should be able to access or change another user's data: this aspect should be controlled by the operating system access rights granted. Users should be able to create their own links and nodes within their private workspace, then change the access rights so that other users may view or edit them as required.

Subsequent authors and workshops have attempted to define the term 'open hypermedia', in particular the Open Hypertext Systems Workshop at Konstanz in May 1994 (Aßfalg, 1994) and the ECHT '94 Workshop on Open Hypermedia Systems at Edinburgh in September 1994 (Wiil and Østerbye, 1994). Following this workshop there have been a series of workshops on OHS held at the ACM conferences. The third was held at

Hypertext '97 in Southampton (Wiil, 1997). Selected papers from this workshop are now available in a special issue of the *Journal of Digital Information* [http://jodi.ecs.soton.ac.uk], and interested readers are referred to the excellent editorial for more information and a summary of the research issues.

Thinking on the subject was summarised as follows in Hall, Davis and Hutchings (1996): The term *open* implies the possibility of importing new objects into a system. A truly open hypermedia system should be open with regard to:

1. *Size:* it should be possible to import new nodes, links, anchors and other hypermedia objects without any limitation, to the size of the objects or to the maximum number of such objects that the system may contain, being imposed by the hypermedia system.

2. *Data formats:* the system should allow the importation and use of any data format, including temporal media.

3. *Applications:* the system should allow any application to access the link service in order to participate in the hypermedia functionality.

4. *Data models:* the hypermedia system should not impose a single view of what constitutes a hypermedia data model, but should be configurable and extensible so that new hypermedia data models may be incorporated. It should thus be possible to interoperate with external hypermedia systems, and to exchange data with external systems.

5. *Platforms:* it should be possible to implement the system on multiple distributed platforms.

6. *Users:* the system must support multiple users, and allow each user to maintain their own private view of the objects in the system.

No one system implements all of the aspects of openness as described above. Open hypermedia systems are largely still in the province of the research laboratory, although commercial versions of some of them are available, including DHM (Grønbaek and Trigg, 1992) and Microcosm (Davis *et al.*, 1992; Hall, Davis and Hutchings, 1996). They all vary considerably in implementation and scope.

By these definitions, the way in which the World Wide Web is currently used makes it a closed hypermedia system, although it is quite possible to implement an open hypermedia system within the WWW environment and a number of groups are currently working on this (including work such as DLS (Carr *et al.*, 1995), Chimera (Anderson, 1997) and the use of Dexter (Grønbaek, Boovin and Sloth, 1997)).

HDM

One of the difficulties encountered in performing the design of hyper-media applications is how to represent the results of the design process. Implementation mechanisms are not appropriate as they typically cannot be used to capture the abstractions required by a design. The alternative is to use informal or formal design-specific representations. However, informal representations, such as natural language and storyboards, can result in ambiguity, cannot be effectively used to reason about the design, and do not provide an effective mechanism for comparing alternative designs.

The alternative is to use formal design representations, often based on a design model of the hypermedia application. These models are typically intended to provide a framework or language which can be used to compare and document the specifications of applications and communicate them between analysts, designers, implementors and clients. One of the best developed hypermedia design models is HDM (literally, Hypermedia Design Model) (Garzotto, Paolini and Schwabe, 1993).

HDM incorporates a set of design elements which are used to define an application. The application is composed of typed *entities*, which are in turn composed of *components*. *Entities* and *components* are connected by *structural links* or *application links*. An HDM *schema* is a set of *entity* and *link* type definitions, and a *schema instance* is a set of actual *entities* and *links*.

HDM provides a framework in which hypermedia applications can be described and analysed. This in turn implicitly leads to a top-down process for the development of applications. This methodology is not, however, explicitly part of HDM. Indeed, HDM provides a framework for hypermedia development, but does not address the development process itself.

An important point to make is that HDM is a design model (i.e. a model of the design of an application) not a design method (i.e. a set of activities required to create the model). Nevertheless, the model does inherently imply which elements need to be designed, and hence can be viewed as indicating a methodology even if it is not explicitly defined.

For example, the design includes a set of entities, so a designer must perform an activity where these entities are identified.

OOHDM

Whereas HDM is a design model, the Object-Oriented Hypermedia Design Method (OOHDM) (Schwabe and Rossi, 1995a, b) is a design method, i.e. a series of activities for carrying out the design and implementation of hypermedia applications. In OOHDM applications are developed using four stages of development, carried out in an incremental process, with each stage typically focusing on some specific design issue. The result is that an object-oriented model of the application is constructed.

The first stage of development in OOHDM is domain analysis, where a conceptual model of the application is constructed using a combination of conventional OO modelling technique primitives and extensions added specifically for the hypermedia domain. The concern at this point is primarily for the application domain semantics, and does not consider application structure or functionality.

The second stage is navigation design, where user profiles are used to guide the design of the navigational structure of the application. The nodes in OOHDM represent views onto the conceptual classes, and links are derived from the conceptual relationships defined during the previous stage. In essence, this should theoretically improve the maintainability of the application, since the application-specific navigation structure is conceptually separated from the application-independent domain knowledge. The result of this stage is a collection of nodes, links, access structures and navigation contexts.

The third development stage is abstract interface design, where the interface is essentially modelled by defining perceptible objects in terms of interface classes, which are in turn defined as aggregations of interface primitives (such as text fields). The behaviour of the interface is also specified by considering responses to events and communication mechanisms between interface and navigation objects.

The fourth and final stage is implementation, in which interface objects are mapped to implementation objects.

The OO techniques used in OOHDM modelling, such as classification, inheritance (generalisation and specialisation) and aggregation, provide an expressiveness in the modelling that facilitates abstraction of the design and implementation and reuse opportunities based on the use of design patterns. The specific separation of domain, navigation, interface and implementation also means that maintainability of the application is improved.

One of the aspects which OOHDM does not address, except implicitly as being based on an iterative model, is how the various phases should be coordinated and at what stages it is appropriate to be focusing on different aspects. This also has the possibility of making it difficult to obtain a sense of project closure. OOHDM also does not address early lifecycle activities such as feasibility studies, development of initial proto-types, project planning and estimation, etc. Despite this, OOHDM is one of the more advanced hypermedia design methods available. Similar work on OO modelling of hypermedia applications has also been performed by Lange (1993) on EORM (Enhanced Object Relationship Model), though this does not provide as clear a differentiation between domain analysis and navigational design.

Hypermedia Design Environments

Jocelyne and Marc Nanard have been investigating various issues related to design environments and their role in the hypermedia design process (Nanard and Nanard, 1995). In particular, they have looked at the characteristics of design environments which are required in order to suitably facilitate the design process. Their work has not focused on formal design models, but has considered general human-factor aspects, and has been based on sound practical observations of design activities. In particular, they did not look at the design activities themselves, but the way in which these activities have been carried out. In particular, they say (Nanard and Nanard, 1995):

> 'Designing is not simply following a formal design technique. It is an incremental and opportunistic human activity that takes place in an two-axis space. . . . One axis represents the stages generally identified in formal design methods. The second represents categories of the designer's mental activity. Actual design activity is not a simple set of steps along the "method steps" axis. Rather it is like a Brownian motion within the activity space.'

Nanard and Nanard point out that results from psychological studies indicate that any creative process (including the design of hypermedia) involves an opportunistic mental process. Any final result is typically the result of numerous iterations and backtracking. Indeed, activities along the mental process axis include generating material, organising and structuring, reorganising and updating, and evaluation. These activities are carried out in a complex and chaotic but natural fashion. Indeed, the quality of the result is often dependant upon the complexity and richness of these activities.

On the basis of these observations, Nanard and Nanard argue that any hypermedia design environment needs to support both the abstract models typical of formal design approaches as well as the specific instances of a design which support the cognitive processes mentioned above. Designers should be able to design a model at an abstract level and then instantiate the model, or design a specific instance and then conceptualise this to obtain the abstract model. Such an approach, with a rapid feedback loop between abstract models and instances, facilitates evaluation and process recursion, and hence improves the resulting design quality.

Designing for Comprehension

Thuring, Hannemann and Haake (1995) have looked at how issues of cognition and human information processing can be used to improve hypermedia design. They begin by differentiating between applications designed for users who wish to wander through an information space, and applications that have been designed to assist the user in specific directed learning or specific problem-solving. They then direct their focus onto the latter category of applications.

Thuring *et al.* point out that in cognitive sciences, comprehension is characterised as the construction of a mental model of the knowledge being conveyed. The readability of a document or hyperdocument (i.e. hypermedia application) can be related to the effort required to construct this mental model. Readability can be improved by strengthening coherence and reducing the cognitive overhead.

Two forms of coherence are identified as particularly important for constructing a mental model: local coherence, which ties fragments of media together; and global coherence, based on conclusions or concepts from large sections of media. In hypermedia this relates to intra- and inter-node relationships. Intra-node coherence can use traditional writing skills; inter-node coherence, however, requires additional or new skills.

This requires the use of suitable forms of information structure such as aggregation and mechanisms for conveying this structure.

Cognitive overhead relates to the use of mental resources for activities other than the immediate understanding of the information being presented. Examples include the effort required by readers for navigation, orientation and user interface adjustments. The effort for these activities can be reduced by providing suitable clues to the reader.

Thuring et al. (1995) identify a series of ten cognitive design issues which are important in addressing issues of coherence and cognitive overhead:

How to increase the coherence of a hyperdocument?
- I1. How to appropriately indicate semantic relations between information units?
- I2. How to reduce the impression of fragmentation?
- I3. How to aggregate information units?
- I4. How to provide an adequate overview of the hyperdocument?

How to reduce the reader's cognitive overhead?
- I5. How to indicate the reader's current position?
- I6. How to show the way that led to the reader's current position?
- I7. How to present the options for reaching new nodes?
- I8. How to support navigation with respect to direction?
- I9. How to support navigation with respect to distance?
- I10. How to reduce additional effort for user-interface adjustment?

From these issues, a number of design principles are developed:

- P1. Use typed link labels (I1, I2)
- P2. Indicate equivalencies between information units (I1, I2)
- P3. Preserve the context of information units (I1, I2)
- P4. Use higher order information units (I3)
- P5. Visualise the structure of the document (I1, I2, I4, I8, I9)
- P6, Include cues into the visualisation of structure which show the readers current position, the way that led to this position and navigation options for moving on (I5, I6, I7)
- P7. Provide a set of complementary navigation facilities which cover aspects of direction and distance (I8, I9)
- P8. Use a stable screen layout with windows of fixed position and default size (I10)

The design principles could be used not only as the basis for manual design activities, but could be used to provide indications of the type of actions which design tools should support. For example, the developer of a design tool could incorporate a mechanism for evaluating the consistency of user interfaces or screen layouts.

Many of the above concepts and principles have been incorporated into various tools developed within GMD-IPSI (Integrated Publication and Information Systems Institute of the German National Research Centre for Information Technology). These include SEPIA and DOLPHIN, which have been designed as cooperative authoring environments.

SEPIA and DOLPHIN

SEPIA (Structured Elicitation and Processing of Ideas for Authoring) (Streitz *et al.*, 1992) is a hypermedia authoring system based around both synchronous and asynchronous collaboration on the production of documents by a group of authors. This includes collaboration on the different activities of the hypermedia authoring process (such as planning of the document, organising the structure for the content of the document, and generation of the actual document itself).

The application supports both individual and synchronised work. When working synchronously, all authors have a shared view of the document. In loosely coupled mode each user works independently, but can see the results of the other users operations. In tightly coupled mode, all users see the same thing and act together. SEPIA uses the concept of 'activity spaces' to explicitly support the development of hypermedia documents within the context of a cognitive model of the activities involved in hypermedia authoring. For example, SEPIA actively supports the representation of argumentative structures and rhetorical organisation of the hypermedia information. The result is hypermedia documents that have been developed collaboratively and which have enhanced navigability and comprehensibility.

SEPIA supports text, graphics, pictures and sound as the contents of nodes, and operates via a graphical interface. It ensures synchronisation of different users by using Cooperative Hypermedia Server (CHS) and a database management system which provides persistent object store and retrieval mechanisms for hypermedia objects (Figure 10-1).

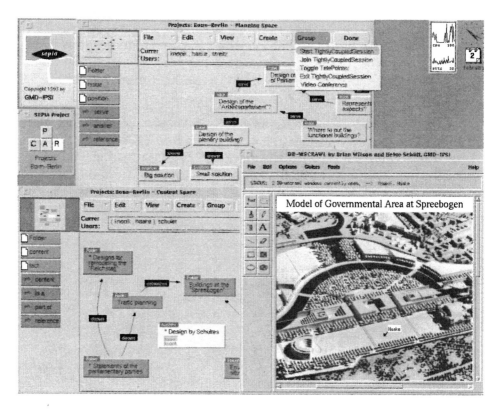

Figure 10-1

SEPIA (Structured Elicitation and Processing of Ideas for Authoring) (Copyright 1996 by GMD-IPSI, reprinted by permission)

SEPIA has been used in a number of subsequent projects, including POLI-WORK (a hypermedia-based document management system for public administration), VORTEL (heterogeneous workflow management systems) and MuSE (SEPIA has been extended to become a unified user-interface to multimedia systems engineering documents).

DOLPHIN (Bapart *et al.*, 1996; Streitz *et al.*, 1994) is another collaborative hypermedia system. The design of DOLPHIN resulted from an analysis of the types of information and structures used in face-to-face meetings (such as group brainstorming). This resulted in a system which supports more informal structures within a general hypermedia document structure and representation framework. This is combined with a pen-based user interface and interaction possibilities based on gesture recognition (such as drawing a cross over an element on the document to delete the element). It thus provides coexistence and smooth transformations between free hand scribbles, a simple node and link model and more formal typed nodes and links (as in SEPIA – indeed, DOLPHIN provides a smooth interface to SEPIA to allow documents prepared with SEPIA to be used within DOLPHIN).

The design of DOLPHIN is closely related to the design of the meeting room, and the provision of networked computers for each participant around the meeting room table and a large interactive electronic white-board. Besides operating the whiteboard with a cordless pen, group members can also interact with it and modify information on the whiteboard from their networked computers using the cooperative functionality of DOLPHIN. Furthermore, people can work not only in this 'public space', shared by all connected users, but also in an individual private space. The data model used by DOLPHIN allows, beyond conventional hypermedia functionality, the representation of dependencies between documents created in different meetings and different workspaces.

Typically, with DOLPHIN, documents are prepared before a meeting, then used and modified interactively within the meeting, and finally, processed and finalised after the meeting. DOLPHIN documents can contain both various media, as well as hyperlinks to other documents. Figure 10-2 shows a typical screendump from a DOLPHIN session.

Design-Oriented Evaluation of Hypermedia

Work by the Hypermedia Laboratory at the Department of Electronics and Information, Politecnico di Milan, has been looking at evaluation issues within hypermedia. In particular, much of the focus has been on what the research group refers to as design-oriented evaluation (Garzotto, Mainetti and Paolini (1995)) – a heuristic evaluation of a hypermedia application based on analysis of the application using a suitable design model with general usability criteria. Garzotto *et al.* identify the following dimensions for analysing a hypermedia application:

- *Content*: the pieces of information included in the application.
- *Structure*: the organisation of the content.
- *Presentation*: how content and functions are shown to the users.
- *Dynamics*: how users interact with, and move amongst, the information.
- *Interaction*: use of an applications dynamic functionalities.

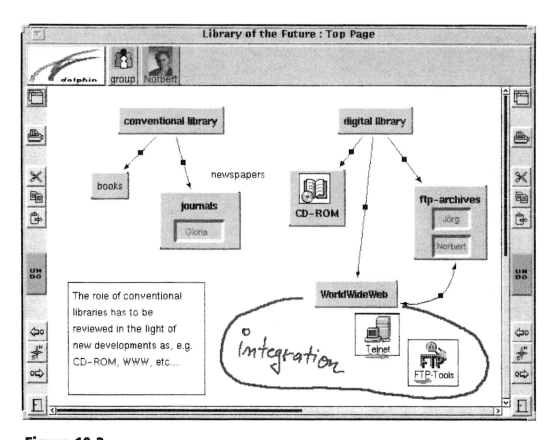

Figure 10-2

Screendump from a DOLPHIN collaborative meeting session (Copyright 1996 by GMD-IPSI, reprinted by permission)

They then make the point that for a systematic analysis of an application we need a suitable design model with which the application can be described. Once an application has been described, various heuristics can be applied to the description. For example: richness, ease, consistency, self-evidence, predictability, readability and reuse. Garzotto *et al.* admit that a user-oriented evaluation (typified by usability tests) can modify the results of design-oriented evaluations. Nevertheless they will usually concur, and design-oriented evaluation can guide the development up to the point at which user evaluation can occur.

More recent work by Paolini and Garzotto has been looking at the Systematic Usability Evaluation (SUE) project, which provides a framework for usability evaluation. The framework identifies three main stages: off-line work, heuristic evaluation and experimental testing.

In the off-line work, the evaluation is essentially planned and designed. The application level being evaluated is first identified (generic features of all applications such as look and feel, category-based evaluation such as hypermedia information richness, or domain evaluation such as characteristics of an encyclopaedia). A suitable model for evaluation at the selected level is then chosen, such as the use of the HDM model of a hypermedia application. Usability criteria are then identified, which can be measured from the selected model, such as consistency and predictability mentioned above. Different criteria may be selected for different user models. For each criteria, a set of abstract tasks are identified which will lead to an evaluation of the criteria.

In the heuristic evaluation, abstract tasks are used to define concrete tasks which can be performed. These tasks are applied by an expert as the basis of a design-oriented evaluation, and the results are used to identify potential problems with the application which can be rectified at the design stage. It can also be used as the basis for identifying end-user concrete evaluation tasks which can be carried out during experimental testing.

Designing for Change

During much of this book, we have been talking about the importance of a suitable development process, including design activities. One of the most significant of these design activities is the creation of a structure for the information space. However, in many cases it will be difficult to predetermine this structure, perhaps because the structure is created as part of the use of the application (for example, when the boundary between authoring and usage – or writing and reading – becomes blurred). It may also be because the structure evolves constantly over the lifetime of the application.

Research at the Department of Computer Science of Texas A&M University has been looking at designing 'spatial' hypermedia which addresses this particular problem. Many of the aspects they have investigated also have a significant impact on how we address maintenance in hypermedia systems.

Marshall and Shipman (1995) point out that factors which are important in spatial hypermedia include the ability to freely create and move nodes, and the ability to express relationships by spatial proximity and visual cues (as distinct from specific link mechanisms). Spatial hypermedia separates symbols of information from content, and the symbols are used to create 'hypertextual' meaning, but using implicit and information relationships. Marshall, Shipman and Coombs (1994) investigated the application of spatial hypermedia applications in an experimental system called VIKI.

Results indicate that spatial hypermedia provide a valuable model of hypermedia which addresses the needs of applications where the structure of the information space cannot or should not be predetermined. The result is a significant change in the way in which the development process would be carried out. The information structure can evolve during use as a natural reflection of the human interaction with the computational elements of the application. Results also show that spatial hypermedia can provide a valuable means of visualising the information structure and provides feedback for navigation.

Hypermedia Support for Computational Applications

Much of the focus of this book has been on dedicated hypermedia applications. This is, in some respects, an overly-constrained view. Hypermedia applications have much to gain by being combined with other applications. Indeed, we defined one of the primary goals of hypermedia as:

Hypermedia Goal 2

To support the carrying out of actions which facilitate the effective use of information.

The focus here is on facilitating effective use of information. In many cases, this information will exist in other applications, either as a part of the information resources of that application, or as a direct outcome. There are several ways of addressing this goal: one is obviously to build mechanisms into the hypermedia applications which allow it to interface to these other applications. This is partly the goal of open hypermedia systems (such as Microcosm which will be discussed in a later chapter). An alternative approach is to design hypermedia functionality directly into these alternative applications. As an example, consider the situation where a conventional CAD tool is augmented with hypermedia functionality so that elements of the CAD drawings can be annotated with cross-referenced hypermedia elements. Indeed, it may even be possible or appropriate to treat the elements of the CAD drawing as hypermedia elements in their own right, with the defined spatial relationships as a special type of hypermedia 'link'.

Bieber and Kacmar (1995) state they believe that this area – of hypermedia support for computational applications – will be the area where hypermedia will have its greatest impact. The conventional hypermedia issues of document management and object presentation are of secondary importance. What is important is that the hypermedia is able to augment the computational or analytical functionality. This augmentation may be in the form of support for linking to the computations carried out, or explanation of these computations, backtracking through analysis steps, links which initiate more detailed calculations, etc. Bieber and Kacmar investigated the role each component of a computational application could play in supporting hypermedia functionality. Apart from the hypermedia component of an application, they looked at the interface and computation components. The hypermedia component was based on a philosophy of 'maximum access' to information.

In a computational application, possible links can exist between any object and its meta-information (such as a definition, value, attribute type, etc.), operations connecting input and output data, structural relationships (such as between items in the CAD drawing example given above), different views of the same data or object, and spatial, temporal or other process relationships. Many of these types of links could be calculated automatically. Indeed, it is likely that they would need to be, given that they would exist within applications where the quantity of information and the rate and complexity of the way in which it changes within these applications are very large.

Zypher

The Zypher research project (Demeyer, 1996) attempts to apply various advanced object-oriented software engineering techniques to the development of open hypermedia systems. In particular, aspects such as object-oriented frameworks and design patterns are used in supporting the design of open hypermedia. A major focus of the project has been handling the need for flexibility in the design of hypermedia systems. This flexibility is considered critical for handling the ever changing requirements, demands and structure of hypermedia applications.

The focus of the work has been in supporting the tailorability of applications as a way of providing flexibility. This tailorability exists at three different levels: domain level tailorability, where new formats or presentation mechanisms can be integrated, is managed through the use of OO style frameworks for domain applications; system level tailorability, where services such as concurrency control and caching can be added or adapted, is supported through the use of meta-object protocols; and configuration level concurrency, where the coordination of system components is adapted, is managed through yet another meta level.

Concept Maps

Concept maps are a visual language which is based on the representation of concepts and the relationships between them. Although they typically can take a wide variety of forms, the underlying basis of concepts and their inter-relationships has been widely used as an educational tool. Concept maps have been used to address two significant problems with respect to information structure within Hypermedia.

First, Gaines and Shaw (1995) have been investigating the use of concept maps as actual components within hypermedia systems. They have developed a general concept mapping system which supports collaborative development of concept maps. They view concept maps as a complement to other forms of media within hypermedia applications – being used as the basis for semi-formal active diagrams which facilitate understanding of the structure of the information space.

Robertson (1997) has taken a different approach, and has investigated the use of concept maps in the hypermedia design process. In particular, he has looked at how concept maps and techniques which have been developed for creating concept maps can be adapted to the problem of creating hypermedia structures. This includes using techniques based on concept mapping in determining how to partition the information space (i.e. what concepts should be the basis of hypermedia nodes), and how to decide which relationships between concepts are important (i.e. what links should we support).

Anecdote

Although there has been recent interest in hypermedia design, there is currently a dearth of hypermedia design tools. In addition, much would be gained from having a design tool which is integrated with implementation into a cohesive development process. Anecdote, developed by Harada *et al.* (1996) at NEC USA, Inc., is a multimedia design and implementation tool (with support for hypermedia linking) based around the use of storyboarding.

The tool allows the developer to create an initial prototype application by designing the structure of the application using storyboards. Initially, 'surrogate media' can be used to populate the elements within the storyboard – such as the use of simple sketches instead of images or videos. This means that the application can be readily simulated to perform evaluations and refine the initial prototype application. As the development proceeds the surrogate media can be progressively replaced by the final content, providing a mechanism for incremental development of an application. This process is illustrated in the screen-dump from Anecdote shown in Figure 10-3.

Anecdote allows developers to choose different approaches to the development of the application and different styles of application. The approach can be top-down (complete creation of a prototype structure before beginning the addition of low level detail) or bottom-up (creation of individual content before progressive integration of these elements into a higher level structure). The application storyboard design can be graphical (such as the use of sketches) or textual (which can be descriptive). The final application style can be timeline-based or hyperlinked. Typically, the development will use a combination of these approaches and styles and alternate between them as appropriate.

Anecdote lacks a number of features which are important in large-scale hypermedia application development, such as the separation of the information structure from the application presentation (Anecdote does, however, incorporate a template mechanism which allows the definition of presentation styles and scenario structures). Nor has Anecdote yet been evaluated in the development of a large-scale hypermedia application, though at the time of writing, this is currently being carried out. Despite this, Anecdote illustrates a possible approach to solving a number of significant problems, the most obvious of which is the provision of an environment which facilitates an incremental approach to development. The provision of storyboard-based prototypes at an early point of the

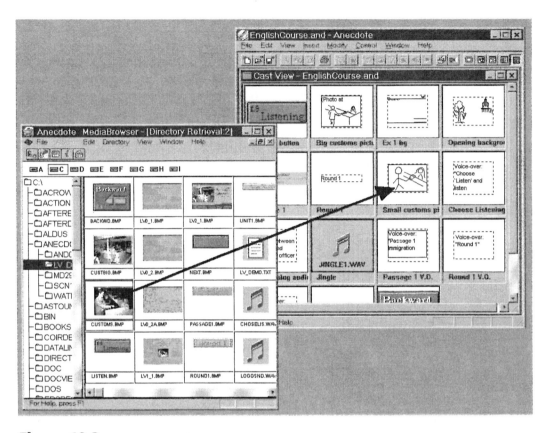

Figure 10-3

Anecdote Media Browser and Cast View. The arrow is superimposed over the screen image to illustrate the drag and drop operation. (Copyright NEC USA, Inc. Reproduced with permission of NEC USA, Inc.)

development also provides active support for scenario and structure analysis, effort and resource estimation and development scheduling.

HART

The HART (Hypermedia Authoring Research Tool) project was carried out by the HyVIS (Hypermedia and Visual Information Systems) Group in the Faculty of Engineering at the University of Technology, Sydney (Robertson, Merkus and Ginige, 1994). The aim of this project was to develop an effective methodology to convert text to hypertext. Rather than use a 'computer centred' approach, HART places the human at the centre of the conversion process, using the computer to augment the human's expertise. The system provides both procedural guidance and intelligent assistance to assist the user in the hyper-component identification process. By providing software tools to assist the human in the editorial process, it was found that both the overall cost and the time involved can be reduce to a commercially acceptable level. Additionally, it is believed this approach will result in better hypermedia systems being developed.

10.4 Research Comparison

It would be naïve to expect that every research project was attempting to address the full range of issues which face hypermedia developers: given research projects will be investigating specific issues (though in doing so, they may often provide insights into other areas). Saying that a specific research project (or even commercial product) does not address certain issues is not a criticism, rather it is a reflection of the focus of the work.

To assist in illustrating what areas different research projects are considering, we have listed the main issues and features of hypermedia applications and development being actively considered by researchers. For each of these areas, we have listed several of the research projects covered in detail in the next five chapters (Table 10-1). These are the projects which should provide a good insight into possible approaches to addressing the given issue. This should provide both a better understanding of the intention of the research work, and a guide as to which research projects or systems would warrant closer scrutiny where an interest in a specific issue exists.

It is worth noting that the above information can be used in two ways: first, if we are interested in approaches to addressing specific issues, then we can identify those systems which would warrant closer attention; secondly, the table can be used to identify the primary focus of interest of the researchers for each project. For example, we can see that the developers of the Matilda system were primarily interested in information management (during both development and use of an application). The next five chapters consider these interests in significant detail.

Table 10-1

Research issues

	Research project	Other research
Effective navigation	Matilda, RMM	OOHDM
Searching and indexing	Microcosm, Hyper-G	
Cognitive management during browsing	Matilda, Microcosm	
Information contextualisation	Matilda, AHM	
Link/content organisation and validity	Microcosm, AHM	HART
Information structuring	RMM, Matilda, Microcosm	OOHDM
Information presentation	AHM	
Use of different media	AHM, Microcosm	SEPIA
Application maintenance	Microcosm, Matilda, Hyper-G	
Information reuse	Microcosm, Matilda	
Development process management	RMM, Matilda	HDM, OOHDM, Anecdote
Cognitive management during devel.	Matilda, Microcosm, Hyper-G	HDM, Anecdoate
Development productivity	RMM	Anecdote
Collaborative development	Hyper-G, Microcosm	SEPIA, Dolphin

11

Matilda, MGraphs and MIST

Who'll come a waltzing Matilda with me
　　(Waltzing Matilda, A. B. Patterson)

Chapter Goals

Matilda is a hypermedia framework, associated information models and tools which focuses on scalable information representations. This chapter aims to show the importance of an effective information model, and how this can impact on the development approach. The objectives of this chapter are to show that:

- Matilda is based around a novel representation which separates application-independent information from application dependant information. The representation is intended to be highly scalable.

- The Matilda representation makes extensive use of abstractions of information to support flexible browsing.

- Matilda does not actively address development process, but the model and the tools which are based on it have an implicit process.

- A major goal of the Matilda project is to actively support reuse of information.

11.1 Introduction

The Hypermedia and Visual Information Systems (HyVIS) research group within Computer Systems Engineering at the University of Technology, Sydney is engaged in research in hypermedia information modelling, approaches to large-scale hypermedia development, use of image data in hypermedia, hypermedia databases, computer vision, image and video representations, image quality assessment and related topics.

In this chapter we primarily discuss several related projects from this research group: the Matilda hypermedia framework; the MGraph hypermedia information model; and the MIST information structuring tool.

The Matilda framework provides a structure within which applications, tools, applications and development models and approaches can be researched and investigated. The framework separates the information domain (which contains viewpoint or application independent information, i.e. information which is invariant) from the application domain (which contains information that is viewpoint dependant). The framework is based around the capturing of the different forms of information contributing to a given application, and hence aims to improve the possibility for information reuse and maintainability.

MGraphs (Matilda Structured Graphs) are a visual formalism for modelling the structure of information within the Matilda framework. A visual formalism provides a mathematical definition which consists of a data structure, structure preserving operations (such as browsing and editing) and an associated visual notation that facilitates visualisation of the structure or a portion of the structure. MGraphs provide a mechanism which allows browsing of information networks using arbitrary abstractions on both information components and semantic relationships, thereby facilitating both an understanding of the information structure and the ability to navigate effectively within this structure. By considering MGraphs in this chapter, we should be able to investigate how alternative information representations can be used to provide an alternative (and possibly more effective) paradigm for browsing an information space.

MIST (Matilda Information Structuring Toolset) is a set of tools which allows a hypermedia author to identify and record the meta-information contained within the information used in hypermedia applications (based on the MGraph model). MIST uses many of the concepts outlined above with respect to browsing the information and its structure at varying levels of abstraction through suppression of detail, and supporting the generation of incomplete or partial structures.

Matilda, Mgraphs and MIST are still prototype research projects. At the time of writing, they have yet to be fully evaluated on any large-scale projects, and are still the focus of considerable ongoing development and evolution. Despite this, many of the ideas which are embedded in their design can provide useful insights into possible effective approaches to the development of large-scale hypermedia applications.

11.2 Matilda Concepts

Most of the work on Matilda, MGraphs and MIST starts from a number of fundamental precepts. The first of these is that the process of developing hypermedia applications is essentially about handling information. Like the development process for any complex application, hypermedia development should incorporate an appropriate process. In the case of hypermedia, this process should address issues regarding the handling of the information, and this will be increasingly true as these applications become more complex, and the information content of applications grows (both in quantity and diversity).

The developers of Matilda claim that most current approaches to hypermedia development are confused by the tendency to cloud the distinction between raw data and the information represented by that data, between the data content, the structure of the data, and the inter-relationships between the data. Similarly, current development paradigms for information applications do not usually take into account issues beyond the immediate functionality of the given application (with a few notable exceptions, such as those described at the end of Chapter 10). This results in information applications which are difficult to maintain, difficult to develop, difficult to reuse, and which have poor functionality and usability. A common example of these problems is the use of markup languages such as HTML, where the information content, syntactic structure and semantic relationships are embedded into a single document, making reuse of the information and maintenance of the application difficult.

Given these observations, the HyVIS group has focused much of its research effort on architectures or frameworks within which improved information handling applications can be developed. If we are to develop a framework for improving the handling of information in the hyper-media authoring process, then we need to consider the requirements for such a framework. The logical place to start this process is to begin to understand the structure of information itself and the ways in which we use this structure. As such, Matilda is based around a model of the types of information which are captured or used during the hypermedia development process.

It is worth pointing out that many of the ideas included in the work by the HyVIS group owe their origin to analogies with the field of software engineering. Traditionally, software was predominantly handcrafted (much as hypermedia applications are currently handcrafted). As software applications grew in scope and complexity, this approach broke down, with many applications failing to deliver the required performance or being completely unmaintainable. This was (and still is) addressed through the development of appropriate sophisticated software engineering paradigms, process models, methodologies, techniques and tools (Gibbs, 1994). The focus within software development has shifted away from technical constraints and issues (such as software coding) towards broader issues (such as appropriate paradigms and process models) which resolve problems like software maintainability and reuse. A fundamental premise in most of the HyVIS work is that a similar shift needs to occur within hypermedia information applications – away from specific technical considerations towards the broader issues of information engineering – such as suitable paradigms, frameworks and processes.

The following subsection has been extracted from work by the HyVIS group, and included verbatim, as it illustrates some interesting ideas of the HyVIS group.

Authoring with Matilda

Prior to discussing the specific approaches which have been adopted, it is worth raising a number of issues. The resolution of these issues within an authoring paradigm is critical if we are to significantly improve the effectiveness of the hypermedia authoring process, and the quality of the resultant applications (in terms of usability, interactivity, and especially maintainability):

- *Handling of large applications*: the size and scope of applications is growing considerably; any attempt to develop an authoring process or application needs to consider how to cope with this. In particular, any information representation or authoring process needs to be easily scalable. This particularly applies to scalability in terms of cognitive issues. A major constraint of current applications is the lack of support to assist the author in handling the large information space. This is also reflected in a number of the following points.

- *Accessibility*: the authoring paradigm adopted must explicitly address problems associated with the access (both by the author and user) to the information space. For example, during the authoring process, the author is initially working with an unstructured or poorly structured information space, and needs explicit support in manipulating this space while ensuring access to the information contained within it.

- *Partially complete representations*: related to the above point is that, during the authoring process, the information space (especially within the under-development application) will be constantly under manipulation. The authoring paradigm should ensure that even partially completed representations of the applications information space can be utilised, accessed, evaluated, etc. Typically, this is not the case with most current applications – where under-developed applications will contain dangling links, incorrect structuring, etc.

- *Reasoning about the information*: if the authoring paradigm supports an information representation which allows reasoning about the information, then the authoring process can use this reasoning to provide more intelligent support to the author. For example, if the model provides support for suggesting semantic relationships based on alternative semantic relationships and information structure, or for suggesting decompositions of information into a lower level structure, then these can be used in generating the information structures to be used.

The Framework

The Matilda framework (Multimedia Authoring Through Information Linking and Directed Assistance) is shown in Figure 11-1. This framework is aimed at supporting research into many of the issues identified above, especially those related to information reuse, application maintainability and the authoring process.

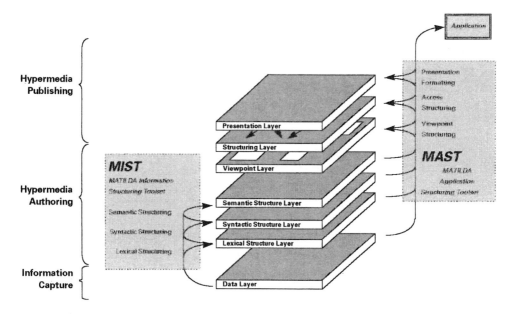

Figure 11-1

The Matilda framework

The Matilda framework aims to make explicit various forms of information (and *meta*-information). In particular, application-independent information (such as the underlying syntax) is separated from the application-dependant information (such as presentation information). At present, research has been predominantly focusing on the information domain. The framework makes explicit the meta-information which is either embedded in the media, or in the way in which the media is interpreted.

The information domain is decomposed into four primary layers (shown in Figure 11-1). The bottom layer is the raw data layer, representing the constituent media files (such as a raw text file, a MPEG video file or an Excel spreadsheet). The next level up makes explicit the lexical structure of these media files, identifying the components within the media at an arbitrary level of granularity (such as a word or chapter in the text, or a scene in a video). The third level identifies the syntactic structure between the various lexical components (such as a chapter containing various sections), and the fourth level makes explicit the semantic relationships within the information (an image and some text relate to the same object).

The application domain codifies the information which will be application-specific. In particular, a specific set of viewpoints on the information is identified (such as a given application-specific structure, and mapping of information content into this structure), followed by the interlinking of the information which the application is to use. Finally, presentation can be identified as the final layer of information to be included in the application.

It makes sense, given that the information structure has been broken into application-independent and application-specific, to also break the processing of the information down. The Matilda framework separates the authoring process into information and application structuring. The information structuring processes (which are the basis of the Matilda Information Structuring Toolset – MIST) are responsible for identifying and formalising the structure of the information. The application structuring processes (which are the basis of the Matilda Application Structuring Toolset – MAST) use this information structure to generate specific applications. It is important to note that this does not imply a specific process model – though we do envisage that these two toolsets will be used in conjunction with each other in an iterative fashion. Further details of the Matilda framework are given in Lowe and Ginige (1996).

Before continuing, let us make explicit the meaning of an *information framework*. The purpose of the Matilda framework is seen as being the provision of a structure or *framework* within which we can refine our ideas on information handling and hypermedia authoring. The framework guides us in investigating information representations, various aspects of the development process, and broader issues such as information reuse and application maintainability. This is achieved through the development of an appropriate architecture, which can then incorporate suitable data models, tools, etc.

MGraphs: A Structured Graph Formalism

An important issue which needed to be addressed as part of the development of the Matilda framework in general, and MIST in particular, was the structure of the information to be represented. This needs to take account of both information theory, as well as the authoring processes identified above. Although the Matilda architecture provides an overall information structure, it does not provide specific information models required to develop a working application. This has been achieved through the development of a set of information models based on an adaptation of the structured graph visual formalism (Lowe *et al.*, 1996; Lowe and Sifer, 1996).

Structure graphs were originally designed to address the need for handling graph-based information at an arbitrary level of granularity and summarisation, without losing context. A structured graph is a network of nodes and links, a node hierarchy and a link hierarchy. Each node may have several link inputs and several link outputs, each of which may have several node producers and consumers. Formally, the node and link hierarchies are ordered sets. The structured graph formalism also defines browsing and editing operations: the browsing operation allows an arbitrary cross-section of nodes to be selected, with a summary graph being automatically produced for these nodes; the editing operations also allow direct editing on any summary graph (such as changing a link or moving a subgraph).

The structured graph formalism has been adapted to model the information structures used within Matilda. One of the primary goals of the information model is that it should provide a mechanism for managing the incredible complexity which is typical of information spaces. One of the primary mechanisms used to manage complexity in almost any domain is abstraction. Many hypermedia models provide a mechanism for abstracting content – the most common being variations of composition of nodes into 'parent' or 'abstract' nodes. However, no model has yet adequately addressed abstraction of the information inter-relationships. The MGraph (Matilda Structured Graph) model aims to address both content abstraction and link abstraction: the content abstraction occurs using a node ordering, and the link abstraction occurs using a link order.

This is best illustrated using a simple example, as shown in Figure 11-2 (based around an information representation of Shakespeare's *Macbeth*). In this example, the circles represent lexical elements, or information components, at various levels of granularity (an entire image file or an object within the image, the entire text of a play, or single statements spoken by one of the characters). The squares represent syntactic elements, or the structural relationships between lexical elements (which can be either containment relationships or contributing relationships, which the formalism tells us are simply unresolved containment relationships). Notice that this allows us to specify different partitionings of a parent's lexical elements (such as the temporal partitioning into acts, or the instructional partitioning into various characters and commentaries). The graph also includes semantic relationships between the various lexical and syntactic elements.

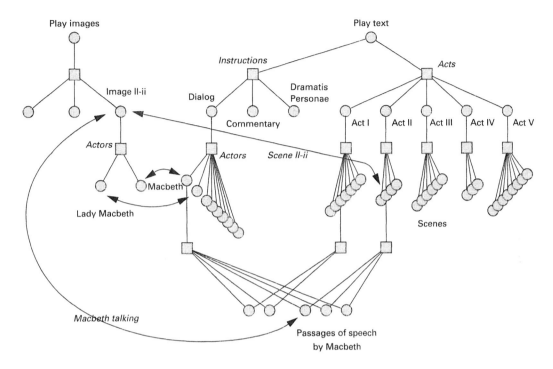

Figure 11-2

An example MGraph, showing the node order and a set of links

The node order shown in Figure 11-2 can be used to provide summarisation of information. One element not shown in Figure 11-2 is the link order, which provides a mechanism for summarising links. This means that if we show a summarised graph, say just the two top nodes in the figure, we can use the link order to automatically determine the most appropriately summarised links between these nodes.

The structured graph formalism can be used in handling issues, such as reasoning about the information and supporting browsing through abstraction of information. For example, we can simplify the browsing of a network by suppressing detail below a certain level in the graph, or zooming in to specific sections of a graph. Similarly, the structured graph formalism actively supports editing of the large information structures. For instance, we can initially add unresolved semantic links between parent nodes of an incomplete graph during the initial creation (such as between *Image II-ii* and *Act II, Scene ii*), which will later (when required) be resolved to a link between the relevant children nodes (such as the image and the specific passage of speech by *Macbeth*). Similarly, the reverse can apply – given an existing semantic link at a low level, we can generate implied semantic links between parent nodes when suppressing low-level structural elements. Essentially, the formalism, and its implementation as a set of data models, allows us to handle large complex information structures in a consistent, effective and scalable fashion.

MIST

The Matilda Information Structuring Toolset (MIST) is the implementation of the information management concepts outlined above. Essentially, MIST is a toolset which allows us to identify and record the meta-information contained within the information used in hypermedia applications. This includes the identification of lexical components, syntactic structure and semantic relationships. MIST uses many of the concepts outlined above with respect to handling large information applications. This especially relates to browsing the information and its structure at varying levels of detail through the suppression of detail, and supporting the generation of incomplete or partial structures.

The core philosophy behind the development of MIST is that it should provide a scalable, extensible mechanism for identifying and recording the structure of information in an application-independent fashion. A number of issues were identified as critical in the development of MIST. The two most significant of these were:

- *Support for structured graph formalism*: the architecture adopted for MIST must be able to provide active support for the underlying information representation and associated formalism. In particular, the architecture needs to consider the mechanism which will be used to provide an interface between the information structures and the browsing and editing tools. A good example of the types of interface paradigms (such as graphs, trees, sets) which can be used is given in Feiner (1988).

- *Open and Extensible*: MIST should be relatively open and extensible, supporting both the gradual evolution of existing components and integration of additional applications or new components into the overall framework. The need for openness in the architecture goes beyond research applications. For commercial applications, the level of assistance provided to the author in the structuring process will evolve over time, as more intelligent support is provided. This concept is well recognised in a number of existing open hyper-media applications, such as Microcosm (Hall, Davis and Hutchings, 1996).

The architecture of MIST was developed based on the above principles, the basic structure of which is shown in Figure 11-3. MIST consists of a core information repository and MGraph module which provides the graph-based interface to the repository (actually, the repository and MGraph interface are not considered part of MIST, but the central elements of both the MIST and MAST Matilda tools), the main MIST user interface, and a series of extensible structure and media browsers. It is these browsers which provide the core functionality in terms of browsing and editing the information structure.

The two elements which require some explanation are the structure browsers and media browsers. The structure browsers are used to provide views onto the information space. A typical view may be a

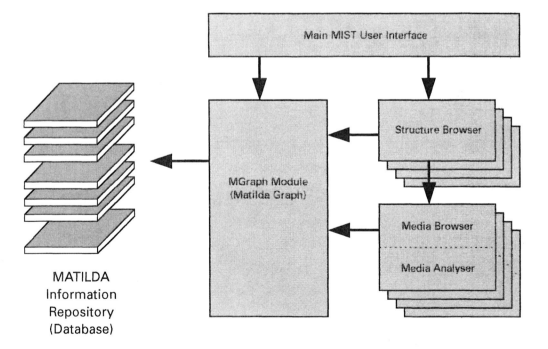

MATILDA
Information
Repository
(Database)

Figure 11-3

The MIST architecture

section of the graph, a display of the node or link ordering, or some other arbitrary collection of nodes satisfying a given query. We can open multiple browsers to provide different views or perspectives of the same information space. The MGraph module actively supports different types of views onto the information representation. The modular nature of the architecture means that, as different types of structure browsers are developed, they can be readily integrated into the overall application.

While the structure browsers manage the overall information space, the media browsers are used to manage individual nodes of information within this space. For each type of media (text data, images of varying formats, video components, audio elements, etc.), a separate media browser can be created. These browsers can then make use of information analysis tools to provide sophisticated intelligent assistance to the author when handling the information components. A structure browser can interface to these elements and launch the appropriate media browser when required. Each of the interfaces between components has been specifically designed for modularity within the application, allowing additional components (especially browsers) to be readily added to the application as needed, resulting in a flexible open architecture.

An example of the various MIST applications is shown in Figure 11-4. This includes the main MIST interface and the Browser Selector used to select a browser to browse either structures or media information. Also shown is one structure browser (used to browse the node ordering) and a media browser (showing one of the image lexical elements from the structure shown).

It is worth noting that all information elements in the structure (including lexical, syntactic and semantic elements) can be annotated with attributes. The specifics of the attributes are dependant upon the type of element being addressed. Grosky (1994) addresses this issue quite well, in proposing a taxonomy of information types which can be applied to both component attributes and relationships (information bearing content based, non-information bearing content based, content independent). In this particular case, the attributes cannot only be used to define the characteristics of the various elements, but also to define separate mappings. For example, it would be possible, in a structure browser, to request only viewing those syntactic structures which have been created by a specific designer, or after a specific date.

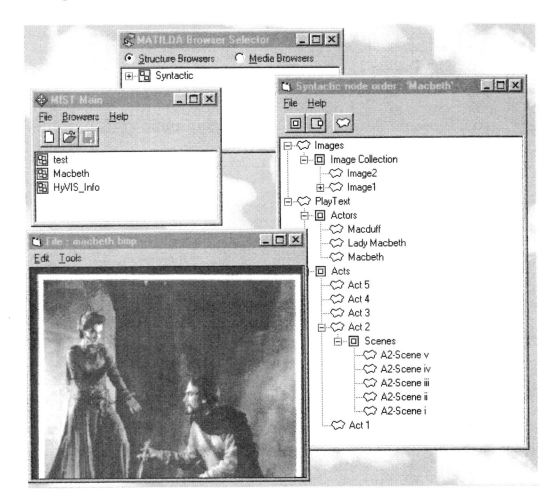

Figure 11-4

Example of the main MIST interface, a structure browser and a media browser

11.3 Dealing with Product Issues

Navigation and Browsing

One of the main factors affecting a user's ability to navigate and browse within an information space is the support provided to assist a user in comprehending the structure of the information space. Matilda and MGraphs provide various mechanisms aimed explicitly at addressing this particular issue. The most significant of these mechanisms is the use of graph structures which supports abstractions of the graph representations.

An analogy which has been used by the developers of Matilda is useful to explain the mechanisms for browsing. When we physically navigate from one location to another, such as driving from New York to Washington DC, we use a level of abstraction with respect to the physical space which is relevant to the distance we are travelling (which is in turn supported by suitable mechanisms for travelling). When we walk from our house to our car, we need to be aware of the specific surface we are walking on – so that we don't, for example, trip on a step. When we drive from our house to a motorway we use a map showing the local streets, but do not need to be aware of the shape of the street surface. When we are on a motorway, local streets become irrelevant and we use a more abstract map showing motorways and major roads. We then reverse the process at the other end of our trip. When we leave the motorway we again look at a street map.

Navigation within Matilda is based around using an analogous form of understanding the information space and moving about within the space. If we wish to travel a short conceptual distance we can navigate at a high level of detail, whereas if we wish to travel a considerable conceptual distance, we can move to a high-level of abstraction and then navigate at that level. As a comparison, navigation in the Web is typically at the lowest level of abstraction. Even when we travel a long conceptual distance we remain at this low level (equivalent to driving from New York to Washington on local streets and back roads – something which may sometimes be interesting, but not very straightforward or rapid).

As an example, consider the case where we are currently viewing information related to publications by the HyVIS research group. If we decide that we wish to see information related to the author of one of these papers, we can navigate directly to the selected publication and thence to the author following conventional hypermedia links with the information presented. However, consider the situation where, in viewing the publications, we remember that earlier we intended to try to find publications on 16th century Florentine art. Such a relationship is obviously likely to represent a considerable conceptual distance (the only relationship being the concept of 'publication'), and hence won't be linked in the conventional sense. Using the MGraph paradigm, we could ask for the HyVIS publications to be abstracted, and specify that this abstraction should occur based on the idea of publications rather than material related to HyVIS.

The developers of MGraphs have recognised that typically the complexity of the relationships would be impractical to create using conventional authoring. Rather, it would require a combination of automated analysis techniques or the generation of links based on usage patterns, i.e. the first time the connection between HyVIS publications and the general category of publications, and hence to the publications on 16th century Florentine art, was requested, it would not be available but could be created based on the navigation patterns of this initial user.

Another important aspect of the approach taken by MIST is that it provides separate tools for understanding content and structure. The content is viewed using various media browsers (which can be extended and adapted to suit the presentation of different types of media). The structure of the information space is presented using an assortment of structure browsers, which can also be adapted as appropriate. The use of structure browsers means that users are able to explicitly perceive the information inter-relationships and readily place content into the overall structure. The extensible architecture of MIST means that, as mechanisms evolve for assisting users in understanding structure, they can be easily integrated into the application.

Cognitive Management During Browsing

Matilda uses a number of mechanisms to reduce the cognitive overhead associated with browsing of information within hypermedia. A useful way to demonstrate these is to consider the cognitive design issues by Thuring, Hannemann and Haake (1995). The first of these issues related to reducing cognitive overhead is to ensure that the reader's current position within the information space is indicated. Matilda achieves this explicitly through the use of the structure browsers, which always show a given view onto the information space, and in which the active content can be readily indicated within these views.

The next of Thuring's design issues focuses on providing feedback to the user on how they arrived at their current position. Matilda does not explicitly provide any support for providing navigation traces, but this could be readily integrated into the various structure browses.

The third relevant design issue is related to the presentation of options for reaching new nodes. The main contribution of Matilda in this respect is the separation of structure and content and the subsequent use of browsers which are specifically designed to allow the user to see the structure, or any arbitrary viewpoint onto the structure, including the local region of the information space. The user does not need to expend cognitive effort on developing a model of a structure which is only presented implicitly (through the connections denoted by the provided links). Once the local structure can be seen, the possible navigation paths become obvious. In particular, different perspectives on the structure support different types of navigation. If the node order is presented, then the user can see the structural relationships amongst the content, and hence possible structural navigation paths. If the link order is presented, then the user is able to see the structure of the information semantic inter-relationships. Finally, if a cross-sectional graph view onto the network is shown, then the semantic connections between the information components can be seen and these can be used as the basis of navigation (much as in conventional hypermedia).

The fourth and fifth design issues by Thuring *et al.* are support for navigation based on direction and distance. By direction, Thuring *et al.* mean aspects such as support for forward navigation (i.e. into new information spaces), backward navigation (i.e. retracing a path which has been previously followed), or other variations such as movement to a higher level of abstraction, or into more detail. By distance, Thuring *et al.* are referring to the difference between following a link (or some other navigation mechanism) to a closely related node as compared to jumping to a totally unrelated information component. Matilda handles both of these aspects quite well. By providing node and link orders which give varying levels of abstraction on both content and structure, the user can readily navigate between varying levels of abstraction. The consumer/producer relations which connect the semantic links to the content provide forward horizontal navigation at any given level of abstraction – and hence navigating varying distances. This is illustrated in Figure 11-5. The only navigation aspect not effectively implemented in Matilda is backward navigation, i.e. history lists or information trails, though this type of functionality could be readily added.

Thuring *et al.* also identify reduction of additional effort for user interface adjustment as an important mechanism for managing the cognitive burden. This particular aspect has not been addressed within Matilda.

Information Contextualisation

Although contextualisation of information was not explicitly addressed by Matilda, it is handled in various implicit ways. The most significant

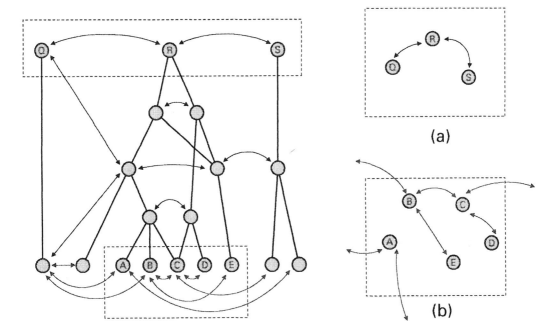

Figure 11-5

A typical structure browser can provide a view onto the underlying MGraph. View (a) shows an abstract view covering great conceptual distances, whereas view (b) shows a high detail local view where navigation is localised

of these is that information is always available within the context of a given structure. Within this structure, a number of aspects are specifically relevant to information contextualisation.

First, the MGraph representation supports different partitions of an information space. This works both top-down (a given abstract information element can be subdivided into more specific elements in different ways) and bottom-up (a given element can belong to different abstractions). This concept assists in providing important contextualisation information. For example, the node order can tell us that the Shakespearean quote 'The deed t'is done' belongs both to the more abstract elements 'Act II Scene II' and 'passages spoken by Macbeth' (both of which, in turn belong to 'The play Macbeth'). This concept is similar to Nelson's (1995) idea of multithreading, where any given concept exists as the intersection of numerous different conceptual threads which combine to provide a unique context.

MGraphs go one step further and allow these threads to be represented at suitable levels of abstraction. Rather than view the context as being either local or global, MGraphs allow the definition of arbitrary continuum of levels of abstraction, and hence context. Local context and global context are not viewed as two different perceptual elements, but as two different extremes of the same concept – that a concept exists relative to other information which provides the context. MGraphs capture this idea and attempts to provide a mechanism for representing it and presenting it to a user in a useful fashion.

Other aspects of contextualisation, such as managing the presentation context (like using a uniform look and feel for information which has a common context) is not dealt with by Matilda. Indeed, it is viewed as an issue which should be resolved either by the design of the user interface, or possibly automatically handled by the presentation interface. There is some question as to whether this is appropriate, and only further experience with Matilda will confirm or deny the validity of this approach.

Finally, it is worth noting that Matilda does not yet address the issue of presentation context. When constructing a hypermedia presentation, we may want to ensure that the immediate context in which information is presented (and how the timing and spatial arrangement is organised) is controlled by the navigation path. For example, if we follow a certain link we may wish all the information being presented to be removed from the screen. Matilda does not have a mechanism for supporting this, though it may be able to be implemented (with some difficulty) using the link attributes.

Link and Content Validity

Matilda does not address content validity in any explicit way. The only mechanism within Matilda which impacts on content validity is the way in which information structure is handled. Since the structure is made so explicit within Matilda, even to the extent (as mentioned above) of supporting what effectively amounts to multiple concept threads, it will be difficult to add material which is out of context or erroneous within the current context. Having said this, there is certainly nothing to stop a developer adding material which is incorrect or inappropriate.

Similarly, a developer is able to add a link which is invalid. Matilda, however, provides certain mechanisms which make this less likely than in many other systems. First, Matilda does not require that a link be added only between the most detailed information. In some systems, this is required. For example, when authoring for the Web a developer has no alternative but to add links between concrete elements (since the Web does not provide any inherent form of abstraction of information elements). In Matilda, the underlying MGraphs support initial addition of links between abstract levels, and then progressive refinement of these links as the implementation progresses.

Consider the situation where we are constructing an MGraph for representing Shakespeare's *Macbeth*. If we add a new node representing a video clip which shows several actors in a production of the play, we may wish to add a link from each of these actors to the relevant section of the *Dramatis Personae*, i.e the section of text at the beginning of the play describing each of the characters. In a conventional system, if these sections of text have not yet been marked up then the link cannot be effectively added – the author would need to interrupt the work on the video clip, mark up the text appropriately, and only then add the link, after which they could (hopefully) return to the interrupted work on the video clip. In Matilda, even if the text was not marked up, the link could be added at the lowest level abstraction above the text (for example, the whole *Dramatis Personae*, or the entire text of the play). This link could then be refined at a later time, after the content structuring had been refined. Such an approach means that the author is more likely to focus correctly on the task at hand, and hence make correct and appropriate links.

Information Structure

The structure of information and how it can be represented in an effective way (for both development and utilisation) is the core focus of most of the work on Matilda.

The approach to managing structure in Matilda is substantially different from most conventional hypermedia systems. Most existing systems treat the structure of the information space either as something which is superimposed on isolated components of information in order to facilitate navigation amongst these components (such as in the Web), or as an orchestrated presentation with which the user interacts (such as in multimedia-based presentations and systems such as AHM). In comparison, Matilda treats the structure as something which is inherent in the information itself. Indeed, the structure is the interpretation of the underlying data, and hence is as important to the effective use of the application as the data itself. With this in mind, the information structure is captured and made explicit as an integral part of the development process.

Rather than superimpose a layer of structure which happens to be appropriate to the end goals of the application, the underlying structure is identified and captured independently of the application. Only when the specific application is being built on top of this inherent structure is consideration given as to which elements of the structure will be appropriate to use within the context of the application. In fact, in some applications, an over-arching application structure may not be needed at all, and the inherent structure of the content may be sufficient.

This indicates one of the main differences between Matilda and most other systems – Matilda provides a very distinct and fundamental separation between the structure which can be viewed as inherent in the information and the structure which we wish to capture and use within a given application. Some holistic theorists, such as Nelson, would claim that all information structure is inherent in the data ('everything is connected to everything else'). You could then go one step further and claim that it is only the application which provides a 'sieve' to select desired structures, and hence no structure has meaning outside of the context provided by an application. However, this overlooks the fact that we can identify commonality of context between applications. For example, we have an assumption of a certain language rules and certain commonality of experience which provides a common interpretation between all applications.

It is worth pointing out that Matilda has yet to be used within a broad range of applications and on very large scale systems. One possible criticism of the approach being adopted by Matilda is that the application-independent structures will be so large and complex that it will never be possible to effectively create these structures. It is only within the constraints set by an application that the complexity is reduced to a managable level. There are several possible answers to this criticism. First, the original aim of Matilda was to capture the application-independent structure as an application was created, so that structure could be reused in other applications. It does not necessarily require that the entire complexity of the inherent structures be generated for a particular development effort.

The developers of Matilda are also looking at the use of automated and semi-automated tools which can be used to assist in the creation of these structures. Unfortunately, at present this work is not yet sufficiently advanced to allow an evaluation of how effective this approach might be.

Finally, there is every possibility that this approach might provide an entirely different paradigm for hypermedia systems where the conventional development process of creating final applications is abandoned in favour of an approach which is in many respects more like Vannevar Bush's original concepts (see page 37). Users navigate within the information space, adding their own connections as they browse, thereby building up the complexity of the structures. The process of development then becomes simply the identification of suitable trails or perspectives within this already existing (and continually evolving) structure. Ongoing work may provide some answers as to whether this is a reasonable paradigm.

Management of Different Media

The research questions surrounding how different media can be handled within hypermedia were not a prime focus of the development of Matilda. As such, Matilda only peripherally addresses this issue. The most obvious related mechanism is the use of specialised software media browsers which provide a vehicle for presenting arbitrary media. The architecture of the Matilda Information Structuring Toolset (MIST) is such that new media browsers can be added at any time to manage different media forms. Indeed, there is no reason why media browsers could not be created that handle composite media types (say, an image, text and associated audio clip), though these have not yet been implemented.

The MIST structure browsers treat all media as the same, i.e. as information packets, albeit of varying levels of complexity. No differentiation is made between lexical elements containing different media types, or even if a given lexical element in the structure actually contains any data or is defined entirely by its semantic and/or syntactic relationships to other lexical elements.

Matilda has not addressed those aspects of managing different media related to timing between elements, such as synchronisation, integrated presentation and possible generation of events based on media conditions. In this respect, Matilda is essentially closer to a conventional hypertext system rather than a hypermedia system. Similarly, the levels within Matilda where presentation of different media in a cohesive fashion is defined are still being developed.

11.4 Dealing with Process Issues

Application Maintenance

One of the original aims of the development of Matilda was to investigate mechanisms for improving the maintainability of large scale hypermedia applications. Although the development effort has moved away from this goal slightly, it has nevertheless made some interesting contributions in this area.

First, and probably most importantly, Matilda has explicitly separated the information domain from the application domain. This means that in developing applications, the structure of the information is not clouded by application considerations, and *vice versa*. These two different elements can be manipulated independently of each other, for example, by defining the presentation independently of the structure we can readily maintain or change the entire look and feel of the application without affecting the underlying structure. Obviously, the converse is also true.

An additional element which assists in the maintainability of applications is that the underlying information representation (i.e. Mgraphs) has been designed in such a way that even as it is being edited or maintained, it is always self-consistent and so can still be effectively browsed. This means that, during maintenance, the structures can still be used to support the development, thereby reducing the burden on the developer.

Reuse

One of the prime foci of the work on Matilda was reuse. In particular, the developers of Matilda wanted to investigate ways in which the information which is generated as part of the development process could be captured and hence reused. To explain this in a little more detail, consider the following scenario. We are creating a series of Web pages, and as part of the development of these pages we start with a series of original legacy documents. We analyse these documents, separate them into various components, and then recombine these components into a series of new Web pages. We also identify specific key phrases which become the anchors for links between these pages.

This development is shown schematically in Figure 11-6. In a typical Web development, as we decompose legacy documents and create Web pages

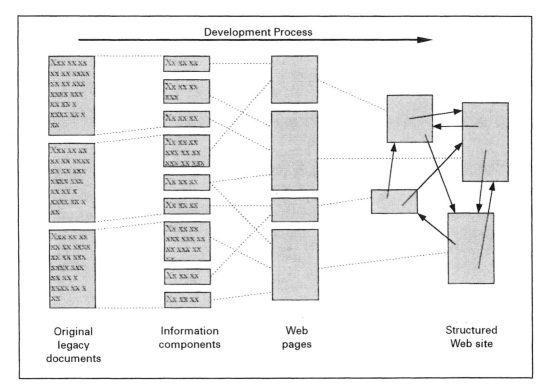

Figure 11-6

In a typical Website, we lose information on the original structure of the information

from the resulting components, we lose information related to both the original structure of these components, as well as possibly even the existence and bounds of these components.

What we have as a result of such a development effort is a collection of Web pages containing material composed from a number of sources. All intermediate information, such as the bounds and origins of the intermediate information components, has been lost. To reuse information such as this, a developer will need to either repeat the original decomposition of the legacy data, or attempt to decompose the Web pages.

Matilda has attempted to circumvent this problem by capturing and making explicit the various forms of information used in the creation and/or use of hypermedia applications. This includes the bounds of any information elements used during the development (i.e. identification and storage of all lexical components), the ways in which these relate to each other at a structural level (syntactic elements) and a conceptual level (semantic elements), the ways in which we combine these to form an application (viewpoint and structuring elements), and the way we present them to a user (presentation elements). Each of these forms of information is explicitly captured and can be reused.

Although Matilda provides a mechanism for capturing the elements which can be reused, it does not provide any explicit indication of how these elements should be identified as potential candidates for reuse within a development project. This is left entirely up to the developers.

In addition, whereas support is provided for reuse of information used within the application, no consideration has been given to reuse of development artifacts such as application specifications, design outcomes, evaluation data or processes, process knowledge or development plans.

Supporting the Full Lifecycle

Although Matilda does not provide explicit support for the development lifecycle, there are two aspects worth mentioning. The first of these is that because Matilda has a well-defined separation between information and application structure, there is an implicit support for the separation of the development process into these two domains. This is, in particular, shown by the creation of the two separate tools for handling the information domain (MIST) and the application domain (MAST).

Although never made explicit, the result is that the development would invariably contain two distinct threads – creation of the structure of the information space, and the creation of the application which uses this structure. Each thread is likely to involve specific analysis, design and implementation phases, though this is not discussed by the developers of Matilda. Certainly, the broader lifecycle aspects such as feasibility analyses, planning, requirements analysis, evaluation, etc. are never discussed.

The second aspect where Matilda impacts on the lifecycle relates to the approach taken to development. A conventional waterfall lifecycle approach to development is inherently top-down. Unfortunately, most hypermedia development practice exhibits a strong combination of both bottom-up and top-down approaches. Indeed Nanard and Nanard (1995) point out that, to be effective, any development approach needs to actively support rapid alternation between top-down and bottom-up approaches. Matilda facilitates exactly this approach. Information structures can be created at a high level of detail, and then abstractions built on top of these detailed elements, or the abstractions can be created first and then refined into detail. In either case, the information structures remain consistent and can be readily manipulated and browsed at all times.

Supporting Process Management

The seven layer model used by Matilda – for the different layers of information – can provide a suitable basis for managing development deliverables. It may be possible to determine the scope of material expected at each layer (along with heuristics for the relative effort in generating each layer), and hence to both plan and measure development progress.

There is some doubt as to whether this is appropriate, though, as the development process for hypermedia (and especially in the type of development supported by Matilda) is very much an iterative and incremental process. This means that it is likely to be very difficult to effectively evaluate progress simply by measuring the completed proportion of given information layers. Further experience with Matilda and the associated development tools would be required before this question could be determined with any degree of confidence.

Cognitive Management and Supporting Enhanced Productivity

These two issues have been combined for Matilda, since they are dealt with in very similar ways. In particular, Matilda attempts to enhance the productivity by providing an environment which focuses the development effort in such a way that the cognitive burden on the developer is minimised. In particular, Matilda allows the developer to focus on one area of the information structure at a time. As described previously, the use of abstractions means that a developer does not need the detailed content for both ends of a link to exist before that link can be added. This means that links can be added into the structure at any time (and at any level of abstraction).

Another possibly more significant, aspect is that MGraphs are self-consistent even during editing. This means that partial information structures can be used during the development to assist with further development. For example, if we add some new content, and then insert links from this content to other regions of the information space, then any existing structure can be readily used to assist in locating the appropriate destination of the links.

One aspect not addressed by Matilda is the provision of assistance in reducing the cognitive effort associated with managing a development project. This includes aspects such as planning, evaluation against plans, etc.

11.5 Conclusions

As with most of the systems described in this chapter, Matilda and its associated components was developed as a research tool to investigate mechanisms for addressing specific issues and problems within hypermedia. It has, of course, also evolved over time. As such, it only addresses a number of the given issues in a peripheral manner. Nevertheless, it provides some interesting approaches which impact on most of the issues described.

In particular, although the Matilda project was initially started with the aim of addressing large-scale development issues of maintainability and reuse, the underlying information representation (MGraphs) which was developed as part of Matilda has provided an alternative focus to the work – that of representing information in a way that facilitates access despite the complexity inherent in large information spaces. Matilda provides a significantly different, and in some respects more complex, approach to the modelling of information and its structure than is typical of most of the other systems and projects described in this book.

The information models are based around the precept that a core mechanism for managing complexity is abstraction. In hypermedia this abstraction needs to be not only for the content, but also for the structure itself. In other words a successful model for representing the information in large hypermedia systems must be able to facilitate the appropriate abstraction of the semantic associations between information elements.

It is this idea which has driven the most recent work on Matilda. This in turn impacts on aspects such as cognitive management during both development and use (information can be viewed at a suitably abstract level), supporting the contextualisation of information (the location within an information space can be identified), and maintenance and reuse of information (structure is captured and explicitly represented).

As mentioned previously, this approach to representing and manipulating information has the potential to significantly change the way in which we build hypermedia systems. Unfortunately, Matilda is still very immature as a development tool, and has not yet been sufficiently widely used to determine whether it does indeed provide a viable alternative.

11.6 Further Information

For more information on the Matilda hypermedia framework or any other aspect of the work described in this chapter, the following sources of information are available. The following Website contains information on Matilda and the other projects by the HyVIS research group:

> `http://ise.ee.uts.edu.au/`

Alternatively, the developers can be contacted at:

Dr David Lowe
Contact address: Faculty of Engineering
University of Technology, Sydney
PO Box 123 Broadway Sydney
NSW 2007 Australia
Email: `dbl@ee.uts.edu.au`
URL: `http://www.eng.uts.edu.au/~dbl`
Phone: +61 2 9514 2526
Fax: +61 2 9514 2435

12

Microcosm

Everything is deeply intertwingled
(Ted Nelson)

Chapter Goals

Microcosm is one of the most successful open hypermedia systems. This chapter shows how a flexible approach to the management of not only content but also structure can simplify many aspects of the development. The objectives of this chapter are to show that:

- Microcosm is an open hypermedia systems which separates the management of links from the management of content, and places no requirement for markup on content.

- A core goal of Microcosm was to reduce hypermedia authoring effort.

- Microcosm actively supports the concept of generic links – links which relate to general content that can appear in numerous specific locations.

- Microcosm is based on an architecture which uses numerous filters that can manipulate links (and hence structure) in very flexible ways.

- The Microcosm approach is particularly effective for managing bogth content and flexible access to this content.

12.1 Introduction

The question the Microcosm team set out to tackle was, and indeed still is, how do you set about building fully cross-referenced versions of very large electronic archives and information repositories? A fuller discussion of the original motivations for the Microcosm project can be found in Hall, Davis and Hutchings (1996), which includes a description of the team's initial work with the Mountbatten archive.

The problem was approached from the team's background in building resource-based applications using hypermedia systems. When dealing with very large information systems, it was considered that the main issues for the hypermedia designer/author were the problems of working with very large numbers of documents and links, the increasingly highly multimedia nature of electronic information, and the fact that different users will approach the information repository from different perspectives. In collections of unstructured information there is no natural beginning or end; no assumptions can be made about the background knowledge of users, nor when they are likely to come across a particular subject, topic or concept for the first time.

All these problems are apparent when we consider the material available in the rapidly growing global network of unstructured information facilitated by the World Wide Web. Designers of material destined for dissemination on the Web face the same issues and problems today as the Microcosm team set out to tackle in 1989. For structured information, designers are increasingly using databases to store documents and their associated structure (level in hierarchy, next page, previous page, etc.), but for large, unstructured digital repositories such as historical archives, corporate information systems, etc., while the documents may be stored in a database there is no inherent structure to help guide the user around the information. For both structured and unstructured information, the management of cross-referencing large sets of documents using associative links was also a focus of the Microcosm project.

The project was first formally reported in Fountain et al. (1990), which includes the initial design guidelines for Microcosm together with a description of the first prototype implementation. One of the project's foremost aims was the need to reduce authoring effort. With very large collections of documents, manual hypermedia authoring is far too time consuming to even contemplate. The use of mark-up languages such as SGML can only partially ease the problem. Additionally, if the hypermedia links, once created, are embedded in the documents themselves and are only allowed to be position-dependant rather than content or context dependant, it is extremely difficult for those links to be reused in other documents, even though semantically they might be equally applicable elsewhere. It is virtually impossible for authors to keep track of the links they have created, let alone to pass this information onto others, and it is also very difficult to create different hypermedia webs for different users without the development of sophisticated link management facilities.

Another objective of the project was to create a system that would enable links to be applied to read-only media such as CD-ROM and informa-

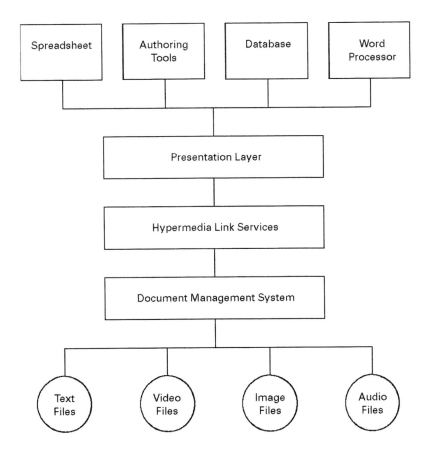

Figure 12-1

The Microcosm philosophy

tion available in formats or application programs over which the system has no control. An overall aim was to enable links to be made to and from information of any media type or format, and to enable all users to be hypermedia authors, not just the creators of the original information.

As a result of this analysis, the team resolved to build a hypermedia system which imposes no mark-up on the data to which the links can be applied, and which provides a link service that can in principle be applied to any media type and to data in any third-party application. This philosophy is embodied in the design of the Microcosm system, and leads naturally to the separation of information management into three layers (see Figure 12-1).

In later versions of the system, the architectural model has been extended to more explicitly address the role of filters in the Microcosm architecture, which is discussed in the next section. This architecture allows for a spectrum of dynamic link types to be defined, in particular the generic link, which enable the destination of a link to be resolved at run-time calculated on the basis of the content, and possibly context, of a source anchor rather than simply its location in a document. The links are stored in link databases, or linkbases, and multiple linkbases can be in use at any one time, thus creating different views on the data depending on the linkbases in use. The Microcosm architecture permits three levels of access to multimedia information, namely – browsing (using the hypermedia link service), searching (using information retrieval technology) and structured (such as the hierarchical catalogue structure in the document management system). In this chapter, we concentrate on the features and design aims of the original Microcosm system, but also discuss more recent Web-based developments.

12.2 Microcosm Concepts

The consequences of these design principles were the need to develop a link management system and a method of allowing links to be applied to applications that are not under the control of the hypermedia system, such as other authoring tools, database management systems, word processors and graphics packages. The overall aim was to keep the system as open as possible so that link following was just one of the many types of actions that could be applied to an object in a data file; in other words, to produce a generalised multimedia information management environment based on the availability of an open hypermedia link service (Davis *et al.*, 1992).

The separation of data and link structure permits the reuse of existing data without affecting it in any way. This creates the potential for any user of the system to be a hypermedia author. Creating a hyper-media structure becomes a separate activity from creating a multimedia dataset, since the hypermedia links essentially form a meta-layer of data that can be applied to any appropriate set of multimedia information. This would enable hypermedia authors to publish sets of links that can be applied to information already published on read-only media such as CD-ROMs or on the WWW. Similarly, publishers could produce multi-media datasets with different sets of links targeted at different users, either compiled into fairly static publications or dynamically available to users who are comfortable with a more flexible information processing environment.

The core of Microcosm is in essence a set of communication protocols that enable the integration of all types of information processing tools, including a hypermedia link service. Users may create their own resources, using software packages of their own choice, and simply incor-porate these resources into the body of information of which Microcosm is aware; users may connect information together using links, or may annotate information; they may navigate through materials by a rich spectrum of navigational link-following devices and searching and querying mechanisms. Having located appropriate information, they may manipulate the data using the tools that created the data in the first place, then they may publish resources and links, or maintain them in a private work space.

A central feature of Microcosm is that it maintains all information about links, including link anchors, separately from the node component data; the node component data is untouched by Microcosm, and may thus continue to be viewed and manipulated using the application that created it. This approach makes it possible to:

- Integrate third party applications easily.
- Generalise links.
- Make links in read-only data.
- Maintain alternative sets of links (webs), and
- Build and use link-processing tools.

In keeping with the principle of allowing third party applications to continue to access their data, Microcosm does not import node component data: the Microcosm storage layer *is* the file system. Microcosm does, however, keep various document attributes over and above those that are maintained by the file system, such as an extended description of the file, a logical type for the file, the name of the author, the viewer that Microcosm prefers to use for this format of data, and any number of keywords and user-defined attributes. These attributes are maintained by the Document Management System (DMS). Users may then access any file from the standard file system browser or file manager, or they may access files using the file manager supplied with Microcosm, which displays the files using their extended descriptions and organises them hierarchically by their logical types.

The Link Service Model

Microcosm consists of a number of autonomous processes which communicate with each other by a message-passing system (Figure 12-2).

The messages which Microcosm components send to each other to communicate have a very simple structure – each consists of a variable number of fields, called tags, which in turn comprise a tag name and a tag body. The name is a simple string uniquely identifying the tag, while the body contains a value for the tag. The most important tag in any message is the 'action' tag, which tells the process receiving the message what to do which the other tags in the message. Typical values for 'action' tag bodies are 'follow link', 'make link', and 'show links'. The message contains no instructions for interpreting its contents; instead, it is up to the receiving component to know whether it understands the message and, if so, what to do with it.

There are a variety of mechanisms for generating messages, but the most important is through interaction between the user and the system. *Viewers* provide the interface via which messages may be created and actions initiated. For example, the most common interface is the Text Viewer which provides a menu – the 'action' menu – with a number of menu items, each of which when selected generates a message with a different 'action' tag-body, such as 'follow link'. The name of the menu item and the message generated when that item is selected are not bound together, so the 'follow link' action could be generated via a menu item labelled, for example, 'tell me more'.

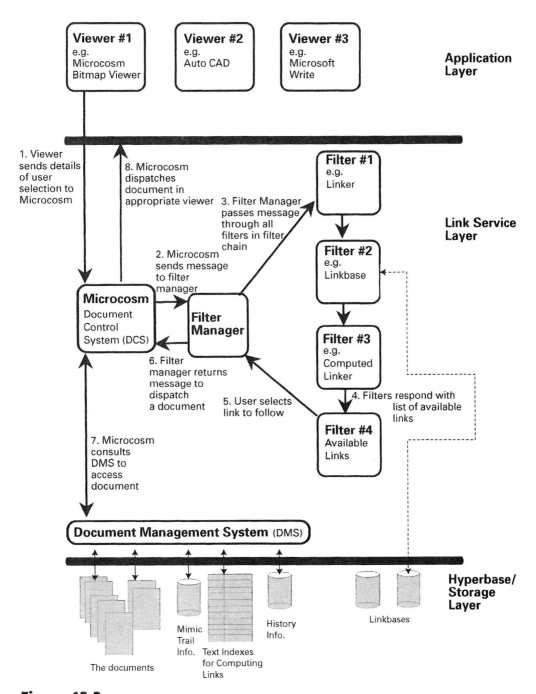

Figure 12-2

The Microcosm link service showing typical message passing

Viewers and Filters

To access the Microcosm link service the user interacts with applications known as *viewers*, which are applications that can display the required format of data. Within the viewer the user may make a *selection*, and initiate an *action* based upon that selection. Typically, this is achieved via a menu option as described above, but the interface to this mechanism is entirely viewer-dependent. The selection may be anything, for example a text string from a text viewer, which could be Microcosm's own Text Viewer or a commercial word-processing package, an area of a picture, an object in a drawing or a cell in a spreadsheet. Some fully aware viewers may have the ability to display buttons, for example the Microcosm Text Viewer, in which case the user may double-click on these buttons, rather than needing to select a text string and choosing an item from the 'action' menu in order to follow links. In Microcosm, a button is simply a binding of a selection and action that shortcuts the usual process. There are three main classifications of viewers in Microcosm: fully aware, semi-aware and unaware. These are described in detail in Hall, Davis and Hutchings (1996) and Davis, Knight and Hall (1994). Using the selection-action metaphor for selecting source anchors means that it is quite possible to follow Microcosm links from content viewers that have no method of communicating with Microcosm (unaware viewers in Microcosm terms), such as standard Web browsers (Davis, Knight and Hall, 1994).

When an action has been initiated, the viewer arranges to send a message to the Document Control System (DCS). Each message contains:

- The content of the selection.
- The action chosen by the user.
- The identifier of the source file.
- Information about the position or context in which the selection was made (if possible).

Microcosm then dispatches this information in a message to the *Filter Manager*, which arranges to pass the message through all the filter programs that are currently installed and that have registered an ability to handle messages containing this particular action. *Filters* are programs or processes that can communicate with Microcosm, and which can handle all the message protocols with the Filter Manager. In the current version of Microcosm (as illustrated in Figure 12-2 above), the filters are connected in a chain topology, although this aspect of the system has evolved over recent years as the various distributed versions of the Microcosm link service have been explored (Hill and Hall, 1994; Goose *et al.*, 1996). Each filter in the chain sees, and has the opportunity to respond to, any messages sent by the Filter Manager. Filters can block messages, ignore them, alter them or create new ones.

An important example of a filter is the Linkbase filter which, on receiving a 'follow link' message, looks up the source anchor (the object that has been selected in the viewer) in the database of links (or linkbase), and if successful, creates a new message asking to dispatch the destination file and display the destination anchor. The last filter in the chain is usually the Available Links filter, which traps the messages relating to links found back to the DCS which displays it for the user to select from.

Linkbases provide the primary hypermedia functionality in Microcosm, and currently support three primitive link types:

- Specific links, which are position dependent (i.e. point-to-point or point-to-node) and can be presented as buttons,

- Local links, which are defined on the content of the source anchor selection but only within a particular document (i.e. they are only resolved if the source anchor is selected in that particular document, the destination does not have to be in the same document), and

- Generic links, which are defined on the content of the source anchor selection wherever the source anchor selection occurs.

Microcosm also supports whole documents as link types, i.e. node-to-node links. Links are uni-directional and the system supports multimedia destinations for all types of links. There is no limitation on the number of linkbases that can be installed at any one time; indeed, it is standard practice to include at least three, one providing links supplied by an original author, one providing generic links to background material, glossaries, dictionaries, etc., and one containing links private to the individual user. Links can either be made manually by the user selecting the source and destination anchors and the type of link, or system-generated by various mechanisms.

Microcosm has always embodied a declarative model of link authoring (Hall, Davis and Hutchings, 1996) with the view that links, whether authored manually or automatically, represent relationships between objects, and as such, can be reusable across many different datasets. The team has always argued that links should only be made position-dependant in a document when that is absolutely necessary, and that the system should enable the author to declare what information is linked to what, and in what context, rather than having to describe how this is effected (Hall, 1994).

Another important filter that is currently part of the standard Microcosm system is the Computed Linker, which is invoked when the user selects a piece of text and initiates a 'compute links' action. It applies information retrieval techniques to attempt to identify text-based documents or sections of documents that have the most similar vocabulary to the text in the source selection. To achieve this, it uses an index of all the text-based documents within the current application area. The index is created using a utility program provided with the Microcosm system. However, since the Microcosm architecture is of the 'plug-and-play' variety, it is straightforward to replace this in-built search engine with any third-party software that can communicate with Microcosm.

Other examples of filters are given in Hall, Davis and Hutchings (1996). Because the architecture is so flexible, almost every process that the system designers want to include in the system is implemented as a filter. For example, all the Microcosm built-in navigation tools, such as the history mechanism and the guided tour facility, are implemented as filters. The team have also experimented with using a number of information processing tools, such as databases, Prolog rule bases and neural networks, as filters to generate 'links' to relevant information for users.

12.3 Dealing with Product Issues

Navigation and Browsing

The 'lost in hyperspace' problem is well documented, but over the last few years research has shown that this effect largely occurs if link following is virtually the only navigational method. Even the earliest Web browsers provided search facilities as well as link following capabilities, which was part of the reason for their success. Microcosm provides multiple navigational methods, so that the user is able to browse information, locate new information easily, recall information that has previously been visited, and follow trails through information left by others. There are three main methods of access to information, as shown in Figure 12-3.

These are browsing using the hypermedia link service, searching using the 'compute links' mechanism and structured access through the Document Management System (DMS). In general, the quality of information retrieved varies according to the method of navigation applied. For example, following a specific link takes you to a particular piece of information because the creator of the link has decided that the relationship between the source and the destination is important. Such links may be thought of as high quality, but there may not be many such links because of the effort involved in creating them. On the other hand, a generic link may be followed from any place that its source anchor occurs. The generic link, once created, will be available from many places, but the quality of the relationship discovered may be lower because of the general nature of the link. In the extreme, it is up to the user to decide whether a relationship found as the result of a 'compute links' action is relevant, since the system will return all files that Microcosm is aware of that contain the chosen source anchor, whatever their context.

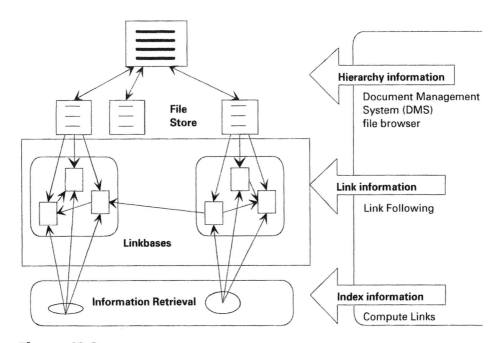

Figure 12-3

Levels of access to information provided by Microcosm

The Document Management System is a hierarchically organised catalogue of all the files in the current application, which is the term used in Microcosm to define a particular set of data files and links. The same set of files may have any number of different representations in the DMS, each representation defines a different Microcosm application.

Other navigation devices in Microcosm include the history and mimic filters. Microcosm provides a simple history mechanism that keeps a list of all the documents a user has seen in a given session. The user may view the history list in terms of either the document descriptions or the method by which they arrived at that document, and select a document to return to. Histories may be saved, edited off-line and reloaded between sessions. In Microcosm, because links are not all point-to-point (for example, generic links) it is not straightforward to define a 'back' button, and users are advised to use the history device to retrace their steps.

Mimics are guided tours or trails through a given set of documents. These allow one user to show another a route through a set of resources, but the user is still able to diverge from the trail and return to it at will. The easiest way to create a trail is to load a saved history.

Cognitive Management during Browsing

The graphical user interface of the DMS enables users to access files directly, in the same way as they would in any hierarchically organised file store. Studies show that users find it very easy to locate information in this way because the methodology is so familiar. When navigating a large application, they tend to follow a small number of hypermedia links at a time, returning regularly to the file browser to re-orient themselves and begin a different line of inquiry. As mentioned previously, it is the richness of the multiple navigational methods provided by Microcosm that helps reduce the 'lost in hyperspace' effect.

However, the Microcosm link model with its many-to-one (generic) links and plug-and-play filter architecture that enables dynamic link generation, precludes against developers easily being able to provide visualisation tools. Once you move beyond the simple point-to-point link model, the ability to draw maps or plans is significantly reduced. Using the information in the linkbases, local maps that show all the links *from* a particular document are relatively easy to produce. They were provided by the research version of the system, but didn't make it to the commercial version because the developers found that they were rarely used.

Another important aspect of Microcosm from the very beginning was that the system allowed for multiple windows of information retrieved by the user to be displayed at the same time. This is in contrast to standard Web usage, for example, where the browsers only allow one document to be displayed at any one time. Allowing the user to determine how much information (how many documents) are displayed on the screen helps orientate them as they navigate the information, but it also relies on the user being reasonably competent at manipulating windows. To accommodate users who do not have this ability, the Microcosm interface can be customised by the author to restrict the number and/or type of documents that can be open at any one time, depending on the type of application they are authoring and the target audience.

Information Contextualisation

The Microcosm model allows for the development of filters that determine what links are offered to which users in what context. These processes were originally called filters, because it was assumed by the early developers that with such a powerful link model, the user would be overwhelmed with possible links, which would therefore need to be filtered to make the system usable. In the event, it is only now as we move into the world of large-scale distributed hypermedia systems that this is actually becoming the case. Until relatively recently, except in the research version of the system, most filters created were there to generate links rather than filter them out.

Because of the basic Microcosm message passing architecture and link formats, it is easy to conceive of filters that process the links which have been generated in response to a user query and filter them, according to the context in which the user is making that query, for example by detecting the context from some information about the current file or user selection. Similarly, links could be filtered using some algorithm that matched them against a previously obtained user profile. The possibilities are endless. However, at the moment this work is largely the realm of the research laboratory.

In the current commercial version of Microcosm, the raw approach is to separate the links on authoring into separate linkbases, so that the user can change the context in which they are making a query by changing the linkbases. For example, if the user is navigating a set of files on British history in the Tudor period, then they would use linkbases also associated with this period, so that any link on the text string Queen Elizabeth would be likely to yield information associated with Queen Elizabeth I rather than the current Queen Elizabeth. This approach is also illustrated very nicely in the use of Webcosm, the Web vesion of Microcosm, to apply links provided by the linkbases to documents available on the Web.

Link and Content Validity

One of the main advantages of an open hypermedia system is the ability to reason about and process the links independently of the documents to which they might be applied. Microcosm adds to this the ability to generate links dynamically in various ways, which produces a powerful system for managing hypermedia links in changeable data. But herein lies one of the main disadvantages as well – that of link integrity. There are two distinct link integrity problems that might occur in a system such as Microcosm, namely the 'editing problem' and the 'dangling link' problem.

As described above, the declarative nature of Microcosm encourages authors to use generic or local links wherever possible, and typically 50% of such links have end-points that are at the 'top of the document'. The editing problem only occurs with documents containing specific links, or for links whose destination is a specific point in a document. So in a typical application it is not a major problem, and for large-scale applications the advantages of using generic links, etc. far outweigh the disadvantages when the editing problem occurs. Nonetheless, it is very frustrating for authors to have to deal with it, especially in small-scale applications with a lot of specific links.

In Hall et al., (1996), the Microcosm team suggest a number of methods of dealing with the editing problem:

- Preventing it from occurring in the first place by, for example, adopting a publishing model which dictates that only documents that are fixed in content maybe linked with position dependent links.

- Using link service-aware tools to edit (this is more like the Hyper-G approach).

● Applying just-in-time techniques to detect when a document is loaded or a link is followed that a document has been edited and effecting the necessary link repair (this approach can only be used with viewers that are fully-aware of the link service).

The dangling link problem occurs when a position or document dependant link anchor occurs in a document that has been moved or deleted without the hypermedia document management system, or hyperbase, being informed. The problem is not unique to Microcosm, and may occur in any hypermedia system where the storage layer may be accessed from outside that system. The World Wide Web suffers particularly from this problem. Microcosm has advantages over some other systems in handling the dangling link problem because all documents registered in a Microcosm application are known by unique identifiers, which are resolved to file names and paths by the DMS only at the time that the file must actually be located.

So long as the DMS is updated to point to the new file position, then all links will remain valid. The dangling link problem only occurs when users move or delete files without informing the DMS. The default behaviour on attempting to follow a link to a non-existent file is simply to report the problem to the user and to ask the user to attempt to point the system at the file so that the DMS can update itself. If links point to files that are not registered as part of the DMS, then Microcosm suffers from the same problem as say the World Wide Web, but at least problems can be corrected easily in the linkbase(s) rather than having to search for documents pointing to the non-existent files. Hall *et al.* (1996) also discusses solutions to the problems of version control and concurrency in open hypermedia systems such as Microcosm.

Information Structure

As mentioned previously, Microcosm maintains a database of all files of which it is aware, known as the DMS. The hierarchical organisation of the files in the DMS is shown in Figure 12-4.

The DMS displays the logical organisation of the files in the current application as prescribed by the author. Files can be part of any number of Microcosm applications, but only one application can be used at any time. Within an application, files may be assigned any number of different logical types which describe where the document will appear in the Select

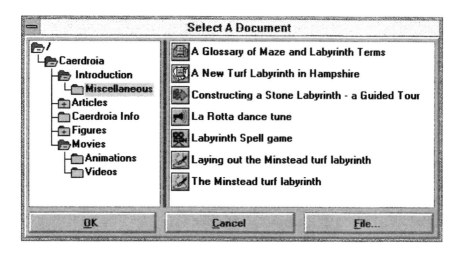

Figure 12-4

The interface to the DMS, showing logical types and descriptions

a Document Window hierarchy. The Select a Document Window allows the author to assign the logical type by dragging and dropping the file into the appropriate directory. The author can therefore structure the information in the application for the user in a number of different ways, thus providing multiple navigation paths to the same information. This has proved to be particularly useful in educational applications. Despite the advantages that the DMS provides for information management as described here and above, the concept of an 'application' can be limiting, since ideally the user would want to be able to move seamlessly from one application to another. This would require some concept of a meta-data layer such as that provided in the Matilda model (see Chapter 11).

Management of Different Media

The ability to handle multimedia data was always central to the design of Microcosm. The designers worked to the principle of developing a system that would support the philosophy of being able to link to and from any data type. Some hypermedia link services take a 'chunky' approach, allowing only node-to-node links. This approach obviously has limitations, in that it does not allow the user to create or follow relationships between individual objects within the nodes. Most hypermedia systems accept that any text span within a text document could be a potential anchor for a link source or destination. The problem to be faced when extending this metaphor to dealing with non-textual data is in defining what constitutes an anchorable object.

Even with multimedia data types of which Microcosm 'knows' nothing, Microcosm can provide all the functionality of a sophisticated browser and a multimedia database, and can add the value of node-to-node linking, or where one end of the link is a text node, it can provide object-to-node or node-to-object linking. When considering the extension of this framework to support object-to-object link for any data types, it is important to emphasise that Microcosm makes no assumption about how an anchor will be expressed. The viewer determines the semantics of the anchor description; the linkbase will store whatever it is told to store (so long as it can be represented by ASCII text), and when requested to resolve a link from an anchor will compare whatever data is sent by the viewer with whatever is stored. So it is up to the programmer of the viewer to determine how to represent an anchor.

The easiest way to represent an anchor within a bitmapped picture is to use the coordinates of a rectangle or polygon which surrounds the object of interest. This allows the user to create specific link anchors and buttons in both source and destination documents. The more difficult and interesting problem in Microcosm is how to map the concept of a generic link onto pictures. This problem will be discussed more generally later, but the Microcosm designers produced an interesting compromise solution for bitmapped pictures by allowing users to create selections in pictures tagged with keywords or phrases. These anchors are treated just like buttons and stored in the linkbase like any other button link, but when the viewer starts running it queries the linkbase for any buttons belonging to this data and the tagged anchors are highlighted in the picture in the same way as 'normal' buttons in text. The difference is that the user can follow any generic links defined on the text tag when they click on the button highlighted in the picture.

There is clearly a degree of effort involved in identifying objects in pictures and manually tagging them with their associated concepts, but this approach can be very useful in particular applications, such as the linking of a large number of bitmaps generated by CAD models, where the names of the objects in the model are well-defined, for example, buildings in a city map or part numbers in the circuit diagrams of a machine. Extending this idea, it is relatively easy to define generic links on objects in files generated directly by an object-oriented drawing package, because the drawing package handles the relationship between the name of the object and the pixels in the display that represent that object. A similar approach can be taken to defining links in spreadsheet applications.

It is relatively easy nowadays to display temporal media such as audio and video files using standard software tools such as the Windows Media Player. However, when considering finer grained linking into and out of such files, there are a number of issues that need to be considered:

- How will a source anchor be represented in such media?
- How will a destination anchor be represented in such media?
- How will the system present the presence of an anchor to the user?

Given a large resource (such as a video film or an audio CD), how will the system know:

- What part of the whole should be represented to the user?
- How may discrete multimedia be synchronised?
- What is the meaning of generic links in such media?

The Microcosm team didn't attempt to tackle the sychronisation issue in the way that, say, the Amsterdam team did (see Chapter 14) but did produce a Microcosm-aware Sound Viewer and a Microcosm-aware Video Viewer to experiment with the other issues. These are described in Hall *et al.* (1996).

Taking the concept of generic linking in non-text media to its ultimate extreme requires the ability to apply content-based processing and matching techniques to media other than text. This is of course a difficult and as yet unsolved problem in the general case. Work is in progress, however, to extend the Microcosm system to include both generic and 'compute' linking capabilities for non-text media as part of the MAVIS project at Southampton (Lewis *et al.*, 1996).

12.4 Dealing with Process Issues

Application Maintenance

The open hypermedia research community argue that one of the main aims behind the development of open hypermedia systems and link services is increased maintainability of hypermedia applications. Certainly, increased support for application maintenance was one of the main aims of the Microcosm project. A key to this is the separation of links and documents, and management of each. The Document Management System supports the maintenance of the documents within an application and provides a number of different ways for documents to be identified, and the 'compute' links facility provides for the retrieval of text documents by means of indexes. By querying the linkbases it is possible to find out what links have been made, when and by whom, as well as their source and destination anchors.

The concept of storing structural (navigation) links in databases along with the documents they refer to is now well-established for large-scale Web site maintenance. Microcosm extends this idea to associative linking as well. Clearly, the down-side of the separation of links and documents is the extra effort involved in maintaining link integrity, as mentioned above, but the Microcosm team would argue that this is a price well worth paying to support associative linking in large-scale applications, where more than one author is involved either at the same time or over time.

The use of generic links helps to reduce authoring effort, and also to ease maintenance problems, because each generic link defines a class of links, which only has to be defined once and is applicable across the whole application to which that linkbase is applied.

Reuse

The issue of reuse was also a central focus in the Microcosm project. The team focused not just on document, or even hyperdocument, reuse, but also on link reuse. Links are treated as separate objects which can be processed and analysed separately from documents, and generic links can be reused in any application with an appropriate context. For example, it doesn't make a lot of sense to apply a set of generic links generated on the basis of the entries in a UNIX manual to a set of documents about English literature, or *vice versa* (although some interesting relationships can be found by applying links to a set of documents out of context!).

The Microcosm architecture enables different views of the same set of documents to be presented to different users, either by associating different logical types to the files in the application in the DMS, or by using different combinations of linkbases. The link service can be applied to any application that can communicate with it, although there are different levels at which this can be applied (see the above description of Microcosm viewers). The filter architecture of Microcosm allows for the dynamic generation of links through whatever algorithm is defined in the particular filter, which in principle allows for the generation of highly adaptive hypermedia applications, though in practice these are still very difficult to create successfully because we know so little about how to build dynamic user profiles. In the more recent work of the team at Southampton, the filter architecture of Microcosm has evolved into a framework of communicating agents to further support this type of research (Goose *et al.*, 1996; Pikrakis *et al.*, 1998).

Supporting the Full Lifecycle and Process Management

The broader lifecycle aspects are not explicitly addressed in Microcosm. The philosophy encourages evolutionary development of applications, and is very much resource-based. The approach to design can be both top-down and bottom-up for both documents and links. Authors are advised first to collect together the resources they want to use in an application and to classify them according to whatever logical types they choose in the DMS hierarchy. At this point, the documents are already accessible through two different access mechanisms in the DMS: first, direct access to the files through the graphical user interface; and secondly, through the database which allows query-based access on any field (author, keywords, etc.). Text documents can also be accessed through the search mechanism of the 'compute' links facility.

Once the resources have been assembled, the author can start making links between the resources. There is currently no particular support for specific linking and the creation of buttons; it is up to the author to decide what items if any in each document should be linked in this way to other resources in the application or elsewhere. Specific links and buttons enable the author to suggest navigation routes through the application to the user, the design of which needs careful consideration. Buttons also help give the structure to the application (next page, home page, etc.). In Microcosm these could be handled by a separate presentation environment, such as Toolbook or Authorware, but increasingly nowadays users expect access through standard Web browsers, so it is up to the application designed to decide whether the structural links should be handled in the standard (embedded) way using HTML pages or stored in the Microcosm linkbase. For large scale applications, when the documents are all stored in a database, current practice is tending towards the storage of the structural links similarly. Microcosm extends this concept easily to the storage of associative links which enhances process management.

The generic and local link facilities allow for a form of top-down linking, which encourages the author to consider the main concepts in an application or an individual document, and to decide how these should be represented or defined using links. For example, if the application has a glossary, it is very easy to define using an automated batch process all the terms in the glossary to be the source anchors for generic links whose destinations are the glossary entries for the corresponding terms. A similar process can be used for any associated dictionaries or other reference material. The author may also choose to create generic links, for example on the names of all the major characters or places in the application to a collection of biographies or a gazetteer, respectively. The possibilities are endless. Local links are used to provide a generic-type link, but one that is only defined within the context of a particular document.

For large scale applications, developers are advised to consider the following process for generating associative links between documents in a manageable way. As every document or resource is entered into the DMS (either manually or automatically through some sort of batch process), its associated keywords are registered in the DMS database. The application is then immediately searchable at this meta-data level, as well as directly through the DMS and through the 'compute' links index. Generic links are then generated, again either manually or automatically, using the document's keywords as source anchors and with the associated document as the destination of the link. This automatically gives the documents a 'pull', and it can be accessed through browsing whenever another document or resource refers to that keyworded concept. This is limited to exact matches on the keyword in the current implementation, but research versions have extended the source anchor matching process to include synonym matching, and to address the issue of checking the context of the selection of the source anchor, for example if the user selects the word '*tank*' as the source anchor for a link, does the context imply a fish tank or an army tank?

It is worth noting that the use of powerful search and analysis engines to generate sets of associative (generic) links for large sets of documents has been enhanced considerably in the Web version of Microcosm.

Cognitive Management

The separation of links into databases, the use of dynamic (generic) linking and the ability to access the information in the application through various different means (hierarchical structure, indexing, keywording, browsing) all aid cognitive management during development. Authors can easily find out what information is in the system and what links have been established, and can view any number of resources on the screen at any one time. For manually created links, an easy graphical user interface is provided for selecting the source anchor and document, the destination anchor and document and describing the link to be created. Links can be edited and manipulated in the linkbases, and different linkbases can be used to help define the context of the links. The generic links in the linkbase effectively produce a conceptual index to the documents in the application if the process of creating them has been systematically based on the use of keywords as described above. Researchers in the group are working on the development of a new notation which addresses the issue of support for design and cognitive management during the development process for multimedia applications, including support for the management of specific linking and buttons.

For large scale applications the research team are working on the development of 'modular hypermedia authoring', which enables developers to break-down the authoring of a large scale application into modules, in a similar way to the same process in software engineering. To support authoring in multimedia applications, the team are extending the idea of using content-based retrieval techniques to define source anchors in non-text documents mentioned above, to include a multimedia thesaurus that enables different media representations of the same concept to be used to represent that concept; for example, an image of a face, a name or a video clip might all represent the same person in this concept database.

Supporting Enhanced Productivity

One of the main motivations behind the original design of Microcosm was to reduce the authoring effort for large-scale applications. The introduction of generic and local links was one means of doing this. The other was the introduction of the filter architecture to both support dynamic link generation by means of the most appropriate method for an application, and to 'filter' or 'customise' the sets of documents and links offered to a user. The team have since developed the idea of the filter architecture into a framework of communicating agents (De Roure *et al.*, 1996; Pikrakis *et al.*, 1998) and are experimenting with different types of agents to both support application development and the customisation of the application for different users. The results of this work are being applied increasingly to the Web version of Microcosm.

12.5 Conclusions

The Microcosm model of hypermedia application development is very much an information-centred model, and the approach to authoring and design is resource-based. Microcosm is an open hypermedia system and provides a link service that can in principle be applied to any information resource. The principles of information access at many different levels, generic linking and the filter architecture were all introduced into the original design to provide support for the development and cognitive management of large-scale hypermedia applications. The emphasis in the design has always been on dynamic configuration, late binding of links and a move towards the use of agents to support link authoring and management.

Microcosm became a commercial product in 1995, and is sold and developed by Multicosm Ltd (see below). It has always been in essence a desktop application. Distributed versions were developed by the research team (Hill and Hall, 1994; Goose *et al.*, 1996) but for both the commercial and research teams the phenomenal growth of the Web meant that any distributed version needed to be compliant with the Web environment.

The benefits of keeping links separate from content are just as applicable to the Web as any large-scale hypermedia information management system, if not more so. In 1994 the research team began to develop a version of the Microcosm link service for the Web. This project became known as the Distributed Link Service (DLS) (Carr *et al.*, 1996). The design of the DLS initially mimicked the Microcosm design in the Web, but later moved to a proxy server implementation for pragmatic development reasons. Some of the more advanced features of Microcosm, such as the interactive query-based interface to the linkbases and the ability to apply links to any type of documents (not just Web documents), have been lost, but the essential philosophy of Microcosm, that of providing a light-weight link service that supports powerful mechanisms to support link authoring and management, has been retained. The architecture of the DLS includes the provision of an agent framework (evolved from the original Microcosm filter architecture), and the system is being success-fully applied in a number of research projects, such as an electronic journals project.

The DLS is being commercially exploited by Multicosm and the commer-cial version is called Webcosm. Both the DLS and Webcosm make use of the powerful combination of search/content analysis engines and generic links to automatically generate associative links for large sets of Web documents.

12.6 Further Information

For more information on Microcosm, the DLS and Webcosm, or any other aspect of the work described in this chapter, the following sources of information are available. The best source of information regarding the original Microcosm project is probably the following book:

Hall, W., Davis, H. and Hutchings, G. (1996) *Rethinking Hypermedia: The Microcosm Approach*, Kluwer Academic Publishers, ISBN 0–7923–9679–0.

Information regarding research developments can be found at the group's Website

```
http://www.mmrg.ecs.soton.ac.uk/
```

and information regarding the commercial products Microcosm and Webcosm can found at

```
http://www.multicosm.com/
```

Alternatively, the developers can be contacted at:

Professor Wendy Hall
Contact address: Department of Electronics and Computer Science
                    University of Southampton
                    Southampton SO17 1BJ
                    UK
Email: wh@ecs.soton.ac.uk
Phone: +44 1703 592388
Fax: +44 1703 592865

Contact details for Multicosm Ltd can be found at their Website

http://www.multicosm.com/

13

Hyper-G and Hyperwave

Structure without life is dead. But life without structure
is un-seen

(John Cage, 'Lecture on Nothing', Silence, 1961)

Chapter Goals

Hyper-G is a client-server, Internet-based hypermedia system which
provides session support, access control and a rich data model. This
chapter demonstrates ways in which an alternative system to the
Web can provide functionality which improves both usability and
development. The objectives of this chapter are to show that:

- Hyper-G, like the Web, is client-server based. Unlike the Web,
  connections to servers are maintained for the duration of a
  session, allowing more effective access control and logging.

- Hyper-G has adopted a rich data model which includes links
  between flexibly defined anchors and document collections
  (which form a document hierarchy).

- Hyper-G document collections allow contextualisation of information.

- The Hyper-G anchor-link model allows flexible management of
  non-text media and maintenance of link consistency

- Hyper-G has evolved into Hyperwave – a system which inter-
  operates with the Web but provides most of the advanced
  information management features of Hyper-G.

13.1 Introduction

Hyper-G was conceived in 1989 at The Institute for Information Processing and Computer Supported New Media (IICM) at the Graz University of Technology. During the 1980s, IICM had been undertaking research on videotex systems and hypermedia in the form of Computer Aided Instruction systems. Using this experience, the idea was conceived for a system which combined the expertise that had been developed in these areas, yet circumvented their design problems (such as the confusion of content and structure). The result was Hyper-G. The developers of Hyper-G claim 'Hyper-G represents the first of a new generation of Internet information systems – it provides real hypermedia, supporting tools for structuring, maintaining and serving heterogeneous multimedia data including text, images, digital audio and video, PostScript and 3D scenes'. During the 1990s, Hyper-G continued to develop and eventually evolved in a commercial system – Hyperwave.

In this chapter we focus on Hyper-G and Hyperwave, and the various components which form Hyper-G (such as Amadeus and Harmony) and Hyperwave. In particular, we consider how Hyper-G helped address a number of the problems discussed in this book, including aspects such as user orientation and contextualisation and information maintenance and consistency.

At the heart of Hyper-G are several relatively simple concepts. The first is that the traditional hypermedia node-link model (such as that adopted for the WWW), although adequate for supporting navigation, is not sufficient for effective document management or information contextualisation. A second concept is that Hyper-G uses session-based connections to servers so that it is possible to more easily support interaction styles involving state information. Finally, the design of Hyper-G is based (at least partially) on the concept that a uniform and consistent structure as possible is desirable, and that strong control over the objects (documents, links, etc.) in a hypermedia system is critical.

The outcome of these concepts is that Hyper-G is a complex set of standards, protocols, tools, applications, and a very rich data model. Hyper-G is essentially a distributed hypermedia system which works across networks and can co-exist with (or indeed, interoperate with) the World Wide Web. Indeed, Hyper-G can be viewed as an extension of the Web, even though it was developed in parallel with the Web.

Hyper-G has reached the point where it is now a significant commercial success (as Hyperwave), and is being used in a number of substantial installations. Hyperwave is continuing to evolve as a successful commercial product. The current research work on Hyperwave continues to be undertaken by researchers at IICM, in conjunction with the Institute for HyperMedia Systems (IHM) of Joanneum Research, with the help of a very large number of other organisations all over the world.

In this chapter we largely focus on Hyper-G rather than Hyperwave, primarily since we are considering the research focus and issues which led to the development of the system, though in most cases the descriptions are just as valid for Hyperwave.

13.2 Hyper-G Concepts

Hyper-G is a distributed hypermedia information management system. It comprises a complex set of tools and protocols which allow multi-user access and management of multiple media documents across the Internet or local networks. Figure 13-1 shows a typical session involving the use of Hyper-G to browse information.

The data models and information management techniques used in Hyper-G facilitate full-text retrieval, ensuring automatic link consistency, links to and from multimedia documents, document security, access control and straightforward interoperability with other Internet protocols such as WWW, FTP, Telnet and Gopher. Indeed, Hyper-G can be seen as a sophisticated form of Web Server which extends the conventional Web model.

Hyper-G Architecture

Hyper-G, like most Internet-based information management systems, is client-server based. The server stores, organises and manages specific content, and is responsible for managing sessions and requests for information from clients. The clients (either native Hyper-G clients such as Harmony or Amadeus, or conventional WWW browsers) are used to visualise both content and/or meta-information about the content or other server operations which is retrieved from the server, or to provide new content to the server (thereby acting as an authoring tool).

Hyper-G, however, has a fundamental difference to other client-server systems, such as the Web. Conventional Web client-server communica-

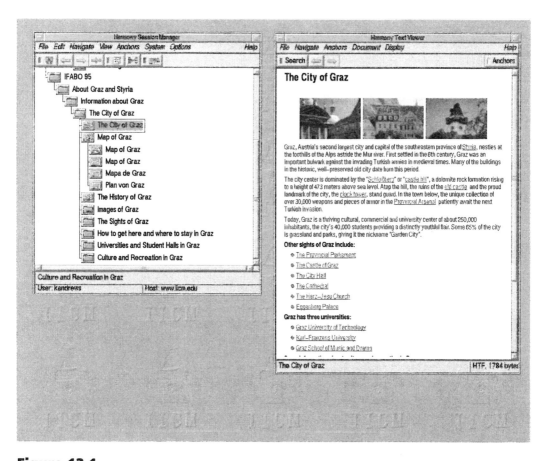

Figure 13-1

Typical Hyper-G browsing session

tion is essentially stateless, i.e. a new connection is established by the client with a (possibly different) Web server each time a request is made. Hyper-G, however, is based on establishing a connection with a single server for the entire duration of a session. All communication from the client then goes through this single server, though this server can contact other servers for information on behalf of the client (Figure 13-2). This use of session-based connections and a local server (which acts as a proxy for other servers) allows Hyper-G to support aspects such as user authorisation, document annotations, communication minimisation (since a new connection need not be established for each request) and improved security management.

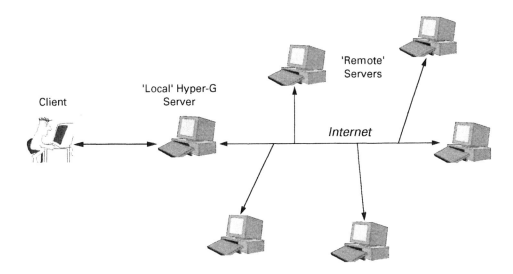

Figure 13-2

Client-server architecture of Hyper-G. (Reprinted from Maurer, H (1996) Hyper-G now Hyperwave: The Next Generation Web Solution by kind permission of Addison Wesley Longman Ltd.)

Hyper-G was originally developed to work most effectively with its own native Hyper-G clients. However a gateway (or rather a protocol converter) exists within the Hyper-G server which allows it to interoperate with conventional Web browsers (such as Netscape's Navigator or Microsoft's Internet Explorer). Much of the advanced functionality supported by Hyper-G can only be accessed easily using the native Hyper-G browsers (we discuss both Hyper-G servers and clients in more detail below). It is worth noting that Hyperwave has moved away from dedicated clients, to the use of standard Web clients. This will be discussed in more detail below.

Being a distributed system, Hyper-G also supports multiple users. However, the communication protocol used between server and client supports manipulation of the information as well as viewing, and therefore the Hyper-G clients can be used for authoring. As a result, Hyper-G can be considered a multi-author environment which allows concurrent updates by different authors while continuing to be used to serve information for browsing. The server of course supports appropriate user identification and authorisation.

Document Management

If we split the term 'hypermedia' we obtain *hyper* and *media*. *Hyper* refers to the associative linking within hypermedia applications. We shall consider how Hyper-G manages this in the next section. If we look at the second part of the word, *media*, then essentially we are considering the multiple media content which is used within hypermedia applications: text, images, audio, video, graphics, music, etc. This content is typically stored as 'documents', which must be managed in some way. Most hypermedia systems have very poor document management facilities, and it is this area where Hyper-G provides significant advantages.

The designers of Hyper-G introduced the concept of a *collection*, an object which acts as a container for other Hyper-G objects (including documents and other collections). Every document or collection in Hyper-G must be part of a collection (with the exception of the server's root collection). The result is a collection hierarchy (Figure 13-3). Note that the hierarchy for a given server must be free of loops. The Hyper-G server enforces

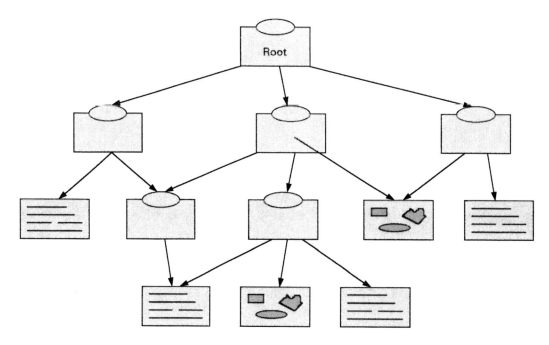

Figure 13-3

The Hyper-G collection hierarchy. (Reprinted from Maurer, H (1996) Hyper-G now Hyperwave: The Next Generation Web Solution by kind permission of Addison Wesley Longman Ltd.)

these requirements. It is also useful to note that a given document can belong to more than one collection. For example, a document describing Ronald Reagan could belong to both 'Actors' and 'Politicians' collections.

The collection hierarchy is a valuable tool for managing documents, in much the same way that a conventional file directory structure on a computer can be used to organise files. Whenever a new document is added to the system it must be added to a collection. Therefore, it will automatically be available to users, unlike the WWW where added documents require suitable links to be added from other related documents

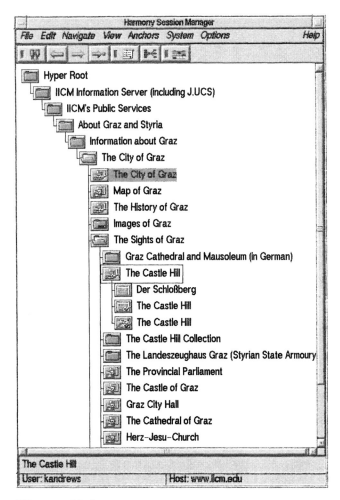

Figure 13-4

The Harmony collection browser

before it becomes accessible. This means that the maintenance effort is reduced.

Hyper-G also uses the document hierarchy as a browsing tool for users. A user can locate a document by browsing the hierarchy like a sequence of menus. Support for this type of browsing is built into the Hyper-G clients, and is also used (though less effectively) in the Web interface. If we reverse the process, and navigate using conventional hypermedia linking, then the document hierarchy can still be shown to the user, and used to provide feedback on their location within the document structure. An example of this feedback is shown in Figure 13-4, which demonstrates the use of the collection browser within the Harmony Hyper-G client.

A collection may contain a special document called the *collection head*. If a user browses a collection (rather than an actual document), then rather than just listing the items within the collection, the collection head is displayed by the client. Hyper-G also supports two special types of collection. The first is a cluster, a collection which contains a set of documents that should typically be viewed together in some form. Layout and synchronisation information can be attached to the cluster, though most current implementations do not use this information. Clusters can be used to support concepts such as compound multimedia documents and multilingual documents.

The second special type of collection is a sequence, which is an ordered collection of documents (or sub-collections) which should be presented in sequence. For example, a typical guided tour would use a sequence to provide the desired set of steps to follow. The relationship between normal collections, clusters and sequences is shown in Figure 13-5. Collections allow a user to select from a list of items; clusters allow the user to visualise the items together; sequences let the use view the items one after another.

Finally, it is worth pointing out that documents and collections are both supported by a rich attribute model. Attributes include elements such as the owner, name, creation, modification and expiration dates, access price (for billing purposes) and access and modification permissions. These attributes allow sophisticated management of the documents. For example, it is possible to automate a process whereby when the document (e.g. a conference announcement) expires, it is automatically removed from one collection (e.g. upcoming conferences) and added to a different collection (e.g. passed conferences). Hyper-G also supports

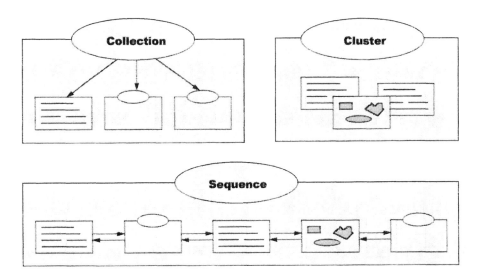

Figure 13-5

Hyper-G collection types (Reprinted from Maurer, H (1996) Hyper-G now Hyperwave: The Next Generation Web Solution by kind permission of Addison Wesley Longman Ltd.)

controlled access so that only authorised users can access given documents, and charging for documents.

Link Management

Whereas the use of collections provides a mechanism for managing documents, Hyper-G also provides support for associative linking (making it a *hyper*media system). The data model adopted is similar to the WWW model of nodes and links, but provides somewhat more flexibility through the ability to define anchors for all forms of media and in quite flexible structures.

Before discussing the linking mechanism, it is worth explaining that the Hyper-G data model is based around the definition of objects and relationships between these objects. Objects include a number of the concepts already discussed: documents, collections (including clusters and sequences), users and groups of users, and servers. A final object type is an anchor, which can be either a source anchor or a destination anchor (the difference will be explained shortly). Anchors are used to define a region of a document. This region can be a section of text, a fragment of an audio clip,

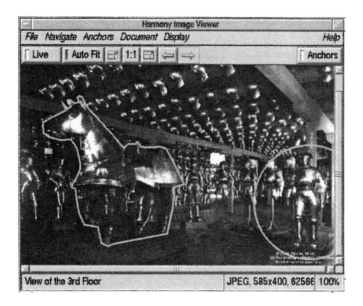

Figure 13-6

Source anchors in an image document

a (moving) region within a video sequence, etc. Figure 13-6 shows several anchors in an image document. Also, anchors, like all other objects, have a set of specified attributes, including an owner and access rights. This means that anchors can be created which will only be accessible to specified sets of users.

Hyper-G also defines specific types of relationships between the objects. A relationship between a collection and a document or between a collection and another collection defines the collection hierarchy discussed above. A relationship between a document and an anchor attaches the anchor to a specific document. It is important to note that anchors are defined separately from the documents, i.e. unlike the WWW, where anchors and the links which lead from them are defined inside a document, Hyper-G treats document and anchors as two separate types of objects.

The final type of relationship exists between a source anchor and destination anchor, document or collection. It is this relationship which provides the hypermedia links between the content. A user can select a source anchor and then follow the link attached to that source anchor. If the destination is an anchor, then the defined region of the document

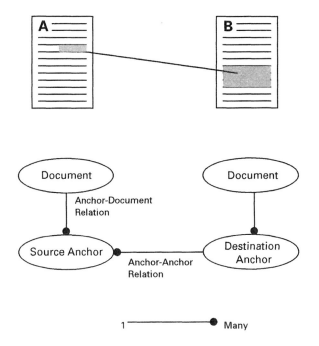

Figure 13-7

Anchor-anchor and anchor-document relations. (Reprinted from Maurer, H (1996) Hyper-G now Hyperwave: The Next Generation Web Solution by kind permission of Addison Wesley Longman Ltd.)

attached to the destination anchor is presented. If the destination is a document, then viewing starts at a default location within the document. If the destination is a collection then the collection is presented. An anchor-document and an anchor-anchor relationship is shown in Figure 13-7.

In Hyper-G the link relationship is implemented by storing the details with the source anchor. This means that a source anchor can only be linked to a single destination, though an anchor, document or collection may be the destination of many links. This means that Hyper-G is only able to implement **1–1** links and **n–1** links, but not **1–n** links or **n–n** links (i.e. multiple destination links). Two possible solutions are to provide overlapping source anchors, and to link to a collection of the destinations.

There are several important consequences of the way in which Hyper-G represents anchors and links. First, because anchors are not embedded into documents, but exist as separate objects, it is possible to delete a document which previously had a number of anchors (and corresponding links) and then add a new document, and have the new document use the same anchors. This is an important maintenance consideration. For example, if we edit or change an image, we do not lose any anchors which we have defined.

A second major benefit is that, unlike the WWW, it is simple to define and use overlapping anchors. For example, we can have a section of text which has two anchors which overlap. How this is handled when browsing is client-defined, but a typical example would be to have the client ask the user which link they wish to follow.

An even more important consequence of the above approach is that the anchors and links can be logically viewed as a separate linkbase (even though internally the Hyper-G server stores all objects, such as anchors, document descriptions, collections, users, etc. in a single object database). This is similar to Microcosm, discussed in the previous chapter. The use of a 'linkbase' allows much more flexible management of links and anchors. Since Hyper-G requires anchors to be attached to a document (via a relationship) for the anchor to be used, it does not provide support for generic links like Microcosm. Theoretically, this could be added by allowing anchors to be defined which specify a matching content, rather than a region of a document. However, this has not been implemented.

One final observation worth making is that Hyper-G anchors can be based on any media type. This means that inherent support exists for linking between any types of media. Unfortunately, the Web does not provide support for links from media other than text and images. This means that Hyperwave (which uses Web clients) cannot take advantage of this aspect of Hyper-G's support for linking.

Hyper-G/Hyperwave Servers and Clients

A number of software components which implement the concepts described above have been developed. These include a Hyper-G server (which formed the basis of the commercial Hyperwave server) and various Hyper-G clients. The server has been implemented for a number of Unix platforms and for Windows NT. Hyper-G clients exist for Windows (3.1, 95, NT) and Unix systems. Hyperwave uses conventional Web browsers (such as Microsoft Internet Explorer and Netscape Navigator) and as such clients are available for almost all platforms.

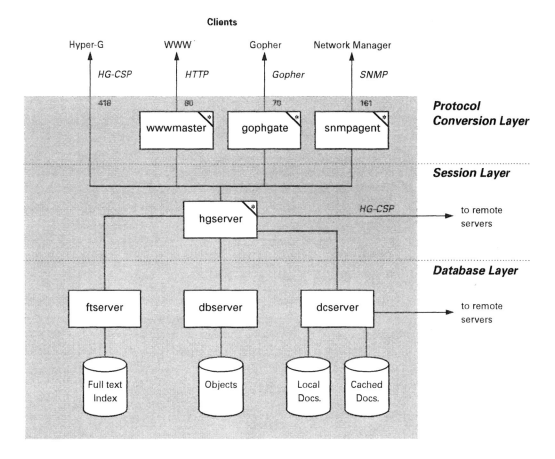

Figure 13-8

The Hyper-G Server architecture. (Reprinted from Maurer, H (1996) Hyper-G now Hyperwave: The Next Generation Web Solution by kind permission of Addison Wesley Longman Ltd.)

The Hyper-G server is not a monolithic software program. Rather, it is a set of components based around a three layer architecture. This is shown in Figure 13-8. The top layer is the protocol conversion layer, which allows the Hyper-G server to interoperate with other Internet protocols: WWW, Gopher, FTP, Telnet, etc. This consists of a series of gateways which respond to (or generate) requests using the relevant protocols. For example, the WWW gateway listens on port 80 of the server for HTTP requests and interprets these according. Since the Web does not support sessions, the gateway generates and manages a session for the Web client (such as Netscape Navigator) requesting information. The HTTP request is interpreted, converted to a suitable HG-CSP request (the native Hyper-G protocol) which is passed to the main Hyper-G session layer, and then accepts a response which is converted into a suitable Web page.

The middle layer, the session layer, manages connection sessions. A separate instance of the *hgserver* module is created for every connection/ session. This module accepts native HG-CSP requests and obtains the appropriate information from the relevant databases. These databases form the third layer of the server architecture. The server manages a database of documents, a database of objects including collections, anchors, users, groups, and document objects (which reference the actual documents) and a full-text index to use for rapid searches on the documents and the object attributes.

The server has sophisticated mechanisms for managing the structure of the information. For example, when a user requests a document which is stored on another server, the current server will communicate with the second server to obtain the document, and then this document will be cached for further use. The server also uses an algorithm (p-flood) to ensure that consistency is maintained across different servers. The server also ensures aspects such as information consistency and user access control.

A number of Hyper-G specific clients have been developed to communicate with the server. These include Harmony (for Unix systems), Amadeus (MS-Windows 3.1, 95 and NT), Easy (simple PC-based client for applications such as information kiosks) and HGTV (a terminal viewer). We shall briefly describe Harmony as it has the highest level of functionality.

Figure 13-9 shows the primary Harmony interface. The main interface contains a session manager (shown on the left of the figure) which has the main application menu, toolbars, status area, and the collection browser (which occupies most of the window). A user can use the session browser to locate documents or collections which can then be selected and viewed. When a document is opened for viewing the relevant document viewer(s) are opened. At present Harmony has viewers for text, images, video, postscript, audio and 3D scenes. Most of these viewers recognise various file forms (for example, the image viewer recognises GIF, JPEG, TIFF and PNG). Figure 13-9 shows the Harmony text viewer.

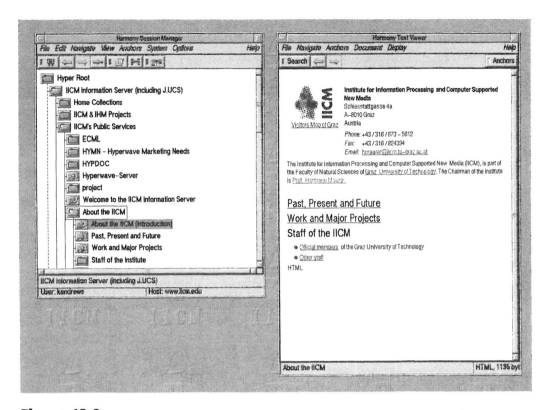

Figure 13-9

The main Harmony user interface

The session manager also provides a history list (to allow the user to backtrack through their navigation path), bookmarking, the ability to view and edit attributes of the various objects (where the user has appropriate permissions), and a powerful search mechanism. Further still, Harmony can be used to add new objects (such as documents, collections, anchors, links) to the server, thereby acting as an authoring tool.

There are two final tools which Harmony provides which are important to discuss: the Local Map and the Information Landscape. The information map, shown in Figure 13-10, provides a graphical representation of the relationships associated with a selected object. This can include hyperlinks, annotations and inline images. Both those objects which link to the specified object, and those which are linked from the specified object are shown. The information map can be used as an additional navigation mechanism, following links by repeatedly selecting objects which are the

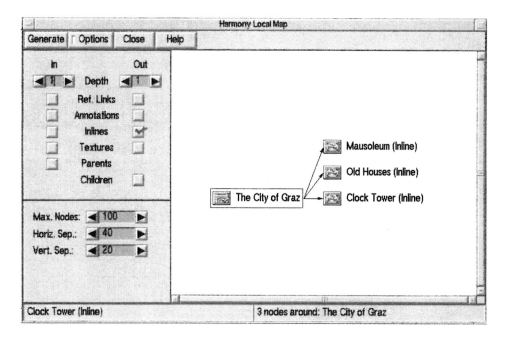

Figure 13-10

The Harmony local map

destination (source) of links from (to) the object of focus, and making them the focus. It can also be used to assist in maintenance, in that it is possible to see exactly which objects are related to an object which is being edited or deleted. The information map is also tightly coupled to the collection browser so that a change in one is reflected in the other.

Figure 13-11 shows the Harmony Information Landscape. This is a three-dimensional representation of the collection structure. In this view, collections are shown as flat boxes, with actual content shown as taller blocks (with the height reflecting the document size). The Information Landscape, like the collection browser, can be used to navigate amongst the various collections and documents: objects can be selected and activated and the user can 'fly' over the landscape or directly to specified objects (using the mouse to control the flight).

Before we conclude this section it is worth noting that Hyperwave has moved away from using dedicated clients, towards the use of standard Web browsers. These browsers will (after being suitably configured to

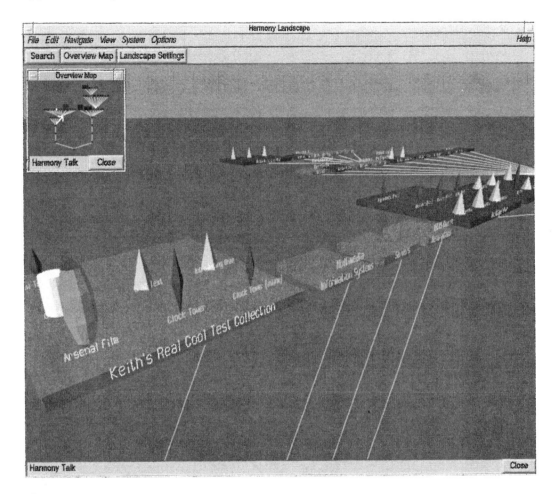

Figure 13-11

The Harmony information landscape

access appropriate proxy servers) be used to access full functionality from Hyperwave servers through the use of Java applets. These Hyperwave applets will be used within the browsers to support some of the more advanced Hyperwave functionality. This will enable Hyperwave to become more fully integrated into, and interoperable with, the WWW, while maintaining the advanced functionality developed for Hyper-G. This means that the Hyper-G clients such as Amadeus and Harmony are no longer used with Hyperwave.

The Hyperwave server utilises a language called *Place*. This is a meta-HTML language, which allows the appearance and function the user interface to be configured. Essentially, Place is used to define templates which contain both HTML and 'placeholders' (hence, the name). When a user access the server from a conventional Web client, the template is used to create the HTML page which is returned to the user. The place-holders within the template are replaced by appropriate information relating to the current object (such as a document or collection). It is therefore possible within Hyperwave to define the look and feel of the interface which is presented within conventional Web browsers (rather than proprietary clients). The result is that the various interface components found within the Hyper-G clients (such as the collection hierarchy, navigation controls, collection head and collection elements, etc.) can all be combined into a single Web page.

13.3 Dealing with Product Issues

Navigation and Browsing

Hyper-G supports effective navigation and browsing of hypermedia information structures in a number of flexible ways. Let us begin by considering information access. Like many hypermedia systems, Hyper-G provides three orthogonal methods of access to information: searching, navigation through a hierarchical structure, and hyperlinking. Hyper-G supports searching of both metadata (i.e. object attributes) and full text searching of the detailed content. It is worthwhile noting that the ability to search on the object attributes will often lead to significantly improved precision in the results returned from the search. For example, we can search for the word 'Brown' in the *Author* attribute, and avoid retrieving information on the colour brown. The attributes are also indexed for faster searching.

Users can access information using the normal structural organisation of the information space. As discussed previously, Hyper-G supports the concept of collections. These collections result in a natural hierarchical organisation of the information space. We can use these collections (and the resultant hierarchies) to navigate within the information space, moving up and down within the collections. Finally, Hyper-G obviously supports conventional hyperlinking. It is worth noting that Hyper-G supports overlapping anchors, and hence a single piece of anchor text can be linked through multiple anchors to multiple destinations. When a conventional Web browser is being used as the front end for Hyper-G this cannot be supported, so multiple destination links would need to be represented as a collection. When XML becomes commonly supported by Web browsers, it will be possible to provide support for multiple destination links.

An important aspect of effective navigation is the visualisation of the structure of the information space. Support for visualisation is a very important aspect of Hyper-G. The elements discussed above (such as both full text and metadata searching and hierarchical organisation of information spaces using collections) are used to present the structure of documents to the user. For example:

- Information from the link databases and metadata can be used to produce local maps (using standard graph drawing mechanisms). Figure 13-12 demonstrates a typical map. This provides a strong indication of the overall structure of the flat document structure.

- Collections and link databases can be combined to produce three-dimensional landscape visualisations. The collection structure recedes into the background with the documents placed in the foreground. Links are overlaid onto this structure. A typical example was shown in Figure 13-11. Such an approach extends conventional maps to include a degree of abstraction which can be particularly useful in managing large information spaces. This capability is built into Harmony and will be available in standard Web browsers for the commercial version through the use of Java applets.

- A recent concept which is still under development is the use of 'information pyramids', as shown in Figure 13-13. The Information Pyramids approach utilises three dimensions to compactly visualise large document hierarchies. As applied to Hyper-G (or more likely, Hyperwave) a plateau will represent the server root and other plateaus on top of the root plateau represent collections and documents under the root. Different icons are used to represent different objects.

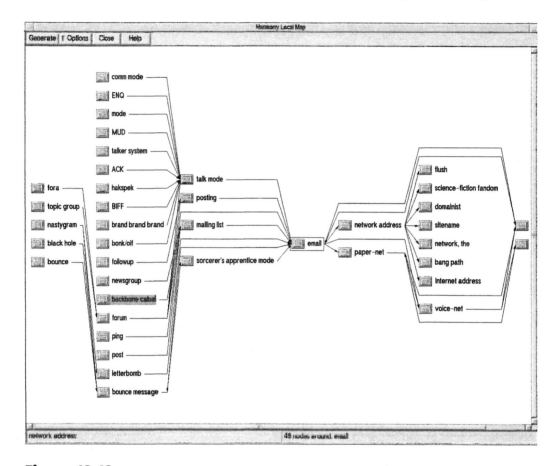

Figure 13-12

Example of Harmony local map

Cognitive Management During Browsing

An important aspect of cognitive management in using hypermedia applications and systems is assisting the user in understanding their location within the information space, i.e. addressing the 'lost in hyperspace' problem. Hyper-G addresses this problem in several ways. The simplest mechanism is by enforcing a specific structure for Hyper-G applications. Hyper-G requires that all documents and collections must be part of another collection (except, of course, the server root). The information space for an application can therefore be described by the hierarchical set of collections. This constraint means that we have a consistent frame-

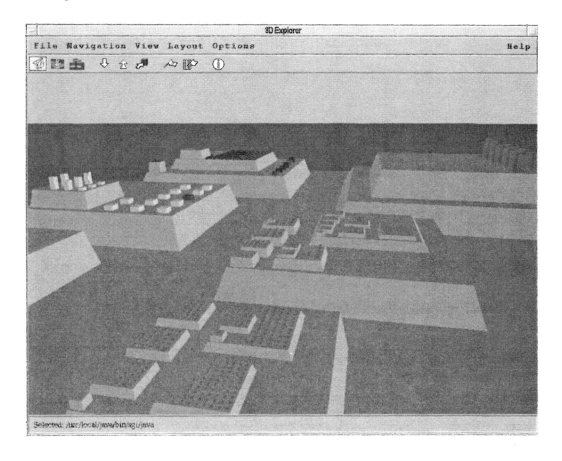

Figure 13-13

Example of information pyramid

work for visualisation of all applications – and hence in reducing the cognitive burden in managing applications.

Beyond simple management of the structure of the information space, Hyper-G also assists the user in knowing where they are within the information space. Harmony supports this through the use of 'location feedback'. This shows the user their current position in the (global) collection hierarchy.

Location feedback synchronises the various different views of the data. When an object is selected in the Local Map and is not already visible in the collection browser, a path to that object is opened up automati-

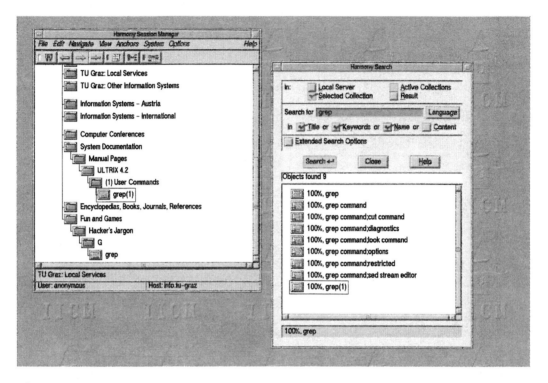

Figure 13-14

Using the collection hierarchy to provide location feedback

cally. Users can gain an understanding of the context in which the object is embedded through its location in Hyper-G's (or Hyperwave's) collection structure, prior to any decision to view it. If you follow a hyperlink (either directly or via a local map) to a different point in the collection (or in another collection), the collection opens up so that the user can see where they are. This means that the user can always see where in the collection hierarchy is the currently viewed node.

Information Contextualisation

Location feedback also provides a valuable method of contextualising information. An illustrative example is given in Figure 13-14. In this example, the user is searching for the word 'grep' in the title and key-words attributes of all objects (collections, clusters, documents and anchors) on a local Hyper-G (or Hyperwave) server. The result is a list of nine matching objects; two text objects and seven anchors. Single-left-clicking an object in the search result list selects the object and activates location feedback (as it does in the Local Map). This is illustrated in the figure.

Because of the location feedback, when the user clicks on the objects in the result list they can see from the collection context that the first grep text document in the result list belongs to the collection 'G' in the 'Hacker's Jargon' and the second belongs to '(1) User Commands' in the 'ULTRIX 4.2' manual pages. This provides valuable context information. Assuming that the user is looking for a description of the UNIX grep command, it is now possible to make an educated choice between the two documents, before retrieving either of them.

The above example is a specific case of a general principle. The collections within Hyper-G provide a valuable contextualisation aid. We can gain a considerable amount of information about an object – including an understanding of it's context, from the collection(s) to which it belongs.

Link and Content Validity

Ensuring link and content validity is one of the main strengths of Hyper-G/Hyperwave. Links are stored and maintained in a link database separate from the content. This approach, supported by an integrated document management system, allows the system to maintain complete knowledge (and control) of the elements being interlinked. Consequently, when documents or links are edited the system can automatically detect any dangling or invalid links. It is therefore possible to ensure that all links are at least syntactically correct – though of course this does not guarantee the semantic correctness of links. The ability to edit documents with Hyper-G/Hyperwave links was initially only available through Harmony or Amadeus clients, but is it now possible through standard Web browsers.

This operates by storing the content of a document independently from the links and anchors. The content and anchors are reconstructed for the purpose of editing and viewing. For HTML documents, the server parses the HTML, stores the links (identified by <A> tags and HREF's) in the link database, the title and any keywords in the attribute database, and the text contents in the document database. The document is again reconstructed for editing and viewing. The database therefore effectively manages link integrity and consistency. Version control is also being integrated into later versions.

Although Hyper-G does not explicitly address semantic validity of content and links, this is inherently supported to a limited extent through the structuring mechanisms which are used. For example, by including objects into collections, the collection gives a context against which content validity can be evaluated. This assists the developers in ensuring that specific objects have content which is appropriate to the object's location within the structure. Also, by having a well-defined structure, link authors are more likely to be able to identify suitable link destinations.

Information Structure

Hyper-G explicitly addresses the issue of information structuring through the use of collections. Collections provide a strong mechanism for managing the organisation of the information space. The collections used in Hyper-G do not form a strict hierarchy. Objects can be in multiple collections, though the server checks for and explicitly disallows cycles. We can view collections as directed acyclic graphs. Collections can therefore be used to support essentially any form of information structure. For example, a hierarchical tree can be readily supported by ensuring that any object belongs to only one collection. A matrix structure can be created by generating two sets of collections (for the matrix 'rows' and 'columns'), and a given object must belong to one collection in each set. Similar principles apply for other structure forms.

The main difference between this approach and a more free form structuring (such as exists in conventional Web pages) is that Hyper-G collections provide a very explicit mechanism for separating the structure from the content – an important aspect in a number of areas, including cognitive management, maintainability and reuse.

It is worthwhile pointing out that the ability for an object to belong to multiple collections means that Hyper-G allows multiple views on the same data. For example, a given email message could belong to a collection for a specific author, another collection for emails on a specific topic, and a further collection for emails on a specific date. Each of these collections (or rather, sets of collections) provides a different viewpoint on the data.

Although collections can be used to manage the underlying data structure, Hyper-G does not provide any explicit mechanism for managing the hypermedia structure of an application. For example, it is perfectly feasible to create overly complex hyperlink networks within a Hyper-G application. It should be acknowledged, however, that the strong contextualisation provided by the combination of collections and location feedback makes this less of a problem than in many other hypermedia systems.

Management of Different Media

Management of different media is another strong point of Hyper-G. The Hyper-G designers always envisaged an extensible hypermedia system that would support linking from and to any media type. From the beginning, the Harmony viewer supported links in numerous file formats (for example postscript, images, MPEG and audio as well as text).

The specific mechanism used by Hyper-G to support anchors depends upon the media type. For example, in image data polygons are used to specify image regions which define the boundary of an anchor. This anchor information is stored as attributes of the links (in postscript, the attribute contains a page number and the x,y coordinates).

Indeed, because of the mechanism used, the anchors can define not only flat structures but anchors of almost any form. For three-dimensional models, it becomes possible to define anchors which are regions of 'space' within the 3D model. The most significant difficulty then becomes appropriate presentation and selection of the anchor within the browser.

Hyper-G also provides explicit support for different languages. Where a given element is stored using multiple languages (as part of a cluster), the element which most closely matches a user's specified preference can be displayed. For example, documents, captions, attributes, etc. can be stored using multiple languages. At the simplest level this can be used to support a multilingual interface. This approach could, however, be readily extended to cover more complex scenarios. For example, it should be possible to store images or audio documents in different formats (or different resolutions or qualities) and then have the most appropriate document retrieved based on some criteria. For example, a user operating across a slow modem connection could automatically retrieve lower resolution images and more highly compressed audio than a user operating with a direct network connection. Such an approach provides a mechanism for direct and automatic adaptation to the system being used to access to information.

Finally, it is worth noting that although clusters can specify layout and synchronisation information, this concept has not yet been adequately explored as a mechanism for coordinating different media. For example, it is not possible in Hyper-G to directly specify coordination behaviour such as having certain viewers remain, and other to be removed when a link is followed. For example, if we have information related to a tour of a museum, then we may at one point in time be presenting an image of a specific museum room, some text on the artifacts in the room, and some general background music. If we select a link in the text page which takes us to another room, we may wish to change the text and image information, but leave the music unchanged. Hyper-G does not provide a straightforward mechanism for achieving such functionality. (To see one approach to providing this functionality, consider AHM described in Chapter 14.) Although Hyper-G does not support this directly, the concept of overlapping collections supported by appropriate use of the attribute model could be used as a basis for indicating media relationships.

13.4 Dealing with Process Issues

Application Maintenance

Hyper-G addresses the issue of application maintainability very effectively. Basic application maintenance was one of the main aims for the designers of Hyper-G. This is achieved in a number of ways, including appropriate use of collections, searchability and separation of content, links and attributes into relevant databases.

We can begin by considering the use of collections. These provide the author with a strong mechanism for combining documents into manageable units. Provided that the collections are used in a consistent fashion, it becomes possible for the author to readily identify sets of documents based on some criteria. For example, if the author wishes to make a change to all documents related to specific individual, then it is (at least in theory) simply a matter of selecting the collection related to these documents. This approach will only break down when the collections are either not used consistently or do not provide a structuring which is consistent with desired modifications.

Hyper-G also makes every object searchable, so it is relatively straightforward to locate specific items (and identify their related collections). This is a very important aid in the maintenance of large systems.

Probably more important than either of the above factors is the separation of collections and links (i.e. structure), document attributes (i.e. metadata) and document content (i.e. data), and their storage in separate databases. This means that changes can be made to either content or structure without affecting the other. For example, links can be added or removed, independently of the content. If we make changes to the content or links then the consistency of the structure can be automatically checked. Since the system maintains a tight document control, it becomes much simpler to ensure link integrity. It is essentially impossible to make changes which result in invalid structures (such as dangling links).

The attribute model used by Hyper-G also provides a basis for improving maintainability. It is possible to include attributes related to the maintenance of the information. For example, we could include an attribute which specifies an expiry date for a document. Beyond this date the document becomes invisible to the user. Attributes can also be used to support versioning of information, though this is being integrated more fully into the Hyperwave commercial version of the system.

Hyperwave is also being extended to include support for workflow for industrial and business clients. This will also play a major role in facilitating the maintainability of applications.

Reuse

Hyper-G supports information use explicitly, but does not provide any substantial explicit support for information reuse. Let us look at the implicit support first. At a basic level, the separation of structure and content means that content can be more readily reused. The use of collections means both that content to be reused can be more readily identified, and its context made explicit (a common problem with reusing content is that the context is not obvious, and when it is reused the context changes and hence the information is no longer appropriate). Similarly, the separation of content and structure also means that the structure is made more explicit, and therefore it is more straightforward to reuse the information structure (though not necessarily the specific implementation of the structure).

It is also worth noting that, whilst Hyper-G allows individual objects to be copied to an application, this can only occur at the document level (i.e. Hyper-G does not have an explicit mechanism for reusing content at a lower level than the document). Also, links are position dependant within a document. This means that reusing hyperlinks is not straightforward as they are highly document dependant.

Hyper-G also makes it difficult to reuse content by overlaying different hyperlink structures on the same content. At present there is no mechanism for partitioning the link database to allow multiple sets of links overlaying the same content.

Supporting the Full Lifecycle and Process Management

Hyper-G does not provide any built-in support for the overall development process (nor was this the intention of Hyper-G). Nevertheless, it does assist with the development process in a number of ways. First, a number of design methods for hypermedia include some mechanism for either clustering information or designing categories of information. For example, RMM includes the design of 'entities' which are essentially classes of information nodes. The clusters or classes are typically instantiated to obtain information nodes or documents. These clusters map very well to the collections in Hyper-G. In other words, Hyper-G provides an inherent support for a very common design artifact. Where a specific design methodology is not being used, it is still desirable to undertake some form of classification and grouping (recommended by Jakob Neilsen for hypermedia design for prototyping the structure of collections (Neilsen, 1995)).

In practice the structural design of a hypermedia application is typically both top-down and bottom-up. Again, although Hyper-G does not provide explicit support for either case, it does provide certain functionality which can assist with the process.

The ability to define collections can be an important aid in top-down design. It means that it is possible to create a hierarchy of collections, and hence design and visualise the document structure prior to creating any specific content. This means that the structure can be created, manipulated and evaluated without the difficulty of managing the content within this structure. Collections can also be used in a bottom-up approach. We can identify existing information, nodes or documents, and then progressively cluster these using collections.

There is, however, little support for the middle section – the identification of the links which should be made. Like most systems, Hyper-G does not explicitly support this, but it does provide various tools which can assist in this process. For example, the ability to undertake full searching on the existing content can be an important aid in the identification of suitable hyperlinks.

Other aspects of the development process are also supported (to varying extents) by Hyper-G. For example, Hyper-G allows different categories of users (and hence developers) and user authentication to be specified. This can be a valuable versioning and development tool. Sections of the content and structure can be designed and implemented, and then locked from further changes.

It is also worth noting that, since Hyper-G has direct and tight control over the documents and structures, it becomes much more straightforward to both undertake comprehensive testing and evaluation, and to automate much of this testing (such as the checking for invalid links).

The developers of Hyper-G and Hyperwave are looking at certain tools which have the potential to provide significant assistance during specific parts of the development process. For example, work is being undertaken on techniques for semi-automatic link creation using thesauri. This would allow the system to analyse existing content and make suggestions for links based on existence of appropriate synonyms.

Cognitive Management during Development

With a system such as Hyper-G, the same tools which are useful for users in terms of supporting effective navigation during browsing, are also useful for authors during the development process. For example, the search facilities in Hyper-G (where everything is effectively indexed) can greatly assist authors in locating appropriate link destinations, without incurring the cognitive burden associated with managing the entire information space.

Similarly, the use of hierarchically layered collections allows authors to more easily identify the appropriate location for new content. Again, the author need not have a comprehensive understanding of the entire application structure in order to be able to locate specific content. The visualisation tools are also important for similar reasons.

Another important aspect is that as information is added to the Hyper-G database it immediately becomes available for browsing. Further, the databases are always consistent, so it is impossible to ever have a Hyper-G application which is 'incomplete' in the sense that it cannot be used. This can be compared to a Web application under construction which will typically contain numerous invalid links, incomplete pages, etc., often to the point where it become unnavigable. This characteristic of Hyper-G is a very important aspect in terms of assisting developers manage an applications during the stages when it is incomplete.

Supporting Enhanced Productivity

The support for productivity provided by Hyper-G depends largely upon the scale of the application being constructed. For small applications, developers can create the pages using conventional Web development tools (such as Microsoft Frontpage) and then, using a custom tool (called *hwupload*), load these pages into the Hyperwave server. Subdirectories (of Web pages) can be modelled as collections on the server. This approach allows developers to take advantage of the sophisticated development environments which are becoming available for the Web.

These Web development environments typically provide advanced page or document design and implementation. However, they do not manage the large scale structuring of information spaces very well. As such they are useful for developing small scale applications but present significant problems when developing large-scale sites.

Where the material already exists (for example, in a large-scale document management system), Hyper-G does not provide any support for migrating the documents. At present, this must be completed manually, though tools are currently under development which should assist with this process.

13.5 Conclusions

Hyper-G has evolved over the last eight years, and now Hyperwave is a commercially successful system. A number of the ideas which drove the initial development of Hyper-G, or even some of the features which were incorporated into the various Hyper-G components, have yet to be realised in Hyperwave. This has partly been a result of the desire (or possibly the commercial need) to interoperate with existing Web servers, clients and protocols. Nevertheless, Hyperwave provides a number of features which help address various limitations of existing hypermedia systems. Foremost amongst these are more effective document management (and subsequent improvements in maintainability) and improved orientation and contextualisation of users.

The research team for Hyper-G and Hyperwave foresee various directions for ongoing research. One possible area is the development of support for more document formats and enhanced gateways for alternative protocols (such as Gopher and FTP). These enhancements become less relevant though with the integration of Hyperwave into the current WWW environment.

Other more interesting directions of research (at least from a hypermedia development perspective) are the integration of improved document management facilities into Hyperwave. This could include support for automatic classification of documents, automatic generation of links and version management and configuration control. Consideration is also being given to support for collaboration mechanisms and active communication of media (such as allowing users to subscribe to specific collections in a way which notifies them of changes). Finally, Hyper-G continues to be used to investigate mechanisms for visualising both information and the structure of context of that information.

13.6 Acknowledgements

We wish to thank Keith Andrews for his invaluable notes, comments, feedback and discussions. These assisted immensely in the compilation of this chapter. We would specifically like to acknowledge Keith's contribution in providing figures 13-1, 13-4, 13-6, 13-9, 13-10, 13-11, 13-12, 13-13 and 13-14 for this chapter.

13.7 Further Information

For more information on Hyper-G and Hyperwave or any other aspect of the work described in this chapter, the following sources of information are available. The best source of information is probably the following book:

Maurer H (1996) *Hyper-G now Hyperwave: The Next Generation Web Solution*, Addison-Wesley, ISBN 0–201–40346–3.
The following Websites contain information on Hyper-G, Hyperwave and the research groups which have worked on these systems:

```
http://www.hyperwave.com/
```

```
http://www.iicm.edu/hg_intro
```

Alternatively, the developers can be contacted at:

Hermann Maurer
Contact address: Institute for Information Processing and Computer
                     Supported New Media
                     Schiesstattgasse 4a
                     A-8010 Graz
                     Austria
Phone: +43 / 316 / 873 – 5612
Fax: +43 / 316 / 824394
Email: hmaurer@iicm.tu-graz.ac.at

Contact details for Hyperwave Information Management GmbH can be found at their Website:

```
http://www.hyperwave.com/
```

14

AHM and CMIFed

Information necessitating a change of design will be conveyed
to the designer after and only after the design is complete.
(Often called the 'Now They Tell Us' Law)

(Fyfe's First Law of Revision)

Chapter Goals

The Amsterdam Hypermedia Model amalgamates ideas from
hypertext and multimedia. The goal of this chapter is to
demonstrate how different media can be effectively integrated in a
way which supports contextualisation of information and
management of temporal media. The objectives of this chapter are
to show that:

● The Amsterdam Hypermedia Model combines the Dexter model
   of hypertext with the CMIF model of multimedia.

● AHM supports composition of multiple media, including temporal media, into flexible presentations with synchronisation
   between the media.

● AHM allows the specification of link contexts, whereby the
   behaviour of different components of a presentation, upon
   following a link, can be specified. This allows improved contextualisation of presentations.

● CMIFed provides a flexible tool for efficient creation of multimedia presentations.

14.1 Introduction

The Interoperable Multimedia Applications group at CWI (Centrum voor Wiskunde en Informatica) in Amsterdam, Netherlands has been researching into multimedia and hypermedia for a number of years. The group is working on authoring software for hypermedia presentations (both implementations and theoretical models), and on operating application and network support for multimedia and hypermedia, in particular synchronization of independent streams. A major focus of the group's work is on developing models and authoring environments which result in flexible interoperable and portable hypermedia applications.

In this chapter we discuss two related research contributions from this research group: the Amsterdam Hypermedia Model (AHM), and the CMIFed authoring tool. The Amsterdam hypermedia model is an amalgamation of basic principles from both the hypertext and multimedia domains. It draws together the Dexter (Halasz and Schwartz, 1994) hypertext model with the CMIF (von Rossum *et al.*, 1993) multimedia model to produce a useful model of the hypermedia domain. AHM extends the Dexter Model by adding a conceptual framework for the inclusion and management of temporal data, the addition of high level presentation attributes, and the incorporation of link context into the model.

AHM is yet to be widely evaluated, and does not address (at least explicitly) many of the process issues which we considered in this book. Nevertheless, it is worthwhile discussing AHM as it is one of the best examples of research aimed at explicitly addressing (at the fundamental level of information modelling rather than application presentation) issues relating to the modelling of context maintenance during the structuring and subsequent use of a hypermedia document, and how to appropriately manage the structuring of dynamic multimedia data in a hypermedia document. In considering AHM, we aim to demonstrate that multiple forms of media can be managed and integrated in a cohesive fashion during development. We also aim to provide some insights into techniques for ensuring that a user maintains their context whilst navigating or browsing within an information space.

The CMIF editor (or CMIFed) is a prototype authoring application which was originally based on the CMIF multimedia model. As AHM was developed (and incorporated CMIF) the CMIF editor evolved to incorporate many of the hypermedia aspects of AHM. Although it is not a comprehensive implementation of the ideas encapsulated in AHM, it is still a useful prototype hypermedia authoring tool, and demonstrates well many of the aspects of AHM.

CMIFed incorporates a number of interesting tools and features which provide a developer with perspectives onto the underlying information structure. Experience with these tools is a useful guide to the types of knowledge that is useful to a hypermedia developer, and how this knowledge can be used to improve the development process.

14.2 AHM and CMIF Concepts

Background

Applications for the authoring of both multimedia and hypertext documents have existed for a number of years. In both cases many of these applications use their own underlying model of the document (either multimedia document or hypertext document). This inhibits the exchange of documents between these applications. A number of attempts have been made to develop 'standard' models which capture the underlying generic nature of documents and hence facilitate the interchange of the documents. Two examples of these models are the Dexter hypertext reference model and the CMIF multimedia model.

The Dexter hypertext reference model

The Dexter hypertext reference model (Halasz and Schwartz, 1994) is a typical example of this style of model for hypermedia applications. The Dexter Hypertext Reference Model evolved out of two small workshops, the first of which was held in the Dexter Inn in New Hampshire in 1988. This model is an attempt to capture the main abstractions which exist in a range of hypermedia applications. Its stated goal is to provide a basis for both comparing hypermedia applications, and improving interoperability.

The Dexter model represents a hypermedia application as three layers (as shown in Figure 14-1). The bottom layer – the *within-component layer* – represents the contents and structure *within* the components of the application. The Dexter model does not attempt to model this layer, but rather leaves the representation at this level up to other reference models

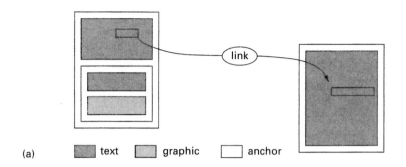

(a)   ▨ text   ▨ graphic   ☐ anchor

(b)

Presentation Specification	Component-specific presentation info.
Attributes	Semantic information
Anchors	Anchor ID	Value
Contents	Data block or pointer to data

(c)

Presentation Specification	Component-specific presentation info.
Attributes	Semantic information
Anchors	Anchor ID	Value
Children	Component ID
Contents	Data block or pointer to data

Figure 14-1

The Dexter hypertext reference model. (a) Dexter components: A composite component (left) is linked to an atomic component (right) (note that there is no representation of time in the figure); (b) atomic component; (c) composite component. (Reproduced from *Hypermedia* **5** (1) by permission of Taylor Graham. *Hypermedia* is now published as *The New Review of Hypermedia and Multimedia* by Taylor Graham, 500 Chesham House, 150 Regent St, London W1R 5FA, UK) designed specifically for modelling the structure and content of particular forms of information. The middle layer – the *storage layer* – is the core of the Dexter model. This layer models the basic node (or component, in Dexter terminology) and link structure of a hypermedia application. A 'database' is composed of a hierarchy of components (which are either *atomic components*, i.e. primitive components, or *composite components*, i.e. composed of other components) which are interconnected by links. Each component contains content (i.e. a piece of data of a specific media type), attributes (which allow a semantic description of the component) and a presentation specification (which determines how the component should be displayed).

The links consist of a set of anchor references each with its own direction and presentation specification – allowing the expression of both simple links and complex multi-source, multi-destination, bidirectional links. The interface between the storage layer and the within-component layer is based around the concept of *anchors*. The within-component and storage layers describe a passive data structure for the hypermedia application. The top layer – the *run-time layer* – captures the functionality to access and manipulate the data structures. This layer revolves around the instantiation of components (i.e. presentation to the user) which can then be manipulated. A *session* entity is responsible for keeping track of the mappings between components and their instantiations.

A number of papers giving a more detailed discussion of the Dexter model and its application to the development of specific hypermedia applications is given in the February 1994 edition of the *Commununciations of the ACM*.

The CMIF multimedia model

The CWI Multimedia Interchange Format (CMIF) was developed as a generic model for the structure of multimedia documents. In particular, CMIF models the time-based organisation and hierarchical structure of information. The model contains data blocks (which contains data of a single media much like the *atomic component* in Dexter), data descriptors (to describe the semantics of the data block), channels (used to provide an abstract output device), synchronisation arcs (to define timing constraints) and event descriptors (to describe the presentation of an instance of a data block). The model also allows structuring of the data blocks using a combination of serial and parallel composites. These elements are shown in Figure 14-2.

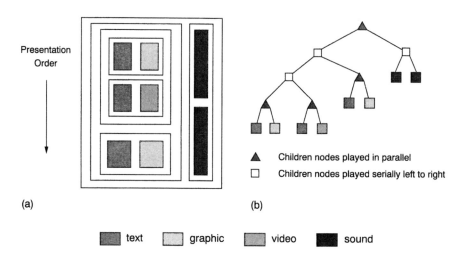

Presentation Order

(a)   (b)

▲ Children nodes played in parallel
☐ Children nodes played serially left to right

■ text   ▨ graphic   ▨ video   ■ sound

Figure 14-2

The CMIF Hierarchy View. (a) Each filled box represents a data block. The rectangles enclosing the boxes represent the hierarchical structuring of the document. The outermost rectangle is the root of the tree. A data block is played before the block beneath it. Data blocks next to each other are started in parallel (unless otherwise constrained by explicit synchronization arcs, not shown here). The shading of the data blocks indicates which channel the data block uses; (b) a tree view of the structure in (a). (Reproduced from *Hypermedia* **5**(1) by permission of Taylor Graham)

Two interesting elements in the CMIF model are the representation of the inter-relationships between the data blocks and the use of presentation channels. The data block inter-relationships are represented using a combination of the hierarchical structuring and the synchronisation arcs. Together, these two mechanisms allow the expression and subsequent validation of the media element structure. For example, we can have a synchronisation arc which indicates that the presentation of one media element always requires the subsequent presentation of certain other media elements and precludes the presentation of others. An example used in many of the CWI examples and demonstrations is support for multiple languages. We can group each set of language elements together, and then include each language in a parallel structuring element implying a choice between them. This facilitates the management of complex sets of media components.

Channels in CMIF are used to provide an interface between the media elements and the presentation. Each media element is allocated to a channel (and a channel can only present a single media element at a time). We can then define the presentation characteristics of the channel. For example, we can have a video channel which is linked to various video data components. This channel can then be assigned to present at a particular location on the application window. Such an approach has several benefits: first, it means that we can structure the multimedia document in a way which allows us to change only those channels which need to change. For example, we can have a music channel which plays background theme music when the document is first started. This can continue to play while other things are occurring, until some other media element requires this channel.

A second benefit is that it means that the presentation specific attributes (such as font size or screen layout) are contained in the channels rather than being embedded into the underlying multimedia information structure. This reflects one of the major aims of the CMIF model – to generate a model which is platform and environment independent. By separating information structure from presentation we obtain a generic structural representation which can remain the same across multiple platforms. We simply need to adjust the channels for each platform variation.

Models and the expression of information

It is worth pointing out at this stage that a representational model such as Dexter or CMIF is quite different from a standard intended to be used for exchanging information or documents. For example, with hypermedia information, SGML can be used to represent and exchange information which has a structure modelled by Dexter. SGML expresses the structure and information within a hypermedia document. Dexter provides a mechanism for modelling the generic structure of the document. We will return to this point at the end of the next section.

The Amsterdam Hypermedia Model

The Amsterdam Hypermedia Model (AHM) was developed to address perceived shortcomings of both the Dexter and the CMIF models within the context of a hypermedia model. The Dexter model allows the composition of information structures and the specification of links between collection of components, but no inherent concept of time is included in Dexter (unless it is included in the within-component layer – but this does not allow the expression of timing constraints between components). Nor does the Dexter model include any concept of context for a link or presentation information beyond individual components. The CMIF model is purely a multimedia model and does not contain any concept of links, and cannot therefore model hypertext or hypermedia information and structures.

AHM attempts to address the shortcomings of both the CMIF and Dexter models by combining them to form a composite model which includes appropriate elements of both. As a starting point for considering how these two models should be adapted or modified the developers of AHM articulated a set of requirements for a hypermedia model. These included:

- *Composition with multiple dynamic media*: although Dexter defines composition, it does not manage the timing relationships between the composited elements. AHM adopted a similar composition mechanism to Dexter (with the exception that composite components cannot contain content). Each composite component can be either a *choice component* (only one of the children components can be played in a presentation) or a *time-dependent component* (all of the children components will be played – note that suitable definition of the synchronisation means that this includes both serial and parallel composition). This approach allowed explicit definition of the structural relationships between media elements during the composition process. Additionally, the synchronisation between both composite and atomic elements is specified using synchronisation arcs, just as in the CMIF model.

- *Higher level presentation specification*: a hypermedia model should be able to specify presentation characteristics of a set of media elements, independently of the structure of the presentation. AHM adopted the channel mechanism of the CMIF model to define default presentation characteristics of the media in the hypermedia document. This separates specification or design of presentation from the structuring of the information.

- *Combining composite components*: a model of hypermedia should allow the expression and analysis of the manipulation of multiple hypermedia structures or documents. For example, if we are to combine several sets of components, then we need a mechanism for evaluating possible conflicts. The most common example of this is with clashes in the use of resources. AHM provides a mechanism for performing this type of evaluation in the form of the

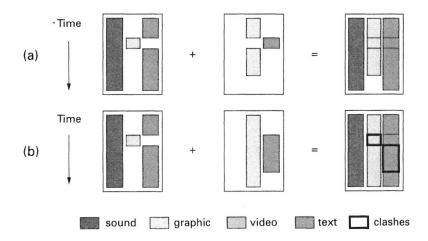

sound   graphic   video   text   clashes

Figure 14-3

Channel representation of composite components. (a) Two components can be combined to form a new composite component; (b) combining the two candidate components produces double use of the channels. (Reproduced from *Hypermedia* **5**(1) by permission of Taylor Graham)

channels. Since various media are allocated to specific channels and have given timing relationships, we can readily determine if, when combining two sets of components or documents, there will be a clash in the use of a channel. This is illustrated in Figure 14-3.

- *Temporal relations*: a hypermedia model should be able to express time-based relationships. These relationships should not, however, be part of the hypermedia semantic link structure. In AHM the temporal relationships are represented using the synchronisation arcs (again adopted from CMIF).

- *Context for links*: a major problem with many hypermedia models (such as that which underlies the Web) is that they do not support the notion of context. For example, if we are to navigate using a link and to subsequently present new information, then what elements of the current presentation should be discarded prior to presenting the new information. For example, if we traverse a link should the background music continue to play? This idea is shown in Figure 14-4. AHM manages this idea by specifying the context for each anchor associated with a link. This context defines the part of the presentation which will be affected when the link is followed.

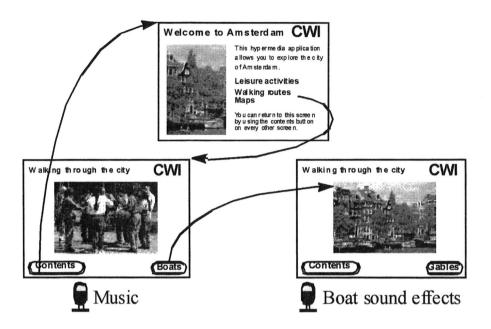

Figure 14-4

In this example, the elements of the presentation which are replaced depend upon whether the contents button or the boats button is selected. (Reproduced from *Hypermedia* **5**(1) by permission of Taylor Graham)

The resulting overall structure of the AHM is a collection of atomic components, composite components (which may be choice or time-dependant), links and channels. The components are similar to those included in Dexter, except for several additions aimed predominantly at handling multiple media types. These include the addition to the atomic component of a binding to a channel and a specified duration, and the addition to the composite component of a set of synchronisation arcs and start times for the children. Other additions include the dereferencing of anchors and the removal of the content from the composite component.

The links in AHM are similar to the links in Dexter, with the exception that each link in Amsterdam also specifies a context which defines the media elements which are affected by the traversal of the link. The channels are essentially as described for CMIF.

The CMIF Editor

The CMIF Editor (or CMIFed) was originally developed as an authoring tool based on the CMIF multimedia model. With the development of AHM, CMIFed has evolved to support some (though not all) of the aspects of AHM. The current version of CMIFed contains some aspects that allow it to be used as a WYSIWYG[9] authoring tool – the author is able to see the presentation as it is constructed – though the tools go beyond simple presentation control functionality. CMIFed contains a number of tools which provide different perspectives on the hypermedia information and facilitate the creation of different aspects of the underlying structures and presentation. The tools include a channel view, a hierarchy view, and a link editor.

The channel view displays the atomic data components mapped onto individual presentation channels. A typical example of the channel view is shown in Figure 14-5. In this example, the channels are shown across the top of the view and time progresses down the view. This view allows the author to control and/or verify which channels will be presenting which media at a given point in time. The channel view also includes the synchronisation arcs which specify timing relationships.

The hierarchy view shows the hypermedia document as a collection of data blocks. The view provides a display of the atomic components and the ways in which they are combined into composite components. The display also provides visual clues as to whether the composition is a choice composition or a time-dependent composition. A typical example is given in Figure 14-6.

The link editor shows the hypermedia links which exist between components. The link editor allows the selection of two components or sets of components (chosen using a suitable filtering – for example, the second set can be based on destinations or sources of the first set). For these sets of components all related links are displayed. An example of the link editor is given in Figure 14-7. It is worth pointing out that the CMIF editor does not implement the full link model from AHM. In CMIFed, the links are untyped and do not contain the contexts which are included in the model described by AHM.

---

[9] What You See Is What You Get – in other words, during authoring the author sees the presentation in essentially the same way as the user will.

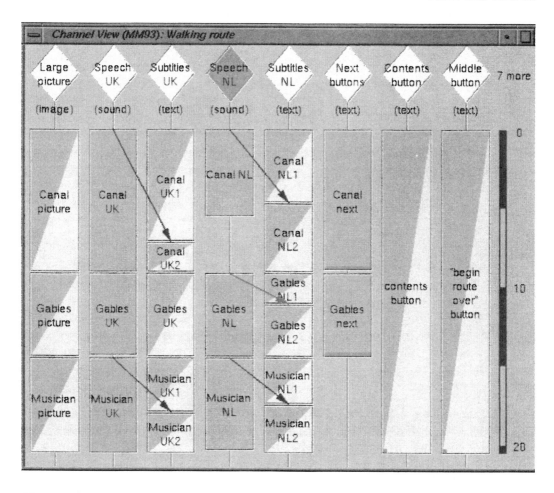

Figure 14-5

Screendump of the channel view from the CMIF Editor. (Reproduced by kind permission of Lynda Hardman, CWI)

Comments

The emphasis in AHM and CMIFed is on document media structuring, i.e. how to handle multimedia information within a hypermedia context. A number of specific hypermedia issues are not addressed, such as the fact that AHM was originally developed to address issues of local structure and the expression and maintenance of the relationships between media components. The model does not inherently address structure at a global level (except as a composite of local structure). For example,

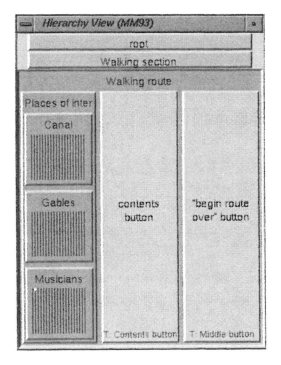

Figure 14-6

Screendump of the hierarchy view from the CMIF Editor. (Reproduced by kind permission of Lynda Hardman, CWI)

issues related to the validity or otherwise of a particular style of information structuring and consistency of the global context are not addressed.

It is worth noting that the implementation of CMIFed places certain constraints which are not inherent in the underlying AHM. For example, CMIFed is a closed hypermedia system in the sense that it does not allow the inclusion of media from other applications (for example, a Word document). This is, however, only a restriction of CMIFed. AHM allows the modelling of components within any media and any format. Additionally, the presentation mechanism is closed – the applications generated using CMIFed can only be presented within its own environment (though work is underway at looking at a mapping from the CMIFed structures to HyTime allowing transfer of CMIFed applications to other environments).

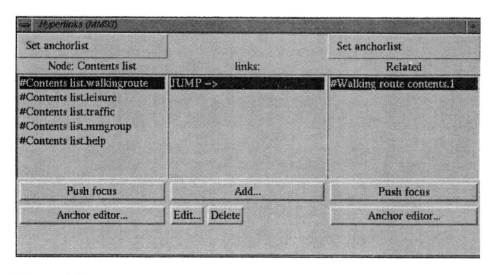

Figure 14-7

Screendump of the link editor from the CMIF Editor. (Reproduced by kind permission of Lynda Hardman, CWI)

14.3 Dealing with Product Issues

Navigation and Browsing

AHM does not provide any inherent mechanism explicitly aimed at assisting a user in identifying or developing an understanding of the overall structure of the information space. Additionally, the current AHM implementation in CMIFed does not provide end-user tools (such as history lists and bookmarks) which are associated with support for browsing and navigation. Nevertheless, it is important to note that these are not criticisms – rather they simply reflect the focus of the research which encompasses AHM and CMIFed. A point worth noting is that aspects such as link history mechanisms are aided by the provision of support for context. This has not, however, been implemented.

Despite the lack of immediate support for traditional navigation mechanisms, AHM does inherently provide support for a number of interesting mechanisms – some of which have been implemented in CMIFed. Probably the most important, in terms of effective navigation and browsing, is the use of presentation channels. Channels help to ensure that an application developed using CMIFed (or any other tool based around AHM) has a consistent look and feel. This is because each data component is bound to a specific channel and the channels are then tied to specific presentation characteristics. Every media element bound to a given channel will be presented with the same characteristics – resulting in a very consistent presentation. A useful lesson from this is that even where channels (or their equivalent) are not supported within a specific authoring environment, 'channels' (or an equivalent such as templates) can be used at an abstract level during the design of a hypermedia application. For example, the presentation interfaces can be designed and each element of the interface assigned a 'pseudo-channel'. The data components can then be linked to these pseudo-channels. Such an approach assists in designing a consistent interface, and ensures that the designer and author remain aware of the presentation dependencies between different data components.

CMIFed has also provided a very consistent mechanism for managing multiple forms of media. Every data component, irrespective of the media type, can be treated in a consistent fashion in terms of the information structuring and synchronisation. The specifics of how different media are handled is left up to the individual channels. As this indicates, a useful design strategy is to provide a layer between the information structure and the presentation which handles different media types.

Finally, it is worth mentioning that AHM and CMIFed provide a model and authoring tool which results in very portable applications. Since the underlying information structure (i.e. composition, synchronisation and linking) of the application is separated from the presentation (i.e. use of channels), applications which are ported from one environment to another will maintain a consistent navigation structure. Adapting an application for different environments will simply be a matter of defining how different channels behave given the available resources (CPU, bandwidth, screen real estate, etc.). This will ensure that we can readily migrate applications from one platform to another. Using this concept as a guide, we can conclude that for any application it is worthwhile during the design stage defining the presentation in terms of the actual information structure rather than the specific presentation characteristics.

Cognitive Management during Browsing

As with support for navigation and browsing, cognitive management during usage was not a primary consideration in the development of either AHM or CMIFed. Nevertheless, there are several observations which we can make.

First, as mentioned above, CMIFed implicitly promotes a consistent look and feel (since the media are played through channels, and all media components bound to a given channel will have consistent presentation characteristics). This consistent look and feel has the end result that users are not burdened (in a cognitive sense) with having to waste effort in understanding the navigation mechanisms, or to constantly readjust to the presentation. Other development approaches achieve a similar result through the use of templates, either at the implementation stage (such as screen layout templates) or at a design stage (such as storyboards).

Secondly (and also related to a consistency of presentation) is that CMIFed explicitly addresses the issue of timing constraints between temporal media. As a result, the timing between different media remains very consistent. Users are not distracted by inappropriate behaviour of temporal media (such as an audio track continuing to play after the text or images change).

A third aspect worth commenting on is that CMIFed develops applications which explicitly maintain the context of information. This ensures that the user is not burdened with having to attempt to understand the context from previously presented information which is no longer available. This is discussed further in the following section.

Information Contextualisation

One of the main contributions of AHM to the research literature on hypermedia is that it explicitly addresses the issue of maintenance of local information context. This is effectively achieved through the use of channels. When a hypermedia anchor is selected and the associated link is activated, the link essentially specifies which structure is to be replaced with new information. As such, it becomes possible for a link activation to modify only very selective components of the presentation. Information is not arbitrarily removed from the presentation when a link is followed, unless it is appropriate for it to be either removed or replaced by other information.

The consequence of this is that we can explicitly specify and design applications where following links is not a matter of switching pages (as is the case with the basic Web paradigm) but rather of providing contextualised information. In the demonstration described by Hardman, Bulterman and von Rossum (1993) the example used is a walking tour of Amsterdam. If the user is presented with a display showing some aspect of Amsterdam and the '*Continue*' button is selected then the generic 'tour' aspects of the presentation (such as the title and navigation buttons) remain unchanged and only the specific contents of the presentation (such as the contents of the video window) change. The result is that the user maintains a context for the information being presented. It is obvious to the user that they are still within the tour. Another example from the Amsterdam demonstration illustrates this quite well: when the CWI logo is selected the presentation remains unchanged except for the commencement of an audio presentation about CWI. Here the source context remains unchanged and the link destination is *also* played.

These ideas can be taken further to provide additional levels of flexible presentation which adjusts to an individual user. The way in which composition is performed in AHM (using both parallel and choice compositions) means that it is possible for the application to have a 'memory' which adjusts as desired. A simple example of this, again from the Amsterdam demonstration, is the support for multiple language presentations. Multiple languages can be provided for each textual and audio component and these are then grouped together and a selection is made between them. Once the selection has been made all material will be presented in an appropriate language, i.e. the context selected by the user of the application is maintained throughout the presentation or usage of the application. Similar techniques can be used to adjust the application to variations such as differing levels of user sophistication and differing gender, ethnic, cultural, religious or political contexts.

Most hypermedia applications do not provide the flexible mechanisms (such as channels and choice composition found in CMIFed) to adjust the context so effectively. Nevertheless, a few lower level mechanisms are often provided. The simplest is the use of background and foreground presentations. For example, in HyperCard (Goodman, 1987) a background card can be defined which can provide a consistent context within a given presentation sequence, as the foreground cards change. A change in the background card will be a sign to the user that the context has changed and they need to refocus their attention. Similar mechanisms can be used in the Web – an unchanging background (however simple – even a single solid colour) will be a sign of continuity of context for the user.

Another mechanism which can be used on the Web to provide a very similar end-result to the use of channels in CMIFed (in terms of maintaining context) is the use of frames. Although still not standardised at the time of writing, many Web browsers support the splitting of the screen space into separate frames. It then becomes possible to modify the content of a selected set of frames while leaving the others unchanged (and hence maintaining the user's context). These do not, however, have the flexibility of channels in CMIFed, and must be achieved in a much more manual fashion.

Having said that AHM provides a model which supports the maintenance of contexts, it is important to point out that it does not provide any mechanism for guiding the design of this contextualisation. This is considered to be beyond the scope of the model (AHM) or the tool (CMIFed), and would nominally be part of the design process prior to the use of the tool.

All of the above points relate to local contextualisation, i.e. the ability of the user to understand the specific environment or context in which the information is being presented (e.g. 'this information is being presented as part of a walking tour of Amsterdam'). AHM does not, however, explicitly address issues of global contextualisation. AHM does not provide any explicit mechanism for assisting a user in orienting themselves within the information space, or for understanding the structure of the information space, though the use of tools such as CMIFed which encourage a consistent structure of the information are more likely to result in a structure which is readily understandable.

Link and Content Validity

Although the content and link validity is not a prime concern of either AHM or CMIFed, through several mechanisms they tend to result in the development of valid structures. First, the link creation tool which has been incorporated into CMIFed supports browsing of link structures in quite flexible ways. For example, it is possible to view all the links related to a given anchor, or all links from a given data component. This means that the author will be able to easily see the range and extent of the links which have been created.

Probably more significantly, the CMIFed authoring tool is in many respects WYSIWYG. In other words, as the application is developed the author can see the content in context in exactly the same way as a user.

Indeed, as component and links are added to the presentation, the display changes to reflect the current state. This means that the author is able to understand in a fundamental way the structure of the presentation and the suitability of the content (especially within the designed context). This will obviously result in authoring which promotes validity of content.

Although AHM and CMIFed do not explicitly address the issue of how to design *valid* links, the functionality provided within CMIFed will help an author in evaluating links as they are implemented.

Another point worth raising, and one which is regularly overlooked in the development of hypermedia applications, is the validity of media synchronisation. Most development tools provide little or no support for ensuring that different media remain suitably synchronised, especially as the context changes and/or links are followed (for example, if we follow a link from a Web page which contains audio to a Web page which does not contain audio, should the audio continue to play?) CMIFed provides several mechanisms for ensuring the validity of the synchronisation of different media, especially during navigation amongst complex hypermedia structures. The most significant of these is the use of synchronisation arcs. They provide a mechanism for representing the relationships between different media and showing when media should be started, continued or terminated. The result is a consistency of synchronisation.

Although the design of appropriate synchronisation constraints is not explicitly a part of AHM or CMIFed, they do provide mechanisms for implementing constraints which are identified during the design process. Indeed, the results of using these mechanisms within CMIFed demonstrate the improvements in application quality which can be achieved by considering synchronisation as a fundamental part of the application structuring (such as terminating an audio track when it becomes irrelevant on following a link).

Information Structure

Although AHM is largely focussed on providing a model for representing the structure of information, it does not provide an indication of how this structure can be identified or designed during the development process. Having said this, it is worth looking at the types of structure which AHM is capable of modelling.

AHM treats hypermedia information in a similar way to the Dexter reference model – as a collection of data components (which can be grouped together to form composite components) and links (which connect the data components) – with the addition of synchronisation constraints and contexts for the links. This style of model of the structure of information applications is incredibly flexible. Indeed, it is in effect a superset of the more constrained information structures (such as hierarchies and linear paths). As such, it is more useful as a general representation, rather than a guide for a specific information structure.

One useful point which is worth making regarding the features of CMIFed is that it is possible to cut, paste and copy entire sections of the structure. It is therefore quite straightforward to develop structures which can then be used as templates (resulting in uniform and consistent structures). For example, in developing a multilingual version of an application, the structure can be created for one language and then easily duplicated for the other languages.

Management of Different Media

In some respects, the real strength of AHM and CMIFed is the way in which they combine multimedia and hypertext. Most existing hypermedia models and authoring tools tend to either focus on the multimedia aspects (such as the flow of the presentation) or the hypermedia aspects (such as the network structure of the information). AHM is probably the strongest of the models which has explicitly attempted to address the inclusion of multimedia information into a hypermedia context (or *vice versa*, a hypermedia structure into multimedia applications).

The main issues which typically have to be addressed in achieving this are synchronisation and structuring of multimedia data, availability and management of scarce resources, and support for interaction with various media. AHM has addressed all of these issues in various ways.

AHM and CMIFed use various mechanisms for structuring information. The choice and time-dependant composition mechanisms provide a technique for organising the information in a media-independent way, whilst still taking into account logical groupings of different media. For example, providing a choice-composition between different audio components which provide the same information in different languages. Although this type of mechanism is not uncommon in hypermedia models, AHM has supported it by binding the components not directly to the presentation mechanisms, but rather to a series of presentation channels.

These presentation channels provide a mechanism for managing media in an application independent way. The channels become the interface between the information components and the presentation engine. Any changes to the presentation (such as changes to the screen layout, display resolutions, etc.) can be implemented by controlling the channels rather than modifying the individual media components. This will obviously result in more robust and portable applications.

The use of the channels has a further advantage. They provide a direct mechanism for handling the scarce resources available to service the higher demands of multimedia information. Multimedia applications are often very resource intensive, especially in terms of access bandwidth (such as retrieving information from disk or a network) and presentation (such as presenting a video on the screen). For an application to be portable and robust, it needs to be able to take into account changes in the available resources resulting either from different platforms or from different operating conditions. For example, we may desire the same application to be able to be used on an application with minimal available resources (such as a low-end PC with low-resolution screen and slow network connection running many other applications) or an application with a large degree of available resources (such as a high-performance workstation with high-resolution monitor and high-speed network connection). It is not reasonable to design an application for the lowest common denominator. We want applications which can adapt to the available resources.

Channels provide a mechanism for achieving this in a very flexible way. The structure of the application can be created independently of the available resources and then individual channels can be tuned to the available resources. For example, we may have a series of images of varying resolutions which are bound to a single presentation channel. The presentation channel can be presenting these images on a low-resolution screen, and will be responsible for adjusting the resolution of the images to suit the resources (in this case, screen real-estate).

This style of adaptation of various media is an integral part of AHM, though it has only been partially implemented in CMIFed. CMIFed has been ported to various platforms, and on each platform the presentation channels are suited to the conditions on that platform. However, the channels, as implemented are not capable of adapting dynamically to varying resource loads (though this will be partly handled by the underlying operating system functionality). Nonetheless, the approach used is a worthwhile concept, providing a mechanism for ensuring flexible adaptation of an application to different sets of available resources. A similar result can be achieved to a certain extent by using design templates or style sheets for the presentation, and binding actual presentation to these design templates, so that an application can be globally adapted by changing these templates. In this respect, channels can be viewed as media specific style sheets.

Another major issue in handling multimedia is the synchronisation of these media. Much work has been undertaken on techniques for ensuring synchronisation between audio and video. Indeed, this is now typically handled directly by the presentation engine. For example, the AVI file format (used for audio/video) interleaves the audio and video media and they can be easily synchronised by the player. The situation is much more difficult when we wish to synchronise media in less obvious ways. For example, we may be presenting text with an associated audio track, and the text should be changed at discrete points in the audio presentation. The text and the audio need to be synchronised in a relatively complex manner.

The synchronisation arcs between atomic components in CMIFed provide a mechanism for specifying these complex relationships. These relationships can be made either with respect to a parent container or to a sibling component and can take various forms as shown in Figure 14-8. Each of the four cases shown in this figure show the components starting at the same time, a component starting a specified time after another, a component starting a specified time before or after the end of another, and the components finishing at the same time. Indeed, the model allows automatic computation of a number of aspects of the presentation timing and synchronisation. For example, the duration of a parent element can be calculated on the basis of the duration and synchronisation of the children components. When an application is presented which has been developed using CMIFed the synchronisation arcs are used to ensure the appropriate synchronisation of the application contents.

One final area of managing multiple forms of media is how they are used to support navigation and interactivity. Most existing hypermedia applications would be more appropriately called multiple media hypertext applications. They tend to be hypertext applications (i.e. the textual information provides the anchors for links, which in turn support the

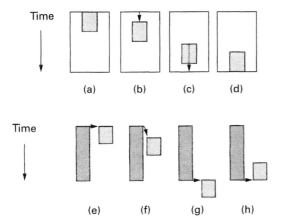

Figure 14-8

Possible timing relationships in AHM. (a) to (d) show relationships relative to a parent, and (e) to (h) show relationships relative to a sibling. (Reproduced from *Hypermedia* **5**(1) by permission of Taylor Graham)

navigation) with the additional media acting only as annotations to the text, but not truly integrated into the application in terms of providing support for navigation. The few minor exceptions to this predominantly revolve around hand-crafted small scale applications where hand-designed image maps have been used to create 'active' images. These applications are however sufficient to illustrate the significantly enhanced functionality which can be achieved with active audio and visual information.

Unfortunately, CMIFed has yet to adequately address the issue of using non-text media to support navigation; whereas text can be readily analysed (identifying the lexical components which can be used as anchors for links) achieving this for non-text media is considerably more difficult. AHM conceptually includes the idea of anchors into non-text media, and these have been implemented at least for images, but not for audio or video information. To the defence of CMIFed, this has yet to be adequately implemented in any existing authoring environment. There is obviously still a considerable distance to go in this area.

14.4 Dealing with Process Issues

Application Maintenance

As has been pointed out previously, maintenance of an application can occur on a number of levels, including maintenance of the application specification, design or documentation, maintenance of the application content, and maintenance of the application structure. Maintenance can also have a number of different purposes – preventative, corrective, adaptive, perfective. Let us consider AHM and CMIFed within this context.

CMIFed is predominantly focused on the structuring of the hypermedia application. It does not explicitly address the development process, and hence does not consider such aspects as either maintenance of applications after the initial development, or the inclusion of maintainability within applications during the development process. Despite this, there are a number of aspects of AHM and CMIFed which result in more maintainable applications than otherwise might be the case.

For example, the use of presentation channels allows an explicit separation between the information structure and the application presentation. All user interface and application presentation characteristics are captured within the channels and are removed from the structuring of the information (using hierarchical containment, synchronisation arcs and link structures). This separation makes it quite simple to easily maintain the interface without affecting the information structure. For example, we can change the position of a video window associated with a given channel within a presentation without being concerned with changing every occurrence of video data bound to this channel.

Similarly, the maintenance of content and the structuring of the content becomes more straightforward when the developer does not need to be simultaneously concerned with the effects of the maintenance on presentation.

Even where the underlying model does not inherently support the separation of structure and presentation (such as on the Web) there are a number of steps which could be carried out which would have a similar end result. First, during the design of the application, the design of the interface should be kept distinct from the design of the information structures. A mapping from the structural components to the interface components can be designed so that, when changes are made to either structure or interface during maintenance, it will be obvious what the effect will be on the other.

A more drastic solution at the implementation level (but possibly more effective for large applications) may be to explicitly store content structure independently of presentation (possibly in a custom designed database) and create the application dynamically from the relevant components as necessary. Simple examples of this already exist on the Web. A small scale example with which we have experimented (Ginige, Witana and Yourlo, 1996) consists of a set of information and structuring data, and CGI scripts which create Web pages with appropriate navigation information dynamically when the pages are requested. This allows very straightforward restructuring of the information space underlying a Website without having to maintain the presentation elements of the Website.

Reuse

As with maintenance, reuse was not a primary concern of either AHM or CMIFed. Aspects of reuse at the early lifecycle stages are not addressed at all – such as reuse of requirements analysis or design considerations. Where reuse does occur however is at the implementation level.

The most obvious example of reuse within CMIFed is being able to reuse elements of the information structure and presentation. For example, within the hierarchy view in CMIFed a user can select a component and copy and paste that component. If this component is a composite then the result is to copy the structure which is inside the component. This techniques has been used within CMIFed to rapidly generate duplicate structures. For example, where an application contains text and audio in multiple languages, the structure for the first language can be created and then duplicated for each addition language.

A word of caution is required here. Directly reusing implemented structure rather than a design for a structure can be dangerous. In the example given above, the structure for different languages is likely to be extremely similar if not identical. In other cases, the structures may be similar but have important though subtle differences. Duplicating an entire structure rather than a more abstract design for a structure may result in the requirement for a tedious cross-checking of every aspect of the structure, or worse still the accidental inclusion of incorrect structural elements.

Admittedly, CMIFed can be used to duplicate high-level design structures, by creating the initial high-level components in a top-down fashion and then performing the duplication before the low-level structure is added.

One major benefit of being able to duplicate structures in this way is that it can result in very consistent application structures. For example, if we have an application which contains sets of information on different countries, then by creating the structure of the first set of information and then duplicating this for all sets, we will end up with a very uniform structure. This will in turn ease navigation problems for a user.

Another mechanism for reuse in CMIFed (again at the low-level design or implementation level) is reusing channel specifications. Since the channels are used to design and implement the presentation aspects of an application, reusing channels allows us to reuse parts of the user interface. For example, we may have a collection of channels including a video channel, several text channels, and an audio channel which are arranged in a specific way to provide a desired user interface layout. By reusing these channels in a new application (and binding the information components in the new application to these reused channels) we will have an identical user-interface in the new application.

Even where a mechanism such as channels is not available in the development environment being used, there are still approaches which can be adopted which have similar impacts on reuse. For example, creating interface templates at a design level will almost always be a useful exercise. The simplest example of these is storyboards. These can be used to provide an indication of the presentation and layout of information and can be readily reused across different applications. At a slightly more pragmatic level we could use implementation templates. As an example, consider Figure 14-9. This shows a Web page which has been designed using frames to have a specific layout. The HTML for the page shows that the content is stored in separate files, and the main page simply defines the layout making reuse of this 'template' very straightforward. In this case, frames are being used in a similar way to channels.

Supporting the Full Lifecycle and Process Management

These two questions have been grouped together, as neither AHM nor CMIFed attempt to address them in any significant way (this was not, after all, the focus of the research for which they were developed).

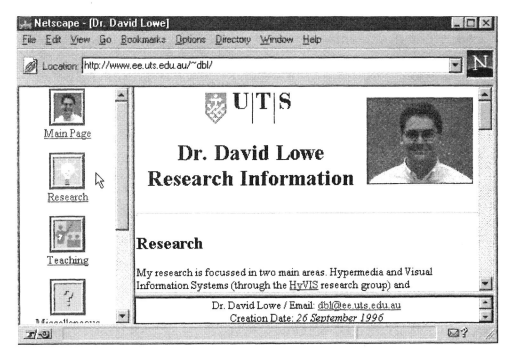

```
<HTML>
<HEAD> <TITLE>Dr. David Lowe</TITLE> </HEAD>

<FRAMESET COLS="140,*">
<NOFRAMES> </NOFRAMES>
   <FRAME SRC="dblindex.htm" NAME="Index" SCROLLING="auto"
        MARGINWIDTH=1 MARGINHEIGHT=1>
   <FRAMESET ROWS="*,50">
   <FRAME SRC="dblmain.htm" NAME="Main" SCROLLING="auto"
        MARGINWIDTH=1 MARGINHEIGHT=1>
   <FRAME SRC="dblfootr.htm" NAME="Footer" SCROLLING="auto"
        MARGINWIDTH=1 MARGINHEIGHT=1>
   </FRAMESET>
</FRAMESET>

</HTML>
```

Figure 14-9

Using frames in a Web browser to support similar functionality to channels in CMIFed

As has been explained, AHM is a model of a hypermedia application, and CMIFed is an authoring tool and not a development tool. In other words, CMIFed is intended to be used for the low-level design and implementation of hypermedia applications. It is assumed that an analysis of the structural, navigational and functional requirements, and high-level design has occurred prior to the use of CMIFed.

One minor point worth raising is that CMIFed is, to a certain extent, a WYSIWYG authoring tool. In addition, the various tools which are part of CMIFed allow rapid changes to be made to the application content, structure and presentation. This means that CMIFed can be used effectively as a rapid prototyping tool to investigate different structures and presentation styles as a method for capturing requirements or as a precursor to the detailed design.

Another consequence of the above considerations is that CMIFed is well suited to an incremental development approach. It is quite feasible to design a small scale prototype and then iteratively refine this to achieve an end application. During each iteration, the current implementation can be evaluated and the next stage of refinement designed. As yet, however, CMIFed has not been used on a large scale project in this way, and so no feedback exists as to the effectiveness of using CMIFed in this style of development process.

Cognitive Management during Development

As has been pointed out in much of the previous discussion, AHM and CMIFed don't address many of the wider development lifecycle issues, being focused on low-level design and implementation. Nevertheless, the tools which are part of CMIFed do assist with the cognitive burden imposed during final development stages, mainly addressing handling and managing of media and the inter-relationships between media components.

The hierarchy view in CMIFed provides the author with a mechanism for managing the structure of the information in a consistent way. The author is always able to view and manipulate this structure, and can view the structure at high levels of abstraction or delve into selected areas of detail whilst other areas remain hidden or summarised. This partially relieves the cognitive burden associated with managing these structures, as irrelevant detail remains suppressed and relevant detail is provided in its appropriate context.

The cognitive burden is also eased by fact that the information structuring is typically based on inherent or logical structures within the information. For example, if we have an application which can be presented using different languages, a logical structure from an author's point of view is that only one of these languages can be used at a given time. This can be represented in the hierarchy view using a choice containment. This means that when the structure is presented, it will be obvious that their is a choice to be made between the different languages.

Another interesting observation is that the hierarchy view makes it difficult to add information components without adding them into a specific section of the structure. In other words, we cannot readily add an item of information (possibly as a temporary placeholder) but leave it unstructured. This may create problems insofar as it reduces authoring freedom and is constrictive, but it also encourages structured development, and ensures that during the development the information is always correct and self-consistent.

The channel view is also likely to reduce the cognitive load on the author. As has been mentioned previously, channels provide a mechanism for separating the information structure from the presentation structure. The channel view is used to provide the bindings between channels and media components. This is presented on two axes; the first axis is a timeline and the second is a list of channels. The author is thus able to look at what information components will be presented at any point in time without being concerned about how they will actually be presented.

One limitation which has been recognised by the developers of the current channel view implementation is that it does not handle well large numbers of channels. As an application grows in scope, the number of presentation channels which are used grows. The current channel view does not have any mechanism for handling these effectively. This has already been demonstrated in the development of a medium size music/art application. The CMIFed developers hope to add additional functionality to the channel view to allow grouping and/or abstracting channels.

Another feature of CMIFed which assists the author in managing the development is the provision of active feedback to the developer as an application is presented. At any point in time the current state of the developed application can be 'executed'. During this execution the channel view will change to show (using suitable colouring) the components and channels which are currently being presented. This makes it easy for an author to understand (and possibly correct) the temporal behaviour and interrelationships amongst the components.

One final aspect of CMIFed which is worthwhile considering is a mechanism, which is built into the various tools, called 'push focus'. This allows any component to be selected and then made the focus of all other windows. For example, a component can be selected in the channel view and then made the focus of the hierarchy view, thereby ensuring that a user can always readily see the structure and context of any component being considered. This will have obvious impacts on an author's ability to ensure that information is always presented in a suitable context.

Supporting Enhanced Productivity

CMIFed was developed primarily to facilitate the inclusion of multimedia data into a hypermedia application in a consistent manner. It was not intended as a vehicle for investigating productivity improvements. We can, despite this, still make some interesting observations about the effects of various elements of the CMIFed functionality on the development productivity.

Many of the aspects described above, which assist in the management of the cognitive burden, will have an obvious impact on productivity. If a developer or author is able to reduce the cognitive overhead associated with the development, then this will evidently reduce the development time required.

Apart from the aspects described in the previous section there are several other areas where CMIFed directly impacts on productivity. Firstly, CMIFed allows the developer to see the presentation of an application as it is being developed. In this respect, CMIFed provides WYSIWYG style functionality, even though the much of the development may be performed with the presentation not directly visible (especially when performing structuring activities using the hierarchy and channel views). The use of an editor which allows immediate viewing of the presentation as an integral part of the development has both negative and positive aspects. Positively, it is likely to make an author aware of interface or presentation problems at an early stage of the development when they are more likely to be easily rectified with minimal effort. Negatively, it is likely to focus the authors attention onto presentation issues and away from information content and structure issues.[10] Insufficient experience has yet to be gained to indicate whether or not a WYSIWYG-style editor is more useful than harmful. It is however interesting to point

---

[10] This is really just a hypermedia version of the long debate about WYSIWYG word processors (such as WordPerfect™ and Microsoft Word™) versus structural document editors (such as LaTeX).

out that in a lengthy discussion on the `comp.infoapplications.` `www.authoring.misc` newsgroup, a large number of experienced Web authors had said that they had spurned the WYSIWYG editors in favour of simple text editors to edit the raw HTML.

Another area where CMIFed has impacted on productivity is the use of automatic calculation of timings and checking of synchronisation consistency. As the duration of components is added and synchronisation between these components is specified, CMIFed automatically calculates such things as the duration of parent containers, and checks that there are no circular synchronisation arcs. Other forms of timing conflicts could also be detected. For example, as shown in Figure 14-3, we could automatically detect conflicts where, because of timing constraints, given channels are being allocated to two different components simultaneously. Automating the detection of this type of problem removes the need for the author to manually cross-check the consistency of all timings.

A final point worth raising is that in CMIFed the process of creating links is quite manual. One of the main productivity problems confronting hypermedia developers is the effort required to create comprehensive link structures. As an example, Microsoft Encarta'95 contains over 300,000 cross-reference links. Using the CMIFed approach of manually creating each link, to create 300,000 links (at 1 link per minute) would take approximately 2.5 person years of work. AHM and CMIFed have not yet provided any significant mechanism to circumvent this particular type of problem (such as automatic link generation, generic links or media analysis tools).

14.5 Conclusions

Given the above responses to the various questions which have been posed, we can make a number of concluding observations. First, it is important to reiterate that AHM and CMIFed were not developed to address many of the issues raised above. AHM was developed as a research vehicle, with a focus on the inclusion of multimedia information into a hypermedia framework. The resulting model (AHM) and authoring application (CMIFed) reflect the historical context of the CWI research group, insofar as AHM has at its core the CMIF model (essentially a multimedia model) and has been supplemented by ideas from Dexter (a hypertext model).

In other words, AHM can be viewed as a multimedia model with hyper-media added on rather than a hypermedia model with multimedia added on. This has the effect that the multimedia aspects (such as media synchronisation and presentation) are handled very well, whereas the hypermedia aspects, such as the modelling of network structures and how they are managed lacks some of the expressiveness found in other hypermedia-specific models. It also means that CMIFed does not address particularly well the traditional hypermedia issues of information structures and their design and management, but does handle multimedia aspects very well.

Another observation is that CMIFed, as an authoring tool, is yet to be validated on a range of large complex applications or projects. Although it has been applied to a number of small scale demonstrations and one medium sized commercial application, not enough experience has been gained to readily understand all the implications of the approach being used. As AHM and CMIFed continue to evolve and be more widely applied the consequences, problems and advantages of the approaches used will become more evident. A major part of this will involve gaining experience in how a development methodology adapts to the mechanisms supported by CMIFed, or possibly how CMIFed determined what is a suitable methodology.

The focus of AHM and CMIFed is very strongly at the low-end authoring of hypermedia applications. There has been no attempt to address issues such as providing methods or tools for understanding the requirements of a given hypermedia application, or performing the high-level structural, information, or functional design. Despite this, it has been observed that the AHM and CMIFed encapsulate many interesting ideas, which in a number of cases implicitly affect how these earlier stage activities may be carried out.

A very good example of this is that the functionality of CMIFed is such that it encourages a strongly iterative approach to the development. So even though CMIFed was not explicitly designed based on a given process model, an iterative model is certainly encouraged. This would in turn mean that any development using CMIFed would need to take this into account.

The strongest points to have come out of the consideration of AHM and CMIFed probably revolve around the impact of the separation of the information structuring and the presentation. This was achieved using the idea of presentation channels. These channels result in applications which are significantly more portable than is traditionally the case, have an enhanced maintainability (since the structure is maintained separately from the presentation) and facilitate reuse (since both structure and presentation can be independently reused).

14.6 Acknowledgements

We wish to thank the Interoperable Multimedia Applications group at CWI (Centrum voor Wiskunde en Informatica) in Amsterdam, Netherlands. In particular we would like to express our appreciation to Lynda Hardman, Dick Bulterman, Maria Theodoridou and Lloyd Rutledge for the various discussions, reviews and comments which greatly assisted in the development of this chapter.

14.7 Further Information

For more information on the Amsterdam Hypermedia Model, the CMIFed authoring tool, or any other aspect of the research work described in this chapter, the following sources of information are available. The following Website contains numerous publications related to the groups research work:

```
http://www.cwi.nl/ftp/mmpapers/index.html
```

Alternatively the researchers can be contacted at:

Lynda Hardman
Contact address: CWI
                  Kruislaan 413
                  P.O. Box 94079
                  1090 GB Amsterdam
                  The Netherlands

15

RMM

... before I had executed half of my design, for the
Machinery was entirely wanting to complete it.
(Epistle Dedicatory, Alexander Pope)

Chapter Goals

The Relationship Management Methodology (RMM) provides an
approach to the design of hypermedia structures. This chapter
demonstrates how a formal approach to the structural design of
hypermedia systems can provide significant benefits, especially in
terms of productivity and application quality. The objectives of this
chapter are to show that:

- RMM is based on the adaptation, from software development,
  of entity relationship modelling. It provides steps for modelling the entities in an application, the organisation of these
  entities, how this is used in supporting navigation, design of
  user-interfaces and run-time behaviour design.

- RMM makes explicit a process model, but the model only covers
  a limited range of the full development process activities.

- RMM utilises a design model (RMDM) which provides a basis
  for representing the resultant application design.

- RMM provides an effective methodology for the class of applications which are highly structured and have high volatility.

15.1 Introduction

Work undertaken primarily within New York University's Stern School of Business has been investigating aspects of hypermedia technology, and especially related to its applications and development processes. In this chapter we focus on one particular project – the Relationship Management Methodology (RMM) developed by a group of researchers including Isakowitz, Stohr, Balasubramanian and Diaz (Isakowitz *et al.*, 1995, 1996).

RMM has been described by its developers as a methodology for the structured design of hypermedia systems. It is essentially a design model and a set of specified design steps which aim to provide a methodology for creating hypermedia applications. The design model is based on a combination of the use of entity-relationship diagrams, and various concepts adapted from the Hypermedia Design Model (HDM, developed by Garzotto, Paolini and Schwabe (1993)).

RMM has begun to be used in a variety of hypermedia development projects. These include financial institutions (e.g. Merryl Lynch), publishing houses (e.g. M.E. Sharpe Inc.), research institutions (e.g. Bellcore) and educational institutions (e.g. Pace University in New York State, Staffordshire University in the UK and the SYRECOS consortium in Luxembourg). Initial feedback from some of these projects is being used in ongoing refinement of the methodology. For example, various extensions such as m-slices (Isakawitz *et al.*, 1996) are aiming to address perceived shortcomings with the initial methodology.

The developers of RMM admit that it is has been developed with a specific class of applications in mind. They provide a taxonomy of applications based on two dimensions: volatility of information and degree of structure.[11] RMM will not be useful or have low usefulness for applications with low structure (such as literary works or news services) since the entity types or classes of information which RMM relies on modelling are not easily identifiable in these applications. Applications with a high degree of structure but low volatility (such as kiosk applications) may benefit from the initial design provided by RMM, but do not gain greatly from the improved maintainability given by a formal design

---

[11] Note that by degree of structure the developers of RMM are referring to the extent of the formal organisation of the information (what we would refer to as syntactic structure), rather than the associative linking or semantic structure which will be present in all applications. With this interpretation, database applications would typically have a high structure whereas literary applications would have a low structure.

process. RMM will be most useful in applications which have both a high degree of structure and high volatility of information (such as product catalogues and hypermedia front ends for legacy database systems).

RMM as useful to consider, as it one of the best examples of research aimed at explicitly addressing the hypermedia *development process* rather than hypermedia products. Although RMM doesn't address the entire development lifecycle (no currently existing hypermedia specific methodology does), it does address the critical stage of design. In considering RMM, we aim to demonstrate the benefits which can be gained from adopting a formal development methodology. We also aim to provide some insights into how a hypermedia development methodology might be developed and then applied.

15.2 RMM Concepts

The Relationship Management Methodology (RMM) addresses the design and implementation of large, complex but highly structured, volatile hypermedia applications. To achieve this, it provides both a model for representing the design of hypermedia applications and a set of steps for developing and utilising this design model in the creation of a hypermedia application.

Figure 15-1 shows the development process which is assumed by RMM and the stages in this process for which RMM provides methodological guidance. As can be seen from this figure, RMM focuses only on the design and implementation stages of the development process. The early life-cycle activities such as feasibility studies, requirements analyses and planning, the late life-cycle activities such as evaluation and maintenance, and the project management activities are not within the scope of consideration of RMM.

RMDM: Design Model

Before considering the actual development method, let us begin by considering the model which is used within RMM. The Relationship Management Data Model (RMDM) is used to represent, using suitable abstractions, the design of a hypermedia application. The developers of RMM make the worthwhile point that existing models of hypermedia systems (such as Dexter) are not appropriate to use in modelling hyper-

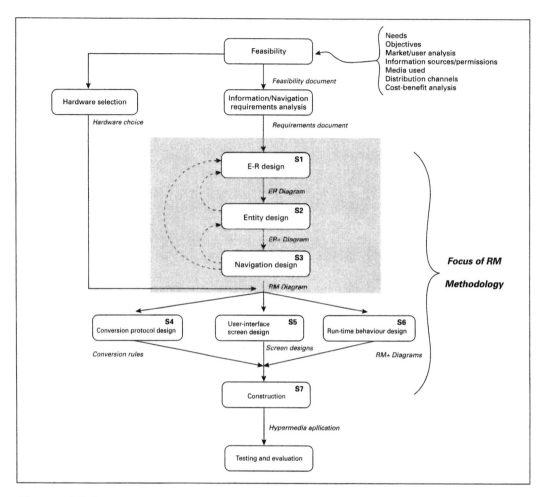

Figure 15-1

Although defined within the context of the full development lifecycle, the scope of the RMM methodology is limited to the design and implementation phases of development. In this figure the arrows are tagged with deliverables from each stage of the development. (Reproduced by kind permission from RMM: A methodology for structured hypermedia design. *CACM* **V** 38:8 August 1995. © ACM)

media applications, as they focus on the internal architecture of a system, rather than modelling a particular application domain.

RMDM is based heavily on HDM (described briefly earlier in the book). Figure 15-2 shows the RMDM modelling primitives. The top four of these primitives are standard entity-relationship primitives and are used to

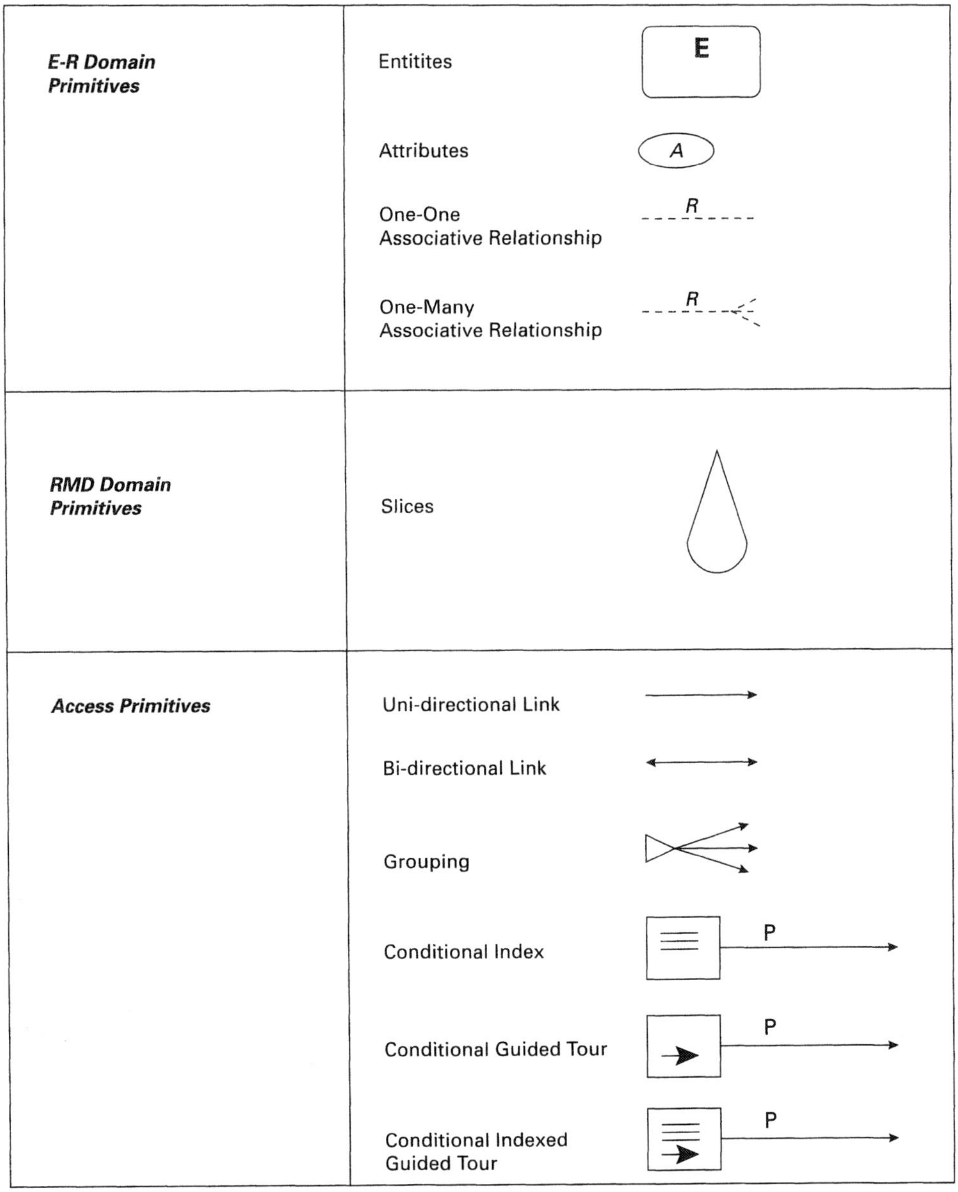

E-R Domain Primitives	Entitites	E
	Attributes	A
	One-One Associative Relationship	R
	One-Many Associative Relationship	R
RMD Domain Primitives	Slices	
Access Primitives	Uni-directional Link	
	Bi-directional Link	
	Grouping	
	Conditional Index	P
	Conditional Guided Tour	P
	Conditional Indexed Guided Tour	P

Figure 15-2

The Relationship Management Data Model (RMDM) primitives. E-R primitives model how information is structured in the application domain. The slice domain primitive models how information is to be presented and the access primitives model navigation. (Reproduced by kind permission from RMM: A methodology for structured hypermedia design. _CACM_ **V** 38:8 August 1995. © ACM)

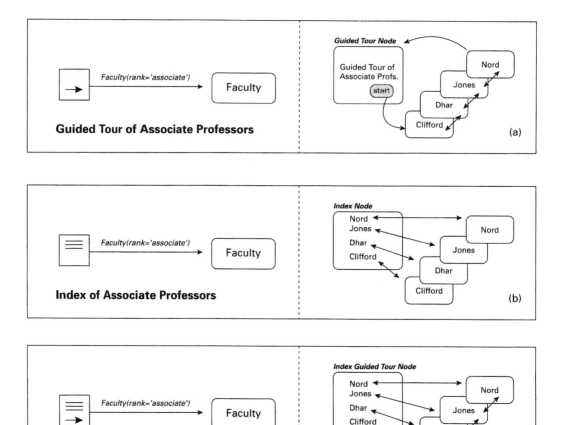

Figure 15-3

Examples of the conditional RMDM access modelling primitives (with conditions specified for each construct). (Reproduced by kind permission from RMM: A methodology for structured hypermedia design. *CACM* **V** 38:8 August 1995. © ACM)

model the applications domain. Entity types and the attributes which belong to entities are used to represent abstract or physical objects. Associative relationships are used to represent domain level associations between these objects. These primitives represent information about the domain which is application independent.

Slices are used to group attributes within an entity together, as the basis for a specific presentation or perspective onto that entity. For example,

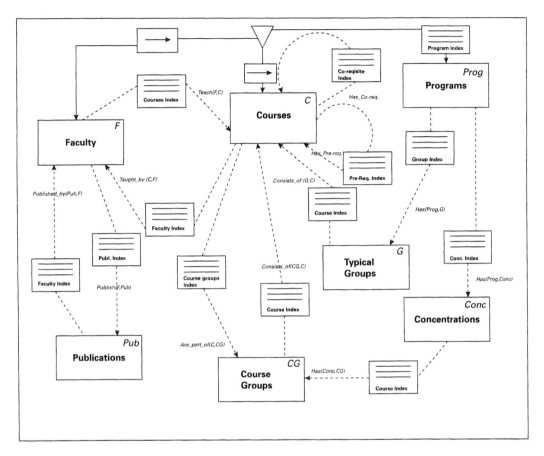

Figure 15-4

RMDM diagram for the Information Systems Department handbook application. (Reproduced by kind permission from RMM: A methodology for structured hypermedia design. *CACM* **V** 38:8 August 1995. © ACM)

we may have a *person* entity which has attributes *name, picture, address, age* and *biography*. In one context we may only wish to have a *name* and *picture*, and in another context we may want *name, address* and *biography*. This would be represented by two appropriate slices. A subsequent addition to RMM, the m-slice, allows modelling of cross-entity groupings. This will be discussed further shortly.

The last set of primitives are used to model application specific access structures. Navigation within an application is modelled by six access primitives. Unidirectional and bidirectional links specify access between slices of an entity. Indexes, guided tours and indexed guided tours (each of which can have certain logic predicate conditions specifying which entities participate) are used to support navigation between different entities. The form of each of these is illustrated in Figure 15-3. Finally, the grouping construct is used to provide a menu-like mechanism which supports access to other parts of the application (such as is typically found on the home page of many Websites). Figure 15-4 demonstrates a typical RMDM diagram.

Recent experience with the basic Relationship Management Data Model has shown that it is limited in several ways. First, it is unable to model certain types of structures. In particular, it is not able, in many cases, to model presentation units of applications. This is particularly true where information from multiple entities is combined into a single presentation unit. Secondly, the model is such that it encourages an explicitly top-down approach to the design of applications. This is, in many cases, highly undesirable.

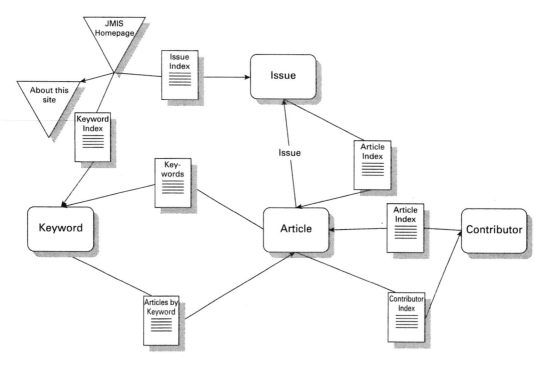

Figure 15-5

RMDM diagram for the Website for the Journal of Management Information Systems (JMIS) (Reproduced by permission of Tomas Isakowitz 1997)

m-Slices

Let us first consider the inability to model presentation units. As an example of this limitation consider the RMDM diagram shown in Figure 15-5. This diagram shows the model (using conventional RMDM primitives) for the Website for the *Journal of Management Information Systems*. As part of the development of this site, we could decide that we wish to design the page shown in Figure 15-6. This page contains a collection of information from the *article* entity (the article title), the contributor entity (the names of authors), the issue entity (the volume and date), as well as information from the relationship between article and issue (the page numbers).

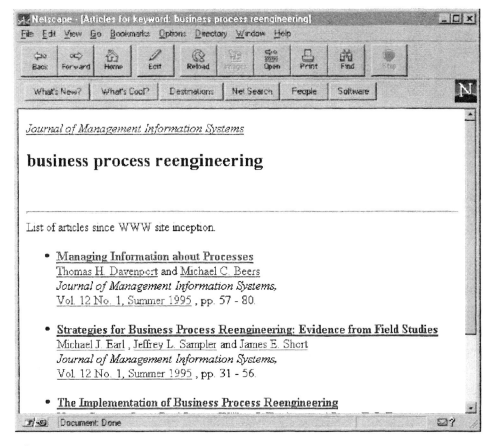

Figure 15-6

This desired Webpage within the JMIS Website cannot be modelled using the conventional RMDM primitives (Reproduced by permission of Tomas Isakowitz 1997)

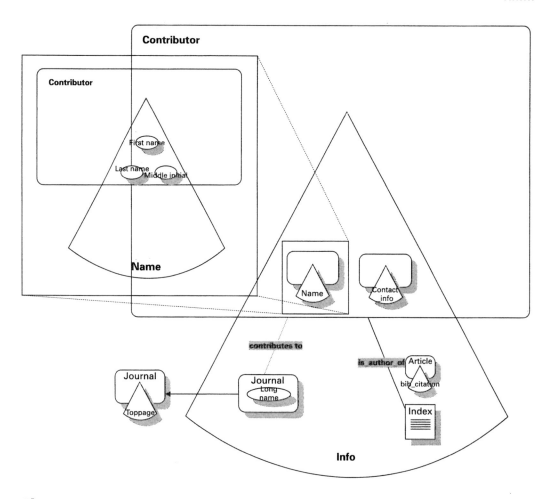

Figure 15-7

The contributor.info m-slice (Reproduced by permission of Tomas Isakowitz 1997)

Conventional RMDM only allows slices to be defined within a single entity, which means that it would not be able to model the presentation unit which is implemented as this Web page. This is corrected by the introduction of m-Slices (the 'm' refers to Russian Matrjeska dolls) (Isakowitz *et al.*, 1996). These new slices allow the modelling of presentation units which incorporate information from a collection of entities, or even relationships. This is illustrated in Figure 15-7, which shows a slice containing information from a number of entities. It is important to emphasise that m-slices model what information is to be part of a presentation unit, and not how this information will actually be presented. Finally, it is worth mentioning that m-slices can be nested allowing complex presentation units to be readily modelled.

In terms of changes to the basic RMDM model, m-slices replace both the conventional slice primitive, as well as the grouping construct.

Application diagrams

The version of RMDM described above (with or without m-slices) lacks the ability to model presentation level information and encourages a strongly top-down development process. A recent addition, aimed at addressing these problems, is the introduction into RMM of the application diagram.

The application diagram is aimed at explicitly showing the presentation units and the interconnections between these units, which go to make up the application. A typical application diagram is shown in Figure 15-8. In this example, each presentation unit corresponds to a HTML template, which when instantiated with data will result in a specific Web page. The star that appears in the *Journal* presentation unit means that every other page has a link that connects to this unit.

RMM Method Steps

RMDM provides a mechanism for modelling the structure of a hyper-media application. The real strength however lies in RMM's definition of a set of procedures for creating and utilising this model. As mentioned previously, the method focuses on the design and implementation stages of development. The steps in the method were shown in Figure 15-1. One point worth making is that in the original RMM these steps were seen as a linear progression (with possible feedback paths resulting in an iterative development). With the addition of the application diagram to the RMM tools, the second and third steps are typically carried out in parallel. This is discussed further in the relevant section below.

Step 1: E-R design

During this step, the information domain of the application is analysed and modelled using an entity-relationship diagram. The E-R representation is well known, and is able to model information structure in a broad

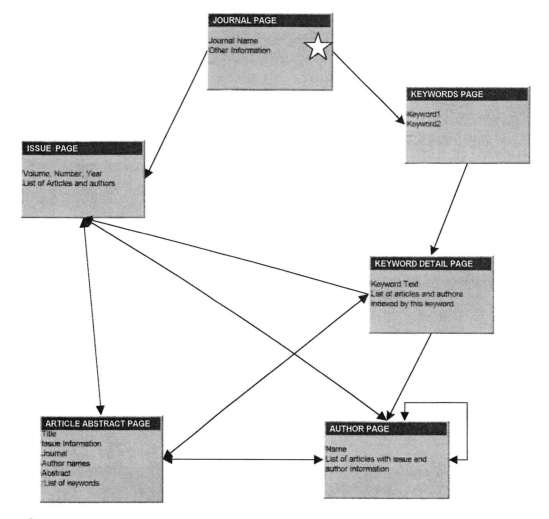

Figure 15-8

The application diagram for the JMIS Website. All classes of Web pages and links amongst them are shown (Reproduced by kind permission of Tomas Isakowitz 1997)

range of domains. During this stage the developer identifies both the entities within the application domain and the relationships between these entities.

Entity-relationship design has been extensively studied in the literature, and is a well-established technique. Within this particular context, the entity-relationship diagram provides an application-independent view of the domain of interest for the application being developed. In developing the E-R diagram, the focus is not on how the information will be used within the context of a specific application, but what information and structure is inherent in the domain. Much of the information captured at this stage will eventually be used within the application, but this is not a prerequisite. For example, the E-R approach helps identify important relationships across which navigation can be supported.

Step 2: slice design

In this step the developer determines how the information in the application will be grouped to be presented to the users of the application, and how they will access this information. In some sense, this can be considered as an identification of the viewpoints or perspectives onto the underlying information represented by the E-R diagram.

This is achieved by the identification of suitable slices (or m-slices) which collect together information from the various entities within the application. The result of this step is a set of slice diagrams such as that shown in Figure 15-7. Each entity also has a default slice which can be used to define the default slice used for any links to that entity.

Apart from the slice diagrams the links between slices which support navigation are also identified. In Figure 15-7, we can see links between the *bib_citation* slice and the *contributor.info* slice, the *issue.toc* slice and the *article.abstract* slice. These links are in addition to any associative relationships defined during the E-R design. In general, the links are between slices within a single entity, and represent structural links to related perspectives of the same entity. The associative relationships defined during E-R design are typically between slices from different entities, and result in semantic or associative links in the final application.

Together the entities and relationships from Step 1 and the slices and links from Step 2 make up the structural components defining the application schema. The output of this step is an enriched E-R model, which is referred to as the E-R+ diagram (which in practice may well be just the original E-R diagram and a collection of slice diagrams). In performing the slice design, the developer needs to consider various issues: how should each entity be divided into slices; which should be the default slice; how should the slices be interconnected; and how should the links be labelled?

Step 3: navigation design

The third step in RMM involves the design of the paths used to navigate amongst the various entities. In the original version of RMM, navigation design begins with the design of the structures supporting navigation between entities based on the associative relationships. Each relationship appearing in the E-R+ diagram is analysed to determine whether it is appropriate, and if so it is replaced by one (or more) of the RMDM access primitives. RMM makes a point of prohibiting individual hard-coded links between entities, as these significantly reduce the maintainability of the application. Next, high level access structures are designed by grouping together items of interest, providing menu-like access to the various material. At the end of the navigation design, the E-R+ diagram has been transformed into a final RMDM diagram.

In the revised version of RMM, which incorporates application diagrams, the goal of identifying the navigation paths is the same, but the process and outcomes are slightly different. The presentation units to be included in the application diagram are identified by selecting all the m-slices which are the target of a link in the E-R+ diagram, and then all links between these m-slices are also included into the application diagram. The outcome, rather than being a RMDM diagram, is the application diagram.

The addition of application diagrams also means that Steps 2 and 3 can be performed together. The result is that this phase of the design can be bottom-up, top-down, or a combination of the two. For example, in a bottom-up approach the designer can initially focus on each entity and then on the more general access mechanisms. In a top-down approach the designer focuses first on the general structures during the slice design, then converts these into lower-level presentation units. In practice, the process is likely to be an iterative approach combining both top-down and bottom-up.

It is also worth pointing out that, during this step, the designers have to identify the components and the way in which they are most likely to be accessed. This means that an understanding of the users and their context is quite important.

Step 4: conversion protocol design

In Step 4 we use a set of conversion rules to transform each element of the RMDM diagram into an appropriate object in the implementation environment. For example, we can define sets of rules which determine how a slice is converted into an HTML page for the Web. At present, this stage is performed manually, though it should be quite feasible to automate this process as part of a CASE tool (or more correctly CAHE tool – Computer Aided Hypermedia Engineering tool).

Step 5: user-interface design

In this step each object appearing in the final RMDM diagram is used as the basis for the design of suitable interface components. Whereas the previous step looks at the structural transformation of the objects into the final application, this step considers how they will be actually presented. This can include aspects such as the look of anchors, button layouts, positioning of video and images, etc.

Step 6: run-time behaviour design

In Step 6 we consider the functionality which supports the run-time behaviour of the application. This includes aspects such as history lists, link traversal, possible inclusion of search engines, etc. Other aspects which might be considered include whether pages should be constructed statically or dynamically as requested, how the underlying data is to be represented, etc.

Step 7: construction and testing

Finally, in the last step the application is actually constructed and evaluated (much as in conventional software development). The details of this stage have not been substantially addressed by RMM, since they will be highly dependent upon the particular platform and environment being used.

RM-CASE

As a brief comment, it is worth pointing out that a CASE[12] tool has been developed to support RMM, called RM-CASE (Diaz *et al.*, 1995). This tool, shown in Figure 15-9, is used to support the design of application using

---

[12] Computer Aided Software Engineering – this might more accurately be called CAHE for Computer Aided Hypermedia Engineering

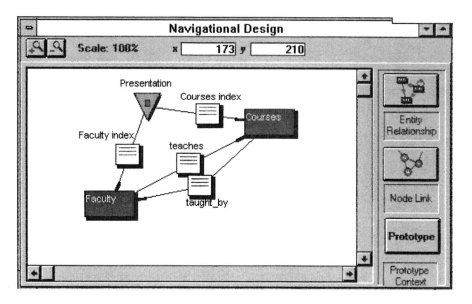

Figure 15-9

A typical screenshot from the RM-CASE tool (Reproduced by permission of Tomas Isakowitz 1997)

the RMM approach. The tool provides support for both the method and the production of diagrams associated with the method.

RM-CASE supports various 'contexts' equating to the stages of development. The first of these is the Entity-Relationship context, which facilitates the construction of E-R diagrams. The slice diagram context supports creation of the slices within individual entities from the E-R diagram. The navigational design context (shown in the figure) allows developers to specify the navigational constructs, and the node-link context supports conversion of the RMDM diagram into an appropriate node-link web for visualisation purposes. The user interface design context allows the interface to be designed and edited (such as associating each node to a HTML template). The hyperbase population context allows specification of the content which will be used in the generation of specific instances of the nodes. Finally, the prototyping context is used to evaluate and test different aspects of the design prior to actual implementation.

It is worth pointing out that design objects (such as entity attributes) are shared between different contexts as appropriate. Any changes made to one context are immediately reflected in the other contexts, so it becomes possible to adopt a very iterative approach to the development, switching between the various contexts as appropriate. This also has the effect of improving traceability within the development process, since a single design object can be easily traced through the various contexts.

Comments

Before considering the specific issues raised with respect to all the research systems we are considering, we make a few comments about RMM which put some of the discussion into context.

First, it is important to point out that RMM is not a full lifecycle method, nor was it intended to be so by its developers. Its focus is largely on the design of hypermedia systems. It doesn't actively address planning, feasibility studies, requirements gathering and specification, evaluation, maintenance or project management. This is not a criticism – it simply means that developers using RMM need to be aware of the scope of activities with which it provides assistance.

Also, RMM does not exist within an explicit process model. Indeed, it could be readily used within a number of different models – though the developers of RMM do make the point that feedback between the various development stages is important. This means that any process model used needs to support an iterative approach to the development.

15.3 Dealing with Product Issues

Effective Navigation and Browsing

The primary mechanism used by RMM in addressing effective navigation and browsing within hypermedia applications is the creation of suitable application structure. A major focus of RMM is the identification and progressive refinement during the development process of the structure of the information space which underlies the application. This structure begins with the inherent structures identified using well-established Entity-Relationship design, and is then refined through the provision of appropriate information groupings and access mechanisms.

A structure based on an entity-relationship analysis is likely to have several benefits, the most significant of which, in terms of supporting effective navigation, is that the structures underlying the application will be based on underlying relationships between the information. These are more likely to be familiar to users of the application, and hence be considered logical. For example, in Figure 15-5 we have modelled the general knowledge that a journal *article* has multiple *contributors*. This fact is also obvious to users of the system, and so is likely to be an appropriate basis for the creation of links.

The RMM development process is also more likely to provide a consistent style of navigation and a consistent look and feel. The entities identified in the initial E-R analysis provide the information base from which slices can be created. These slices then become the presentation units which form the basis of the application. For example, in Figure 15-8, the *Author Page* presentation unit will be used as a template from which pages of information on all authors of articles are generated. Similarly, the links in all of these pages of information will have a uniform behaviour (in this case, being linked to the list of articles the particular author has published). This means there will be a high degree of consistency to the presentation of information, and a high degree of consistency to the structure. The user will be presented with an application which behaves in a very consistent fashion, thereby improving navigability.

Another aspect worth considering is that the design of the information structure can itself be used to assist users in navigation. Figure 15-10 shows a Web page from a site designed using RMM. The page includes a clickable image map which is derived directly from the RMDM diagram generated during the design. This map serves two purposes: first, it assists the user in understanding the structure of the application and where they are within this structure; secondly, it can be used to support, more directly, navigation within the structure. The effectiveness of this will, of course, be highly dependant on how well the map is constructed and how easily it can be interpreted by a user.

A final aspect worth considering with respect to the effectiveness of navigation within applications developed using RMM is the functionality provided within these applications. RMM provides a design step aimed explicitly at addressing this issue, covering aspects such as the design of suitable link traversal mechanisms and support of history mechanisms and search engines. Unfortunately, RMM does not provide any

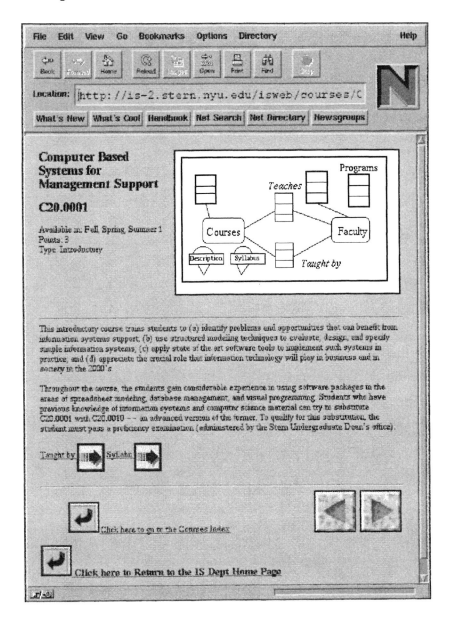

Figure 15-10

This screendump shows a page from a Website developed using RMM. In this case, the clickable map showing the site structure can be generated from the design and serves to both orient the user, and provide an alternative means of navigation (Reproduced by kind permission from RMM: A methodology for structured hypermedia design. *CACM* **V** 38:8 August 1995. © ACM)

indication of how these activities should be carried out, or the criteria to use during this stage of the design. Nevertheless, the explicit recognition of the need to address these issues is an important first step.

Cognitive Management during Browsing

Although cognitive management during the use of applications was not a core focus of RMM, it does address this issue in various ways. First, some of the comments made in the previous section are equally valid in answering this issue. In particular, the use of image maps and a consistent structure will help in these respects; both reduce the cognitive effort required by a user in understanding the structure and where individual items of information can be found within this structure.

In a similar vein, the conversion protocol design stage of the method will help assure that the interfaces are consistent. Again, this reduces the burden on users, as they will not have to repeatedly adjust to differences (trivial or otherwise) in the interface. Where these differences do occur it will be a sign to the user that there is a specific reason for a change in the presentation.

Information Contextualisation

A number of aspects of RMM impact on how support for the contextualisation of information is provided. First, RMM differentiates between associative relationships between entities (during the E-R design stage) and links between slices within a single entity (identified during the slice design stage). The developers of RMM treat the former as semantic associations and the latter as structural links. This differentiation can be important in terms of contextualisation. If we follow structural links (i.e. between slices within a single entity) then the local context (i.e. that of the given entity), remains unchanged. If we follow semantic links, then we are in effect navigating to information based on a new entity, and the local context is therefore changed.

This point can be used in the design of the hypermedia application. User interface clues can be incorporated which alert a user to a change in context. The simplest example which can be readily implemented in almost any environment would be to make the background for the presentation units based on each entity a different colour or pattern.

Another possibility would be changing the way in which windows are managed for the two different types for links.

Another useful contextualisation aid is that it becomes possible to see from which entity a given presentation unit (i.e. slice) is derived. For example, we could place the name of the 'owner' entity of each presentation unit at the top of the page. We could then know, for instance, that a particular Web page is based on a particular 'slice' of information related predominantly to an *author* entity. We can then we can immediately place information within the page into context – such as providing the needed clue that any papers listed in the Web page are papers written by the specified author. This will be particularly true since the entities were explicitly identified as domain objects, which are therefore likely to be familiar to the user.

Sequence context (i.e. how given information relates to other information previously presented in a given sequence of access) is a little more difficult to support in RMM. Although RMM does support the concept of guided tours, these are mainly intended as an access structure, rather than a mechanism for specifying or designing particular sequences of presentation. In essence, RMM does not really address the issue of the sequences of information access which are likely to be useful or effective, and how these sequences can be designed and supported within an application.

Link and Content Validity

Let us first consider content validity. All information in an application designed using RMM must be based on the entities identified during the initial E-R analysis. This means that we are much less likely to spuriously incorporate irrelevant information into the application. This does not guarantee the correctness of the underlying data used in the application – the sources used may still be invalid. It does, however, at least mean that the concepts represented will be relevant to the application being designed. Where we find information at a later stage of the development that we wish to incorporate, this should be added to the E-R model. This will help evaluate the appropriateness of the information to the domain.

In a similar way to supporting content validity, RMM will support validity with respect to links. The E-R diagram identifies not only the key entities, but also the core associative relationships between these entities. Standard E-R analysis techniques can assist in ensuring that these relationships are valid. These relationships are then reflected in the hypermedia links in the final application, which should consequently also be valid.

It is worth pointing out that the mere fact of having design stages where the content and relationships are explicitly identified will in itself be more likely to result in valid content and links. Rather than identifying this information in conjunction with numerous other tasks (when the developer is likely to be focusing on numerous development aspects, and may be readily distracted), much can be gained from a method where the developer's attention is tightly focused on identifying valid and relevant content and links.

One possible problem which RMM may introduce is that there are numerous design stages between the initial identification of content and relationships and the final implementation of the application. This can result in two significant problems: first, when changes are required (for example, if some additional desired content is identified late in the development), it may make developers reticent to retrace so far back in the development process – out of concern for the additional effort required in updating all the intermediate development products. This difficulty may be overcome by providing suitable tool support for the design process, or adapting RMM to a more incremental development process model.

The second possible difficulty relates to the number of transformations the design elements go through. For example, we begin with an associative relationship in the E-R model; this becomes an access structure in the RMDM model, and then a set of instantiated links in a map of the application structure; and finally, is implemented as an actual link in the final application. This sequence of transformations has the potential to reduce traceability and provides opportunities for introducing errors. It is not clear how large a problem this would be. Further experience with large-scale development would be required to evaluate the potential for difficulty.

Information Structure

Before discussing specific mechanisms for creating suitable information structures, it is useful to note that RMM does not attempt to provide guidelines for designing the structure of an application from a global perspective (i.e. What type of overall abstract structure is most appropriate – hierarchical, linear, etc.?). Rather, it develops the information structure by identifying the inherent relationships amongst the information, and using these to build a structure in what is effectively a bottom-up approach. The final structure can almost be viewed as growing from the results of related design stages, rather than being something explicitly designed.

Returning to specific structures, we can begin by reiterating the discussion in the previous section. E-R design and slice design help ensure that we have valid content and links. Having obtained these, they still need to combined into a suitable information structure. The first aspect of this is the way in which the actual presentation units are designed, in other words, we can have valid content but this content must be divided or 'sliced' up in an appropriate fashion. The implication of 'slicing' here is intentional – as that is exactly the way in which RMM addresses this particular issue.

During slice design, the particular presentation units to be used are designed. According to Isakowitz *et al.* (1995) 'It involves splitting an entity into meaningful slices'. The only significant design guideline provided within RMM is that 'it is important to remember that each slice will represent a *whole* for the system [sic – should be application] user. Thus slices should group only related information items but should not contain too much information'. Beyond these observations, RMM does not yet provide guidance on how to effectively design the individual slices.

The introduction of m-slices is aimed at making the representation of presentation units more flexible, but it may make the suitable identification of these presentation units more difficult, since the contents of a slice are no longer limited to the (presumably reasonably cohesive) contents of a single entity. Identification of mechanisms for designing these m-slices would be a fruitful research area. Having made these criticisms, it is important to point out that the situation in RMM is still better than conventional practice. At least the method encourages the developer to pay explicit attention to the way in which information is grouped for presentation.

The second aspect of information structure is how the presentation units are linked together. The situation with respect to links is similar to that with content. The E-R design step identifies the core associative relationships, and the inter-slice links are identified during the slice design, but RMM does not provide guidelines for assisting in identifying suitable links. Nevertheless, having an explicit stage where these are identified is an important initial step in encouraging the design of suitable structures.

One final comment regarding the creation of suitable information structures is that the number of structural building blocks in RMM is relatively small. All forms of structure in RMM reduce to either single links or one of a small set of access structures (indices, guided tours, etc.). In some respects this may be constraining, but it does mean that the user should always be aware of the types of structures which are being used to support the navigation.

Management of Different Media

RMM does little to address issues of the handling of different media. The specific form of media types used in hypermedia applications is not assumed to be text. For example, attributes of entities (which then are incorporated into slices) can be any media type at all. However, RMM does not explicitly consider aspects such as the synchronisation of media, which combinations of different media are most appropriate, how resources for different media are handled, or how different media can be managed to provide suitable contexts when following links (such as is provided by AHM (Hardman, Bulterman and van Rossum, 1993)). Of course all of these issues can be addressed within the framework provided by RMM, but no explicit guidance is provided.

15.4 Dealing with Process Issues

Application Maintenance

Although the RMM methodology does not explicitly contain a 'maintenance phase', it does assist in developing applications which are more likely to be maintainable. Indeed, the application domains which RMM directly targets are highly structured applications that have high volatility. This volatility is largely presumed to be volatility of specific content, rather than volatility of abstract structure, nevertheless, resulting applications still contain characteristics which make them maintainable even in the case of changing requirements or domain.

First, it is worth pointing out that almost any development methodology which has specific deliverables will result in a more maintainable application. The fact that aspects such as design models and decisions are recorded will assist in maintenance, which in general means that maintenance of the application can occur at an appropriate level. If the content changes, then the specific implementation (such as the content of data files) can be updated. If there is a change in the domain of interest, then the design models can be re-evaluated and updated. If the application requirements change, then the maintenance can revert to the original application analysis.

Considering the RMM approach in particular, we can identify several aspects which result in highly maintainable applications. The most significant of these is the separation of domain knowledge, application structure and implementation. The original E-R design captures knowledge about the domain independent of any specific application. Therefore, if the application changes (such as a change in certain requirements), this will not affect the domain knowledge. Similarly, if the domain changes (such as the restructuring of a corporation which maintains Web pages about the structure of the corporation), it is relatively straightforward to see what changes will have occurred in the domain knowledge.

Application structure is captured in the slice diagrams and RMDM diagram (or the application diagram in the revised version of RMM). This is independent of the particular presentation environment. For example, if we change the presentation environment (such as from a CD-ROM to the Web), then the domain knowledge and application structure can remain unchanged and only the implementation needs to be updated.

Finally, it is worth pointing out that RMM develops applications which are inherently maintainable for changes in content, when the structure and domain remain unchanged. For example, consider the addition of new publications to the application represented in Figure 15-4. This application can be inherently template based, with a template for each presentation unit, and each particular instance being generated as required from a combination of a database entry and the presentation template. Content-based maintenance then reduces to simply adding new content to the database.

Reuse

An obvious aspect of reuse in hypermedia is not only to be able to reuse specific content – which is beyond the scope of RMM – but also reuse of other artifacts of the development process. Examples include reuse of requirements, high-level designs, user-interface designs, information structures and templates, etc. Any process that produces intermediate deliverables will of course promote reuse to a certain extent. In the case of RMM, a good example is that domain knowledge is captured independently of the specific application. It is therefore likely that this domain knowledge will be readily reusable across a number of different applications. RMM does not, however, address the issue of how these reusable elements can be identified as potential candidates for effective reuse within a given development process.

The RMM developers make the following point with respect to reuse:

> 'RMM functions as a top-down process, starting with an ER diagram, and concluding with user-interface details. Not only does this constrain software development, but it also discourages re-use because identification of similar functionality is more apparent in a bottom-up approach.'

In this respect, the developers are referring to reuse within a single application, rather than across applications (since with reuse between applications we will presumably have access to all the completed development artifacts).

This observation is addressed by the two modifications to RMM discussed earlier – the m-slice and the application diagram. The m-slice assists in re-use in two ways: first, it captures information about presentation units which can be readily reused in other applications; secondly, in conjunction with the application diagram, it promotes a combined top-down and bottom-up approach to the design of application structures. This means that low-level structures (which are potential candidates for reuse) are identified early in the design process, at a stage when they can still be effectively reused.

Supporting the Full Lifecycle and Process Management

Although RMM (along with OOHDM (Schwabe and Rossi, 1995a, b) and EORM (Lange, 1993, 1994)) is as complete a development methodology as exists, it's major focus is on the design and implementation phases of development. As an illustration both of the coverage of RMM and the process phases which are not actively considered within RMM, consider Figure 15-11. As can be seen, RMM does not actively address aspects such as determination of objectives and constraints, evaluation of alternatives and risk analysis, planning, project management and evaluation.

In many respects this is not necessarily a problem. Many of these activities have tools or methods available elsewhere. For example, Isakowitz *et al.* (1995) make the point that 'feasibility, requirements analysis and testing are undeniably important phases in software (sic) development ... To evaluate hypermedia applications, one can use techniques like those proposed by Garzotto, Paolini and Mainetti ...'. In other words, it

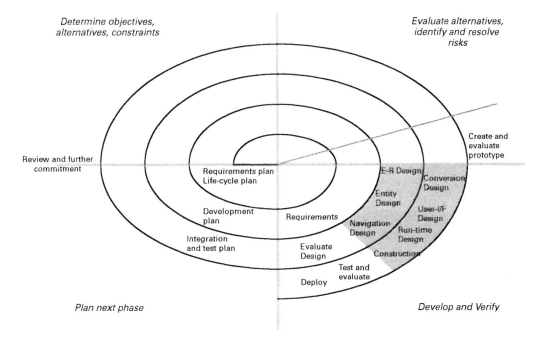

Figure 15-11

The shaded region of the Spiral Model of the Software Development Process shows the major focus of RMM within the context of the entire development process. Similar effects would be obvious if we used alternative process models

is recognised that RMM is not attempting to provide a life-cycle method, but rather a design method which works in conjunction with other approaches which address other aspects of the overall development process.

A major consideration related to the use of a collection of different tools, approaches and methodologies is that project management becomes particularly important. In many cases, the various methods or tools will have been developed based on differing assumptions. For example, RMM is essentially based on a top-down approach to development (though the specific slice and navigation design steps can be carried out in parallel in a combination of top-down and bottom-up). RMM may not, therefore, integrate particularly well with analysis techniques designed for an iterative approach to development, and hence require considerable ongoing feedback from consecutive development iterations to refine the analysis.

Cognitive Management during Development

RMM addresses cognitive management during the development process (or at least those phases of the development on which it focuses) very well. The simplest aspect of this is that it provides a specific set of steps which guide a developer through the design activities. This has several implications: first, it means that the developer is not as burdened with managing the process of design as well as the design itself; it also means that the developer is encouraged to focus on important aspects of the design, and at appropriate stages of the development; also, by providing explicit modelling tools and specifying the deliverables required from each step of development the method ensures that the developer has a consistent basis on which to think about, discuss and design the application. A consistent terminology and notation minimises ambiguity and hence confusion.

Supporting Enhanced Productivity

Very little can be said here that has not been raised in one of the above points. Consistent notation, suitable process steps, improved maintainability and maximising reuse will all aid in supporting enhanced development productivity.

One aspect of productivity which RMM only addresses implicitly is the huge effort required for the two development activities which often dominate development effort: creation of content and cross-linking of information. Creation of the content to be used within applications is essentially beyond the scope of RMM. Cross-linking of the information (i.e. generation of the complex semantic links which provide richness in applications) has only been addressed in RMM as a subset of aspects such as slice design. This may be because the application on which RMM focuses tend to be highly structured domains where the links are between classes of information (i.e. slices of entities) rather than individual instances. Nevertheless, addressing this area would have the potential to result in significant productivity advancements in a broad range of application domains.

15.5 Conclusions

A few final comments regarding RMM may be useful. As has been reiterated several times, RMM is a *design* method rather than a full lifecycle method, and is aimed at a specific class of applications – those involving a very regular but non-volatile structure coupled with a high volatility of content. Bearing this in mind, RMM is particular useful for applications with a class- or category-based structure (such as organisational applications, product catalogues, etc.). Conversely, it is not particularly well suited to applications with an irregular structure, such as hypertext interactive fiction or educational material.

A major strength of the RMM approach is the way in which it separates domain modelling (using E-R design), application structure modelling (using slice and navigation design) and application presentation modelling (using conversion protocol design, user-interface screen design and run-time behaviour design). This approach has the potential to dramatically improve both reuse and maintainability of applications.

A final point is that a worthwhile area of ongoing research or refinement of RMM would be to look at developing the criteria, guidelines and specific details of how each phase of the method carried out. At present, the general approach is detailed, and the issues to be addressed are enumerated. However, in most cases, specific techniques for addressing these issues and developing solutions at each stage are yet to be developed.

15.6 Acknowledgements

We wish to thank Professor Tomas Isakowitz for the various discussions, reviews and comments which greatly assisted in the development of this chapter. Much of the material in this chapter, particularly the descriptions of RMM, has been adapted from other publications on RMM, notably Isakowitz *et al.*, 1995, 1996 and Diaz *et al.*, 1995.

15.7 Further Information

For more information on RMM or any other aspect of the research work described in this chapter, the following Website contains numerous related publications:

```
http://irss.njit.edu:5080/papers/isakowitz/
isakowitz.html
```

Alternatively the researchers can be contacted at:

Prof Tomas Isakowitz
Contact address: The Wharton School
                   University of Pennsylvania
                   1100 Steinberg Hall-Dietrich Hall
                   3620 Locust Walk
                   Philadelphia, PA 19104–6375, USA

16

The Future of Hypermedia Engineering

Only connect
(Howards End; chapter 22, E. M. Forster)

Chapter Goals

This is the concluding chapter of the book. We aim to finish by providing various insights into possible future directions in which hypermedia may evolve, and how we can work towards more effective development. The objectives of this chapter are to show that:

● Currently, the Web is the dominant hypermedia system in use, and is evolving very rapidly. Unfortunately, development practices are not evolving nearly as quickly.

● We can identify three primary product models for hypermedia applications: the publishing model, the presentation model, and the distributed information management model.

● The tools and approaches for managing the development of hypermedia applications are yet to reach any degree of maturity.

● A consideration of issues for the future can help us understand potential directions in which hypermedia may evolve, and therefore give insights into how we can develop applications.

● We mustn't lose sight of fact that development, or even hypermedia itself is not an 'end'. It is only a 'means' for providing information for the sake of developing knowledge which can be used. Development should be carried out within this context – something which is often overlooked.

16.1 Introduction

In this book we have tried to establish a case for viewing large-scale hypermedia developments as an engineering enterprise, and to draw analogies and similarities with the evolution of the software engineering approach to large-scale program development. As more and more people and organisations grapple with the complexities of developing and maintaining large complex Websites, these issues become more apparent, as does the issue of longevity. There are no quick fix solutions available at the time of writing this book, and none obviously on the horizon. It is not possible to produce a fully worked practical case study to illustrate the principles discussed in the book, because the tools to do so don't yet exist. We have tried to illustrate the principles with practical examples throughout the book, but to produce a fully worked case study we would need the equivalent of CASE (Computer Assisted Software Engineering) tools for hypermedia engineering which have still to be developed.

The dominant hypermedia system as we write this book is clearly the World Wide Web. Throughout we have illustrated the points we were making using the Web, which demonstrates the ongoing love-hate relationship hypermedia developers have with it. We love the Web because it provides a common standard for understanding and discussing issues relating to hypermedia development and design, but at the same time, the limitations imposed by the Web model of hypermedia and the current lack of tools to support functions such as hypermedia design, maintenance, reuse, process management or links in non-text data objects can be intensely frustrating. The developers of the Web produced such a flexible and extensible system that the tools we need to support large-scale hypermedia engineering can and are being developed, but the frustration comes from the fact that many hypermedia systems that existed prior to the Web, or that were being developed at the same time, included some of these tools, and the wheel is being re-invented time and time again within the Web community.

On the other hand, the phenomenal growth of the Web has enabled us to see much more clearly the sort of systems that we need to be developing, and in some ways represents the ultimate hypermedia engineering challenge. The very rapid growth of intranets has provided a further impetus for the development of tools to enable organisations to manage and maintain their online information, whether it is in fully hypermedia form or not. The ubiquitous Web browser is now the preferred form of user interface for access to any online information, whether text documentation, spreadsheets, databases or multimedia collections, and every supplier of information processing software has had to provide Web browser access to their system, even if the nature of the processing going on underneath has changed relatively little. This gives us a wonderful opportunity to develop systems that enable all manner of cross-referencing and cross-linking between disparate information systems at the information system level rather than the computer system level. This activity has to be managed, however, or we just end up with spaghetti hypermedia in the same way as early programmers ended up with spaghetti programming.

16.2 Product Models

If you look at sites on the Web today you notice first the concentration on the graphical presentation of the site. In many cases this is highly overdone, and leaves the reader hanging around for hours waiting for the graphics to download. It is easy to draw analogies here with the truly dreadful examples of printing that were produced in the early days of electronic publishing as people experimented with the new medium and were overwhelmed with just what was possible. Once the novelty has worn off, most designers, certainly the professional ones, will have learnt what works and what doesn't, the right compromise between attractive, readable graphics and the time it takes to download the Web pages, how to create a consistent look and feel across the site and what standard features are required to support navigation around the site.

Accepting that we are in an evolving situation in this respect, there are still three basic product models (as described in Chapter 7), although as we look to the future of information dissemination via the Web it is useful to refer to them by alternative terms.

Programming Language-based – The Publishing Model

This is the model that has evolved from Nelson's ideas of non-sequential writing and the development of mark-up languages. Material produced in this mode is highly authored, often by a single author. Links, whether navigational or associative, are usually specifically authored, and their destinations will often be intra- rather than inter-document, so that the material is relatively self-contained. Maintenance is not so much of an issue because the model is similar to traditional publishing in that once it is published that version is fixed. It will be generally modified only by the original author, or group of authors, and the modified version will be published as a new version of the original.

The issue of reuse of published hypermedia documents, or extracts from them, by the original or different authors, is addressed by Nelson's work on transclusions (Nelson, 1993a) but is also tied up with the problems of developing new and workable copyright/IPR laws and internationally accepted methods of electronic (micro) payment. Nelson argues that, once something has been published electronically, it should never be discarded, and that an international system of micropayment will solve the problem of copyright charges for the reuse of previously published material. As ever, he is probably right.

The sort of material that might be produced using this model includes hypertext literature and poetry, technical reports, academic papers, digital archives, etc. Authors will use some sort of programming/mark-up language, such as HTML, SGML or XML, and/or editor, such as an HTML compliant word processor, to create their hypermedia documents. Minimal search facilities will be required by authors – no more than simple find commands and it is unlikely that a fully-fledged database would be required to support an author's, or even a group of authors, collection of documents.

Screen-based – The Presentation Model

This is the model most commonly used in the current generation of Web technology. Almost everyone who has an account on the Internet will have created their own Web page, and the commercial design and implementation of home pages and entire Web sites for organisations of all different types and sizes is now big business. The information is used for public relations, advertising, sales and marketing, so presentation, good graphics design and ease of use is everything.

Many firms who specialise in creating Web sites for major organisations have created their own customised software for the purpose. But for small organisations and individual users there are many software packages on the market to help you create your own home page and Web site. Microsoft's FrontPage is currently one of the best known examples. The software will take imported HTML files, as well as files in other formats, and help you plan the layout of the pages. Embedded links can easily be added to the text, and simple graphical outliners give the author some idea of what links they have created for each page, and their destinations. This eases maintenance for small collections of Web pages, but as discussed throughout the book, does not support the development process for applications of any significant size. Most sites will provide some sort of search facility to enable users to find information that isn't directly signposted, and larger sites may use database techniques for the storage of the documents/files that make up the site.

As a consequence of all this, most Websites of this sort will contain a minimal number of associative links. They are usually designed as a hierarchy, with a well developed home page that signposts the user to the significant information in the site and is itself clearly signposted from all other pages. As you move down the hierarchy the number of associative links in the pages gets fewer and fewer, and at the bottom of the tree tend to disappear altogether. The leaves of the tree are often dead-ends because they are documents that have been generated for other purposes (as reports, or course notes, or whatever) and imported into the site in their original format, They are often not in HTML, so creating links in them is more difficult. Additionally, the effort of creating associative links from these documents and subsequently maintaining those links as the site evolves is too great to make it worthwhile unless there is some development process support for the task.

A classic example of this sort of Website can be found in higher education institutions, where course material is made available to students via the Web. The overall structure and presentation of the material may be organised at a faculty, departmental or course level, but the course content will be provided by individual lecturers and may or may not be in HTML. It will often be material that was produced before the Web became a standard method for dissemination, and imported from whatever word processing system the lecturer uses. Academics are past-masters when it comes to the reuse of lecture material!

It is almost impossible to maintain any sort of associative linking in such sites, either intra- or inter-document, without some sort of support for the process. It is hard enough to maintain any sort of consistency or 'house-style' in terms of the overall structure or navigation of the site, and indeed, on version control. The site will need to be constantly maintained, and the information will certainly change on an annual basis at the very least so that version control becomes important, especially since the lecturers responsible for particular topics will change from year to year. It is also an example of the type of application which would most benefit from a high degree of cross-referencing and cross-linking, because of its educational purpose and the need to demonstrate to the students the interrelatedness of the material.

Information-centred – The Distributed Information Management Model

This model only really applies when the amount of information to be handled is of a significant size. The application will often contain a subset of information that has been generated using either of the two previous models – publishing and presentation – but will also contain information resulting from any number of heterogeneous information processing tools such as word processors, databases, spreadsheets, graphics packages, etc. It may also be distributed across many different servers and maintained at different levels by individuals, groups and/or the organisation as a whole. Examples might be a digital library or a corporate information system.

Distributed information management is the great challenge for hypermedia as we move into the 21st century. Everything in the system is potentially interconnected, and the management of the complex links, relations, associations, between the disparate pieces of information and information systems becomes of paramount importance to the usability of the overall system. The hypermedia or browsing aspects of the system will of course be supported by database and information retrieval technologies. The Web has given us some idea of what might be possible in a distributed environment, and has shown how eagerly users embrace such technology once it is available to them. But there is still a very long way to go before we can truly realise the full potential of such systems.

Hypermedia design is very difficult in large, dynamically evolving systems which have no natural starting point (home page) or structure. Link management is impossible unless links are handled as entities in their own right and/or there is some sort of supporting design process. System designers need to consider how to handle relationships between information elements created and stored in disparate, and often legacy, information systems. Large information systems will contain information in many different formats and media types. It is also important to remember that people will be using such systems for many different reasons and with different sets of skills.

With regard to this model, we are probably at a similar stage as we were with the development of databases in the 1970s. We can see the advantages of overall structure and design, but because the necessary tools and techniques to support this have yet to be developed, we take the link of least resistance and continue to develop in an *ad hoc*, piecemeal fashion. We must also remember that a large distributed information system will be made up of many small systems and applications, the design and development of which will be the responsibility of different individuals and groups. So as with databases, overall decisions about standards, structures, terminologies, etc. are of paramount importance.

16.3 Support for the Process

Anyone can be a hypermedia author now using HTML, but support for the process of hypermedia authoring is still minimal. For groups of authors and for authors/creators of large sites, applications and distributed information systems it is virtually non-existent. Increasingly, designers are using various forms of databases to store Web pages and the information about the structure of those pages. For example, each page can be associated in the database with its home page, previous page, next pages, etc. But the tools to provide access to this information through standard Web browsers are still largely *ad hoc*, often home-grown as add-ons to the database, or customised versions of the tools provided by the database vendors, and there is no support for the hypermedia design process. Databases, by their very nature, are highly structured, and provide little support for the task of designing and maintaining associative links. Tools are required that provide system support for the hypermedia engineering process.

In previous chapters we have described a number of research projects that illustrate the work being undertaken in the hypermedia research community to provide the foundations for the development of such tools. Hypermedia design methodologies, such as RMM and OOHDM, are still in their infancy and are not commercially available, but this work points the way forward as to what will be possible in the future. The RMM developers themselves point out that it is aimed at a rather specific class of application, generally those involving a very regular but non-volatile structure. Other design methodologies have their own strengths and weaknesses; there is no one methodology that provides solutions whatever the problem domain, and this remains a very important area of research and development.

Problems of link integrity, consistency, validity and maintenance are being tackled by a number of teams. We illustrated this type of work using Hyper-G/Hyperwave as an illustration. Hyperwave maintains control over the documents and links in the system by storing everything in a database, links are stored separately from the documents and resolved when the document is viewed, which gives considerable support to the designers of large Web sites. The Microcosm team tackled the same issues but in a different way, creating a loosely coupled link service as part of an open hypermedia system. This is a very active research area, and may have a major influence on the design of future generations of the Web. Indeed, as mentioned previously, there is an active international working group developing an Open Hypermedia Protocol (OHP) designed to enable different models and implementations of open hypermedia systems to be able to communicate with each other.

Work on automatic/system generation of links is also being undertaken by many teams; we used the work being undertaken by the Microcosm team in the use of generic links and the application of dynamic linking to support distributed information management as an example of this type of activity. Here we see the integration of search engines and document content analysis systems with hypermedia tools to enable the automatic or semi-automatic generation of hypermedia links to provide more effective navigation and browsing environments for users.

As the growth of the Internet and high-bandwidth networks continues to accelerate, more and more Web sites contain multimedia information, and users want to be able to create and follow links from within non-text information such as images, sound and video. Projects such as Hyper-G, Microcosm and AHM, among others, have explored the most effective ways to provide such support. There is also a lot of interest in the standards community to extend existing protocols to include this capability. The AHM team have of course taken the work much further, to look at formal models for the support of links in multimedia information and synchronisation issues, and are heavily involved in the design of the SMIL (Synchronized Multimedia Integration Language) protocol.

Other projects such as Matilda have taken a much more holistic approach, and are looking at providing frameworks for supporting all aspects of the development of a hypermedia application or information system, distinguishing between raw data and information, data content, the structure of the data and the inter-relationships between the data.

All these projects and others are contributing to the overall development of support tools and methodologies for hypermedia engineering, although as yet there are none that we know of that claim to provided support for the development lifecycle and process management discussed in this book.

As with all developments in the field of computer engineering, the tools that are eventually developed and used as commonplace by designers will be a pragmatic mix of ideas that have evolved from the research community and the tools that are developed by the commercial software vendors in order to sell more of their products. However, one thing is for sure – we don't have the necessary tools at the moment, but with the phenomenal growth in use of the Internet and the Web, and the resulting headaches for the designers and managers of large information systems, it is only a matter of time before we do.

16.4 Issues for the Future

We are not going to finish this book by too much crystal ball gazing – that is a fool's game when dealing with developments in computer technology – but we can present some of the issues we think are going to become increasingly important. We are of course doing this against the background of a constantly evolving mix of new standards, protocols and products.

Content and Context-based Authoring

As we describe throughout the book, most hypermedia designers and authors today think about linking from the point of view of location – what part of this page should be linked to which other pages. The structural links may be manually or automatically created, but the associative links will be largely manually created, perhaps in response to some overall schematic design process, but the links will be embedded at certain positions in the documents. As more and more information becomes available electronically, people are beginning to focus much more on ways of classifying or describing the content of the data when it is first up-loaded into the system or database.

The whole concept of metadata for unstructured information is becoming as important as it was for structured information in databases, as so many people have always predicted it would. How can you hope to find a piece of information again if you don't 'describe' the nature of its contents when you first enter it into the system. This will aid information retrieval, but it will also help support the process of link creation. The two processes are mutually supportive – you can use information retrieval to create links (this is what you're doing when you use a search engine to identify Web pages) and you can use links to support information retrieval (if someone has taken the time and the effort to make this link, then the information to which it is pointing might be useful).

Typed and semantic links will become increasingly important and, as ever, it will be possible to apply these ideas at many different levels, linking document to document or word to word in meaningful ways. Both the content of the information and its context can be used to help refine the authoring process. As content-based retrieval techniques for non-text data (image, audio, video, etc.) become more developed, they will increasingly be applied to generate links between multimedia documents on the basis of their content, in the same way that links can be generated between text documents using the results of text retrieval systems.

Copyright and IPR

Copyright and Intellectual Property Rights (IPR) are clearly issues that are going to become increasingly important. The Web has very much engendered a culture of 'free to read', and it will be interesting to see if this will be sustained as a result of market forces and if new economic models for authors and information owners to receive payment when people read their material. In the scholarly publishing world, Stevan Harnad (1994) and others have long advocated that journal publishing will move to a 'free to read, pay to publish' model as it all becomes electronic. Commercial entities are likely to recover their costs through advertising as always. But what about the author of the hypertext novel or poem who is trying to make a living out of publishing their material on the Internet?

Advocates of micropayment systems predict that paying to download information from the Internet will become as easy and as relatively painless as using the telephone or watching satellite television. In fact, it is likely that these three technologies will merge at some time in the future so that we will be watching the latest movie one minute and accessing the Web pages of our local supermarket or newspaper the next, all through the same interface. Anything is possible!

How will all these developments affect hypermedia engineering? In a world where potentially anything can be connected to anything, we will have to be careful whether we own the information we want to link to or from. When the Web started to become widely used, some short-sighted governments and organisations started to try to legally prevent people linking to information they didn't own. Such legal challenges arose because the information was being abused, but the principle of not allowing authors to refer to other information on the Internet (i.e link to it) is ridiculous. But are authors in any way legally responsible if they refer their readers to illegal or factually incorrect information? Or can readers sue authors if they incur large costs through following a link in the author's document? In principle, these issues are no different to the same issues that arise in traditional publishing, but because it is so much easier to link information electronically, and the electronic information to which you link can change rapidly, problems can arise that much more easily. Also, if you want to reuse another author's hypermedia document (i.e. to link to it from within your own document collection) do you have the right to copy that document onto your own server under any conditions? Nelson's ideas on transclusions and methods of payment for the reuse of material owned by others will come into their own here.

Taking these ideas a step further, with open hypermedia systems such as Microcosm, it is possible to 'add' links to other author's documents by either 'superimposing' them onto the document by using Microcosm generic links, or, as in the Web version, by embedding HTML commands in the document as it is viewed through a proxy server.

What rights have we to do such things? Do I have the right to publish, or make publicly or commercially available, a linkbase that includes information that will in effect add links to documents over which I have no ownership, even if I make it clear (say, by changing the colour of the link) that this is the case? The hypermedia designers of the future must take all these issues into account when designing their applications.

Distributed Hypermedia Issues

The Web has shown us that distributed hypermedia is possible, but of course, it has also exposed all the problems that this brings with it. One of the most apparent is the need for a universal naming system, so that if you make a link to a file then you know that the link will remain valid irrespective of to wherever that file is moved or however it is renamed in the future. There is also the problem of being able to give guarantees about the amount of time it will take to download a document, which is of course closely related to the issue of caching documents that someone has recently used in case they might want to use them again in the near future. Everyone has experienced the frustration of trying to clear the automatic cache in their favourite Web browser, when they know that the contents of the document has changed but the cache won't let them view the new version. But of course, it is just as frustrating if you have to wait forever to reload a document that you had only been looking at a few minutes previously. These are well known problems in computer science, and increasingly the browsers and document servers will be able to deal with such issues in a more intelligent way.

Building systems to allow for mobile users is also going to become a major issue. Mobile users are going to want access to subsets of hypermedia applications or Websites when they are disconnected from the network or connected by a low bandwidth line. They will need information about whether a link is valid in their current state of connectivity, and/or how long it might take to download the destination file. Designers may need to take such issues into account during the design process.

Cooperative working in distributed systems is also a major issue for the future. In a large organisation, for example, how can users find out who else is accessing the information they are interested in, what is the latest version of a particular report, what is the audit trail of this decision making process? Many of these issues can be described and defined in terms of hypermedia engineering – they were predicted after all in Bush's classic 'As We May Think' article (Bush, 1945) – and the ability to analyse trails and links to support requests for information in a large distributed system is likely to become a standard feature of hypermedia systems in the future, as demonstrated by the MEMOIR project (Pikrakis *et al.*, 1998).

Development Processes and Process Modeling

Development processes for hypermedia will continue to evolve and improve. This will take a number of paths, one of the most significant of which will be the continual improvement of methods for the development of hypermedia (and in particular, Web) applications. In particular, full lifecycle methods (as opposed to simply design and implementation methods) will be developed and refined. The appropriateness of methods for different domains will also be considered – such as determining heuristics for selecting the most appropriate development methods for different hypermedia application domains. The incorporation of development attributes such as adaptability, flexibility and support for creativity into the development methods is also an important future direction.

To support improved development methods there will need to be corresponding improvements in design models, such as HDM (Garzotto, Paolini and Schwabe, 1993). This includes improving their expressiveness in terms of aspects such as modelling user interaction styles, refinement of design languages which complement the graphical notations but provide a basis for reasoning about designs, and consideration of the appropriateness of different design models for different application domains.

Very little attention has yet been paid to hypermedia-specific issues regarding the capture of requirements and the specification of acceptance criteria for hypermedia applications (particularly with regard to usability issues). For an application domain which is ostensibly about supporting the user's information management, there is currently very little attention on how the requirements of different classes of users can be identified and represented. In most cases, this is achieved through relatively informal techniques such as interviews and prototyping. Future research should result in the development of more formal methods of eliciting requirements, resolving conflicts between different requirements (such as a Website's need for advertising funds compared to a user's need for clarity of presentation), and representing requirements in an unambiguous way.

Another area for future improvement is hypermedia development process modelling. At present, most development uses processes adapted from software engineering or similar domains. We will see the development of development processes which are better suited to the hypermedia domain. As a first step in this process, descriptive process modelling will begin to be developed, allowing hypermedia developers to model and then analyse current development practices. Current research is just beginning to look at developing frameworks within which this modelling can occur.

Another important aspect likely to see continual future improvement is techniques for hypermedia product evaluation. This will encompass answers to questions such as: What forms of evaluation are appropriate? What frameworks can be used to support effective evaluation? What intermediate aspects (such as requirements and designs) are suitable for being evaluated? Development of suitable metrics. Development of heuristics to assist in interpretation of metrics. How the results of evaluation can be used to improve both the product and the process which was used in creating the product. How do we plan for the evaluation? What sorts of skills are required to effectively perform evaluation?

Project Scoping

Every business involved in hypermedia development, be that the creation of Websites, CD-ROM titles or SGML documentation, needs to be able to properly budget and plan its hypermedia development projects. This requires an ability to understand the scope of hypermedia projects. Early and accurate scoping of the resource needs of projects is vital to ensure effective project management, risk minimisation, competitive bids for contracts and objective evaluation of bids by clients. As the hypermedia industry matures, clients are becoming more demanding and profit margins are under threat. Without continuous improvement of the scoping and estimation process, it will become increasingly difficult to remain competitive in the hypermedia industry.

There is little knowledge of how to scope and plan projects in the hypermedia domain. As a result, most project planning and subsequent development processes are currently *ad hoc* and ill-defined. In contrast, the characteristics used for scoping software projects are better understood. For instance, approaches such as Function Point Analysis involve considering a system's inputs, outputs, complexity and scope of interface components (or screens), to develop a count of system size which can then be transformed into an effort estimate. Such techniques can be applied quite early in the software lifecycle. No such well developed techniques exist for hypermedia project planners – future improvement will need to identify the important characteristics for early estimation and resource scoping.

Hypermedia scoping research is likely to focus on developing scoping models, accumulating empirical data on existing projects, and understanding the relationships between characteristics of projects and the resources required by those projects. Models, supported by empirical evidence, will provide project management with an explicit understanding of the project characteristics that affect productivity and cost. For instance, it will assist in understanding those characteristics of a development project which can potentially cause large fluctuations in development costs.

Novel Interfaces

For the last decade, windows and direct manipulation interfaces have dominated the market. Most hypermedia systems, including the Web, present link anchors in such systems as highlighted objects (words, pictures, icons, etc.) that the user clicks on with a pointing device to follow the link. There is a case for a more flexible interface to hypermedia systems (Hall, 1994), where users are free to initiate dynamic queries about links (relationships) rather than only being able to access links whose anchors are highlighted in the document. With current interfaces, this is difficult to achieve in a way that users find natural.

The advent of new types of interfaces, such as speech and virtual reality, will enable such flexibility to be introduced into the interface in a much more natural way. The whole issue of speech interfaces to hypermedia systems, for example, is an interesting one to explore. How do you give a spoken command to a Web browser to follow a particular link in the middle of a document? It might be much more natural to describe the object that the link is associated with by speaking the word or the name of the picture, or whatever.

Such interfaces are going to become very important with the development of wearable or more mobile computers. When users are on the move they will not be able to use a mouse and keyboard to navigate around Web pages, and this is another issue of hypermedia engineering that designers are going to have to take into account.

Moving around a virtual world and selecting items with which to interact, such as opening a door to move into a virtual room or selecting a book from a virtual shelf, is essentially another way of presenting a hypermedia interface to an information system. People who play computer games are very familiar with such worlds. At the moment they are very expensive to produce, but increasingly the 2-dimensional world of windows will frustrate users of highly interactive systems. Users will want to customise interfaces to best suit themselves and the task they are performing, and this will increasingly become part of the hypermedia design process.

Agents and Filtering

As in almost every field of computing, intelligent agents will be used to support many aspects of information systems, including search and retrieval, personalisation, customisation, maintenance and classification. They can be used to automatically generate links and to provide personalised hypermedia environments for users. The Microcosm architecture includes a chain of filters, each of which can be a different process that either generates or removes (i.e. filters) links for the user. This has evolved in the MEMOIR system (Pikrakis *et al.*, 1998) to a framework of agents that can provide single or multiple responses to a user's request for information. Such a request could be as simple as the usual hypermedia action of clicking on a highlighted word in a document, which will be resolved by an agent that looks that word up in a linkbase or uses it as the basis for a text search of an appropriate document set.

Agents can be used to personalise the presentation or content of a hypermedia application according to their knowledge of the user or users. In the Web, such agents are being implemented using proxy servers and Java applets. They again represent a move towards more flexible and dynamic interfaces to hypermedia systems. Behind the scenes agents can be used to constantly monitor the information environment, to update links, whether embedded in documents or stored separately in linkbases, and to inform users as required of changes that have taken place, for example when the status of a document has changed. They are going to play a significant role in the future design of hypermedia systems.

16.5 Conclusions

As we write this book, it is clear that the Web community is taking more notice of hypermedia issues. The development of XML (and especially the XLink capabilities) is an illustration of this. Users are expressing the need for more richly linked hypermedia applications, and are beginning to realise that search engines are not the answer to everything. From the discussion in this chapter, it is clear that future hypermedia systems will involve the integration of database systems and search engines with hypermedia linking technology. Part of the design process in future will include an assessment of when to use which specific technologies. When should a link (i.e a relationship) be stored in a database, embedded in a document or resolved dynamically using a search engine or some other knowledge management process, and how do these technologies interact with each other?

It is obvious that hypermedia engineering is barely even an embryonic discipline. We have shown that there is a broad range of issues to be addressed, and many different ways of addressing these. Despite this, little progress has yet been made is creating a consistent, scientific, measurable and repeatable approach to the development of hypermedia. Indeed, we should probably return to the fundamental question of how appropriate it is apply engineering to managing the developing of hypermedia.

It could be claimed that designing applications to manage information is, in many respects, an art rather than an engineering discipline – being based on the creation of complex networks of information which individually carry little meaning, but together convey an effective message. This view is analogous to the situation with writing novels – something which would seem to be obviously art rather than engineering. However, this overlooks the point that much traditional linear writing still makes use of formalised principles and approaches. Structuring a book follows conventional patterns, and once written, editing, correcting, production and delivery are all supported by well established processes.

Returning to the question of whether hypermedia development is art or engineering, we believe that it is both – engineering supporting art. Much of hypermedia development will still be a creative activity, especially with respect to the creation of actual content. We cannot, and should not, try to dictate the creative process, but we can put in place mechanisms (processes, tools, etc.) which provide a framework to support the creative process and help us provide the necessary inputs and use the outputs most effectively.

We mustn't lose sight of the fact that development, or even hypermedia itself is not an 'end': it is only a 'means' for providing information for the sake of developing knowledge which can be used. Development should be carried out within this context – something which is often overlooked.

Appendix 1

Design Principles

A1.1. Design Principles

A large number of hypermedia design checklists and guidelines exist, especially with respect to the Web. In this book we have discussed a number of these design principles. In this appendix we summarise the more significant of these. It is important to note that the justification for these principles varies from supporting cognitive studies to research analysis to current practical experience. In all cases, they must be considered in the broader context of the application goals.

We have not attempted to be exhaustive in this list (there will, after all, always be yet another principle which could be added to cater to specific circumstances). Nor have we tried to categorise the following principles. Indeed, we have simply tried to provide broad principles (with an explanation) instead of specific rules. For example, we state 'keep interfaces simple' rather than 'avoid scrolling text'.

Indeed, the following list is simply intended as a starting point which could be used in at least two different ways: first, it should give a starting point for developing a feeling for good hypermedia design practice; secondly, the following list could be used as a checklist for design reviews. It is also very important to bear in mind that the following principles should always be used within the context of a suitable development process.

Manage bandwidth resources effectively
> Making extensive use of images, audio, animations etc can place heavy burdens on resources – especially communications bandwidths. This can in turn slow down access. Consider alternatives such as using smaller images (and possibly providing a link to the full-size image) and thumbnails, limiting animations, using image and audio file formats which give compression, etc.

Keep screen design simple
> Many hypermedia applications suffer from overly complex screen design. This gives an opportunity to demonstrate coding skill, but results in applications which are confusing and difficult to use to locate appropriate information. As an example, use screen backgrounds which do not detract from the foreground content.

Keep the interface simple
> An overly complex or active interface will distract the user. For example scrolling text and animations will attract a user's

peripheral vision and act as a great distraction. Give the user's the opportunity to focus!

Ensure presentation consistency

The presentation should be consistent. For example, screen layout, modes of emphasis, headings, spacing, etc. should remain consistent in order to minimise the cognitive effort required to interpret each node.

Keep functionality simple

As with the above points, providing unnecessarily complex functionality within an application gives a user too many things to think about and distracts the user from both the users goal and the underlying information being presented.

Avoid the use of cutting edge technology

This can result in two problem areas – lack of stability and lack of support. Stability of the environment can create problems with system crashes, unexpected behaviour, etc. Lack of support means that users may not have access to the hardware, software or experience required to use the application.

Provide location orientation

To avoid disorientation, every node or page in a hypermedia application should contain information which allows the user to identify location. For example, if a hierarchical structure is used, then the page path could be placed at the top of each page, such as:

```
hypermedia/section 1/intro/what is hypermedia
```

Provide location reorientation

To assist a user reorient themselves if they become lost, every page should include a link (or links) to a home page, suitable map, index, table of contents or some other form of representation of the application structure (or in many cases – several of these). In particular, dead-end nodes should be avoided.

Ensure appropriate node size

Users will typically avoid scrolling through a node to locate information unless absolutely necessary. The visibility of important navigation, content and orientation information should be maximised. Similarly, content should not be unnecessarily fragmented. A good rule of thumb is that each node should encapsulate a single core concept.

Ensure a strong structure and communicate this structure explicitly
Users need to be able to develop a mental model or taxonomy of the application structure. This can best be achieved if this structure is made as explicit as possible. As an example, provide an application map and provide a mechanism for showing location on this map.

Provide support for locating information within the application structure
In many cases, users will want to move long distances or gain access to information without knowing the location. Facilities such as search engines can support such goals

Provide evidence of paths already travelled
Navigation can be strongly supported by ensuring that users know when they have already traversed a given link, or visited a given node. An example is the use of changing link anchor colours used in most Web browsers.

Ensure technological compatibility
Many hypermedia applications will be used on systems of varying capability and using different systems. The design should ensure that the application will either work with all possibilities or adapts appropriately to different technologies. For example, with the Web there is often no guarantee that the user will be user a specific browser, so browser-specific facilities should usually be avoided.

Ensure that user customisation does not interfere with presentation
Many hypermedia systems (including Web browsers) allow users to customise aspects such as background colours, screen sizes, etc. The design should ensure that no combination of customisation results in an unusable system.

Avoid focusing the user on the underlying technology
A common mistake in hypermedia design is say something such as 'click *here* for more information on blurbs'. This should be avoided as it focuses the users attention on the underlying technology (such as mouse clicking). An alternative would be to say 'more information on *blurbs* is available'.

Ensure obvious link destinations
The destination of links should be evident from the link context or description. A major cause of inefficiency in use of applications is following links only to discover that the destination is not what was expected.

Maximise structural simplicity

Many elements of an applications structure should be kept simple to minimise navigation effort. Some examples:

- you shouldn't have to jump between nodes to check footnotes.
- links internal to a node should be recognisable as such.
- in lists etc. group material appropriately.
- for sequential material provide next/previous links.

Know your user

Ensure that any presentation metaphor, application structure, etc. is familiar to the users. As an example of a bad design, consider an application for teaching basic physiology which uses an operating theatre metaphor – something with which many users may not be familiar. Knowing the user also implies using appropriate language, jargon, level of detail, etc.

Conversely, the application should be clear about its intended audience so that potential users can evaluate the applications relevance to themselves.

Minimise reader workload

As a general rule, the application should not require the user to do things which can be readily automated. For example, if a mechanism for interaction is provided, and only certain choices are acceptable, then a pull down list might be preferable to a free-form entry field.

Utilise design standards

Many design problems (and especially inconsistencies) can be avoiding by developing (or obtaining) standards and adhering rigidly to these. In particular standards which provide quantifiable guidelines (such as 'all nodes be less than 10k in size') are preferable.

Utilise quality standards

Again, many design problems can be avoided by adopting quality standards. For example, a typical requirement in a quality standard may state that 'which every change, no matter how small, all links should be retested' or 'which every major change, perform an independent aesthetic review on all platforms and do a text-only walkthrough of the application'.

A1.2. Sources

The following sources can be used to obtain additional lists of design principles (indeed these sources were used in assisting the compilation of the above list) and specific design hints and tips:

Yale C/AIM Web Style Guide
   http://info.med.yale.edu/caim/manual/

The Ten Commandments of HTML
   http://www.visdesigns.com/design/commandments.html

Top Ten Mistakes in Web Design
   http://www.sun.com/960416/columns/alertbox/index.
   html

Top Ten Ways to Improve Your Home Page
   http://www.glover.com/improve.html

HTML Bad Style Page
   http://www.earth.com/bad-style/

Elements of HTML style
   http://www.book.uci.edu/Staff/StyleGuide.html

The HyperTerrorist Checklist of WWWeb Design Errors
   http://www.mcs.net/~jorn/html/net/checklist.html

Web Authoring Tips
   http://www.pantos.org/atw/tips.html

Appendix 2

Development Activities

The following is a list of possible development activities which can be incorporated into the development process. Note that the specific groupings given (such as 'management') are not necessarily the most appropriate for a specific process.

Management

Management activities are those activities which contribute to the overall supervision and organisation of the development process. These activities will typically ensure the adequate progression of the development.

- **Project initiation**: this involves the initial concept development, selection of a process and methodologies to follow, and development process initiation. This will often occur in response to a perceived market niche, need or opportunity.

- **Project planning**: covers organisation of activities, timing, work schedules, coordination of resource and skills allocation, and specification of deliverables. This will often involve the use of conventional project management tools (such as project planners and management tools such as GANTT charts). To be performed effectively this requires an awareness of both the activities required for a successful development process and the resourcing required by specific activities. At present this is often based only on experience or general heuristics (such as '1 hour of educational content typically requires 10 hours of authoring effort').

- **Project management**: this encompasses the usual project management operations, such as initiation, coordination, evaluation and administration of activities (typically based on the project plan).

- **Budgeting**: cost analysis and prediction, expenditure management, etc. This will require an awareness of the cost of resources (including 'hidden' costs such as personnel recruitment costs). This will often be particularly difficult as the skills required for effective development are changing rapidly and are typically on the cutting edge of the technology (and hence in short supply and subject to wide variations in cost).

- **Resource management**: this covers resource analysis, resource procurement, allocation, evaluation and utilisation. Different resources will be needed for different development activities. For example, a single computing platform may be needed for the bulk of the development work, but access to a range of platforms may be needed for evaluation purposes). Physical resources include computing hardware (such as computers, scanners, displays, network hardware, storage media, backup facilities), media capture tools (such as video and photographic cameras, and audio equipment), physical space ('where will the content experts work?') and personnel. Logical resources include time, money, and skills.

- **Personnel management**: the effective management of the personnel involved in a development effort is a major concern. This includes analysis of skill requirements (such as programmers, design expertise, user-interface skills, content experts, project managerial skills, etc.), hiring and skill procurement, team building, role assignment, skill development and team management. This can be a particularly difficult task as many of the skills (such as Web 'authoring') are changing rapidly, have a demand much greater than supply and present a particularly difficult moving target.

- **Version control and configuration management**: in many cases, a hypermedia system will be a organic entity in that it will grow, change and expand over the course of the development. As such, it will usually be important that some form of configuration management be used to track and manage the changing system.

- **Project reviews**: a major factor which contributes to the effectiveness of the project management is feedback on progress and problems. These can be partly provided by effective management and consideration of deliverables, but will be supplemented by reviews, walkthroughs, inspections etc. at various stages of the development.

- **Policy management**: management of a project will almost always require an awareness of various factors which impact on the project. In many cases, this should be reflected in a set of suitable development policies. These factors include social (does this system need to be socially relevant, appropriate, etc.), political, legal (including use of trademarks and copyright) and ethical and moral (does the application conflict with social mores?).

- **Standardisation and style**: as with many other forms of development, standards (and the adherence to them) can be important. For example, if a Website is being developed then it may be considered desirable to adopt a 'house standard' for the HTML style to be adopted – to ensure uniformity and consistency. Similarly, consideration needs to be given to the desirability or otherwise of adopting specific data representations (such as JPEG versus GIF images) and information representations (such as adopting SGML as a 'house standard').

- **Test management**: the testing, verification and validation of all aspects of both the development and the resulting product needs to be managed. As with general process management, this is likely to focus on the development and implementation of appropriate test plans. Consideration should be given to not only testing the outcomes of the various activities, but also verifying the processes themselves as a way of improving the process between development projects.

- **Management of documentation**: obviously, an important aspect of any development is documentation. Documentation needs to cover both the development (such as system specifications, design documents, results of prototype evaluations, test specifications and results, etc.), as well as product documentation (installation and user manuals, etc.).

- **Project closure**: finally, at some stage the development project is likely to cease. Consideration needs to be given to winding up the project, reallocating resources, redistributing personnel, etc.

Investigation and Specification

We have grouped all those activities related to gathering information into the category of investigation and specification. These activities will usually revolve around the analysis of specific systems, issues, constraints, resources, etc. which are likely to affect the development in some way (such as a user's needs, resource costs, social constraints or content availability). These investigations should result in an increased knowledge regarding how to effectively develop the system. This knowledge may be as varied as an awareness of why the product the product is being developed, or a comprehensive specification of the required system functionality.

- **Feasibility analysis**: it is important to understand, especially for large projects, whether a project will be feasible. This will be dependant upon a broad range of factors, including financial viability (development costs as compared to product demand or expected gain), cost-benefit analysis, availability of appropriate information sources, and technical viability. An initial step in most developments will be to establish the feasibility of the project. This activity will, to a certain extent, be dependant upon information gained in various other activities (such as an analysis of potential users).

- **Analysis of why**: as with any development process, it is important to acquire an understanding of the purpose and objectives of the application being developed. This will subsequently drive the creation of a set of requirements, and the eventual design and implementation of the system. As an example, consider the difference between the objectives of an educational system designed to assist learning about Shakespearean language and a catalogue system developed for presenting products for sale.

- **Analysis of users**: the development of a system will be greatly affected by the expected users. For example, obviously an educational system will be very different (in terms of content, interaction, navigation methods) if developed for five year-olds as compared to 20 year-olds. An understanding needs to be developed of the target audience: who is likely to use the system to be created, the benefits which are expected for the users, and the characteristics of the users.

- **Analysis of usage**: related to the users of the system is an understanding of how the system will be used. This includes the types of information or knowledge which users expect to gain, the interaction patterns which will be acceptable, the routes of user usage and thinking and responses to the usage. For example, access mechanisms for an encyclopaedia (where indexing and searching will predominate) will be very different from access mechanisms for an educational title (where browsing and guided tours might be more appropriate). An understanding of expected or desired usage patterns will affect the way in which we design the behaviour of the system, the link structures, the interaction mechanisms and the content. Also, the usage patterns may vary between users or groups of users, indicating the need for multiple systems or patterns, or customisability. The use of the system will also impact on the need for security.

- **Analysis of what**: we can consider what material is required in the system. This will include the broad subject area, data requirements, information captured by this data, educational requirements, expected semantics of the information, the level of detail required and the breadth of content.

- **Analysis of where**: in many cases, the location and availability of the information will be significant. There may be a reason for using a specific platform (such as provision to a specific category of users who only have access to a certain platform) or technology (such as the broad accessibility provided by the Web).

- **Analysis of how**: how the information system is to be supported needs to be considered. This will include consideration of the navigation mechanisms which we may want to use, how we will support the information structures, how we will support information access, how we support customisation, and how security can be managed. We are not considering how to implement the system (this is a design consideration), but what are the available options and imposed constraints.

- **Prototyping**: developing a prototype is a valuable mechanism for eliciting information in the process of understanding the system to be developed. The information gained will depend upon the type of prototype developed, but can include user response to a specific look and feel, effectiveness of different interaction mechanisms, and examples of information structures. The prototype can cover anything from a simple mock-up of a screen layout to a detailed but simplified application used to demonstrate behaviour and interaction functionality.

- **Boundary analysis**: in every case the hypermedia system under development will exist within the context of a broader information environment. This environment may be another hypermedia system or system infrastructure (such as Web), or an existing source of information (such as paper-based information). In either case, consideration needs to be given to the interface between the old and the new systems, as well as any other systems which may coexist with the application under development. This would include consideration of the interactions between the systems (and any possible synergy which may be able to be used) and the degree of seamlessness which may be desirable.

- **Consideration of implications**: an application does not exist within a void – it will be influenced by the environment in which it exists. This environment is social, political, ethical and legal, and will have implications for the way in which the system is developed and used. This environment and its implications need to be adequately understood.

- **Analysis of content availability and constraints**: information is obviously central to hypermedia applications. The ability to obtain (within an acceptable cost, and at an acceptable quality) suitable information will impact significantly on the ability to develop a suitable application. Obtaining this information may not be straightforward. It may need to be generated from scratch (requiring appropriate content experts) or captured from elsewhere. In addition, there may be constraints which affect the ability to use the information. For example, it may have associated ongoing usage or royalty costs or copyright constraints.

- **Analysis of application maintainability**: in most cases, hypermedia applications will require considerable ongoing development, evolution or maintenance (particularly where the application is providing access to a dynamically changing system). We need to consider the ways in which the system and its underlying information will evolve, ongoing use of the system, and how information will be updated and maintained.

- **Functional and non-functional requirements elicitation**: the results of many of the above activities can be combined into the final specification of the system requirements. This would cover both functional requirements (such as the required support for interaction and information utilisation mechanisms) and non-functional requirements (such as performance and maintainability).

System Design

A number of activities are related to the design of the overall system, or affect all or many parts of the system. For example, designing the overall system architecture will provide a form for the system, and designing a system look and feel will affect the presentation across all components. We have grouped these activities under the category of system design.

- **Platform and environment selection**: based on the system requirements, we can select the platforms and environments under which we will undertake the development, and on which the final system will operate. This will cover selection of hardware (what computer systems must the final system operate on, what hardware will be used for the development, what information capturing tools we will use, etc?), environments (such as which operating systems will be supported), authoring tools (will we use a commercial authoring tool, or use a customised approach) and presentation engines. The exact components which require resolution will be dependant upon the system requirements. If we are developing a Website, then we may need to consider factors such as whether the site will be hosted by an Internet Service Provider (in which case we need to look at the facilities provided by the ISP), or whether we shall be supporting our own hardware.

- **Application paradigm**: early in the design process (if not even earlier in the original analysis) we will need to select an appropriate application paradigm. In many cases, this will be controlled by the specific application. For example, if the requirements are specifically for a Website then the selection is implicit in this requirement. If the requirement is simply for a system to support an educational goal, then we may have more leeway, and will need to decide between a Web-based application and various standalone alternatives, where the choice between paradigms such as score scripting and iconic flow control will depend (at least partially) upon the type of material being presented.

- **Develop system architecture**: the development of a system architecture can be one of the most critical steps. As pointed out by Rowe, Leaney and Lowe (1996), when we are developing an architecture we are creating a form for the system solution at a time when the implications of the form are probably least well understood. The development of a system architecture will encompass separation of hardware and software functionality, and an identification of system functional components and interactions between these components. For example, we may identify the need for a search engine which interfaces to the hyperbase, which in turn is supported by high-capacity storage hardware.

- **Allocation of system resources**: the system under development will have available a certain set of resources (processing power, network bandwidth, memory, screen real estate, etc.). In many cases, these resources are pushed to the limit by the demands of hypermedia applications. These resources need to be allocated in an appropriate fashion to the various system components, and mechanisms for managing the resources need to be designed. A very simple example is Web applications where bandwidth is constrained. It may be decided that text data and interface elements will always be given priority over image, video and audio data. Video playback can be very processor intensive and may severely constrain concurrent indexing mechanisms. This could be handled through the appropriate use of resource allocation and management.

- **Design application attributes**: at some stage of the design a series of general attributes will need to be considered. For example, the structure of the application will be greatly affected by attributes such as typical node (or page) size, supported link mechanisms, methods of mixing media, etc.

- **Design of content scope, depth and granularity**: an activity which will almost always be required is consideration of the information space or content to be included. The scope of the information space (i.e. where are the bounds of what is included), the depth of the content within this space and the granularity of the information presented are all important considerations. For example, if we are developing a Web-based application to support access to the data provided by a nation's bureau of statistics, then we may need to consider what data to include – do we include just the raw data, internal reports on future predictions, newspaper articles analysing the implications of the data, government policy on data collection mechanisms? The answer to these type of questions will relate back to the original identified purpose of the application and the application requirements.

- **Information representation design**: the mechanism which we use to represent the information which underlies the application is one of the most significant developmental considerations. For example, if we are developing a Web application, then the most obvious possibility is that the information is captured in HTML documents. This may not, however, be the best option. An alternative might be to use a more general SGML representation (designed to fit the application more consistently) with filters developed to map the SGML into the required HTML documents. Other alternatives include options such as storing the data in a hypermedia database (or *hyperbase*) and having it dynamically retrieved and built into HTML via suitable CGI scripts. Whatever the method, it needs to be designed with a view to satisfying the requirements as effectively as possible (including non-functional requirements such as maintainability).

- **Design information viewpoints**: the same underlying data and information can be presented in numerous ways, thereby radically changing how it is perceived (consider, for example, the perspective placed on much economic information by different political parties). It is not sufficient in designing hypermedia systems to consider just the data to include. In many, if not most, cases we also need to consider the viewpoint onto this data we wish to support (the exceptions will be where we are attempting to provide a service for accessing raw data, such as statistical information). This viewpoint will be reflected in how we organise the information, what navigation structures we support, where we place emphasis, and the information presentation. For example, if we omit links between related concepts then we are actively de-emphasising the relationship.

- **Design access mechanisms**: the information contained in a hypermedia application can be used and accessed in many ways – such as indexing, searching and browsing. We need to design the mechanisms we consider appropriate for the application under development, and how these should be integrated. At what points in the application should searching be permitted? How will this searching be supported (dynamically searching the information repositories, searching through static tables generated offline)? What types of indexes do we wish to support? How do the users get access to the search mechanisms? These types of questions are at the core of the types of functionality and interaction we wish to support.

- **Design information taxonomies and structures**: an important aspect of the development of information systems is the way in which we use them to retrieve information. As explained well by Urr (1991), our ability to retrieve information is influenced by our ability to conceptualise the structuring patterns being used, and these structuring patterns are dependant upon useful schemes of classification and information organisation, or information taxonomies. To ensure that the access mechanisms which are developed are effective, we need to design suitable information taxonomies. This means considering the overall information patterns, and then refining these into specific structures. For example, in a recent development of an educational case study (looking at the development of a software system – for use in a software engineering course), the overall information structure appeared as in

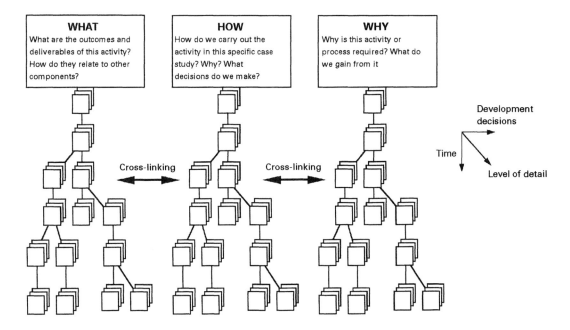

Figure A2-1

Overall information structure for a software development process case study. This case study looked at the application of process to developing a specific software product (in this case it was an elevator control simulation system). The information space was separated into three distinct but parallel 'regions' with matching structures which were made explicit to the user, thereby facilitating the users ability to effectively navigate

Figure A 2-1. An example of a methodological approach to this activity is the use of Entity-Relationship modelling in RMM (Isakowitz, Stohr and Balasubramanian, 1995).

● **Design navigation structures**: related to the information structures (and information viewpoints) are the navigation structures we wish to support. We need to design the paths around the information space that allow a user to browse and navigate. This will need to take into account our overall objectives, the viewpoints we wish to support, and the expected routes of use and user thinking. This activity is one of the most critical, and unfortunately one of the most overlooked – partly because of its difficulty, and partly because of our current lack of understanding as to how to carry this out effectively. It is important to bear in mind that the navigation structures will be greatly influenced by the type of application being constructed. An educational systems will be very different from an information repository which will be very different from a reference work. Also, we can have multiple layers of information navigation structures supported within a single application.

- **Design templates**: in many cases we will wish to design templates for use in the detailed design of various components of the system. These templates can be used to ensure a consistent look and feel (described shortly) by using screen templates or to ensure a consistent information structure by using information templates, as supported to a certain extent by SGML Document Type Definitions (DTD). Templates have the potential to ensure consistency and promote reuse whilst saving development effort.

- **Storyboarding**: storyboarding is a well accepted and well developed design technique. Borrowed originally from animation, storyboarding allows the system structure to be considered, evaluated and refined. Fisher (1994) provides an excellent introduction to the purpose and use of storyboards within multimedia and hypermedia, including how to manage the idea of interactivity within storyboarding.

- **Hyperbase design**: in many cases, especially for large systems, a hypermedia database (or *hyperbase*) will be used to manage the data within the application. The relationship between the hyperbase and the other system components will have been defined by the system architecture, but the data structures within the hyperbase and mechanisms for accessing this data will need to be considered and designed. As commercial hyperbases become more widely available, this activity will be simplified.

- **Design of info capture protocols**: one of the most time-consuming activities (at least at present) in hypermedia development is information capture. This process can be made more effective if suitable protocols are set up which manage information capture. For example, if a project involves the migration of a large amount of legal information from paper documents to hypermedia, then we could set up procedures for scanning the documents, using Optical Character Recognition (OCR) techniques to convert the scanned images, and then using suitable information analysis filters to map the documents into relevant SGML documents. We need to identify the procedures to use and the information filters which are required.

- **Design of global look and feel**: it is invariably important (especially from a user perspective) that the application have a consistent look and feel. We need to consider how this will be achieved. A typical mechanism used in many applications is to adopt an appropriate metaphor. For example, the CD-ROM 'Investigating Lake Illuka' develops investigation and problem solving skills. This uses as the central metaphor a lake environment around which the user can navigate. Such metaphors provide both a degree of consistency and a useful context for the user.

- **Design navigation cues**: the user will obviously need to be able to navigate around the information space. During the design of an application we need to consider how the user will be able to identify the navigation paths available to them. In simple Web applications this is achieved through highlighting textual anchors in some ways. Anything more complex than this simple example requires considerable thought. Navigation cues in image data are difficult to provide (typically being achieved by stating 'this is a clickable image' or making the content obviously interactive – such as making it look like a 'button'). Alternatively, we can avoid navigation cues (or at least the 'button' syndrome) altogether, and allow the user to select content and request any associated links. Whatever approach is adopted, it needs to be consistent and reliable, or the user will lose confidence with a subsequent loss of effective navigation.

- **Design context cues**: as discussed at length early in the book, our ability to extract information from presented data is dependant (at least in part) on the context in which the data is provided. We need to ensure that in designing systems we make this context clear and unambiguous. As a trivial example, in the example given previously in Figure 4-6 we could readily provide three different coloured backgrounds for the three different information regions. This would allow the user to easily understand the purpose of the information being presented ('is it what, how or why?'). Consideration of context is especially important where the user can easily and quickly jump from one context to another without the benefit of an associative link (as would be the case when using indexing rather than browsing).

- **Design security protocols**: there will be cases where we are developing systems which require security for one reason or another. For example, we may have university course material being placed onto a Website which we wish to only make available to registered students, and to provide mechanisms for allowing those students to submit coursework in a secure fashion. The specific security mechanisms will be highly dependant upon the architecture of the system, the sensitivity of the information being protected, and the required level of granularity of protection (e.g. do all users have the same level of access, or are there different categories?)

- **Design tour engines and required tours**: for a number of application domains, especially educational systems, we will wish to provide navigation mechanisms which are more controlled than the more general associative linking. A common example of this is where we wish to guide students along a specific 'learning' path through the information space. In the system shown in Figure 4-6, we have implemented a CGI engine which allows us to specify sequences of arbitrary pages as a tour. The student starts one of a selected number of tours at an opening page, and can then follow that tour by selecting the tour button on each page. At any stage they can deviate from the tour by browsing, but when they again select the tour button, they are returned to the place where they left the tour. Such a mechanism gives a greater degree of flexibility, but requires the use of a tour engine of some form, and the design of tours which are appropriate to the context.

Component Design

Under the category of component design we have grouped those activities which revolve around the design of specific elements of the system.

- **Detailed hardware design**: the specific hardware systems will need to be designed, including aspects such as networking, storage, firewalls, information capture infrastructure, etc. The design will need to take into account the integration of these components into a working system.

- **Design of information capture mechanisms**: the design of information capture protocols was mentioned above. The individual capturing mechanisms will also have to be designed. A simple example would be the design of a filter which is used to parse raw text documents and identify structuring elements (which may be recorded using SGML, automatically marked up as HTML, or decomposed and stored in a hyperbase). More complex examples would be the design of tools to aid in automated or semi-automated segmentation of images, video or audio.

- **Design information structures**: having earlier designed the coarse level information structures, the specific structure now needs to be defined. This would, for example, include the design of the purpose and focus of each individual node, and the way in which the nodes are interlinked. The activity should result in a complete understanding of the scope and topology of the information space.

- **Design search engine and support mechanisms**: if a search engine is being used then the engine itself must be designed, as well as the mechanisms which will support the search engine. This would include the design of tools which generate the data used by the search engine, and which then analyse this data. The integration of the search engine and associated tools into the overall system also needs to be considered.

- **Node authoring**: this activity involves operations such as content allocation, screen layout, presentation design etc., in other words, the design of each individual node. A typical procedure might be the slice design used within RMM. This activity will often require a considerable degree of creativity and possibly content expertise.

- **Link authoring**: in a similar vein to node authoring, link authoring involves the creative design of the specific link mechanisms (consistent with the overall information structure). This will include the detailed design of anchor locations and trigger mechanisms.

- **Link engine design**: where a specific link engine or link services mechanism is being used, the relevant aspects of this must be designed. The extent of this activity will depend heavily upon whether a commercial system which provides link services is being used (such as Microcosm (Hall, Davis and Hutchings, 1996)) and the extent of customisation which is desirable and possible.

- **Installation engine design**: unrelated to the specific product, but still very important, are the design of mechanisms for installing the application. Even if the application is Web-based, there will often be the requirement to install specialised components. For example, a lot of Websites now make wide use of assorted browser plug-ins. Consideration needs to be given to how installation of these additional components will be supported (simply a link to the Website of the relevant plug-in provider, or is something more sophisticated appropriate?).

- **User feedback mechanisms**: in many cases (especially for applications which are networked), user feedback can be important. This feedback may be to the developers ('what do you think of my Web pages?') or to other categories of users ('here is the coursework associated with the course presented on this Website!'). The design and integration of these feedback mechanisms will need to take into account how the feedback is generated and delivered.

- **User evaluation mechanisms**: a growing number of Websites use various mechanisms to collect statistics on the use of the Website (the simplest being a trivial access counter). This type of evaluation can be important to analysing the usage patterns of the application or site. It can be used to highlight information which is under or over-utilised, navigation paths which are never followed, etc. This knowledge can then be used to refine and improve the application. For this to occur we need to design into the system mechanisms for capturing appropriate usage statistics.

- **Detailed run-time behaviour design**: where the application provides complex behaviour patterns we need to design this behaviour. For example, a sophisticated application may be developed which build up a profile of the reactions of different uses and adapts the navigation structures based on these profiles. The mechanism to be support this needs to be designed. Typical examples where this is beginning to occur are Websites that incorporate active or intelligent agents, for example to provide a news source customised to the interests of individual users.

- **Design of synchronisation mechanisms**: obviously, temporal media can play a significant role in hypermedia applications. The design of the mechanisms to be used to support the synchronisation of these media, and their integration into the overall system needs to be considered. This functionality may be supported by the development tools or authoring system being used, in which case consideration can be restricted to the level of synchronisation which is needed. Score or cast scripting authoring tools are well suited to this type of problem.

- **Tour design**: having designed at an abstract level the required tours, the details of the specific tours through the information space can also be considered. This will need to take into account complex factors such as learning theories, desired educational outcomes, and user profiles. The design will have to include the tour routes, the degree of flexibility to be allowed, how the tour is conducted, etc.

- **Interface element design**: the system being developed is likely to incorporate specific interface elements which need to be designed. Examples would include Java applets, three-dimensional VRML spaces, animations, etc. Each of these has to be designed within the context of the overall system, the interactions which are being supported, and the system interface.

- **Design security mechanisms**: where security is being considered, the security mechanisms need to be designed in detail. This may include password protection, encryption mechanisms, etc., and is likely to require the design of components to support this, such as appropriate CGI script or applets.

Production

Having designed the system in detail, the various components can be implemented and integrated into a working useable system. We have grouped all activities which produce items (other than just documentation, plans, ideas or understanding) into the production category.

- **Hardware purchase and setup**: the hardware required for both the system development and maintenance, and the system operation must be acquired and set up. This will usually be carried out very early in the process as most other implementation activities rely on access to the appropriate hardware.

- **Organise copyright permissions**: where necessary, permission must be obtained for use of copyright material. The specific details will depend upon the way in which the information is expected to be used.

- **Presentation engine**: the presentation engine needs to be implemented. If the interface is being custom built, then this will involve use of suitable tools in programming the presentation engine. For example, this may require developing or adapting a HTTP server which builds pages (as they are requested) from an underlying hyperbase or using a language such as Visual Basic to create a presentation interface. Alternatively, specific tools may be used to generate the presentation mechanisms.

- **Link engine**: where necessary, the link engine (and associated link services) will need to implemented. Again, this may involve using or adapting existing system components, or building a link engine from scratch for a dedicated purpose.

- **Information filters**: where filters are being used to assist in the information capture, these will need to be implemented. Various tools can be used to assist in this process.

- **Content creation**: this involves the creation of content which is required and cannot be obtained from elsewhere. This may involve the entering of new text, image generation, audio recording, the creation of animations, etc. This activity can often be incredibly time consuming, and requires the skills of content or domain experts.

- **Content capture**: where content is pre-existing it will need to be captured. This can incorporate scanning in of texts and images, video digitisation, etc. This, along with the following two activities, are often the single most labour- and time-intensive activities to be carried out and can represent a very large proportion of the development costs.

- **Content manipulation**: once the content has been captured it needs to be converted into a form which is appropriate for use in the application. With text this can involve the use of OCR to convert scanned pages into digital text and the use of conversion filters to identify the structure of the text. With other media we may wish to change the data representation for the purpose of storage, compression or transmission. Additionally, as conversion techniques are still flawed (for example, OCR is still not completely accurate), considerable effort and resources can often be spent cross-checking the conversion process.

- **Content editing**: having captured the content we will often want to edit it in some way to highlight or extract specific elements. For example, we may have an image of the US President, amongst a number of other people. If the President is the focus of the information being presented, we may want to edit the image to highlight or extract that part of the image containing the President. Similar operations can be used on other forms of media.

- **Storage of content**: as the content captured or created needs to be stored. This can be in a hyperbase, in an ordinary file system (which would therefore need setting up and managing) or distributed across a network.

- **Generation of interface elements**: elements used to support aspects of the interface (such as Java applets and CGI scripts) will need to be implemented. Often this will require specific programming skills (which are currently changing rapidly).

- **Node authoring**: the individual hypermedia nodes need to be authored. This will involve combining the various media into the specific nodes, which may be a physical composition (where the media become part of the node), a logical composition (where the nodes are effectively views onto underlying data stored separately, and which may therefore be part of multiple nodes), or a hybrid (such as in HTML – where the text is part of the node, but the images are stored separately). If the design of the nodes has been carried out effectively then this activity should be relatively mechanical in nature.

- **Link authoring**: the interlinking of nodes needs to be implemented to create the information structures. This may be through the addition of anchors and links to nodes (as in HTML), or through the separate specification of links in a linkbase without modifying the information nodes (as in Microcosm (Hall, Davis and Hutchings, 1996)). As with the implementation of nodes, if the design is sufficient then this should be a relatively mechanical (if somewhat time-consuming) process. It is worth pointing out that, in practice, the design and implementation aspects of node and link authoring are often carried out as part of the same activity.

- **Development of installation engines**: where required, the installation engines for the application will need to be implemented.

- **System integration**: finally, the various components of the system will need to be progressively integrated. How this is carried out will, to a large extent, be dependant upon the particular process model being used. For example, if a top-down development approach has been adopted, then it is likely that the overall system structure will be implemented at an early stage and the individual elements can be integrated into this structure as they are developed. Alternatively, with a bottom-up approach it is more likely to require significant integration of major components of the system as they eventuate.

There are a number of additional activities which are not directly related to the detailed implementation of the application, but can still be considered part of the production. These are particularly relevant for mass-production items for commercial distribution. This includes production of the release version of the applications (reproduction, packaging, etc.), distribution, sales and promotion. These activities are beyond the scope of this book and are usually the domain of specialist publishers or related organisations.

Maintenance

It will be rare for a hypermedia system to be developed which does not require maintenance of some sort. At the most trivial level, this will involve simple corrective maintenance or refinements as feedback is obtained on the system usage. At a more significant level, in many cases the underlying information will evolve or expand. Whatever the case, we have grouped together in this category all those activities which occur after the 'release' of the application for use.

It is worth pointing out that many of the activities carried out during the development of an application will be similar to the activities carried out during the maintenance of that application. Rather than reiterate these activities, we look at those which differ, or group them in different ways.

- **Maintenance planning**: the maintenance of systems is often left as somewhat of an afterthought. This can create significant problems for several reasons. First, the maintainability of an application needs to be built into the application during the original development. It is not something which can be added into the application after it is ostensibly completed. Also, the effort required for maintenance can be quite significant. This needs to be considered during the original budgeting and planning. The maintenance of a system should be carefully planned and managed.

- **Analysis of maintenance requirements**: during the original development, we should analyse the maintenance requirements of the system. Is the underlying data going to evolve over time (such as changing statistics, product lines or tax legislation)? Are the users going to change over time? Is the technology being used going to evolve. This last point is particularly significant. For example, Websites which appeared cutting edge even 12 months ago often already appear dated. We need to be clear about or requirements for how the system needs to be maintained.

- **Analysis of effectiveness**: progressive improvement of an application will be heavily dependant upon how effectively the application has achieved its goals. To determine this, we need to obtain feedback from users and monitor how they have been using the system. If the system design included collection of usage patterns, then we can analyse these to determine how the system is being used, and consequently how it should be changed.

- **Corrective maintenance**: corrective maintenance involves the correction of errors or problems with a system. These errors may take the form of incorrect information (which requires capture or creation and preparation of new information) incorrect structuring (we may have partitioned the information incorrectly for our goals or needs), and incorrect linking (which can include overlinking and underlinking, links which are inappropriate or confusing, etc).

- **Adaptive maintenance**: adaptive maintenance involves modifying a system to adapt to a changing environment or conditions. For example, as the Web evolves we may wish to take advantage of changes which occur (such as incorporating suitable applets into an application which was developed before Java became widely used). Alternatively, we may wish to use enhancements in hardware performance or migrate the application to additional platforms or environments (such as developing a Macintosh version as well as a Windows version).

- **Perfective maintenance**: perfective maintenance is where the applications underlying functionality is enhanced. For example, we may wish to extend the information space underlying the application or improve the search mechanisms provided. In general, the success with which this can be achieved will be dependant upon the flexibility incorporated into the original design.

- **Maintenance of documentation**: a major factor affecting our ability to maintain a system is the quality of the documentation. This will be true on an ongoing basis, so it is important that all documentation be maintained along with the system itself.

Verification, Validation and Evaluation

We have grouped all activities relating to testing and evaluation into a category of activities. In general, these activities are not aimed at producing the system itself, but at ensuring that the development occurs in an appropriate fashion. In many cases, the specific activities in this category will be dependant upon the specific development process which is adopted. We have, however, given a representative list of activities.

- **Test planning**: as with any aspect of the development process, the testing and evaluation needs to be adequately planned to ensure that it is carried out in an appropriate manner. This will require the creation of testing schedules, test styles, elements to be tested, responsibilities for testing, etc.

- **Prototype evaluation**: if a prototype is used to assist in the capture of requirements and assist in understanding the development, then the prototype will need to be evaluated. This may include consideration of the style of interface, the way in which the prototype is used, the navigation structures which effective, etc. In general, the particular type of evaluation will obviously be heavily dependant upon the purpose for which the prototype was developed.

- **Requirements verification**: once the requirements of the system have been developed, these requirements can be tested against the objectives of the system. If relevant, they can also be checked with the client for whom the system is being developed. Other possibilities include evaluating the requirements for consistency and completeness.

- **Design evaluation**: a design evaluation will ensure that the design is consistent with the requirements of the system. This may involve simulated testing of the designed system, tracing design elements to the relevant requirements (and hence identifying requirements which have not been met), walkthroughs and reviews of the design, and other similar testing procedures.

- **Component testing**: as each element (such as nodes, link structure, interaction element, search engine, information filter) is developed it can be tested. For example, with nodes this may simply be presenting the node to a user to see whether the relevant concept is conveyed satisfactorily.

- **Integration testing**: as with any system involving complex interactions amongst many components, the overall system may fail even when the individual components appear to work correctly. This can be a result of mismatches in the interfaces between the components, for example, the individual link structures may be correct, but when combined the overall cognitive effect may be to confuse the user due to a unacceptably complex information space topology.

- **Interaction verification**: the interaction provided by the system needs to be verified. For example, in a system which uses active agents to dynamically adapt to the user's usage patterns, the interaction between the user, the agents, and the remainder of the system would need to be verified.

- **Navigation verification**: the overall navigation support of the system needs to be verified. This would include consideration of the links and how they are presented, the support for providing the user with a context after each navigation operation, the effectiveness of the overall structuring taxonomy, etc.

- **Information verification**: the application content also needs to be verified. This covers aspects such as evaluation of content completeness and correctness, content relevance, content consistency, the partitioning of the content into nodes or pages, etc.

- **Multi-platform and multi-environment evaluation**: where the system is to be used on multiple platforms or environments, it is important that the system performance be evaluated on each possible combination. This is especially true if the development was restricted to a single platform. The most common example of this style of evaluation is checking the presentation of Web pages (which were developed on one system) using a variety of different Web browsers and machines. There have been many cases where pages were developed and checked on one machine and then released, only to realise that they did not work correctly on alternative browsers (a common cause of this is the use of browser-specific HTML tags or functionality).

- **Performance evaluation**: although the static presentation of a system is important, it also needs to have its dynamic performance evaluated. In other words, are there cases where conditions lead to an unacceptable deterioration of performance? This may be especially true in cases where the hypermedia system is sharing resources with other concurrent processes or programs, leading to either a reduction in the available resources (such as processing speed, memory or bandwidth) or complete unavailability of resources (such as when audio channels on a sound card are being used by another application).

- **Acceptance testing**: finally, the overall system can undergo acceptance testing. If the system has been developed for a client, this is likely to be the final step before the system is handed over. The acceptance testing will be relative to the original system requirements.

Documentation

Rather than provide a long list of documentation activities, it is sufficient to point out that most of the activities listed above will have a component associated with documenting the results of the activity. In many cases (except maybe implementation activities), the documentation produced will be the major deliverable from each activity. The only additional activity it is worth mentioning is the planning of the documentation activities.

- **Documentation planning**: as any systems developer or project manager will be aware, it is very simple to cut costs, and especially time, by delaying (and eventually avoiding altogether) documentation. Documentation, however, is critically important to an effective development process, and as such needs to be planned and managed effectively. This will include an identification of the documents which need to be produced, the scope of the documents, responsibilities, version management, and timing.

Appendix 3

Development Plans and Checklists

The following sections contain both typical outlines for documents resulting from typical development activities and checklists which provide a basis for developmental reviews. It is important to note that the document outlines given are not necessarily intended to be used 'as-is'. Rather, they should be adapted to suit specific circumstances, or used as an indication of the type of issues which need to be addressed.

Much of the information for these plans and checklists derives from the systems and software process management literature. In particular, *Software Engineering Fundamentals* (Behforooz and Hudson, 1996) is invaluable for further reading.

A3.1. Application Development Plan

Table A3–1

Typical hypermedia application development plan outline

I.	Document scope
II.	References, Terminology, Acronyms
III.	Application description
	content, functionality, interfaces, project deliverables
IV.	Contract description (if appropriate)
	contractual commitments and obligations
V.	Product model selection
VI.	Development process selection
	process selection, adaptation, management
	methodologies
VII.	Work breakdown
	project tasks, development activities, reviews
	roles
VIII.	Scheduling
	timing of tasks and activities, milestones, reviews
	responsibilities
IX.	Resourcing
	resources (physical, personnel, skills, time, tools)
	resource management
X.	Risk management
	risk identification, risk management
	contingency planning
XI.	Project management
XII.	Standards and procedures

Table A3–2

Development plan checklist

Is the scope clearly defined? Is the scope consistent with goals? Is the project suitably bounded?

Is terminology defined? Appropriate? Consistent with common usage?

Have all resources been identified? Are resources acceptable? Available? Are tools available? Cost-effective?

Have risk areas been identified? Is risk assessment valid? Are the risks suitably analysed and documented? Are risks acceptable? Is risk containment suitable? Is there a suitable commitment to risk management?

Are cost estimates reasonable? Acceptable? Consistent with experience? Were multiple methods used? Are cost management procedures in place?

Are time schedules reasonable? Acceptable? Consistent with experience? Were multiple methods used? Are scheduling reviews in place?

Is suitable documentation produced? Is the required documentation suitably defined? Is the level of documentation consistent with the project scope? Have standards been defined?

Is the project manageable? Are milestones suitable? Is the reporting frequency suitable? Are the management techniques consistent with company culture and policy?

Does the process include suitable review points?

A3.2.   Application Quality Assurance Plan

Table A3–3

Typical hypermedia application quality plan outline

I.	Assurance plan purpose
II.	Quality assurance management
	organisation, roles, tasks, responsibilities
III.	Reviews
	document and deliverable reviews
	walkthroughs, audits
IV.	Review procedures
	purpose, responsibilites, approaches
	procedures
	entrance and exit requirements
V.	Scheduling
VI.	Traceability
	procedures for ensuring traceability in the development process
	procedures for defect tracing
VII.	Quality assurance tools and techniques
VIII.	Reporting
	Documentation standards
IX.	Review failure procedures
X.	Training
XI.	Risk management
XII.	References and related documents

Table A3–4

Possible scheduled reviews

Development Plan Review

Quality Plan Review

Test Plan Review

Evaluation and review of development tools

Application Requirements Review

Preliminary Design Review

Content and Structure Design Review

Navigation Design Review

Functional Design Review

Application Content and Structure Implementation Review

Navigation Implementation Review

Functional Implementation Review

Maintenance Review

System Hand-over Review

Table A3–5

Quality hypermedia attributes

	Functional
Navagability	Suitable support for navigating within the information space
Info. maps/overviews	Suitable support for users developing a mental model of application structure
Info. trails	User understanding of path travelled
Searching and indexing	Support for locating specific information
Info. contextualisation	Ability to extract valid information from provided data
Info. security and cost	Appropriate management of ownership of information sources
Presentation	Suitable metaphors, appropriate presentation support for interpretation of information.
Customisation	Support for customisation to specific user preferences.
Effective use of resources	Efficiency in use of processing, memory, network bandwidth.
Temporal media	Suitable synchronisation, interaction, presentation.
	Non-Functional (Information)
Link validity	Correctness, relevance, completeness, integrity of information associations and links.
Content validity	Correctness, relevance, completeness, integrity of information content.
Concept organisation	Appropriate and effective partitioning and structural arrangement of concepts.
Consistency/ seamlessness	Structure, functionality and presentation are consistent throughout the application. Application is suitably integrated with related applications.
	Non-Functional (Other)
Efficiency	No or low impact on other applications.
Maintainability	Structured in a way which supports maintenance and evolution. Suitable documentation levels.
Reusability	Ability to utilise elements of analysis, design or implementation.
Reliability and robustness	Appropriate tolerance to incorrect usage or failures in associated systems.
Testability	All aspects testable and verifiable against suitable criteria.
Interoperability/ portability	Meets ability to accommodate growth and change.
Political/social aspects	Suitable content and structure for intended, prospective or possible users.
Cost effectiveness	Cost of developing, maintaining and using application is consistent with gains provided.

Table A3–6

Quality plan checklist

Does the quality plan cover all aspects of the development process?

Are all aspects of the quality plan appropriate for the given application, context and domain?

Is the development team committed to quality assurance? Does the development team understand the purpose of quality assurance?

Are suitable skills available for managing quality? Is suitable training in place for developing these skills?

Are the roles and responsibilities clearly defined? Is suitable staffing available? Are lines of authority suitably defined?

Is the quality assurance process suitably managed?

Is the documentation clearly defined? Appropriate? Adhere to suitable standards?

Are procedures defined for quality failures? Is traceability managed and effective?

Are review procedures defined? Practical? Cost-effective?

A3.3.   Application Requirements

Table A3–7

Typical hypermedia application requirements specification outline

I.	Introduction
	1. Purpose
	2. Application overview
	3. System scope
	4. Definitions, acronyms, terminology
	5. Documents and references
II.	General Description
	1. Content description
	2. Functional description
	3. Application and development constraints
	4. Threats, competing applications
	5. Related work, applications, systems
	6. Assumptions and dependencies
III.	Users
	1. User classification
	2. User expectations and needs
	3. . . .
IV.	Application Information Requirements
	1. Application goals
	2. Content
	3. Structure
	4. User documentation and support
	5. . . .
V.	Application Functional Requirements
	1. Navigation functionality
	Link transitions, orientation, reorientation, maps, etc.
	2. Search and indexing functionality
	3. Security and charging mechanisms
	4. User interfaces
	Utilisation of screen real estate, support for interface mechanisms (mice, keyboards, etc.), windows and panes, etc.
	5. User customisation
	Adjustment of functionality (such as behaviour on link following), presentation, layout, content, structure, etc.
	6. Interfaces to related applications
	7. . . . .

Table A3–7 (cont.)

VI.	Application Non-Functional Requirements and Attributes
	1. Reliability
	2. Maintainability
	3. Interoperability
	4. Application Security
	5. . . .
VII.	Development Requirements
	1. Scheduling and Delivery
	timescales, delivery dates, incremental delivery
	2. Design constraints
	standards compliance, hardware limitations, presentation system constraints.
	3. Documentation
	required documents, structure, standards, etc.
	4. Process
	reviews and reporting, process maturity, quality assurance, etc.
	5. Personnel and Training
	6. . . .
VIII.	Acceptance
	Acceptance criteria, hand-over procedures
App 1.	Client statement of needs
App 2.	Market analysis
App 3.	Feasibility studies, Cost-Benefit analyses

Table A3–8

Requirements specification checklist

Is the feasibility study complete, comprehensive and conclusive?

Is the cost-benefit study complete, comprehensive and conclusive?

Are there any open requirements issues? Are these being suitably addressed?

Are all requirements testable?

Are the requirements stable?

Are all requirements necessary? Unambiguous?

Are content bounds clearly defined?

Are content depths and cohesiveness clearly defined?

Is content structure defined appropriately

Are all functions defined and prescribed? Bounded? Unambiguous? Testable?

Are performance guidelines or requirements specified for each functional requirement? Are these performance requirements testable?

Are all application user inputs and expected behaviours defined for application functionalities?

Can performance requirements be met?

Does the requirements document adhere to required standards?

Have the requirements been evaluated? Accepted by the client?

Do the requirements address all client needs? Are requirements traceable to client needs and goals? Have any discrepancies been resolved?

Have application acceptance criteria been defined and accepted?

Is the requirements scope consistent with the planned development process, schedule, costs, and resource estimates?

A3.4. Application Design

Table A3–9

Typical hypermedia application design specification outline: note that the specific contents will be heavily dependant upon both the application and its domain, and the specific design methods and approaches which have been utilised. The following outline is intended solely as an example of the structure and types of material which may be considered appropriate for inclusion

I.	Introduction
	1. Purpose
	2. Application overview
	3. System scope
	4. Definitions, acronyms, terminology
	5. Documents and references
II.	System Architecture
	1. System decomposition
	2. System components
	3. Hardware design
	4. . . .
III.	Information Content Design
	1. Required content
	2. Content depth and breadth specification
	3. . . .
IV.	Information Structural Design
	1. Content decomposition and concept identification
	2. Content allocation
	3. Application structural design
	4. Navigation structures
	5. Semantic structuring
	6. . . .
V.	Navigation Design
	1. Information access
	2. Navigation paths
	3. Tours
	4. . . .
VI.	Functional and Behavioural Design
	1. Navigation functionality and link traversal
	2. Search engines and indexing
	3. History lists, bookmarking, etc.
	4. . . .
VII.	User-Interface Design
VIII.	Preparation for Publication
IX.	Quality Assurance
	1. Design review
	2. Test planning, procedures and cases
	3. Traceability
	4. . . .
X.	
VIII.	

Table A3–10

Design specification checklist

Is the architecture appropriate? Consistent with goals? Technically feasible?

Are all requirements addressed in the design? Has this been traced?

Is the information content appropriate? Consistent?

Is the functionality consistent with the application content and goals?

Does the design meet the overall application goals?

What quality attributes have been met?

Have design trade-offs been documented? Are these trade-offs acceptable?

Have documentation standards been met?

Is the design complete?

Is the design unambiguous?

Has the design been satisfactorily reviewed? Was the review carried out appropriately?

Is the content relevant? Is the structure relevant? Is the functionality relevant? Is the behaviour relevant?

Is the content correct? Is the structure correct? Is the functionality correct? Is the behaviour correct?

Is the application usable? Does the design support usability and cognitive management?

Does the design facilitate effective implementation?

A3.5. Application Evaluation

Table A3–11

Evaluation checklist

Have acceptance criteria been defined and accepted?

Have suitable test plans been developed and reviewed?

Was testing adequately addressed during all development phases?

Are suitable testing tools and techniques defined, available and appropriate?

Is traceability from user/client needs, through specification and design, to final implementation complete and suitable?

Have test cases been defined and reviewed?

Have all navigation paths been considered?

Have all functional components been considered?

Has behaviour under different environments and platforms been evaluated?

Have system limitations (such as network bandwidth) been tested?

A3.6. Risk Management

Table A3–12

Possible risks and risk management

---

1. **Loss of critical personnel and skills**

   Explanation: In a rapidly evolving field such as hypermedia (and especially the Web) skills are in short supply and high demand. As a result a significant risk is the loss of key personnel during critical stages of a development project, or an inability to obtain certain skills when required.

   Risk management: Staffing with suitable personnel, team building, personnel agreements, subcontracting, cross-training, development documentation, in-house training, rescheduling key people.

2. **Unrealistic schedules**

   Explanation: rapidly changing technology, fiercely competitive markets and inexperience with development efforts for large projects can result in the specification of unrealistic development schedules.

   Risk management: multiple schedule estimation, documentation and use of earlier project schedules, renegotiation with client, incremental development and delivery, reuse.

3. **Unrealistic budgets**

   Explanation: Fiercely competitive markets, high personnel costs and inexperience with costing of large projects can result in unrealistic budget estimates.

   Risk management: multiple cost estimation, documentation and use of earlier project costs, renegotiation with client, incremental delivery and charging.

4. **Development of incorrect content, structure, functionality or presentation**

   Explanation: A major cause of low quality applications (and a resultant failure to achieve desired objectives) is errors in functionality, presentation, content and particularly structure, resulting from an inadequate process.

   Risk management: Suitable domain analysis, prototyping, scenario analysis, user modelling and surveys, suitable formal design methods, developmental reviews.

5. **Constantly changing requirements**

   Explanation: A lack of understanding of potential and a poor understanding of the application goals can lead to a set of requirements which gradually evolve during the course of the development, resulting in a blow-out in development costs.

Table A3–12 (cont.)

Risk management: High change threshold, incremental development, change management, domain and goal analysis, sign-off on requirements.

6. **Failure of external components or subcontractors**
   Explanation: Potential exists for failure of those elements of the development which are beyond immediate control (through failure of contractors, equipment or components which do not meet specifications, etc.)
   Risk management: Benchmarking, inspections, audits, evaluation of contractors, acceptance-based fee schedules, acceptance testing, prototyping.

7. **Changing technology**
   Explanation: Hypermedia technology is changing at a rapid pace. The potential exists for applications to be redundant very rapidly, having a very short valid lifespan
   Risk management: Maintenance planning, technology analysis, technology-independent design, prototyping, utilisation of established technology trends and standards.

8. **Performance shortfalls**
   Explanation: In many cases systems may not provide adequate performance.
   Risk management: Simulation and prototyping, benchmarking, performance analysis.

Appendix 4

Example Case Study – HyperBank

To illustrate many of the ideas presented in this book, we have used a case study as the basis of various examples. The following is the scenario used as the basis of the case study.

The *ABO* (*Archaic Banking Organisation*) is a large commercial banking organisation which provides a broad range of banking products and services and has a large varied customer base. The types of information with which the *ABO* deals is incredibly diverse, both in domain and in structure. Examples include:

- Account information (such as account ownership and transaction details). This information is enormous, but is very well structured and is currently maintained using traditional database technologies. Dedicated software systems are used to provide interfaces to the systems designed to handle transactions, statement mailouts, etc.

- Mailouts (such as announcements and bimonthly newsletters to customers). The bimonthly newsletter is managed by the *ABO*'s public relations office, and is outsourced to a small specialist publisher. The remainder of the material is handled in an *ad hoc* fashion as required.

- Advertising material (such as television and radio advertisements, posters, brochures, and pamphlets). As with the bimonthly customer newsletter, this is outsourced to a third party advertising agency.

- Procedure manuals (such as guidelines for tellers). The bank has a large set of standard paper manuals outlining operating procedures for bank staff. These manuals have been developed using an eclectic mix of technologies scattered through various bank departments.

- Employee information (such as staff details and employment conditions). These are typically maintained by the *ABO*'s personnel department. The employer details are stored in a database which has interfaces to software systems such as salary and retirement fund details. Conditions of employment and related information is managed in various *ad hoc* fashions.

- Administrative information (such as phone lists and contact names). An internally developed text-based system is used to support access to a number of regularly updated lists of information such as 'phone lists, contact names in bank branches and staff availability. In addition, an internal email system is also supported.

- Legal documents (such as relevant legal cases, legal statutes, etc.) The *ABO*'s legal department maintains a large collection of hard-copy legal material which is used in guiding bank operations.

- Operating information (such as current interest rates, the *ABO* share price, and listings of the *ABO*'s assets). This material is managed individually by assorted *ABO* departments.

- Internal newsletters. A fortnightly newsletter is produced by the banks personnel department for internal distribution which contains a variety of information such as a message from the CEO, general bank notices, personal advertisements and general articles of interest.

An important observation is that the information given above is produced from a number of different sources and is used by a variety of users. These users include:

- Current customers: these can in turn be categorised as personal, business, charity and government. They have a range of needs, including savings and term deposits, mortgages, short-term and business loans, etc.

- Prospective customers: these are the people who are not yet customers but have requested information from the bank.

- Potential customers: the *ABO* views *all* people as potential customers, and often targets them through advertising material.

- Staff: as with current customers, these fall into a broad range of categories (which can often overlap). Examples include tellers requiring information on procedures, legal staff requiring details of past law cases, or administrative staff requiring employment details.

- Suppliers: many organisations are suppliers of the *ABO*. For example, the bank has a contract with *HyperTeller*, an engineering firm who maintains the Automatic Teller Machines. *HyperTeller* typically needs access to legal contract information and usage rates on the ATMs.

- Government regulatory agencies: various government agencies, such as the Advertising Standards Board and the Banking Ombudsmen monitor the bank's activities and the information they deal with.

Each of these users will have different requirements which affect the way in which the information sources are managed and accessed. For example, access authorisation and privacy considerations means that security of much of the information is critically important. It is also recognised that the different users have differing levels of sophistication, background knowledge and experience with technology.

Client statement

The *ABO* management has been influenced by the current hype about the Internet, Intranets, the information superhighway and the World Wide Web, and a fear that they might be left behind in the race to adopt these technologies. An internal report has had two main recommendations: the first is that Web technologies have the potential to provide a cohesive and integrated information management strategy; the second is that, to maintain long-term competitiveness, the bank must establish a significant presence on the Web, and use it in supporting access and utilisation of the banks diverse information.

As a result, the *ABO* management has identified as a core strategic initiative for the bank the development of appropriately integrated Web-based applications, collectively referred to as *HyperBank*, to support their current business activities. These applications must support appropriate access to and utilisation of the banks information sources by the diverse user base.

References

Anderson K M (1997) Integrating open hypermedia systems into the World Wide Web, *Proceedings of the 3rd Workshop on Open Hypermedia Systems, Hypertext '97* Southampton, UK.

Andleigh, P K and Thakrar K (1996) *Multimedia Systems Design,* Prentice Hall.

Andrews K and Kappe F (1994) Soaring through hyperspace: A snapshot of Hyper-G and its Harmony client *Proceedings of Eurographics Symposium and Workshop on Multimedia* Graz, Austria.

Apple Computer (1989) *HyperCard stack design guidelines* Addison-Wesley.

Aßfalg R (ed) (1994) *Proceedings of the Workshop on Open Hypertext Systems* Konstanz, Germany, May.

Bapat A, Geißler J, Hicks D, Streitz N A and Tietze D (1996) From electronic white-boards to distributed meetings: Extending the scope of DOLPHIN *Conference Video of the ACM 1996 Conference on Computer Supported Cooperative Work* (CSCW'96) Boston, MA, November 16–20.

Barlow J P (1994) A taxonomy of information *Bulletin of the American Society for Information Science* June/July, 13–17.

Belkin N J (1978) Information concepts for Information Science *Journal of Documentation* **34**(1), 55–85

Behforooz A and Hudson F (1996) *Software Engineering Fundamentals* Oxford University Press.

Berk E (1991) *Hypertext/Hypermedia Handbook* McGraw-Hill.

Berners-Lee T (1991) World Wide Web: An Illustrated Seminar http://www.w3.org/pub/WWW/Talks/General.html

Berners-Lee T (1994) Universal Resource Identifiers in WWW http://www.w3.org/pub/WWW/Addressing/URL/uri-spec.txt

Bernstein M (1990) An apprentice that discovers hypertext links *Proceedings of ECHT '90.*

Bieber M and Kacmar C (1995) Designing hypertext support for computational applications *Communications of the ACM* **38**(8), 99–107.

Bigelow J (1988) Hypertext and CASE *IEEE Software* **5**(2), 23–27

Boehm B (1981) *Software Engineering Economics* Prentice Hall.

Boehm B (1988) A spiral model for software development and enhancement, *Computer* May, 61–72.

Botafogo R A, Rivlin E and Shneiderman B (1992) Structural analysis of hypertexts: Identifying hierarchies and useful metrics *ACM Transactions on Information Applications* **10**(2), 142–180.

Buckland M K (1991) Information as thing *Journal of the American Society for Information Science* **42**(5), 351–360.

Bush V (1945) As we may think *Atlantic Monthly* July.

Campbell B and Goodman J (1988) A general purpose hypertext abstract machine *Communications of the ACM* **31**(7), 856–861.

Carr L, De Roure D, Hall W and Hill G (1995) The distributed link service: A tool for publishers, authors and readers *Proceedings of the Web Revolution: Fourth International World Wide Web Conference* Boston, MA.

Carr L A, Davis H C, De Roure D C, Hall W and Hill G J (1996) Open information services *Computer Networks and ISDN Systems* **28**, 1027–1036.

Chandler D (1994) Semiotics for beginners http://www.aber.ac.uk/~dgc/semold.html

CACM (1995) *Communications of the ACM*, Special issue on designing hypermedia applications, **38**(8).

Conklin J and Begeman M L (1988) gIBIS: A hypertext tool for exploratory policy discussion *ACM Transaction on Office Information Applications* **6**(4), 303–331.

Davis H, Hall W, Heath I, Hill G and Wilkins R (1992) Towards an integrated information environment with open hypermedia applications *ECHT '92: Proceedings of the Fourth ACM Conference on Hypertext* Milan, Italy, 181–190.

Davis H, Knight S and Hall W (1994) Light hypermedia link services: a study of third party application integration *Proceedings of ECHT'94* ACM Press, 41–50.

Demeyer S (1996) *Zypher: Tailorability as a Link from Object-Oriented Software Engineering to Open Hypermedia*,PhD Dissertation, Vrije Universiteit Brussel.

De Roure D C, Hall W, Davis H C and Dale J (1996) Agents for distributed multimedia information management *Proceedings of PAAM'96* London, March.

Diaz A, Isakowitz T, Maiorana V and Gilabert G (1995) RMCase: A tool to design WWW applications *World Wide Web Journal* **1**(1), 559–566.

Egan D E, Remde J R, Gomez L M, Landeuer T K, Eberhardt J and Lochbaum C C (1989) Formative design-evaluation of 'Superbook' *ACM Transactions on Information Science* **7**(1), 30–57.

Engelbart D (1988) The augmented knowledge workshop In: Goldberg A (ed) *A History of Personal Workstations* Addison-Wesley, 187–236.

Feiner S (1988) Seeing the forest for the trees: Hierarchical display of hypertext structure *Proceedings of Conference on Office Information Systems* Palo Alto, CA, 23–25.

Fisher S (1994) *Multimedia Authoring* AP Professional.

Fountain A, Hall W, Heath I and Davis H (1990) Microcosm: An open model for hypermedia with dynamic linking *Hypertext: Concepts, Systems and Applications, Proceedings of ECHT'90*, Paris, November, 298–311.

Furuta R, Plaisant C and Shneiderman B (1989) A spectrum of automatic hypertext constructions *Hypermedia* **1**(2), 179–195.

Gaines B and Shaw M (1995) Concept maps as hypermedia components *http://ksi.cpsc.ucalgary.ca/articles/ConceptMaps/* Knowledge Science Institute, University of Calgary.

Garzotto F, Mainetti L and Paolini P (1995) Hypermedia design, analysis, and evaluation issues *Communications of the ACM* **38**(8), 74–86.

Garzotto F, Paolini P and Schwabe D (1993) HDM – a model based approach to hypermedia application design *ACM Transactions on Information Systems* **11**(1), 1–26.

Gibbs W (1994) Software's chronic crisis *Scientific American* **271**(3), 86.

Gibbs S and Tsichritzis (1995) *Multimedia Programming: Objects, Environments and Frameworks* Addison-Wesley.

Ginige A and Fuller C (1994) Magazine of the future: A vision and a challenge *IEEE Multimedia* **1**(2), 11–14.

Ginige A and Lowe D (1995) Next generation hypermedia authoring systems *Proceedings of Multimedia Information Systems and Hypermedia* University of Tokyo, Japan.

Ginige A, Witana V and Yourlo Z (1996) Use of the World-Wide-Web in the delivery of education – a case study *3rd International Interactive Multimedia Symposium* Perth, Australia, 21–25.

Goldfarb C F (1990) *The SGML Handbook* Oxford University Press.

Goodman D (1987) *The Complete HyperCard Handbook* Bantam Books.

Goose S, Dale J, Hill G J, De Roure D and Hall W (1996) An open framework for integrating widely distributed hypermedia resources *Proceedings of the IEEE International Conference on Multimedia Computing and Systems* Hiroshima, Japan, 364–371.

Grønbæk, K and Trigg R H (1992) Design issues for a Dexter-based hypermedia system *Proceedings of the European Conference on Hypertext 1992 (ECHT '92)* Milano, Italy, 191–200.

Grønbæk K, Bouvin N O and Sloth L (1997) Designing Dexter-based hypermedia services for the World Wide Web *Proceedings of the 3rd Workshop on Open Hypermedia Systems, Hypertext '97* Southampton, UK.

Grosky W (1994) Multimedia information systems, *IEEE Multimedia* Spring, 12–24.

Haan B J, Kahn P, Riley V A, Coombs J H and Meyrowitz N K (1992) IRIS hypermedia services *Communications of the ACM* **35**(1), 36–51.

Halasz F G, Moran T P and Trigg R H (1987) NoteCard in a nutshell *Proceedings of ACM CHI+GI '87 Conference* Toronto, Canada, 45–52.

Halasz F and Schwartz M (1994) The Dexter hypertext reference model *Communications of the ACM* **37**(2), 30–39.

Hall W (1994) Ending the tyranny of the button *IEEE Multimedia* **1**(1), 60–68.

Hall W, Davis H and Hutchings G (1996) *Rethinking Hypermedia: The Microcosm Approach* Kluwer.

Harada K, Tanaka E, Ogawa R and Hara Y (1996) Anecdote: A multimedia storyboarding system with seamless authoring support *Proceedings of Multimedia '96: The Fourth ACM International Multimedia Conference* Boston, MA, 341–351.

Hardman L (1989) Evaluating the usability of the Glasgow Online hypertext *Hypermedia* **1**(1), 34–63.

Hardman L, Bulterman D and van Rossum G (1993) The Amsterdam Hypermedia Model: extending hypertext to support *real* multimedia *Hypermedia Journal* **5**(1), 47–69.

Harnad S (1994) Publicly retrievable FTP archives for esoteric science and scholarship: a subversive proposal In: A Okerson and J O'Donnell (eds) *Scholarly Journals at the Crossroads: A Subversive Proposal for Electronic Publishing* Association of Research Libraries.

Hill G J and Hall W (1994) Extending the Microcosm model to a distributed environment *Proceedings of ECHT'94* ACM Press, 32–40.

Hirata K, Hara Y, Shibata N and Hirabayashi F (1993) Media-based navigation for hypermedia systems *Proceedings of the Fifth ACM Conference on Hypertext* Seattle, WA, 159–173.

Horn R E (1989) Mapping HyperText: an analysis, organization, and display of knowledge for the next generation of on-line text and graphics *Lexington Institute*, Lexington, MA.

Howell G (1992) *Building Hypermedia Applications: A Software Development Guide.* McGraw-Hill

Hughes K (1994) A hypemedia timeline. enterprise integration technologies. http:// www.eit.com/web/www.guide/guide.14.html

IEEE (1991) *IEEE Standard Glossary of Software Engineering Terminology* Spring Edition.

Isakowitz T, Stohr E and Balasubramanian P (1995) RMM: A methodology for structured hypermedia design *Communications of the ACM* **38**(8), 34–48.

Isakowitz T, Kamis A and Koufaris M (1996) Extending the capabilities of RMM: Russian Dolls and Hypertext *Proceedings of the Thirtieth Annual Hawaii International Conference on Systems Sciences* Hawaii, USA. (Also published as 'Extending RMM', CRIS Working Paper series #IS-96–8, Stern School of Business, NYU.)

Johnson S (1995) Quality control for hypertext construction *Communications of the ACM* **38**(8), 87.

Kreitzberg C B and Shneiderman B (1988) Restructuring knowledge for an electronic encyclopedia *Proceedings Intl Ergonomics Association 10th Congress* Sydney, Australia, 615–620.

Lange D (1993) Object-oriented hypermodelling of hypermedia-supported information systems *Proceedings of the Twenty Sixth Hawaii International Conference on System Sciences* Maui, Hawaii, 380–389.

Lange D (1994) An object-oriented design method for hypermedia information systems *Proceedings of the Twenty Seventh Hawaii International Conference on System Sciences* Maui, Hawaii.

Legget J J, Schnase J L, Smith J B and Fox E A (1993) Final report on the NSF workshop on hyperbase systems *Technical Report TAMU-HRL 93–002*, Texas A&M University.

Lewis P H, Davis H C, Griffiths S R, Hall W and Wilkins R J (1996) Media-based navigation with generic links *Proceedings of the 7th ACM Conference on Hypertext* Washington, DC, 215–233.

Lowe D and Ginige A (1995) HyperImages: Using object recognition to navigate through images in multimedia *Proceedings of IS&T/SPIE Symposium on Electronic Imaging* San Jose, CA.

Lowe D, Ginige A, Sifer M, and Potter J (1996) The Matilda data model and its implications *Third International Conference on Multimedia Modelling* Toulouse, France.

Lowe D and Sifer M (1996) Refining the Matilda multimedia authoring framework with the structured graph visual formalism *IEEE International Conference on Multimedia Computing and Applications* Hiroshima, Japan.

Lowe D and Ginige A (1996) Matilda: A framework for the representation and processing of information in multimedia applications *3rd International Interactive Multimedia Symposium* Perth, Australia.

Malcolm K C , Poltrock S E and Schuler D (1991) Industrial strength hypermedia: requirements for a large engineering enterprise *Proceedings of Hypertext '91, Third ACM Conference on Hypertext* San Antonio, TX, 13–24.

Marshall C and Shipman F III (1995) Spatial hypertext: designing for change *Communications of the ACM* **38**(8), 88–97.

Marshall C, Shipman F III and Coombs J (1994) Searching for the missing link: discovering implicit structure in spatial hypertext *Proceedings of the European Conference on Hypermedia Technologies* Edinburgh, Scotland, 217–230.

Maurer H (1996) *Hyper-G now Hyperwave: The Next Generation Web Solution* Addison-Wesley.

Nanard J and Nanard M (1995) Hypertext design environments and the hypertext design process. *Communications of the ACM* **38**(8), 49–56.

Nelson T (1993a) Literary Machines, Edition 93.1.

Nelson T (1993b) *World Enough* Mindful Press (extracted from http://www.obs-us.com/obs/english/papers/ted/tedbio11.htm#page118).

Nelson T (1995) The heart of connection: hypermedia unified by transclusion *Communications of the ACM* **38**(8), 31–33.

Newcomb S, Kipp N and Newcomb V (1991) The HyTime hypermedia / time-based document structuring language *Communications of the ACM* **34**(11), 67–83.

Niblett T and van Hoff A (1989) *Programmed Hypertext and SGML* The Turing Institute.

Nielsen J (1993a) *Hypertext and Hypermedia* AP Professional.

Nielsen J (1993b) Iterative user interface design *IEEE Computer* **26**(12), 32–41.

Nielsen, J (1995) *Multimedia and Hypertext: the Internet and beyond* AP Professional.

Nielsen J and Sano D (1994) SunWeb: User interface design for Sun Microappli-cation's internal web *Proceedings Second International WWW conference '94: Mosaic and the Web* Chicago, 547–557.

Nitecki JZ (1984) The concept of information-knowledge continuum: Implications for librarianship *Journal of Library History* **20**(4), 387–407.

Norman G (1995) *Software Reuse Concise Guide* European Software Institute.

Parunak H V (1989) Hypermedia topologies and user navigation *Proceedings of the Hypertext '89 Conference* Pittsburgh, PA, 43–50.

Pearl A (1989) Sun's link service: A protocol for open linking *Proceedings of Hypertext '89* Pittsburgh, PA, 137–146.

Pikrakis A, Bitsikas T, Sfakianakis S, Hatzopoulos M, DeRoure D, Hall W, Reich S, Hill G and Stairmand M (1998) MEMOIR – Software agents for finding similar users by trail *Proceedings of PAAM'98: The Third International Conference and Exhibition on The Practical Application of Intelligent Agents and Multi-Agents* London, UK, 453–466.

Raskin J (1987) The hype in hypertext: A critique *Proceedings of the Hypertext '87 Conference*,Chapel Hill, NC, 325–330.

Rearick C (1991) Automating the conversion of text into hypertext In:Berk E and Devlin J (eds) *Hypertext/Hypermedia Handbook* Intertext Publications/McGraw.

Robertson C K, McCracken D and Newell A (1981) The ZOG Approach to man-machine communication *International Journal of Man-Machine Studies* **14**, 461–488.

Robertson J (1997) *The link creation problem in hypermedia* Doctoral Thesis, Faculty of Engineering, University of Technology, Sydney.

Robertson J, Merkus E and Ginige A (1994) The Hypermedia Research Toolkit (HART) *Proceedings of European Conference on Hypertext 94* UK.

van Rossum G, Jansen J, Mullender K S and Bulterman D (1993) CMIFed: A presen-tation environment for portable documents *Proceedings of ACM Multimedia '93*, Anaheim, CA, 183–188 (revised version of CWI Report CS-R9305).

Rowe D, Leaney J and Lowe D (1996) Development of an applications architecting process for computer based applications *Proceedings of Sixth Complex Applica-tions Engineering Synthesis and Assessment Technology Workshop (CSESAW'96)* Montreal, Canada.

Schwabe D and Rossi G (1995a) The object-oriented hypermedia design model *Communications of the ACM* **38**(8), 45–46.

Schwabe D and Rossi G (1995b) Building hypermedia applications as navigational views of information models *Proceedings of the Twenty Eighth Hawaii International Conference on System Sciences* Maui, Hawaii, 231–240.

Shneiderman B (1987) User interface design for the hyperties electronic encyclopedia *Proceedings ACM Hypertext '87 Conference* Chapel Hill, NC, 189–194.

Shneiderman B, Brethauer D, Plaisant C and Potter R (1989) The Hyperties electronic encyclopedia: An evaluation based on three museum installations *Journal of the American Society for Information Science* **40**(3), 172–182.

Steinmetz R and Nahrstedt K (1995) *Multimedia: Computing, Communications & Applications* Prentice Hall.

Streitz N, Haake J, Hannemann J, Lemke A, Schuler W, Schutt H and Thuring M (1992) SEPIA: A cooperative hypermedia authoring environment *Proceedings ECHT'92 4th ACM European Conference on Hypertext* Milan, Italy, 11–22. (Also available as: Streitz N, Haake J, Hannemann J, Lemke A, Schuler W, Schuett H, Thuering M (1996) SEPIA: A cooperative hypermedia authoring environment Updated and revised version in: R Rada (ed) *Groupware and Authoring* Academic Press, 241–264.

Streitz N, Geissler J, Haake J and Hol J (1994) DOLPHIN: Integrated meeting support across LiveBoards, local and remote desktop environments *Proceedings of the ACM Conference on Computer-Supported Cooperative Work (CSCW'94)* Chapel Hill, NC, 345–358.

Thuring M, Hannemann J and Haake J (1995) Hypermedia and cognition: Designing for comprehension *Communications of the ACM* **38**(8), 57–66.

Urr C (1991) Will the real hypertext please stand up *Computers in Libraries* May.

Vithanage R (1997) Design of process models for large digital information applications, *Masters Thesis*, University of Technology, Sydney.

West S and Norris M (1997) *Media Engineering: A guide to developing information products* Wiley.

Wiil U K and Østerbye K (eds) (1994) *Proceedings of the ECHT'94 Workshop on Open Hypermedia Systems* Technical Report R-94–2038, Aalborg University.

Wiil U K (ed) (1997) *Proceedings of the 3rd Workshop on Open Hypermedia Systems, Hypertext '97* Southampton, UK, April. (CIT Scientific Report no. SR-97–01, The Danish National Centre for IT Research. http://www.daimi.aau.dk/~kock/OHS-HT97/)

Woodhead N (1991) *Hypertext and Hypermedia* Sigma Press/Addison-Wesley.

Yankelovich N, Meyrowitz N and van Dam A (1985) Reading and writing the electronic book *IEEE Computer* **18**(10), 15–30.

Further Reading

Akscyn R, McCracken D L and Yoder E A (1988) KMS: A distributed hypertext abstraction machine *Communications of the ACM* **31**(7).

Conklin J (1987) Hypertext: A survey and introduction,*IEEE Computer* **20**(9).

Garzotto F and Paolini P (1991) HDM – a model for the design of hypertext applications *Proceedings of the Third ACM Conference on Hypertext* San Antonio, Tx, 313–328. Grønbæk K, Hem J and Madsen O (1993) Designing Dexter-based cooperative hypermedia systems *Proceedings of the Fifth ACM Conference on Hypertext* Seattle, WA, 25–38.

Grønbæk K, Hem J and Madsen O (1993) Designing Dexter-based cooperative hypermedia systems *Proceedings of the Fifth ACM Conference on Hypertext* Seattle, WA, 25–38.

Hall W (1995) Towards industrial strength hypermedia *Proceedings of Multimedia Information Applications and Hypermedia* Tokyo, Japan.

Lehman M M (1991) Why is process important *Proceedings 1st International Conf on the Software Process* Redondo Beach, CA.

Marcus A (1996) *Multimedia Interface Design Studio* Random House.

Parunak H and Van Dyke (1991) Tools for authoring hypertexts In: Berk E and Devlin J (eds) *Hypertext/Hypermedia Handbook* McGraw-Hill, 299–325.

Parunak H and Van Dyke (1991) Toward industrial strength hypermedia In: Berk E and Devlin J (eds) *The Hypertext/Hypermedia Handbook* McGraw-Hill.

Sakauchi M (1994) Image retrieval and image understanding *IEEE Multimedia Computing Magazine* **1**(1).

Shneiderman B (1989) *Hypertext on Hypertext*, Addison Wesley.

Index